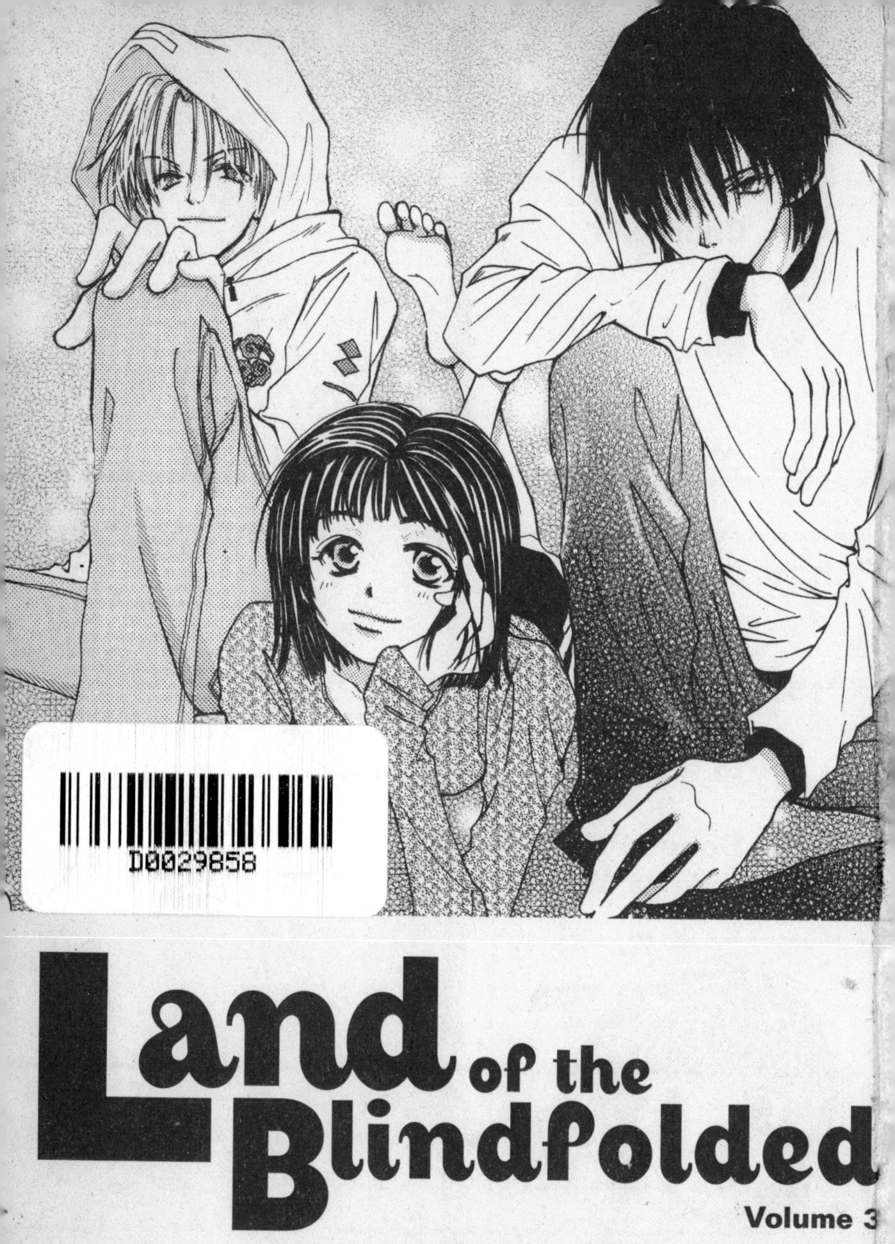

Land of the Blindfolded

Volume 3

By Sakura Tsukuba

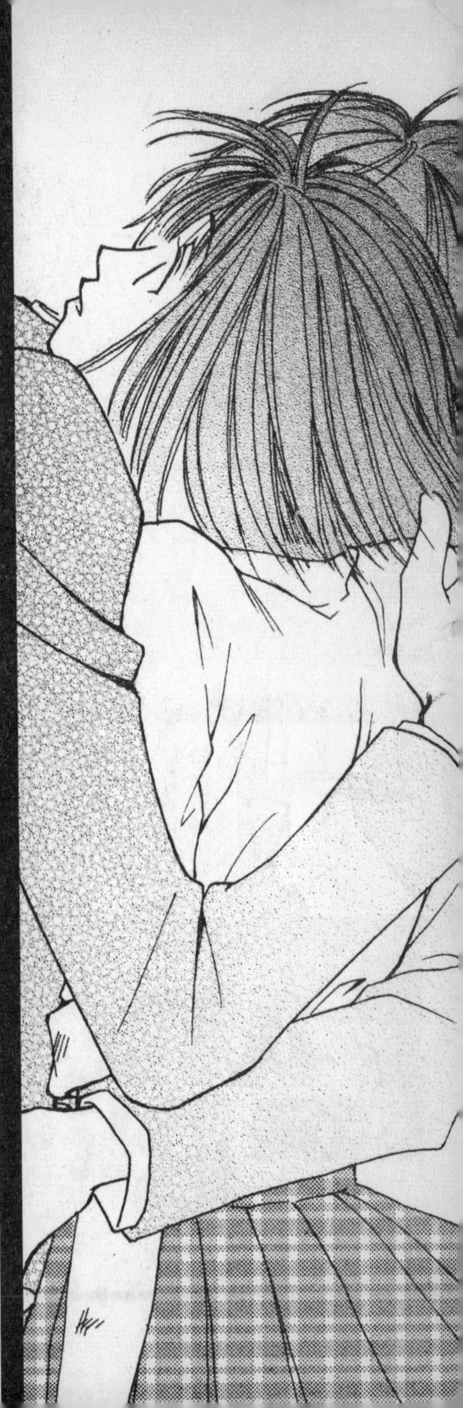

CONTENTS

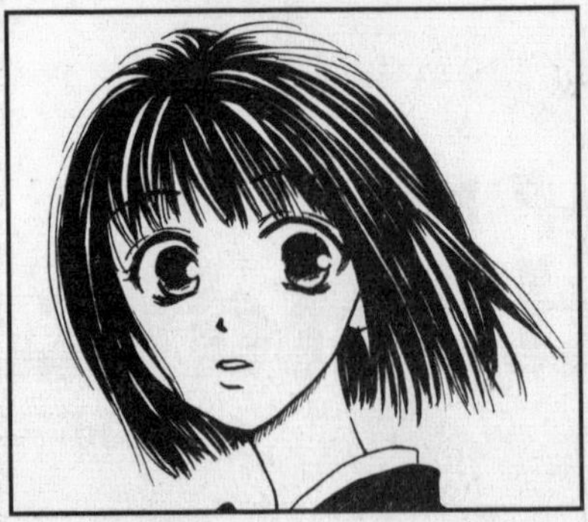

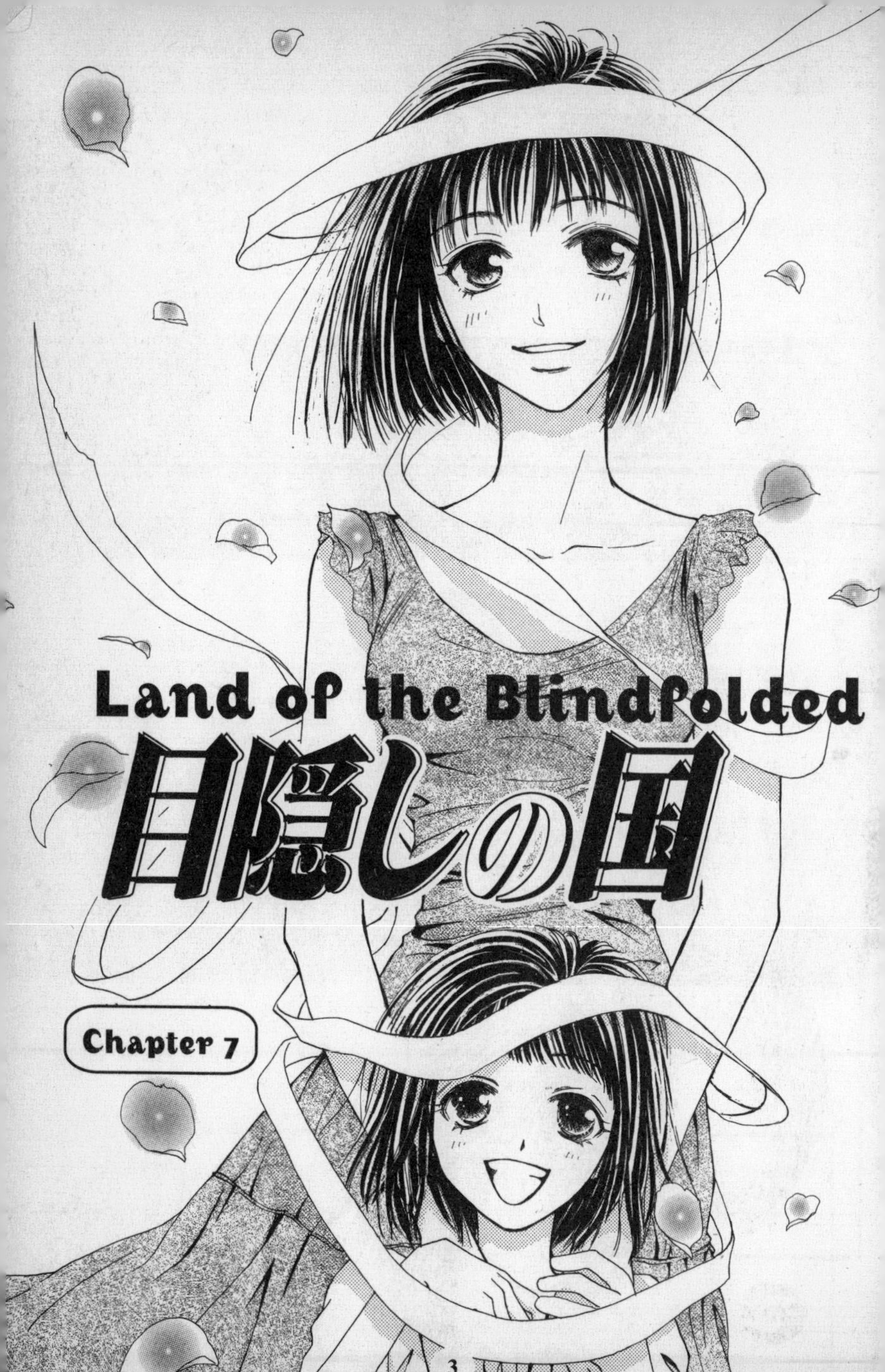
Land of the Blindfolded
目隠しの国
Chapter 7

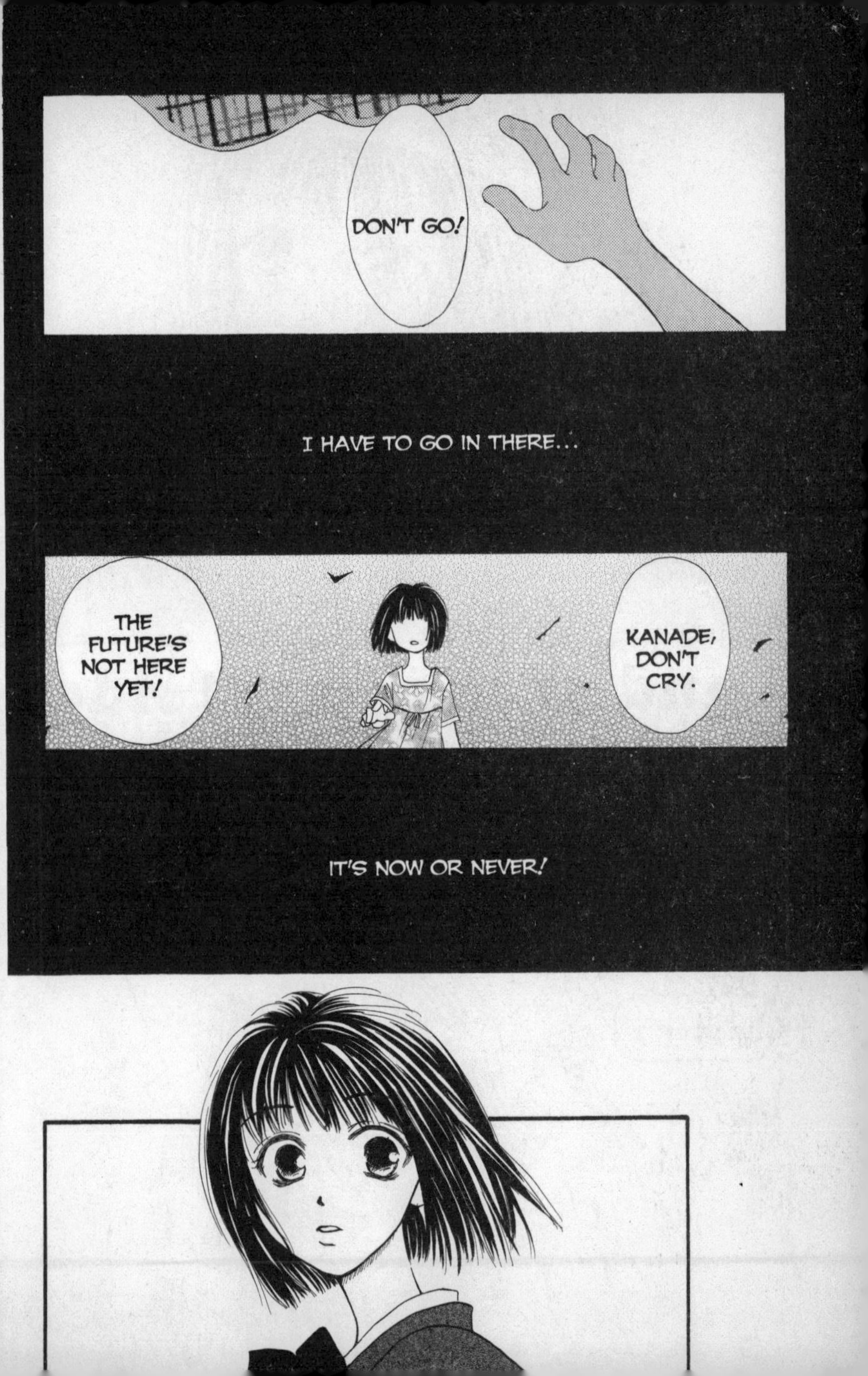
DON'T GO!
I HAVE TO GO IN THERE...
KANADE, DON'T CRY.
THE FUTURE'S NOT HERE YET!
IT'S NOW OR NEVER!

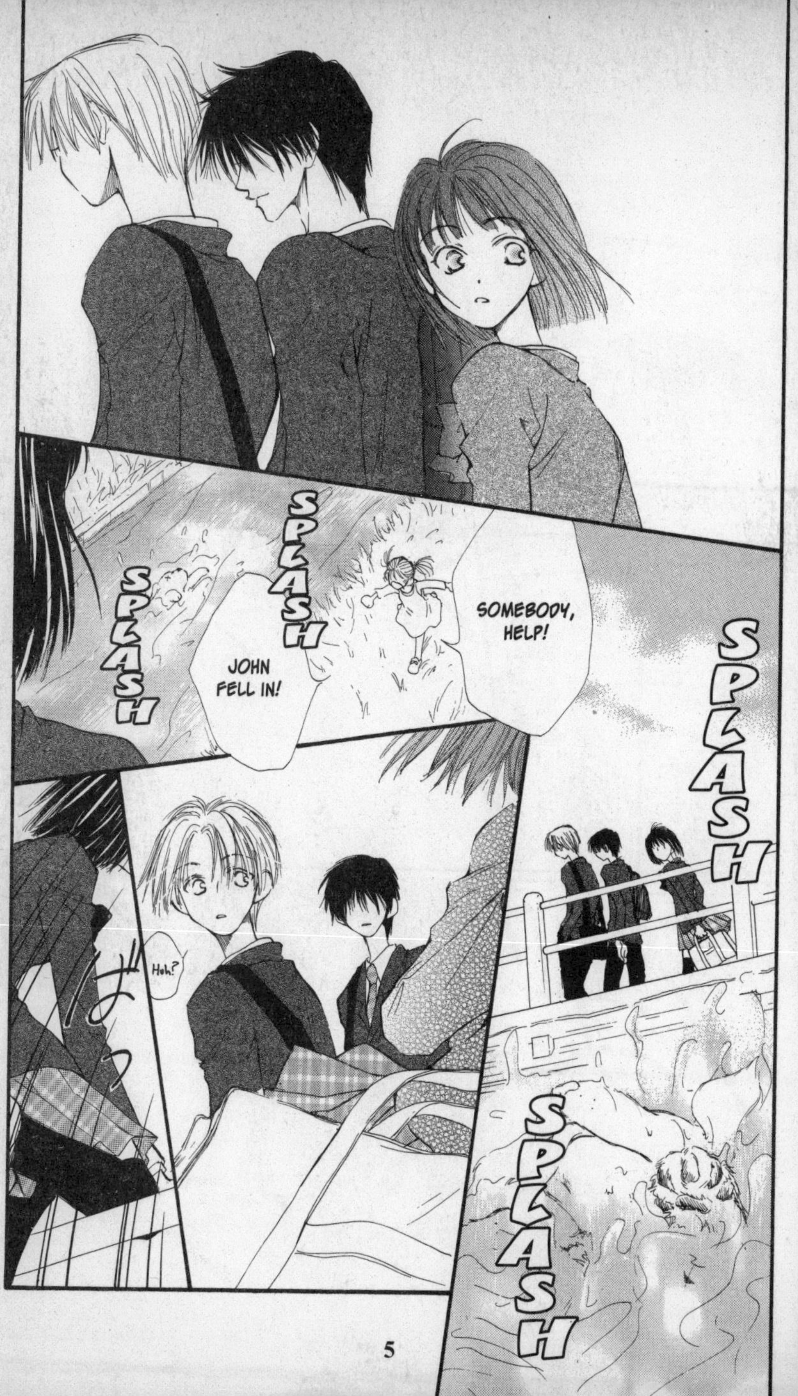
SOMEBODY, HELP!
SPLASH
JOHN FELL IN!
SPLASH
SPLASH
SPLASH
Huh?
ばっ

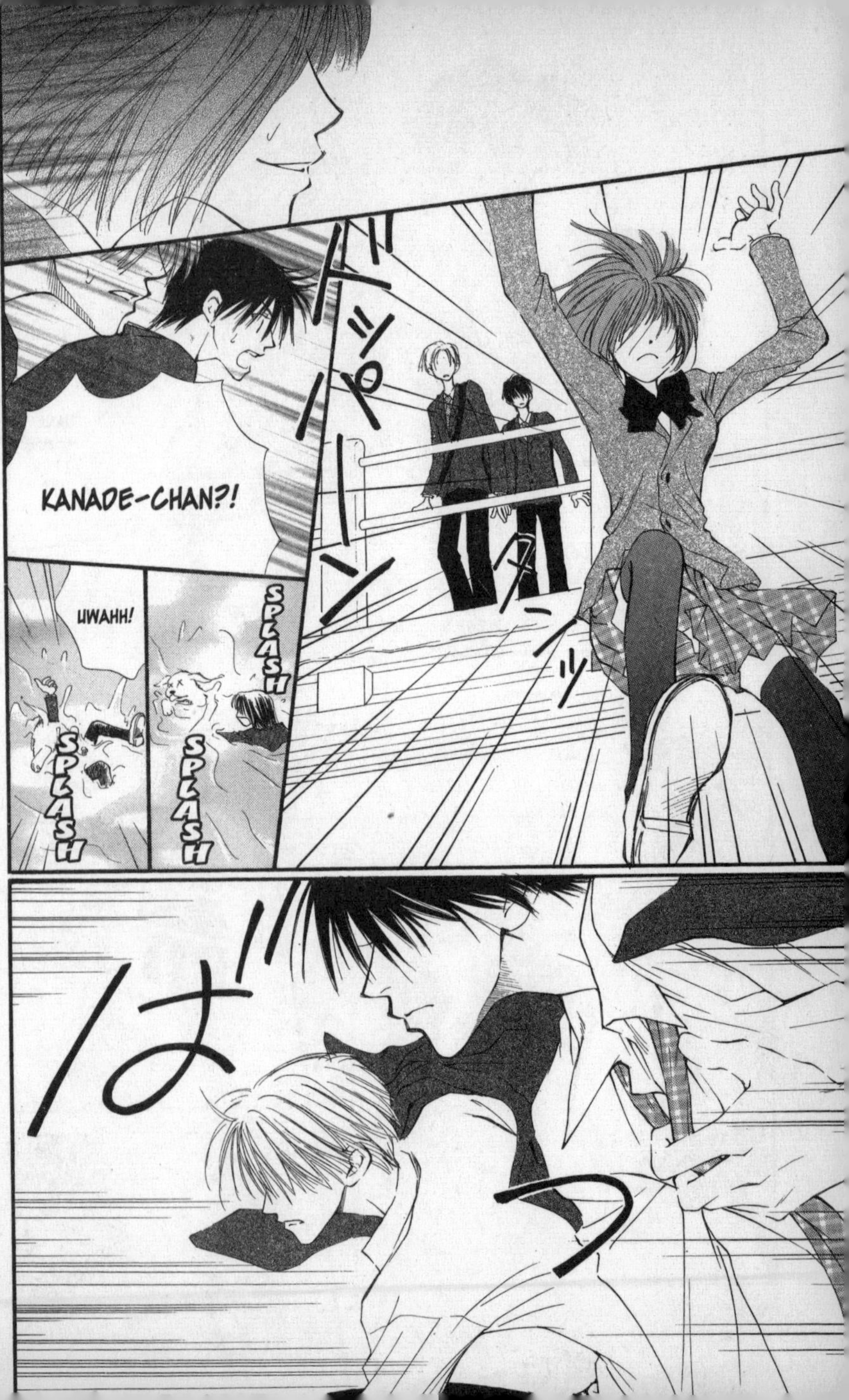
KANADE-CHAN?!
SPLASH
SPLASH
UWAHH!
SPLASH

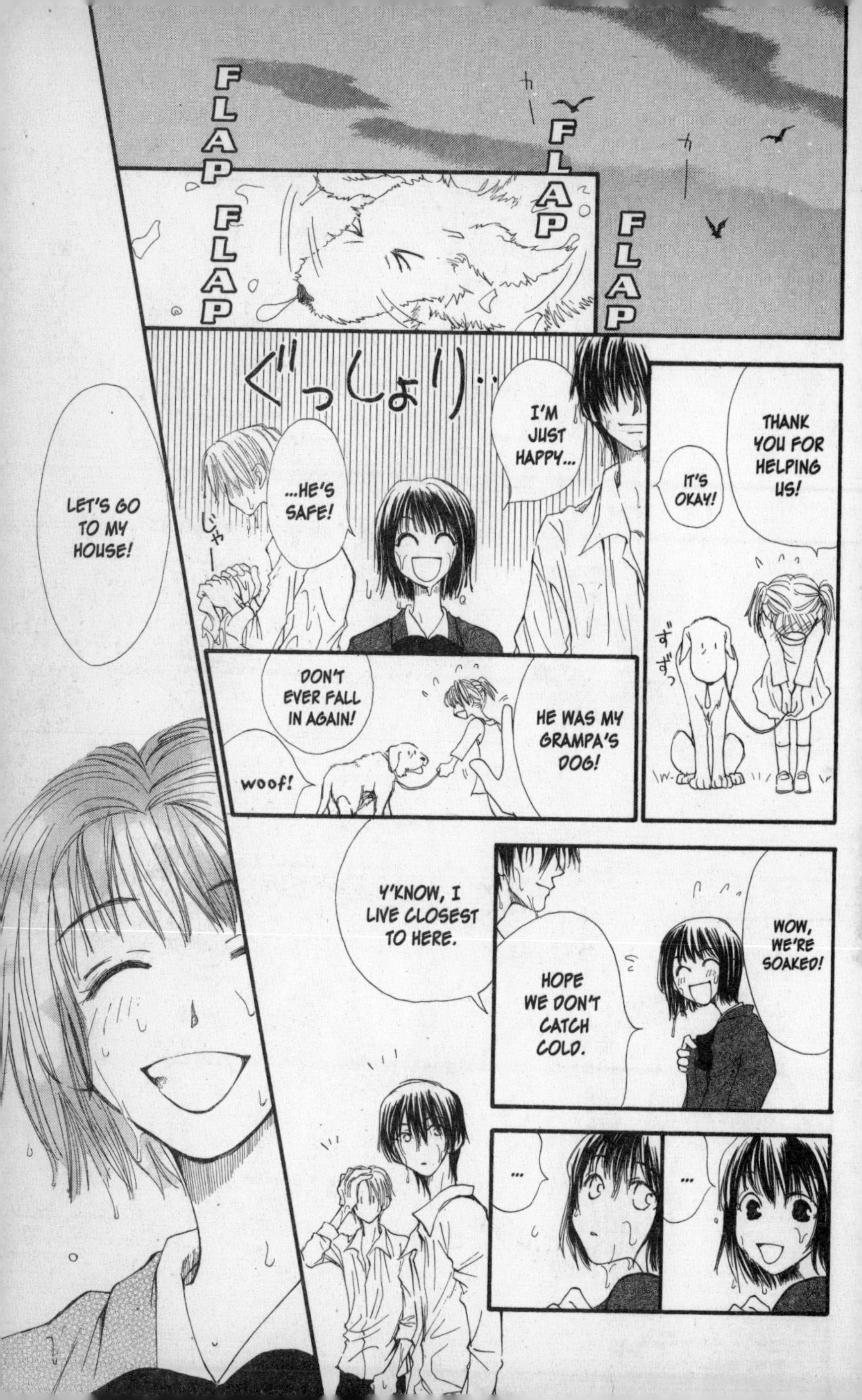
カー
カー
FLAP
FLAP
FLAP
FLAP
ぐっしょり‥
I'M JUST HAPPY...
...HE'S SAFE!
じゃー
THANK YOU FOR HELPING US!
IT'S OKAY!
ずずっ
HE WAS MY GRAMPA'S DOG!
DON'T EVER FALL IN AGAIN!
woof!
WOW, WE'RE SOAKED!
HOPE WE DON'T CATCH COLD.
Y'KNOW, I LIVE CLOSEST TO HERE.
...
...
LET'S GO TO MY HOUSE!

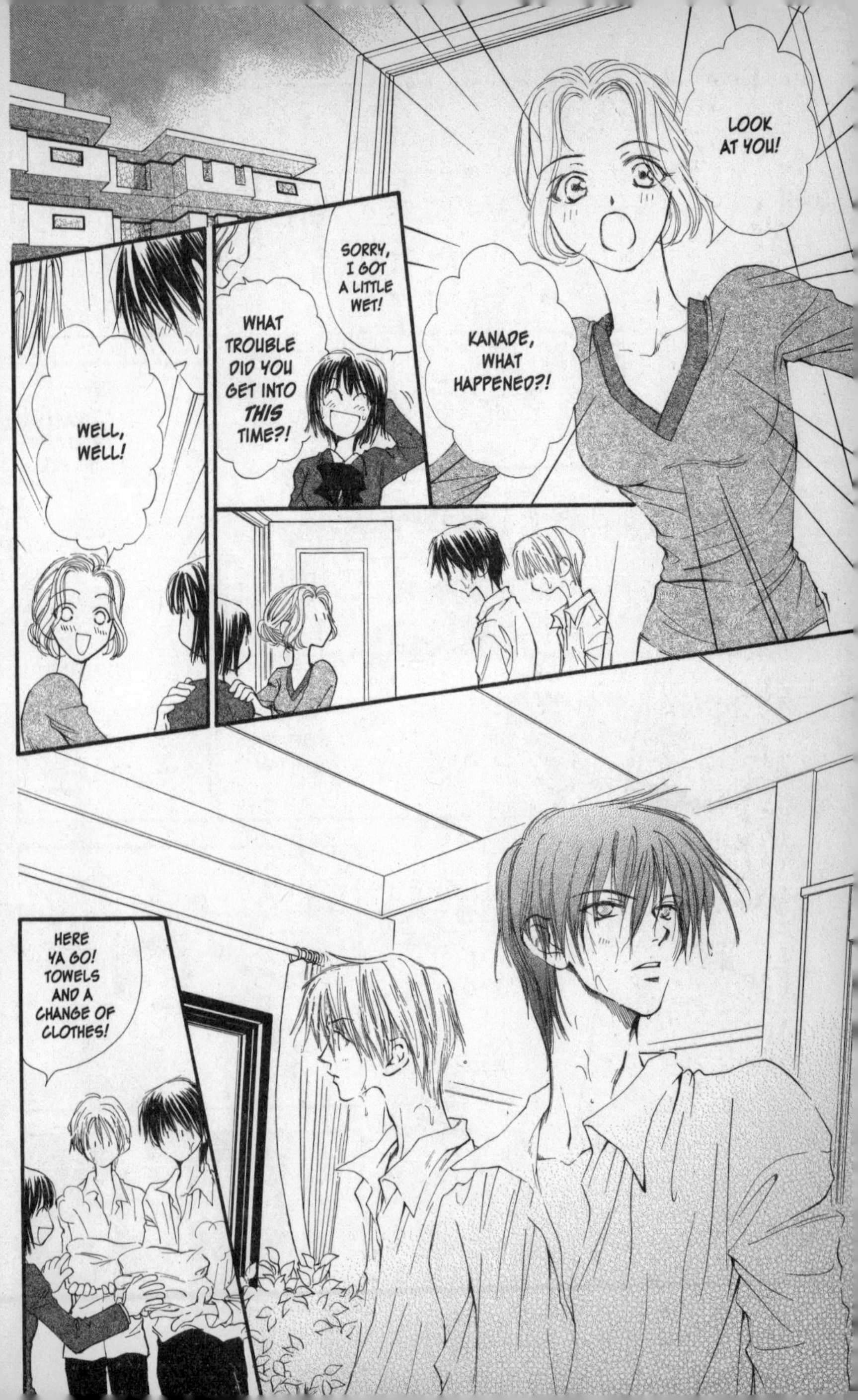
LOOK AT YOU!
KANADE, WHAT HAPPENED?!
SORRY, I GOT A LITTLE WET!
WHAT TROUBLE DID YOU GET INTO *THIS* TIME?!
WELL, WELL!
HERE YA GO! TOWELS AND A CHANGE OF CLOTHES!

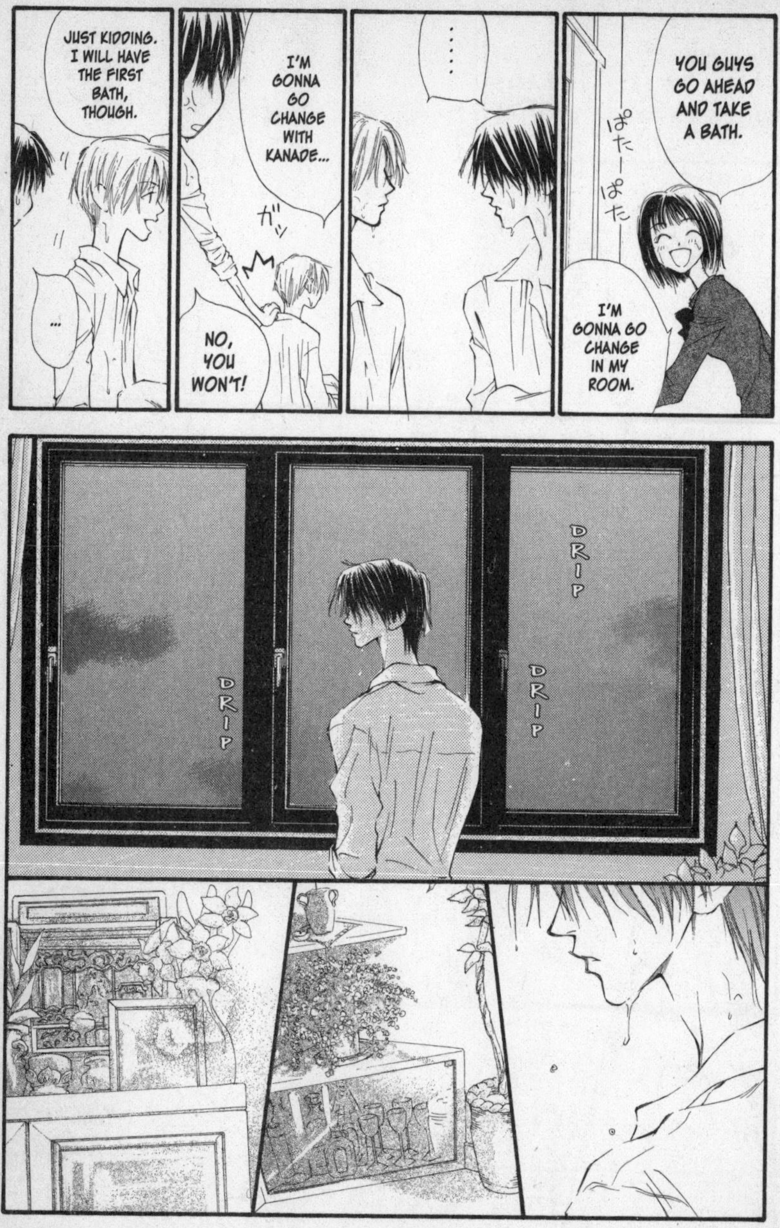
YOU GUYS GO AHEAD AND TAKE A BATH.
ぱたーぱた
I'M GONNA GO CHANGE IN MY ROOM.
......
I'M GONNA GO CHANGE WITH KANADE...
ガッ
NO, YOU WON'T!
JUST KIDDING. I WILL HAVE THE FIRST BATH, THOUGH.
...
DRIP
DRIP
DRIP

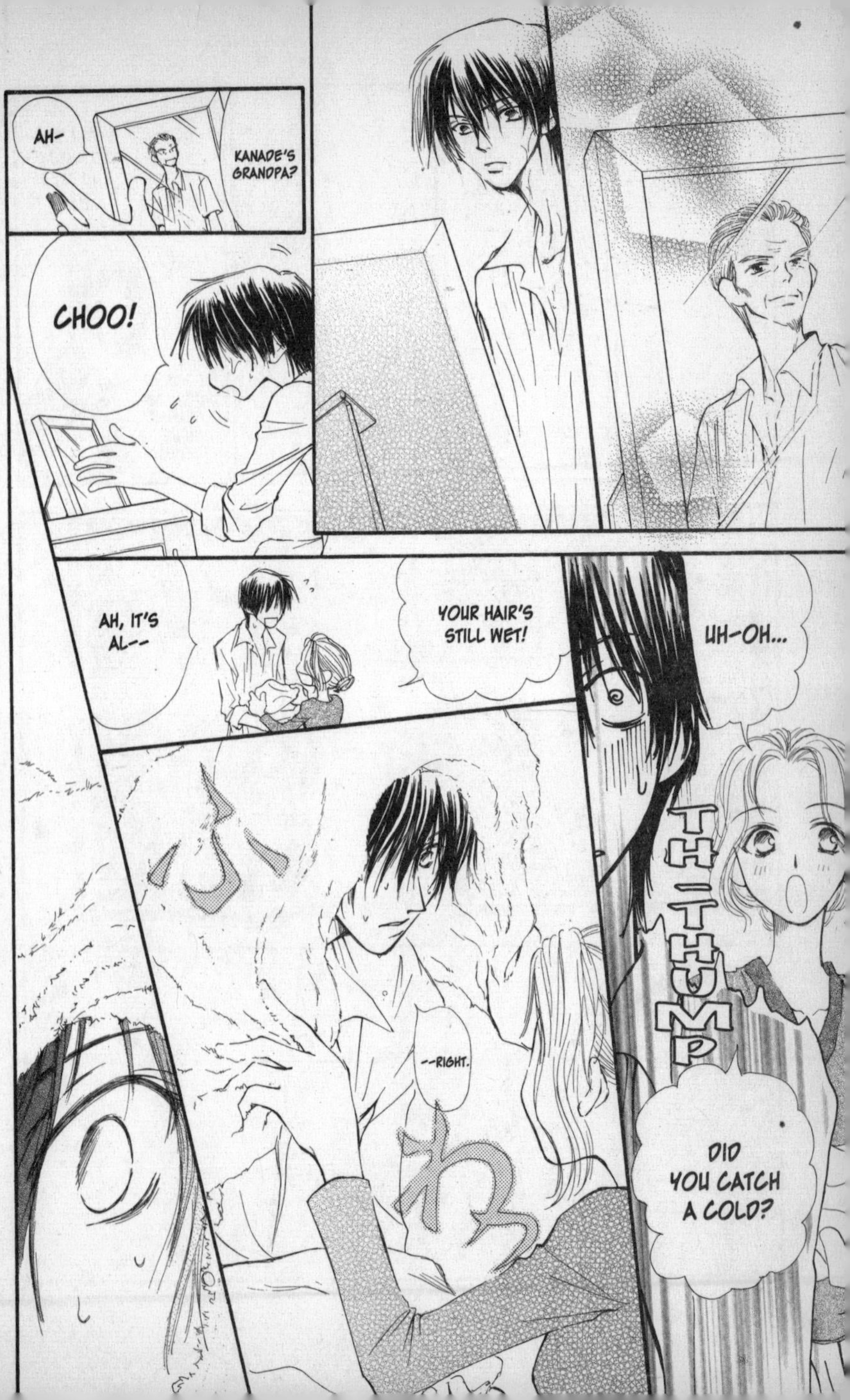
AH-
KANADE'S GRANDPA?
CHOO!
UH-OH...
TH-THUMP
DID YOU CATCH A COLD?
YOUR HAIR'S STILL WET!
AH, IT'S AL--
--RIGHT.
わ

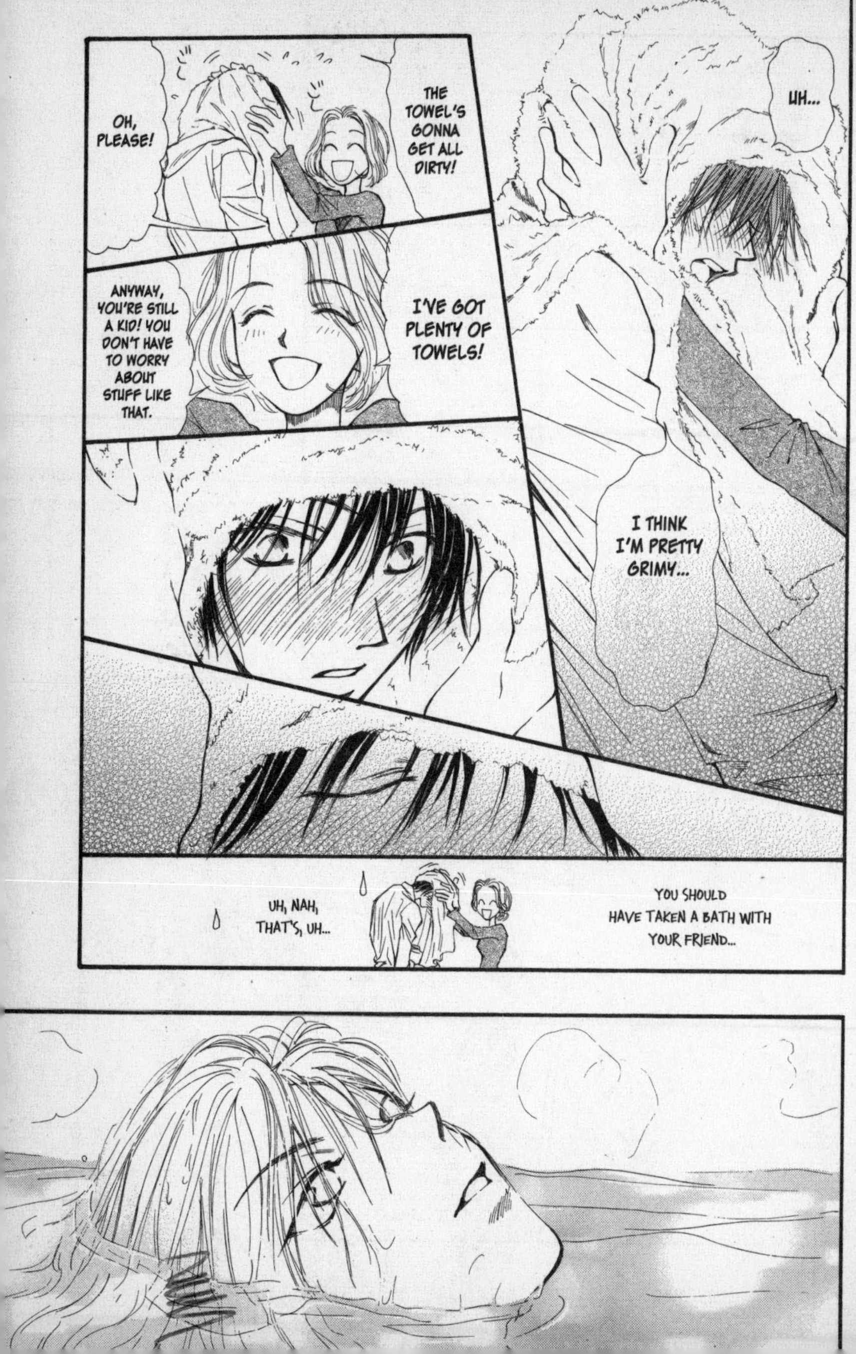
UH...
I THINK I'M PRETTY GRIMY...
THE TOWEL'S GONNA GET ALL DIRTY!
OH, PLEASE!
I'VE GOT PLENTY OF TOWELS!
ANYWAY, YOU'RE STILL A KID! YOU DON'T HAVE TO WORRY ABOUT STUFF LIKE THAT.
YOU SHOULD HAVE TAKEN A BATH WITH YOUR FRIEND...
UH, NAH, THAT'S, UH...

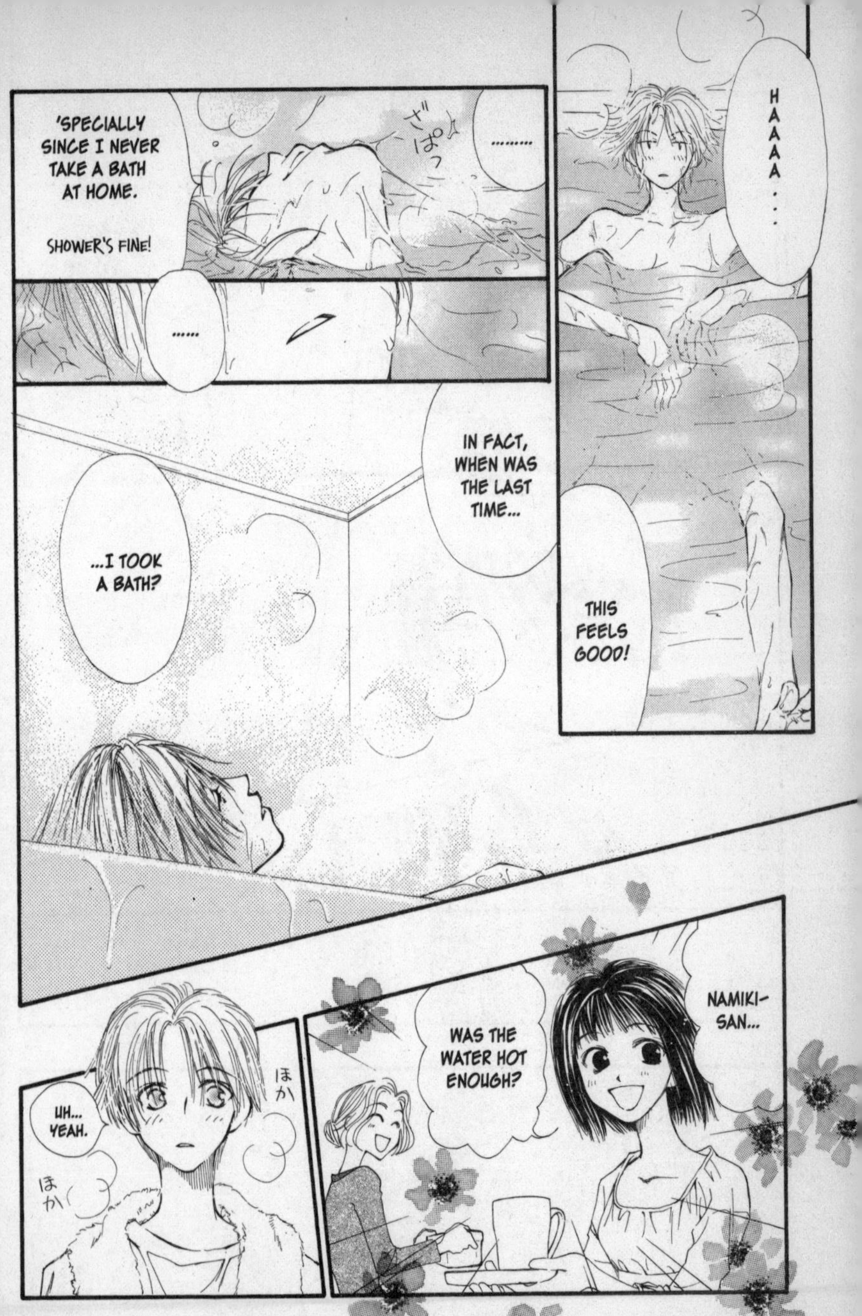
HAAAA...
THIS FEELS GOOD!
ざぱっ
....
'SPECIALLY SINCE I NEVER TAKE A BATH AT HOME.
SHOWER'S FINE!
......
IN FACT, WHEN WAS THE LAST TIME...
...I TOOK A BATH?
NAMIKI-SAN...
WAS THE WATER HOT ENOUGH?
ほか
ほか
UH... YEAH.

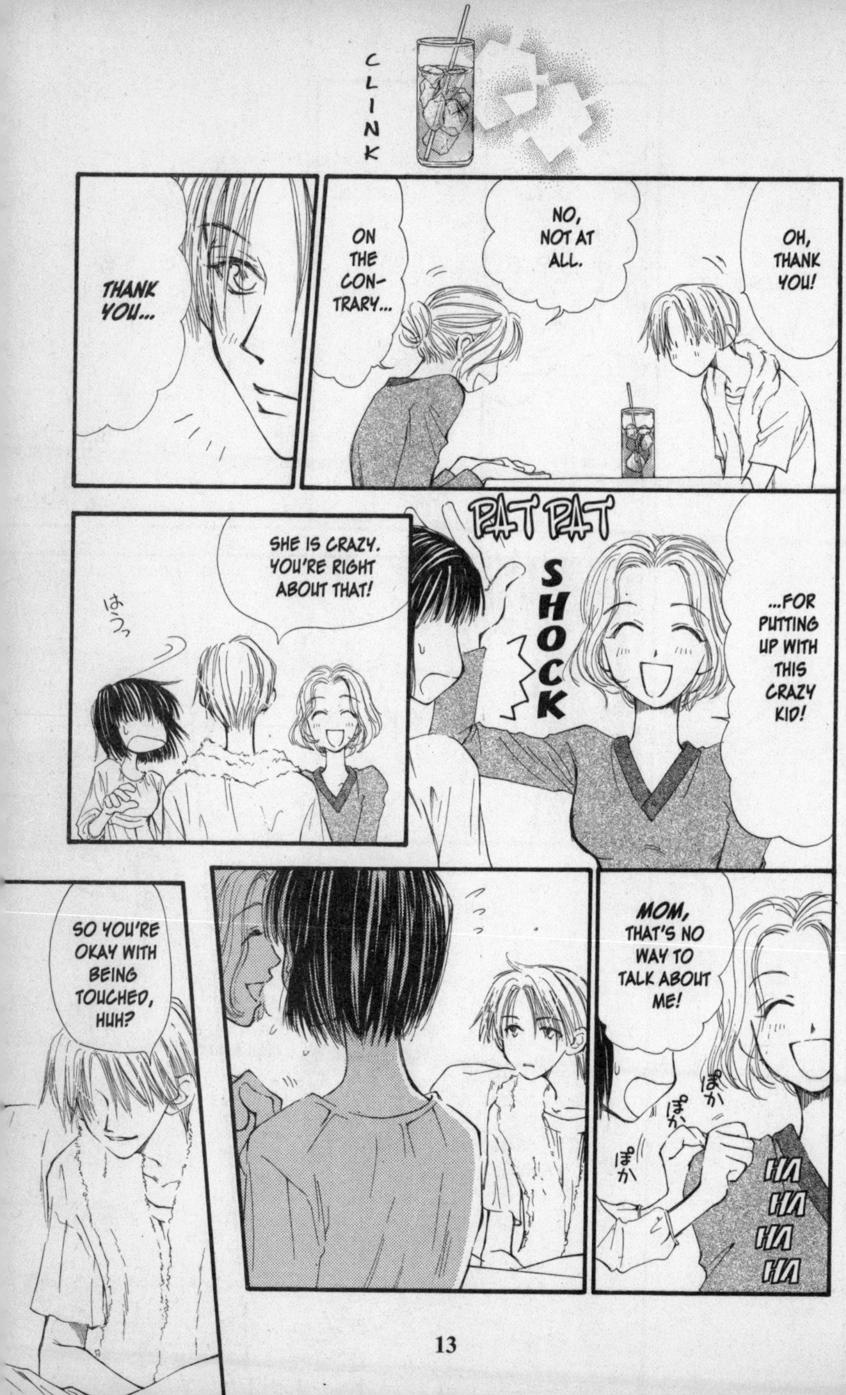
CLINK
OH, THANK YOU!
NO, NOT AT ALL.
ON THE CON-TRARY...
THANK YOU...
PAT PAT
SHOCK
...FOR PUTTING UP WITH THIS CRAZY KID!
SHE IS CRAZY. YOU'RE RIGHT ABOUT THAT!
はうっ
MOM, THAT'S NO WAY TO TALK ABOUT ME!
ぽか
ぽか
ぽか
HA HA HA HA
SO YOU'RE OKAY WITH BEING TOUCHED, HUH?

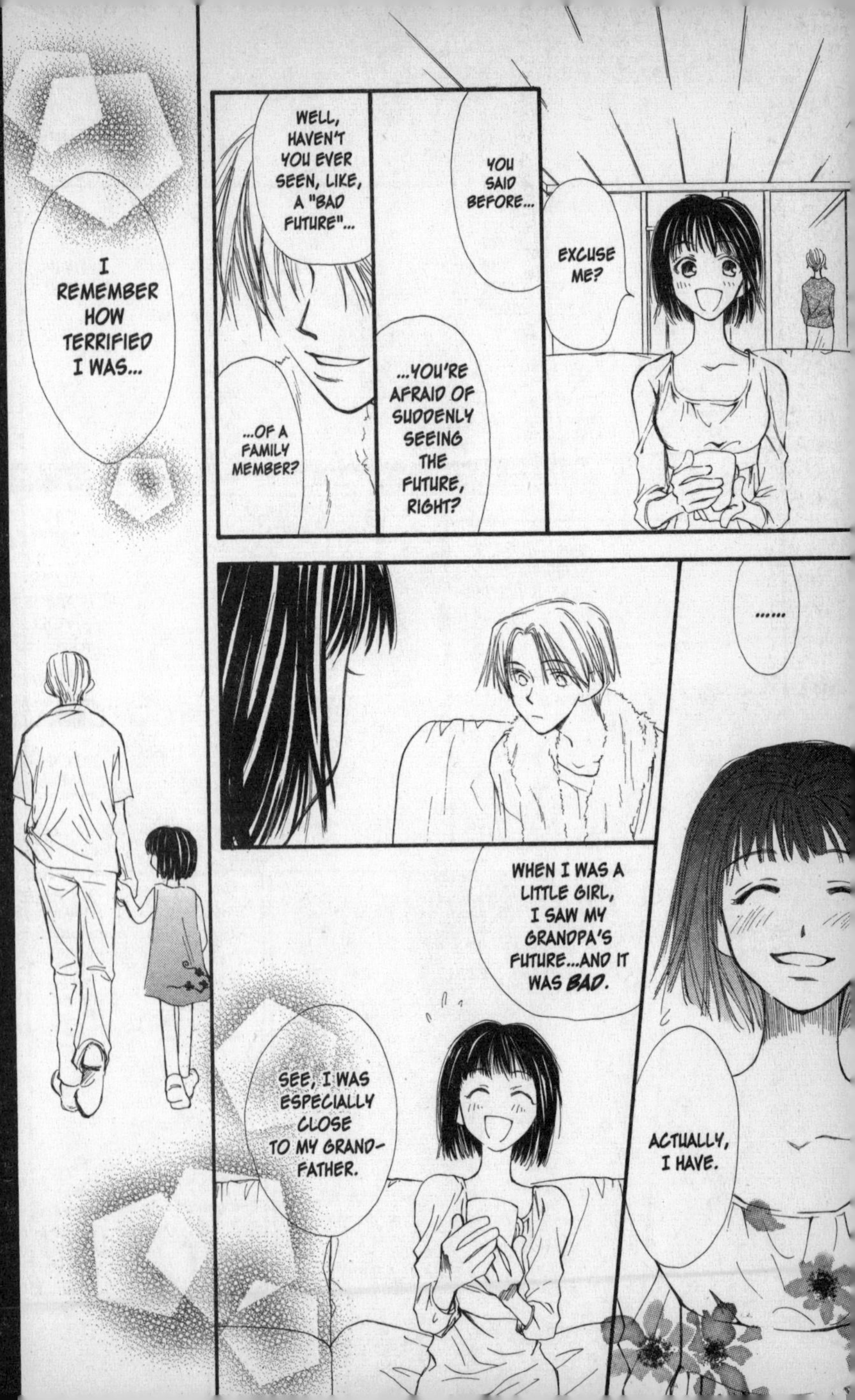
EXCUSE ME?
YOU SAID BEFORE...
...YOU'RE AFRAID OF SUDDENLY SEEING THE FUTURE, RIGHT?
WELL, HAVEN'T YOU EVER SEEN, LIKE, A "BAD FUTURE"...
...OF A FAMILY MEMBER?
......
ACTUALLY, I HAVE.
WHEN I WAS A LITTLE GIRL, I SAW MY GRANDPA'S FUTURE...AND IT WAS *BAD*.
SEE, I WAS ESPECIALLY CLOSE TO MY GRAND-FATHER.
I REMEMBER HOW TERRIFIED I WAS...

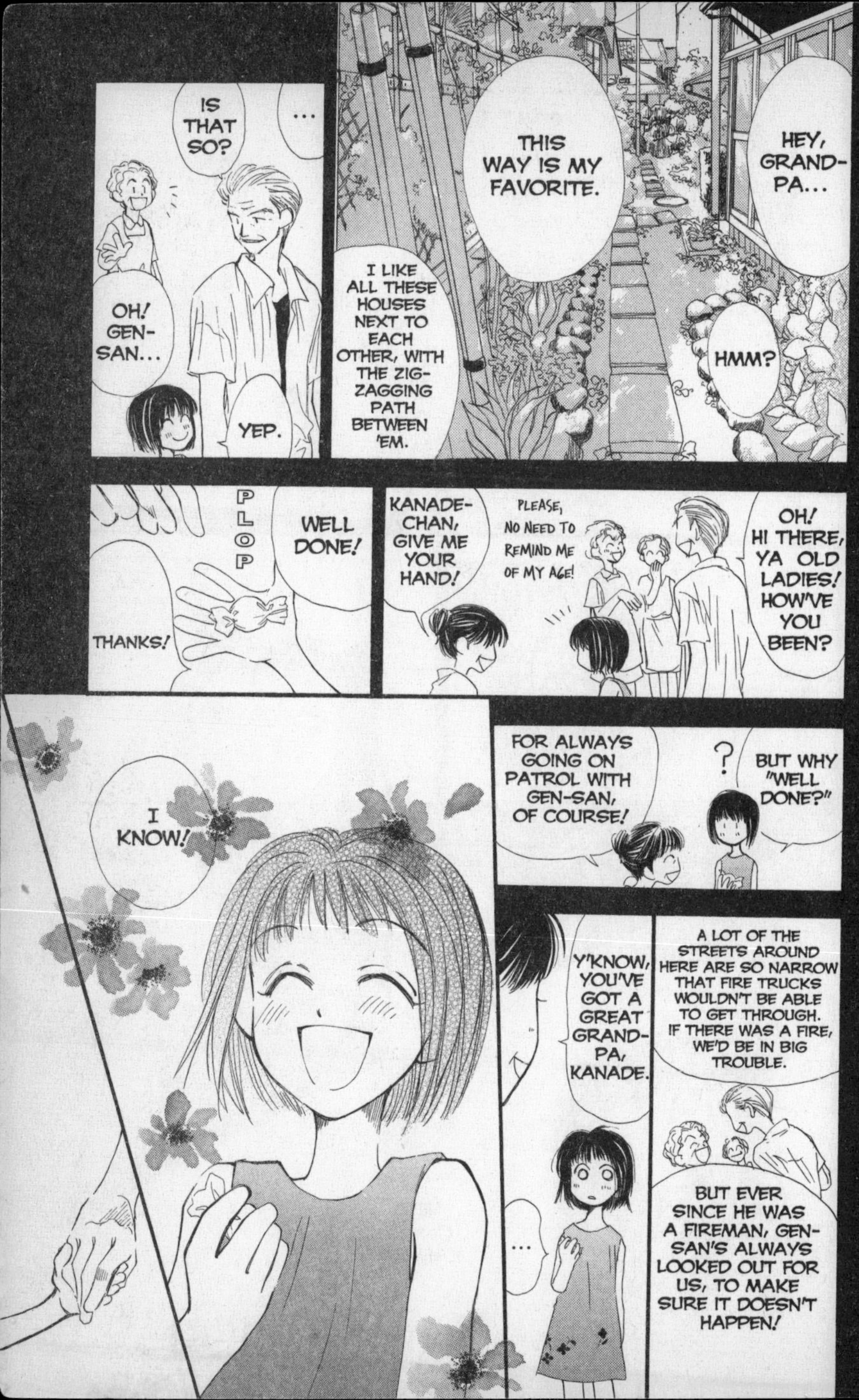
HEY, GRANDPA...
THIS WAY IS MY FAVORITE.
HMM?
I LIKE ALL THESE HOUSES NEXT TO EACH OTHER, WITH THE ZIG-ZAGGING PATH BETWEEN 'EM.
...
IS THAT SO?
OH! GEN-SAN...
YEP.
OH! HI THERE, YA OLD LADIES! HOW'VE YOU BEEN?
PLEASE, NO NEED TO REMIND ME OF MY AGE!
KANADE-CHAN, GIVE ME YOUR HAND!
WELL DONE!
PLOP
THANKS!
BUT WHY "WELL DONE?"
?
FOR ALWAYS GOING ON PATROL WITH GEN-SAN, OF COURSE!
A LOT OF THE STREETS AROUND HERE ARE SO NARROW THAT FIRE TRUCKS WOULDN'T BE ABLE TO GET THROUGH. IF THERE WAS A FIRE, WE'D BE IN BIG TROUBLE.
Y'KNOW, YOU'VE GOT A GREAT GRANDPA, KANADE.
BUT EVER SINCE HE WAS A FIREMAN, GEN-SAN'S ALWAYS LOOKED OUT FOR US, TO MAKE SURE IT DOESN'T HAPPEN!
...
I KNOW!

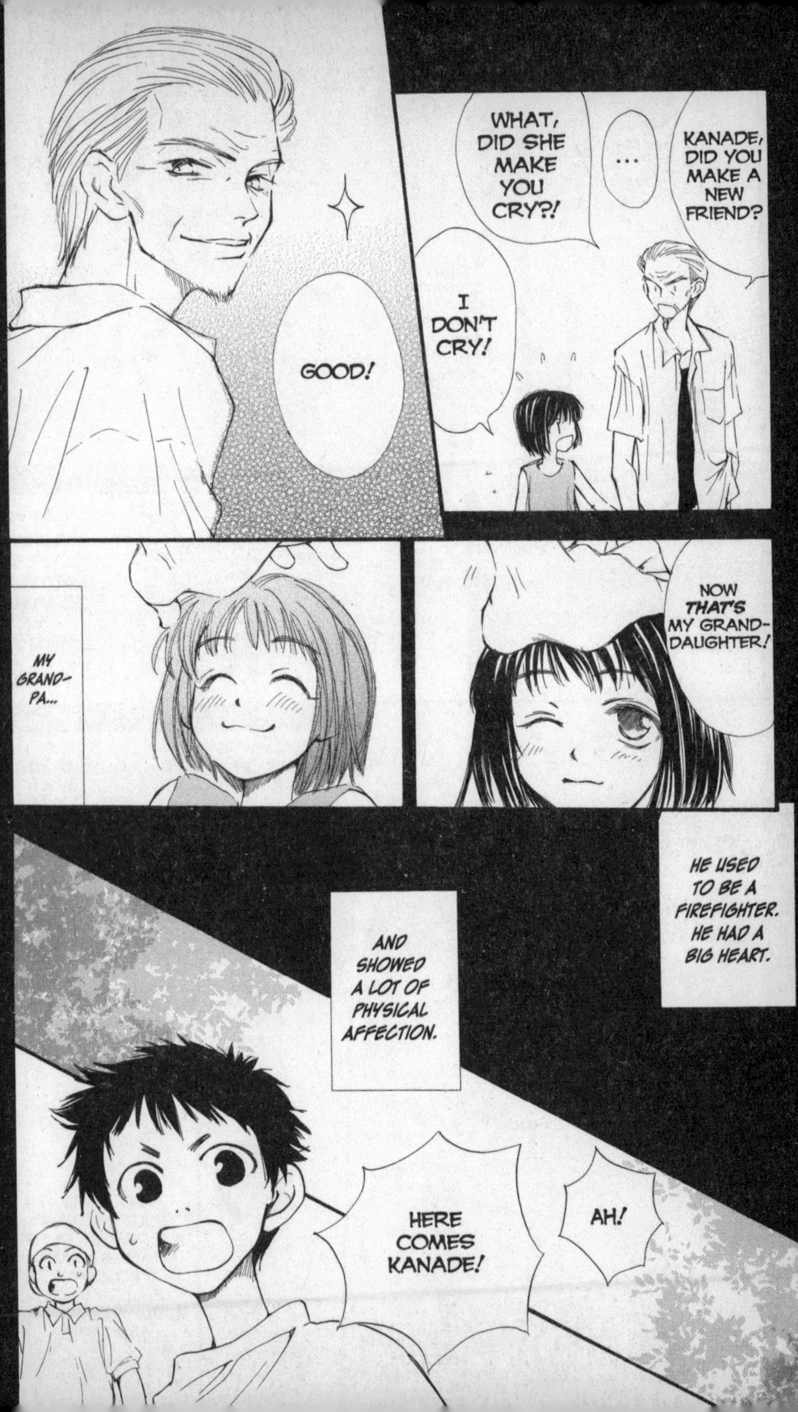
KANADE, DID YOU MAKE A NEW FRIEND?
...
WHAT, DID SHE MAKE YOU CRY?!
I DON'T CRY!
GOOD!
NOW THAT'S MY GRAND-DAUGHTER!
MY GRAND-PA...
HE USED TO BE A FIREFIGHTER. HE HAD A BIG HEART.
AND SHOWED A LOT OF PHYSICAL AFFECTION.
AH!
HERE COMES KANADE!

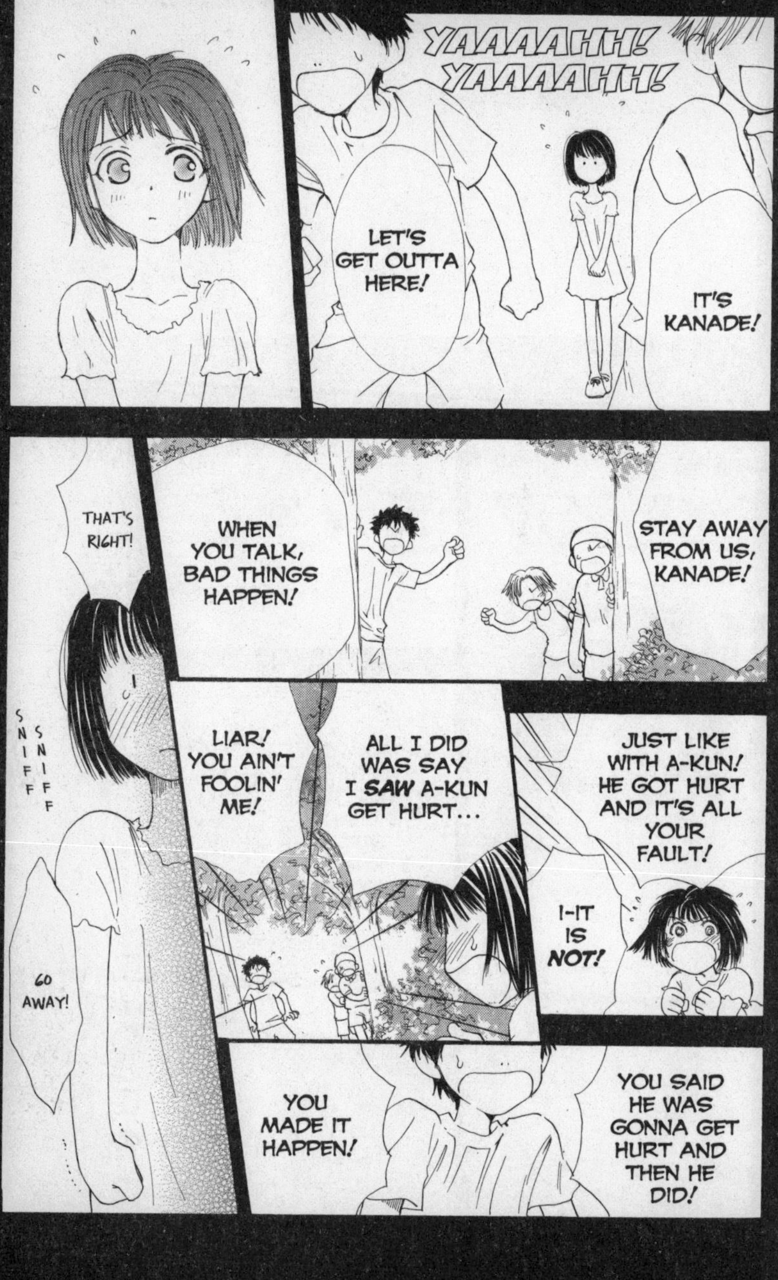
YAAAAHH! YAAAAHH!
IT'S KANADE!
LET'S GET OUTTA HERE!
STAY AWAY FROM US, KANADE!
WHEN YOU TALK, BAD THINGS HAPPEN!
JUST LIKE WITH A-KUN! HE GOT HURT AND IT'S ALL YOUR FAULT!
I-IT IS *NOT!*
ALL I DID WAS SAY I *SAW* A-KUN GET HURT...
LIAR! YOU AIN'T FOOLIN' ME!
YOU SAID HE WAS GONNA GET HURT AND THEN HE DID!
YOU MADE IT HAPPEN!
THAT'S RIGHT!
SNIFF SNIFF
GO AWAY!

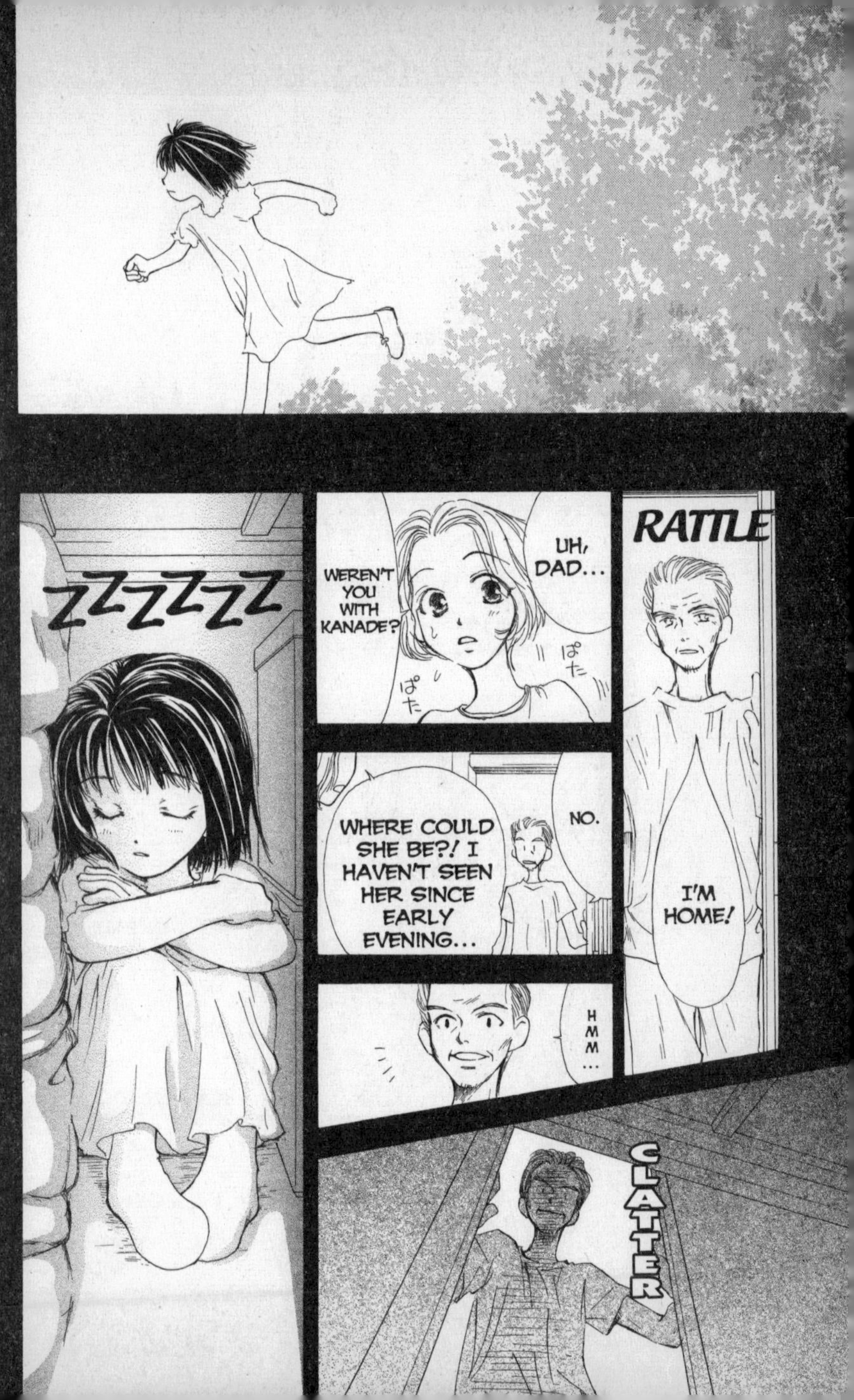
RATTLE
I'M HOME!
UH, DAD...
WEREN'T YOU WITH KANADE?
ぱた ぱた
NO.
WHERE COULD SHE BE?! I HAVEN'T SEEN HER SINCE EARLY EVENING...
HMM...
CLATTER
ZZZZZZZ

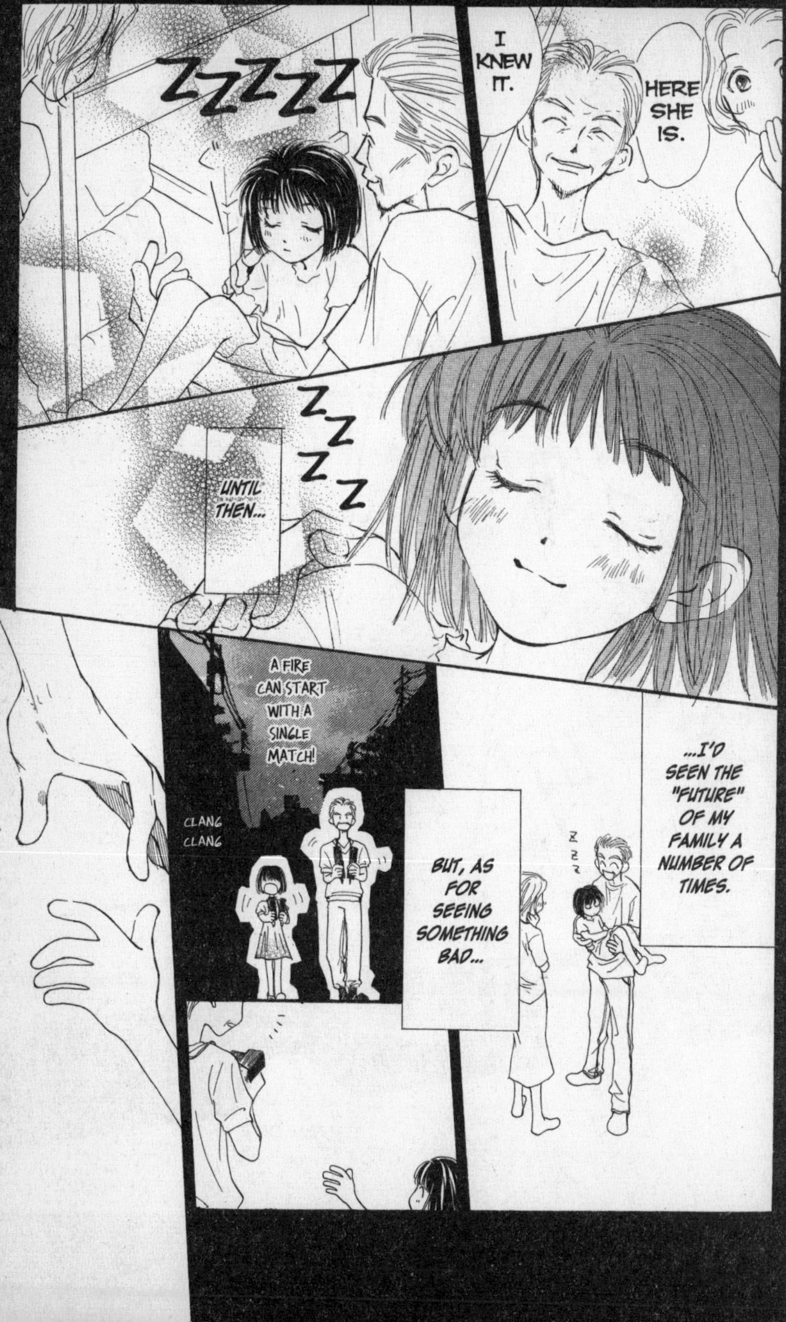
I KNEW IT.
HERE SHE IS.
ZZZZZZ
ZZZZ
UNTIL THEN...
...I'D SEEN THE "FUTURE" OF MY FAMILY A NUMBER OF TIMES.
ZZZ
BUT, AS FOR SEEING SOMETHING BAD...
A FIRE CAN START WITH A SINGLE MATCH!
CLANG CLANG

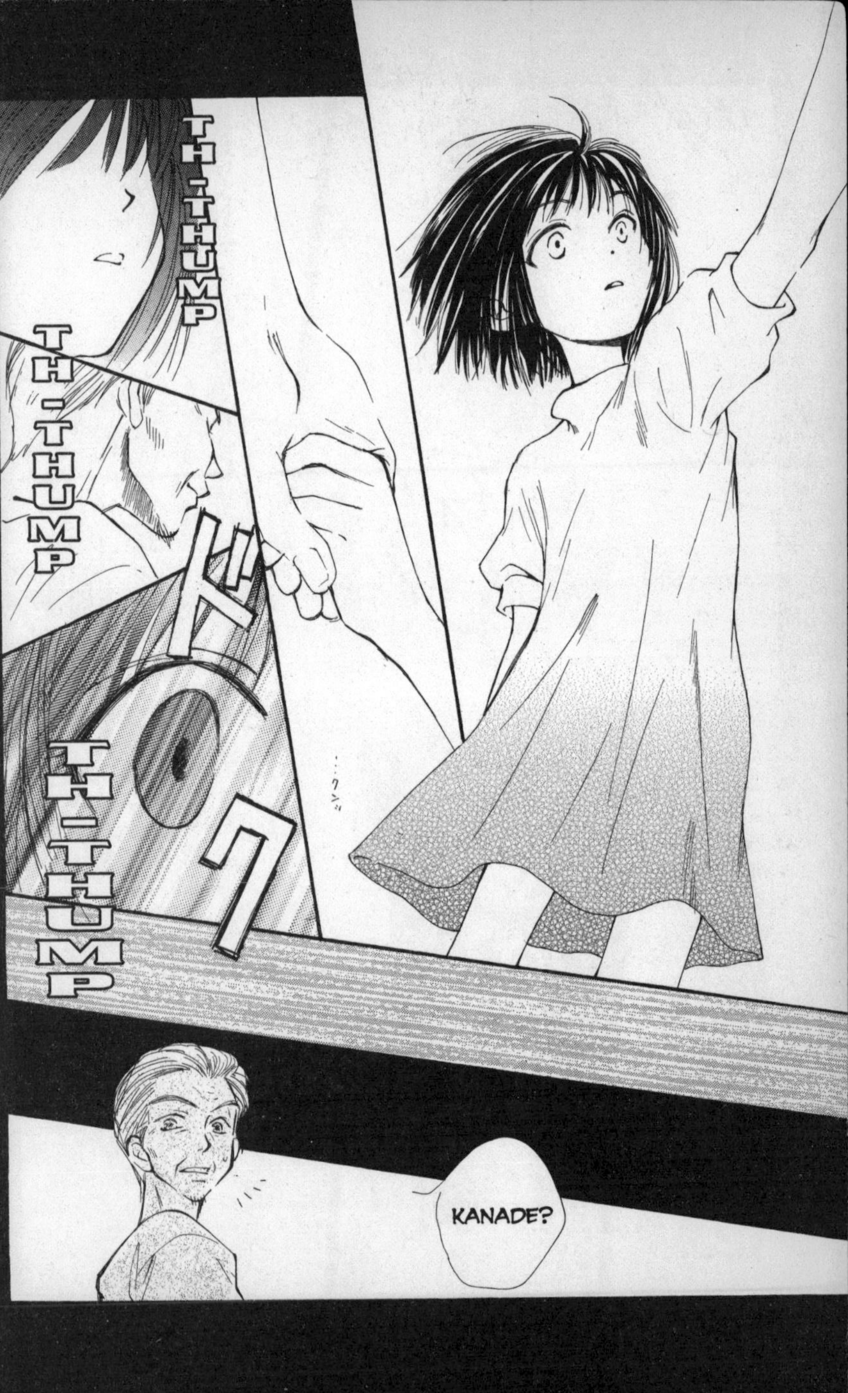
TH-THUMP
TH-THUMP
TH-THUMP
KANADE?

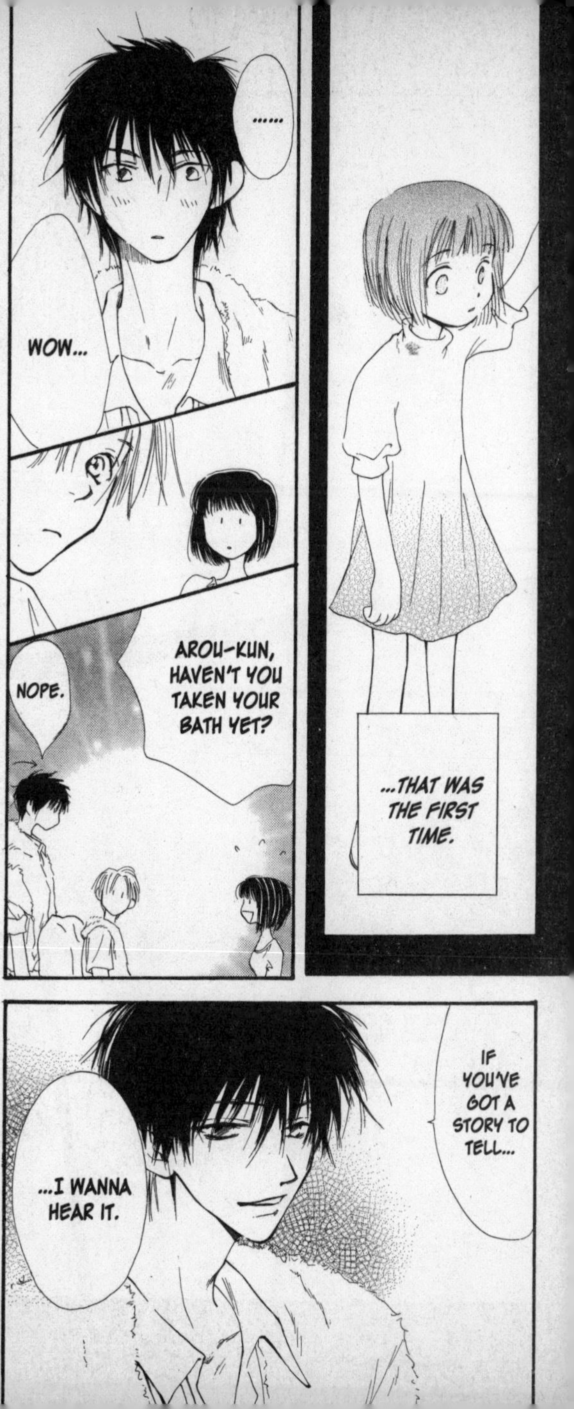
...THAT WAS THE FIRST TIME.
......
WOW...
AROU-KUN, HAVEN'T YOU TAKEN YOUR BATH YET?
NOPE.
IF YOU'VE GOT A STORY TO TELL...
...I WANNA HEAR IT.

SAKURA MAIL

NO. 1

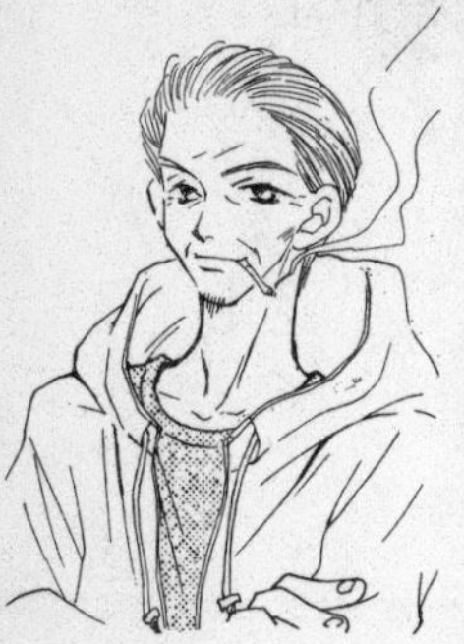

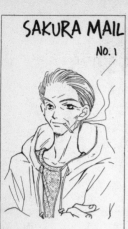

This story came out of my desire to show the people who raised Kanade-chan, and taught her to be the person she is today. Although, I'm sore there are many more people than just the ones in this story... By the way, back when I was still coming up with the characters' names, I thought up the situation of having Arou-kun and Namiki go together forthe first time to the house of the girl (Kanade) they both like and all hell breaks loose. I had lightly drawn the pages before Grandpa's appearance when my editor pointed out that with all the character high jinks, I was straying way off the theme. I hadn't noticed at all! Sigh... Of course, once I got Grandpa in there, I feel like his deep love kind of took over and got me back on track to finish the story smoothly (I think).

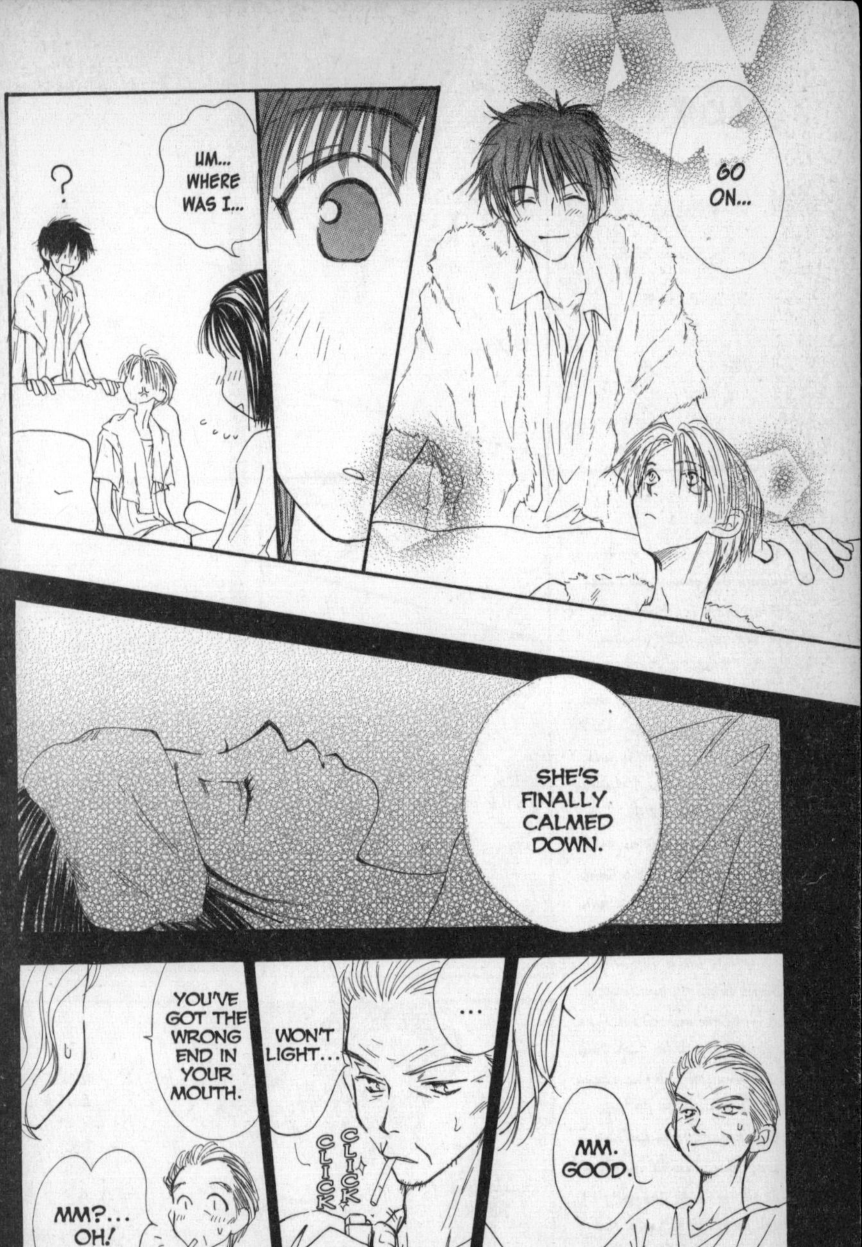
GO ON...
UM... WHERE WAS I...
?
SHE'S FINALLY CALMED DOWN.
MM. GOOD.
...
WON'T LIGHT...
CLICK CLICK
YOU'VE GOT THE WRONG END IN YOUR MOUTH.
MM?... OH!

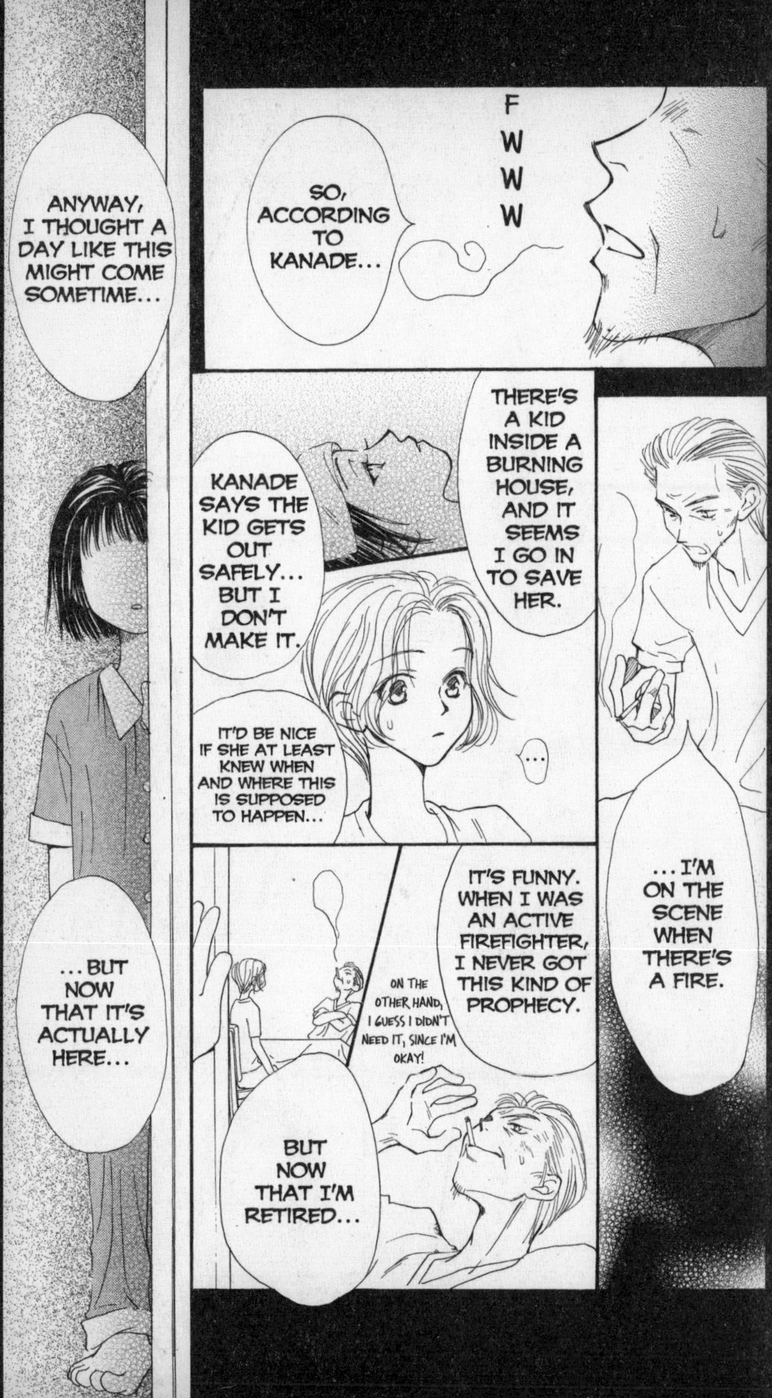
FWWW
SO, ACCORDING TO KANADE...
...I'M ON THE SCENE WHEN THERE'S A FIRE.
THERE'S A KID INSIDE A BURNING HOUSE, AND IT SEEMS I GO IN TO SAVE HER.
KANADE SAYS THE KID GETS OUT SAFELY... BUT I DON'T MAKE IT.
...
IT'D BE NICE IF SHE AT LEAST KNEW WHEN AND WHERE THIS IS SUPPOSED TO HAPPEN...
IT'S FUNNY. WHEN I WAS AN ACTIVE FIREFIGHTER, I NEVER GOT THIS KIND OF PROPHECY.
ON THE OTHER HAND, I GUESS I DIDN'T NEED IT, SINCE I'M OKAY!
BUT NOW THAT I'M RETIRED...
ANYWAY, I THOUGHT A DAY LIKE THIS MIGHT COME SOMETIME...
...BUT NOW THAT IT'S ACTUALLY HERE...

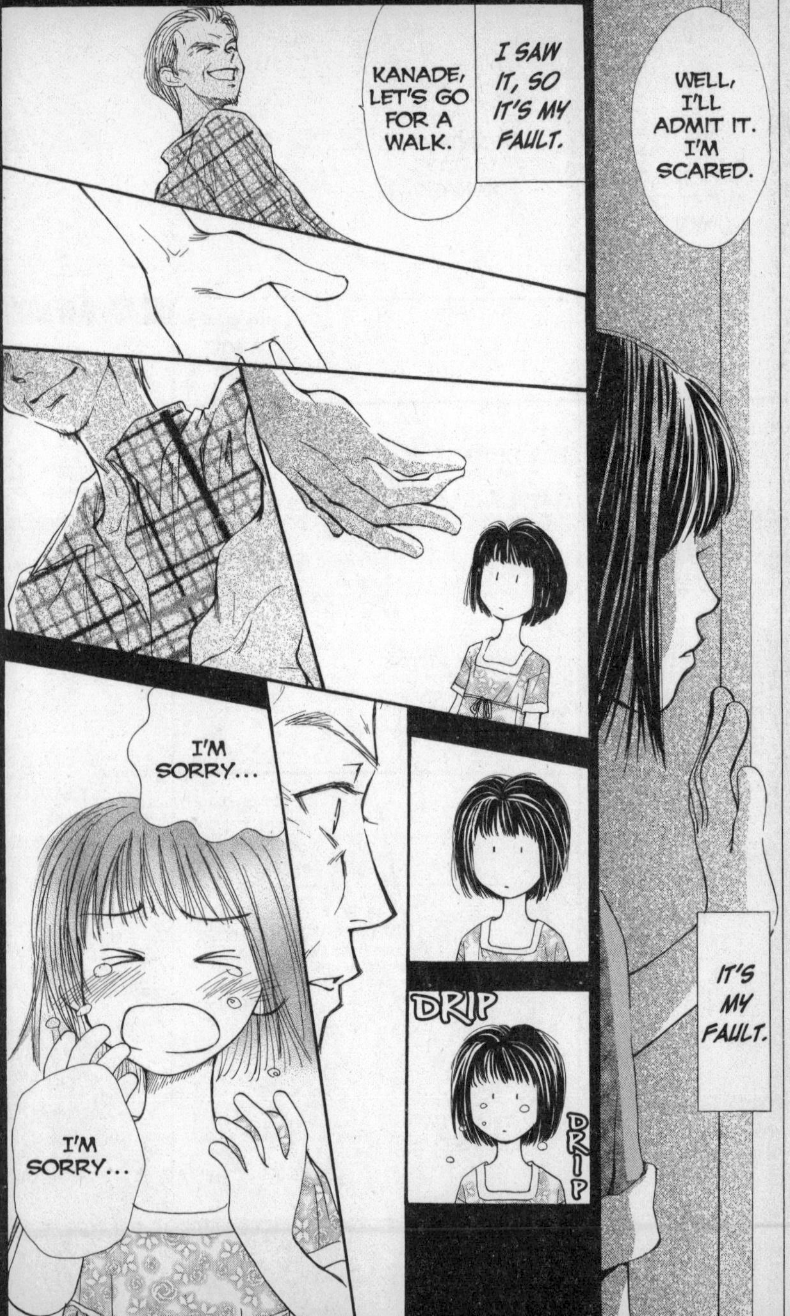
WELL, I'LL ADMIT IT. I'M SCARED.
IT'S MY FAULT.
I SAW IT, SO IT'S MY FAULT.
KANADE, LET'S GO FOR A WALK.
DRIP
DRIP
I'M SORRY...
I'M SORRY...

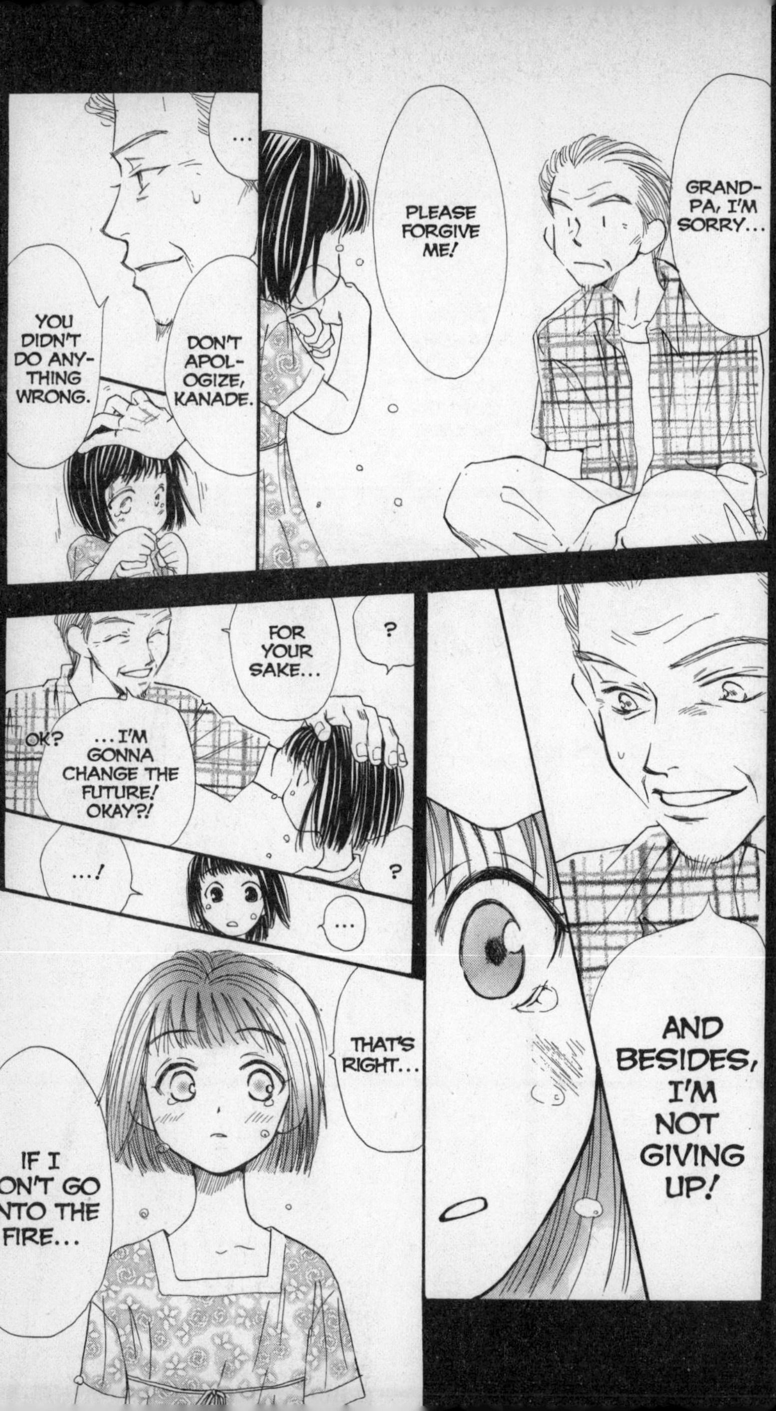
GRAND-PA, I'M SORRY...
PLEASE FORGIVE ME!
...
DON'T APOL-OGIZE, KANADE.
YOU DIDN'T DO ANY-THING WRONG.
AND BESIDES, I'M NOT GIVING UP!
?
FOR YOUR SAKE...
...I'M GONNA CHANGE THE FUTURE! OKAY?!
OK?
?
...
...!
THAT'S RIGHT...
IF I DON'T GO INTO THE FIRE...

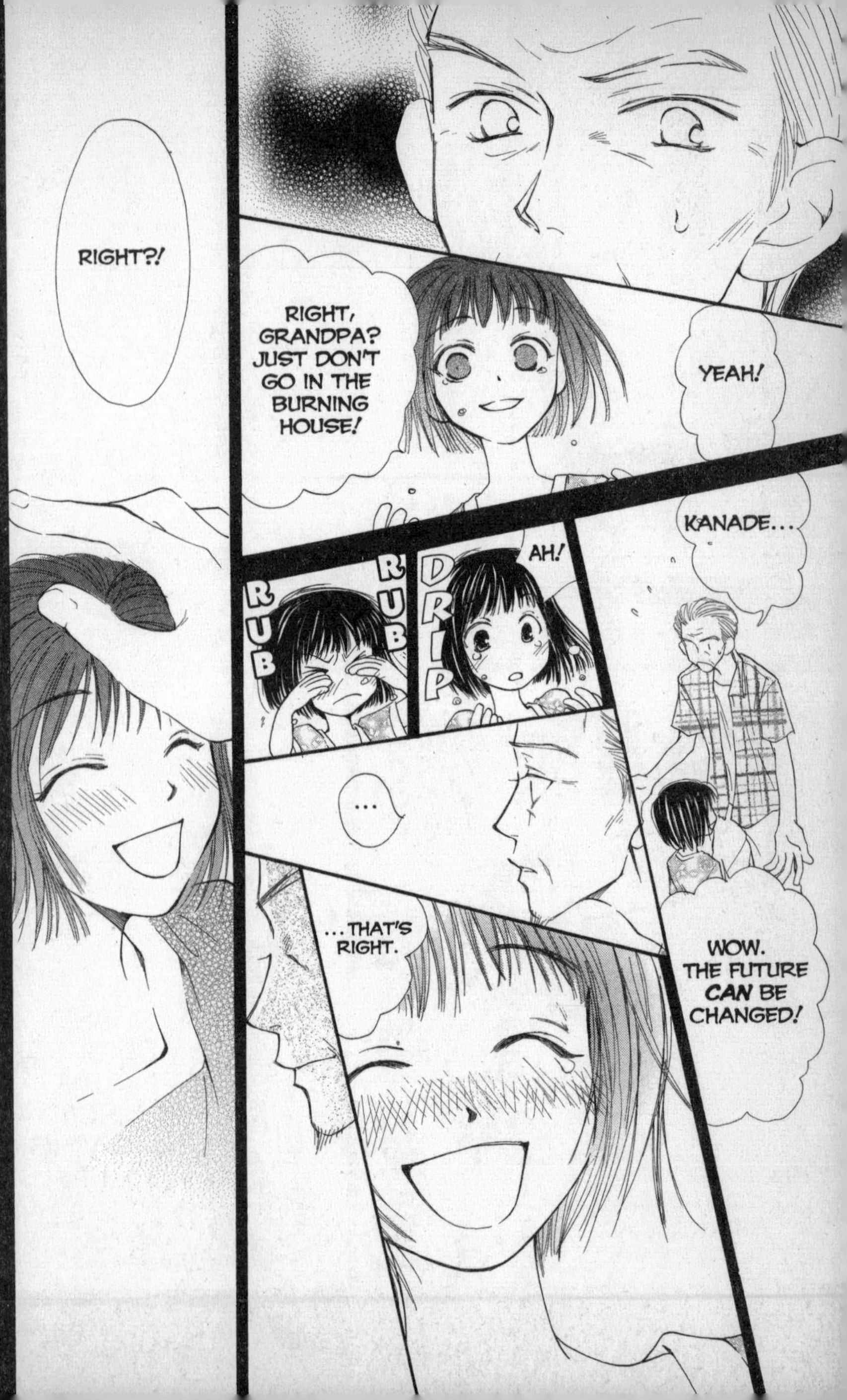
RIGHT, GRANDPA? JUST DON'T GO IN THE BURNING HOUSE!
YEAH!
KANADE...
AH!
DRIP
RUB RUB
...
...THAT'S RIGHT.
WOW. THE FUTURE CAN BE CHANGED!
RIGHT?!

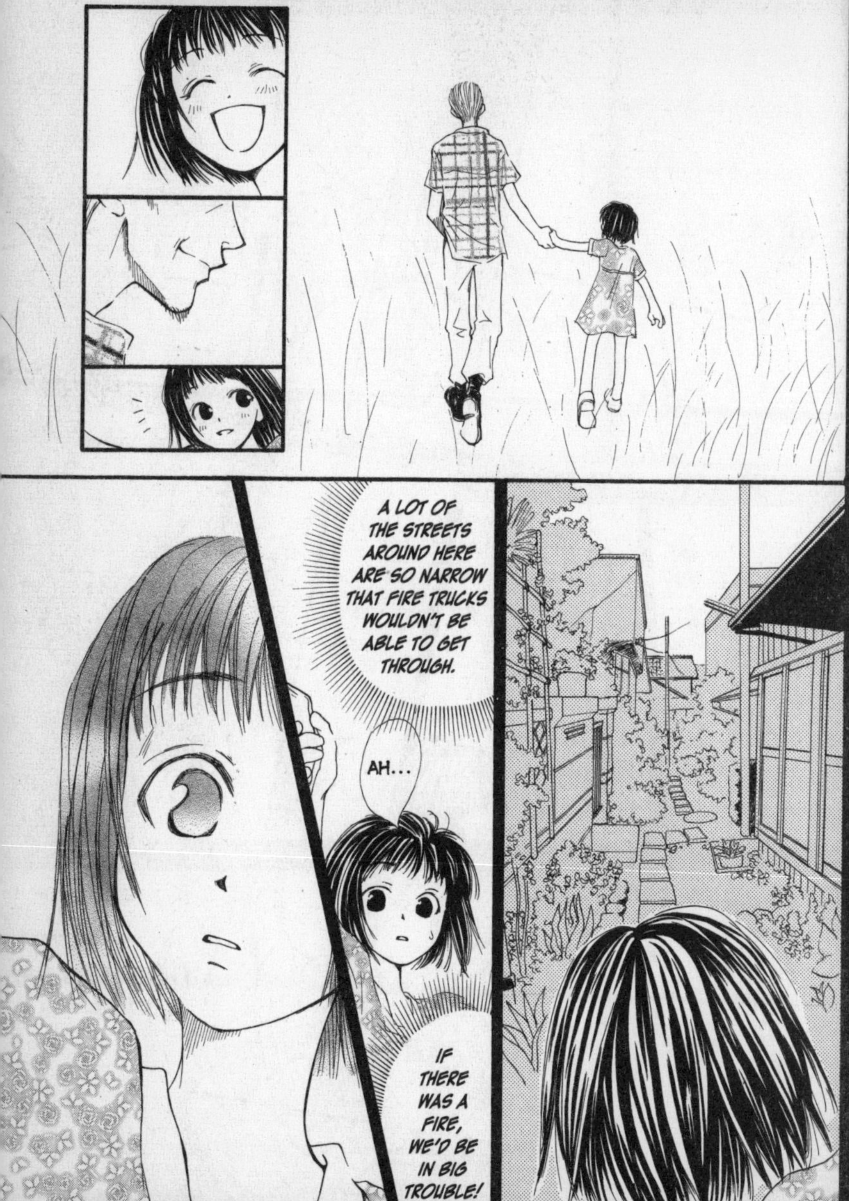A LOT OF THE STREETS AROUND HERE ARE SO NARROW THAT FIRE TRUCKS WOULDN'T BE ABLE TO GET THROUGH.
IF THERE WAS A FIRE, WE'D BE IN BIG TROUBLE!
AH...

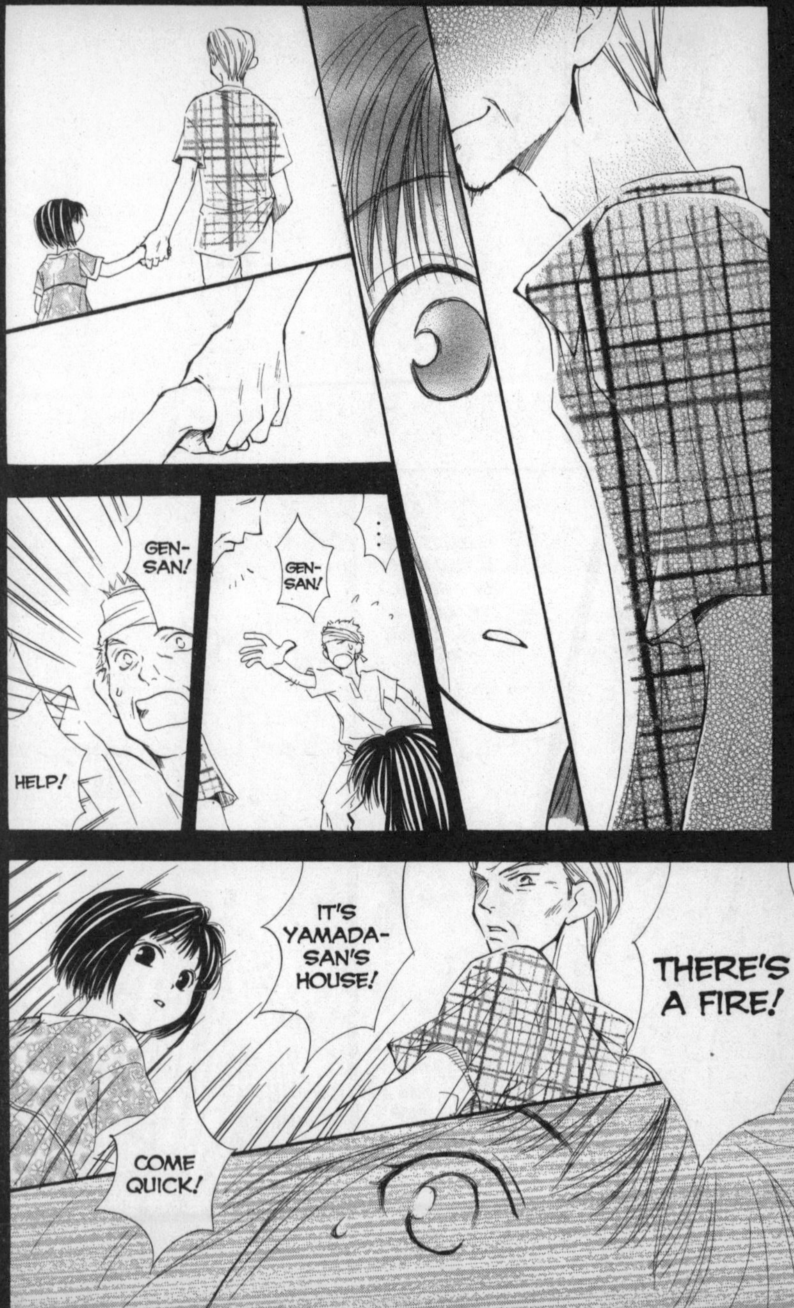
...
GEN-SAN!
GEN-SAN!
HELP!
THERE'S A FIRE!
IT'S YAMADA-SAN'S HOUSE!
COME QUICK!

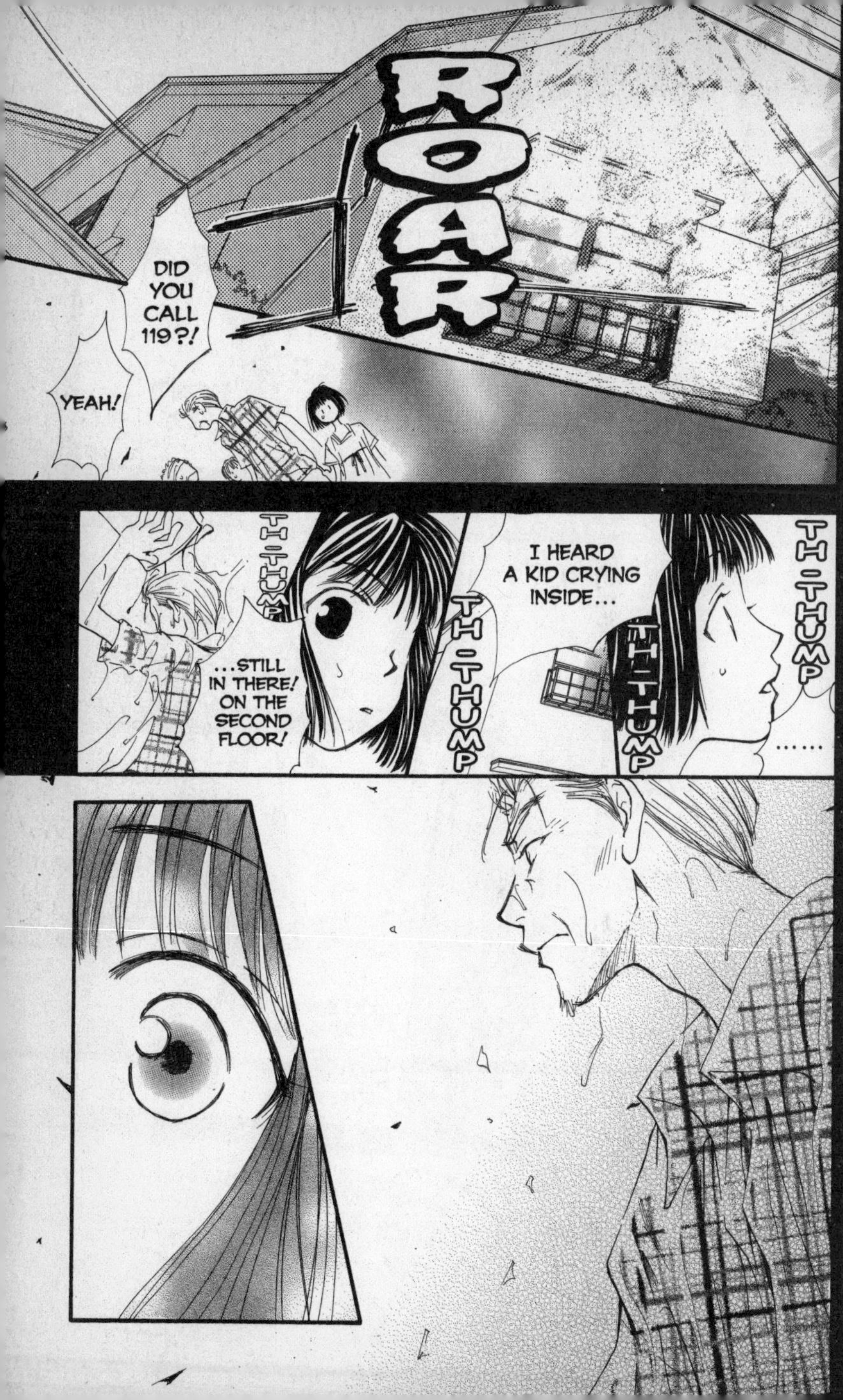
ROAR
DID YOU CALL 119?!
YEAH!
TH-THUMP
I HEARD A KID CRYING INSIDE...
TH-THUMP
......
TH-THUMP
...STILL IN THERE! ON THE SECOND FLOOR!
TH-THUMP

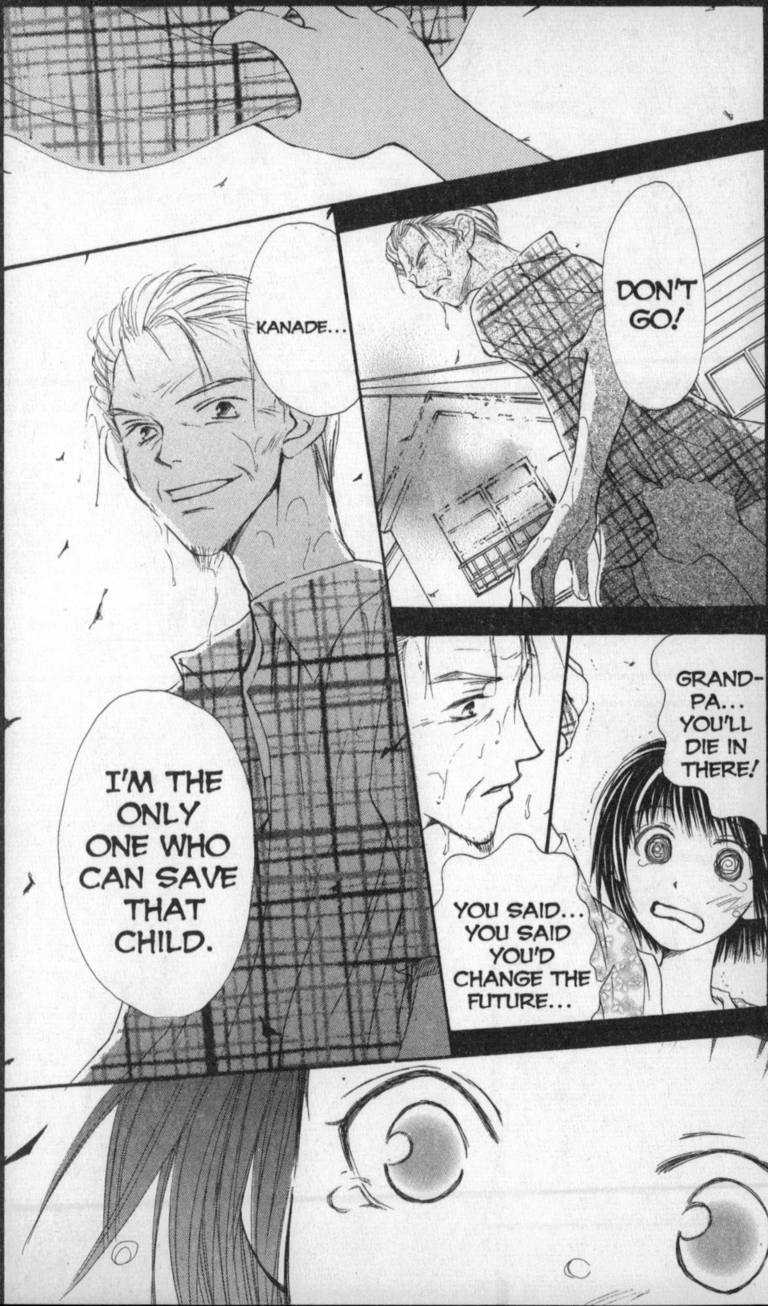
DON'T GO!
GRAND-PA... YOU'LL DIE IN THERE!
YOU SAID... YOU SAID YOU'D CHANGE THE FUTURE...
KANADE...
I'M THE ONLY ONE WHO CAN SAVE THAT CHILD.

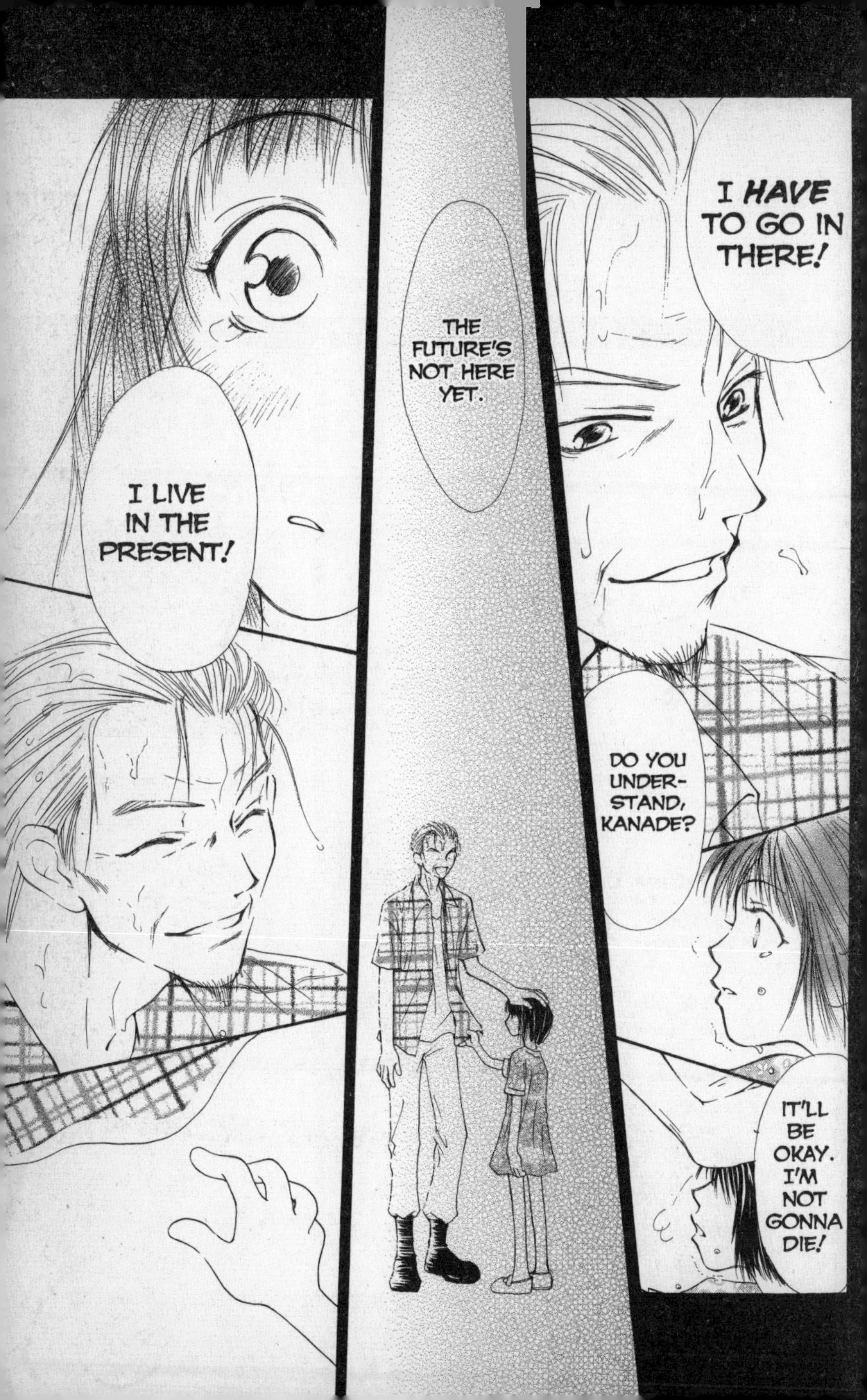
I HAVE TO GO IN THERE!
DO YOU UNDER-STAND, KANADE?
IT'LL BE OKAY. I'M NOT GONNA DIE!
THE FUTURE'S NOT HERE YET.
I LIVE IN THE PRESENT!

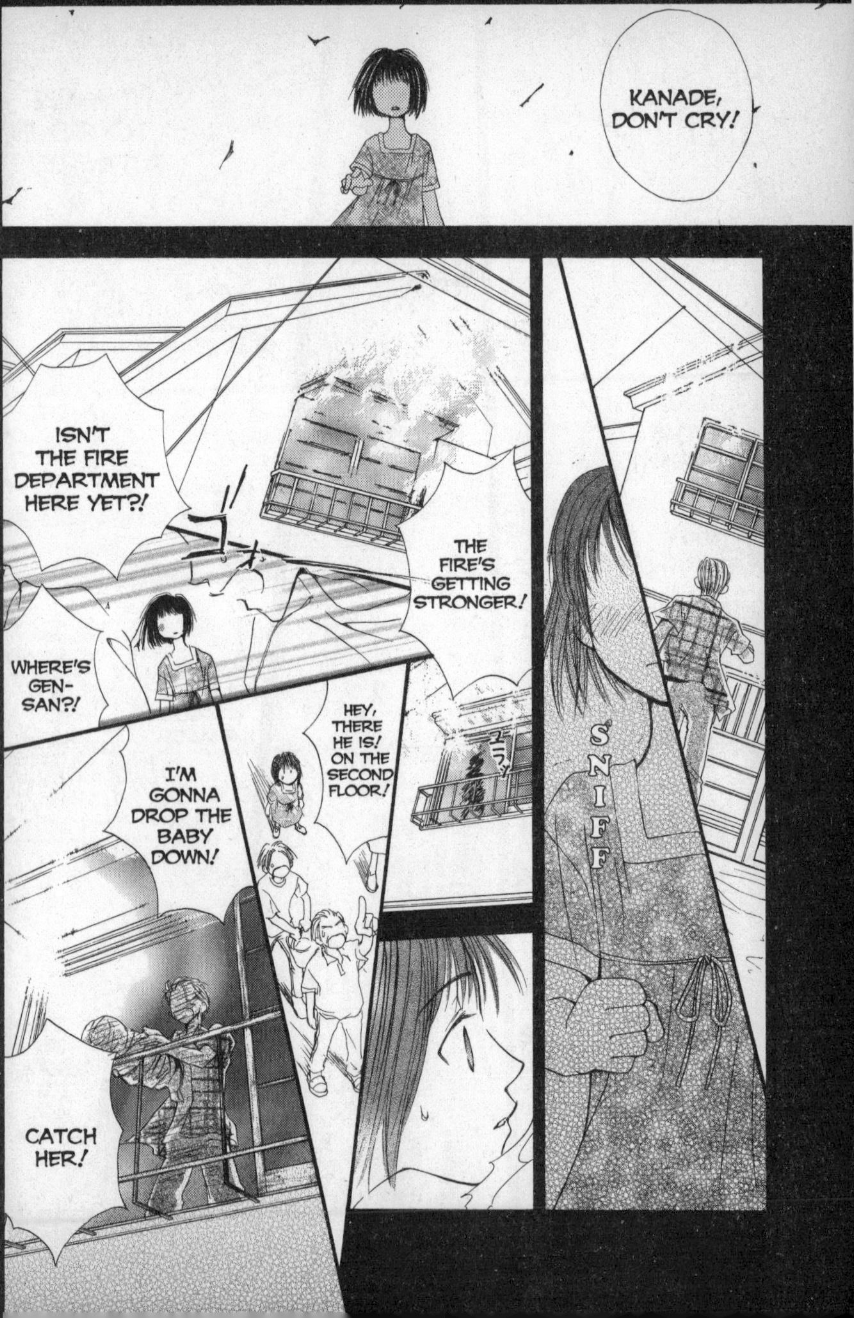
KANADE, DON'T CRY!
SNIFF
THE FIRE'S GETTING STRONGER!
ISN'T THE FIRE DEPARTMENT HERE YET?!
WHERE'S GEN-SAN?!
HEY, THERE HE IS! ON THE SECOND FLOOR!
I'M GONNA DROP THE BABY DOWN!
CATCH HER!

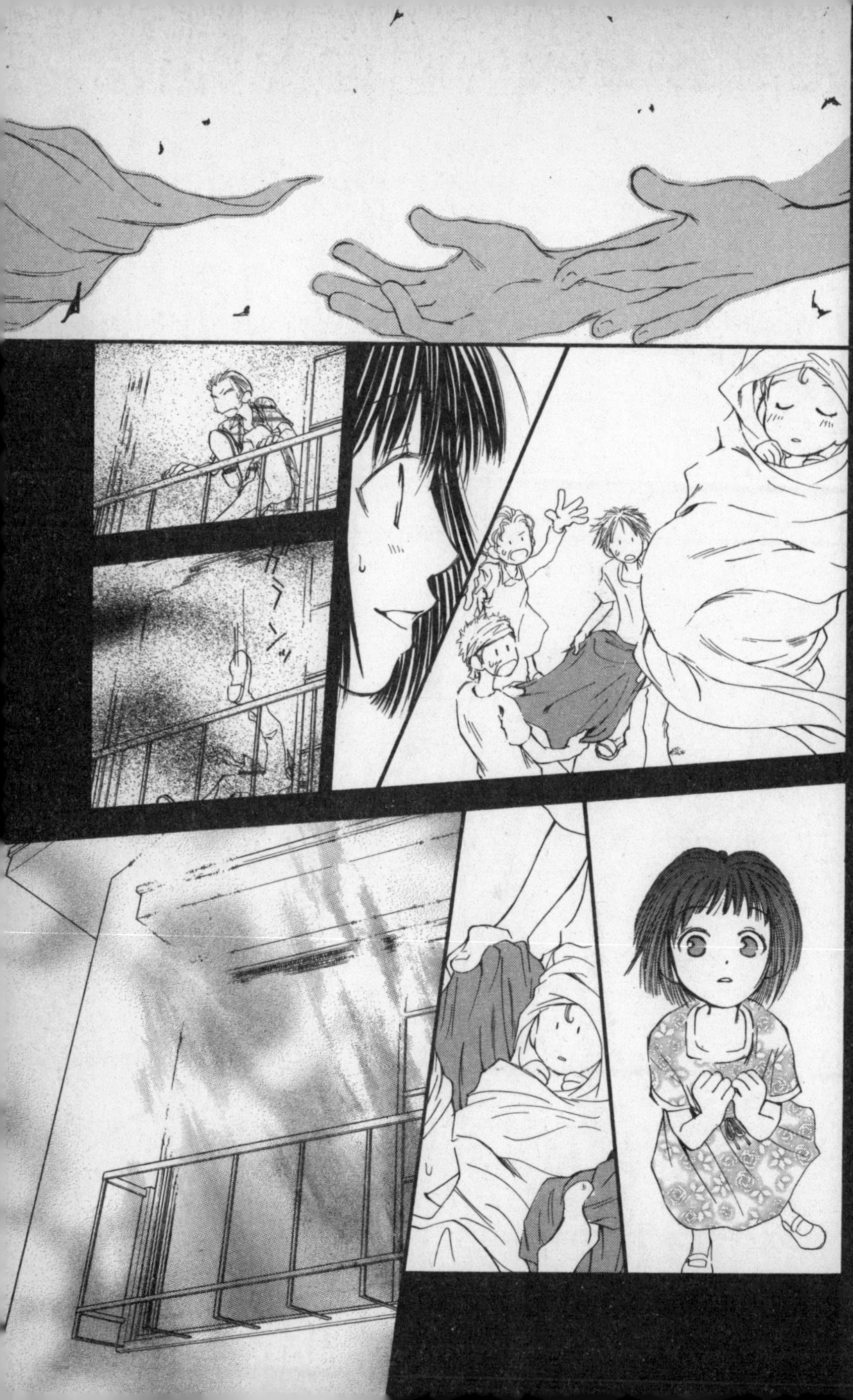

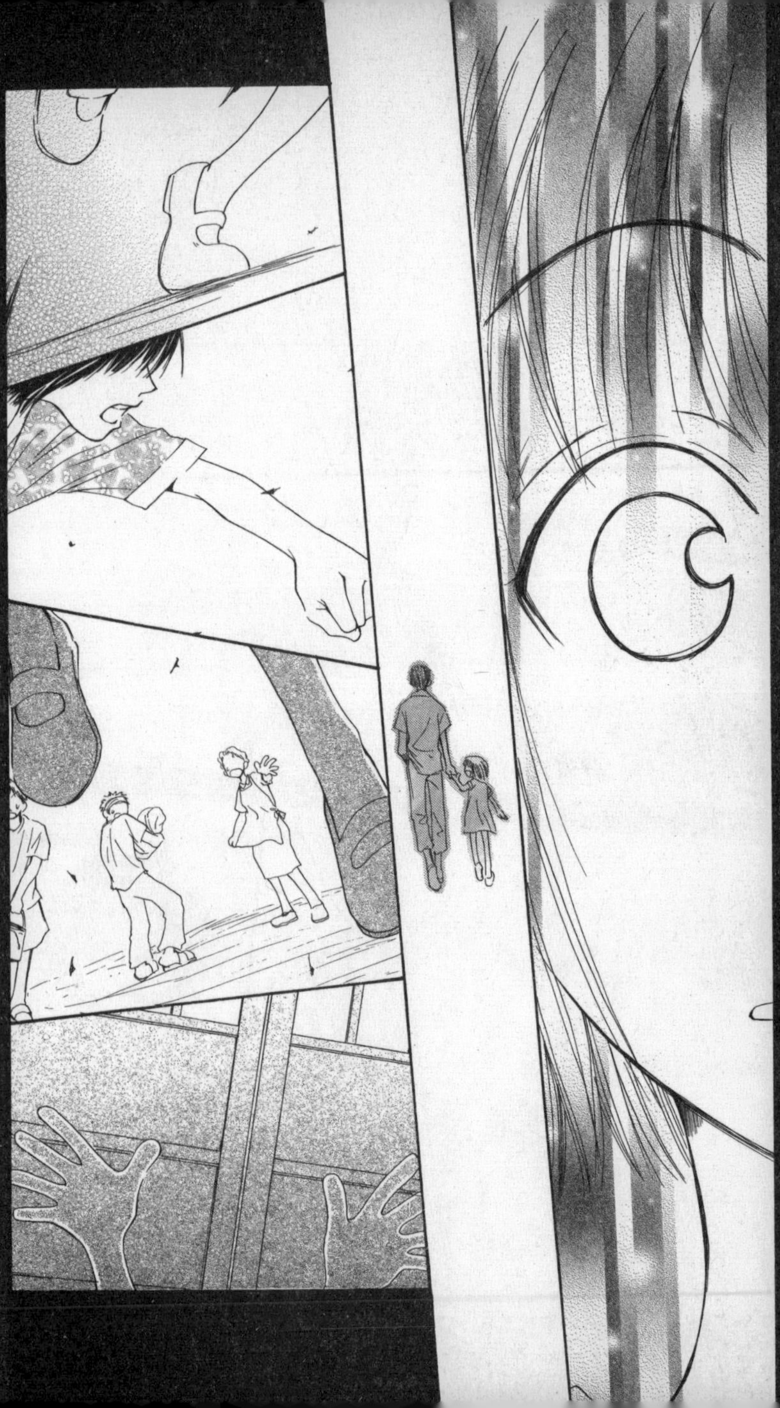

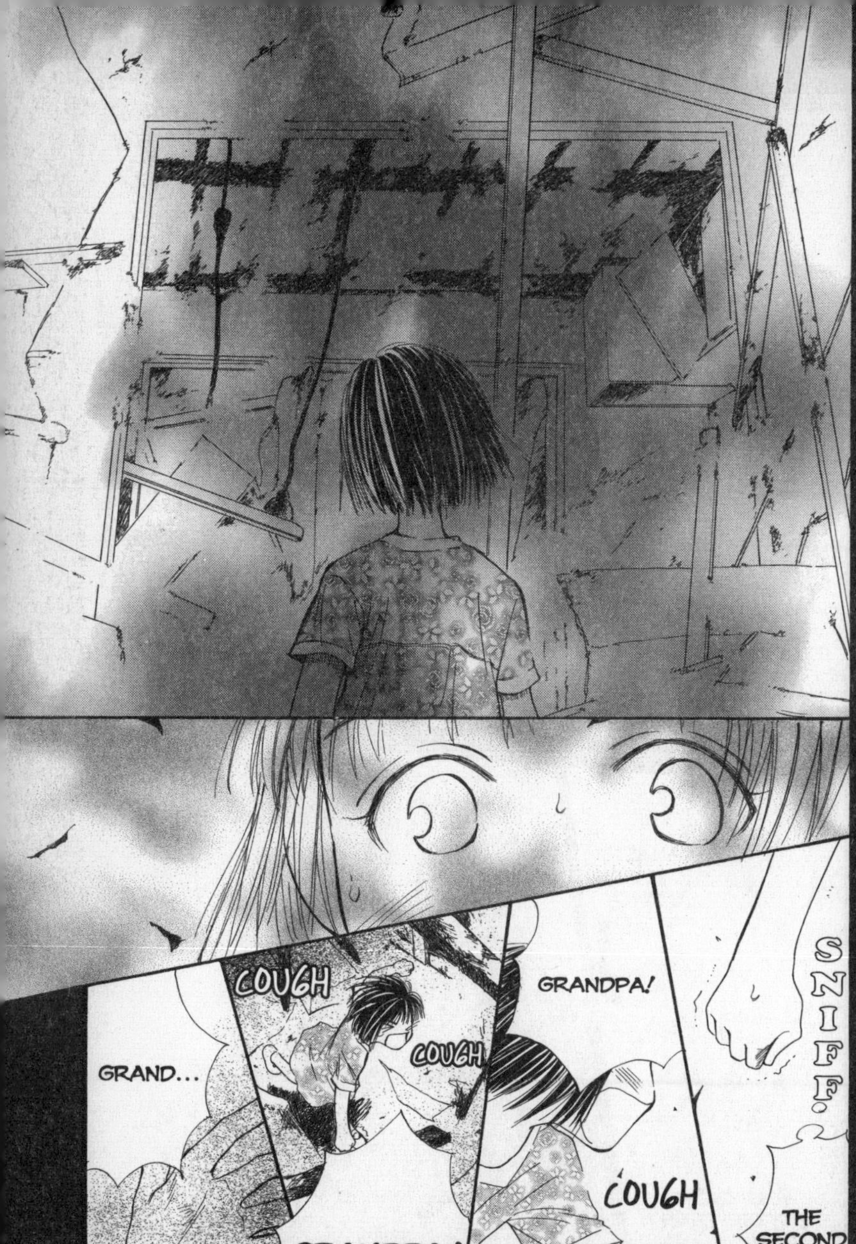
SNIFF.
THE SECOND FLOOR!
GRANDPA!
COUGH
COUGH
COUGH
GRAND...
GRANDPA!

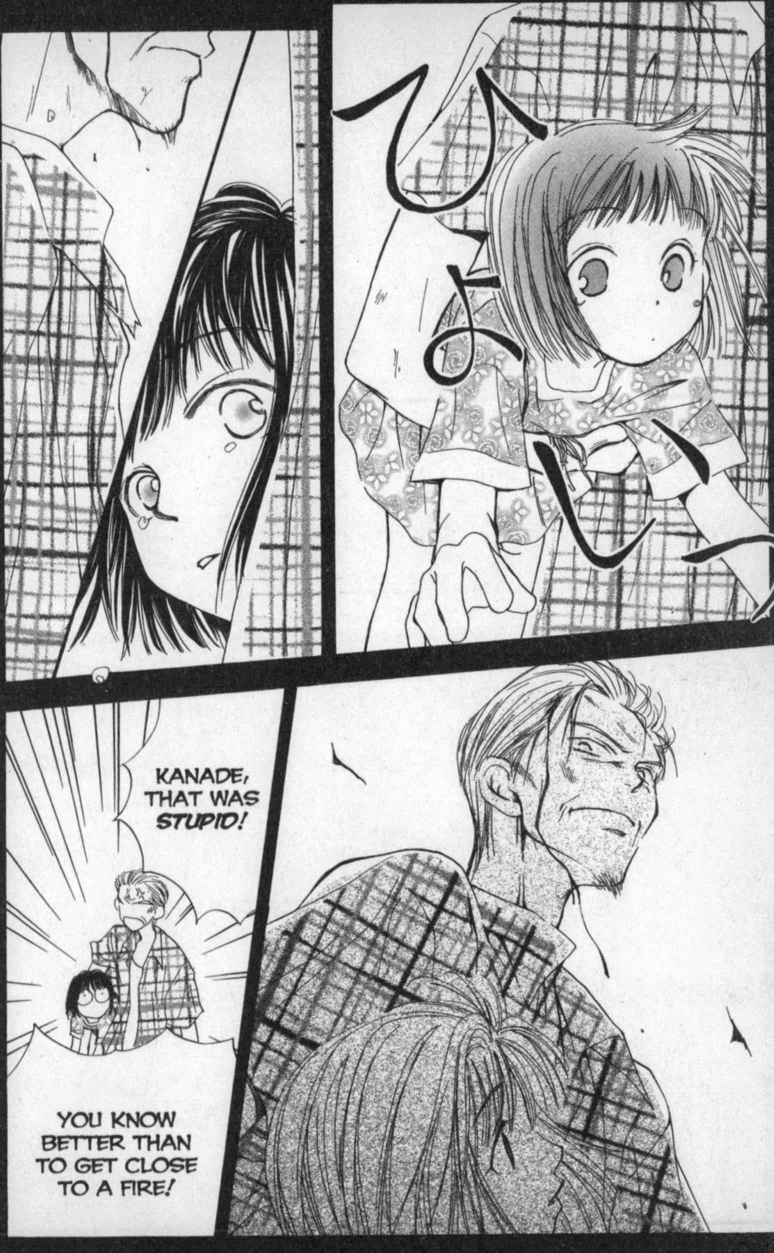
KANADE, THAT WAS *STUPID!*
YOU KNOW BETTER THAN TO GET CLOSE TO A FIRE!

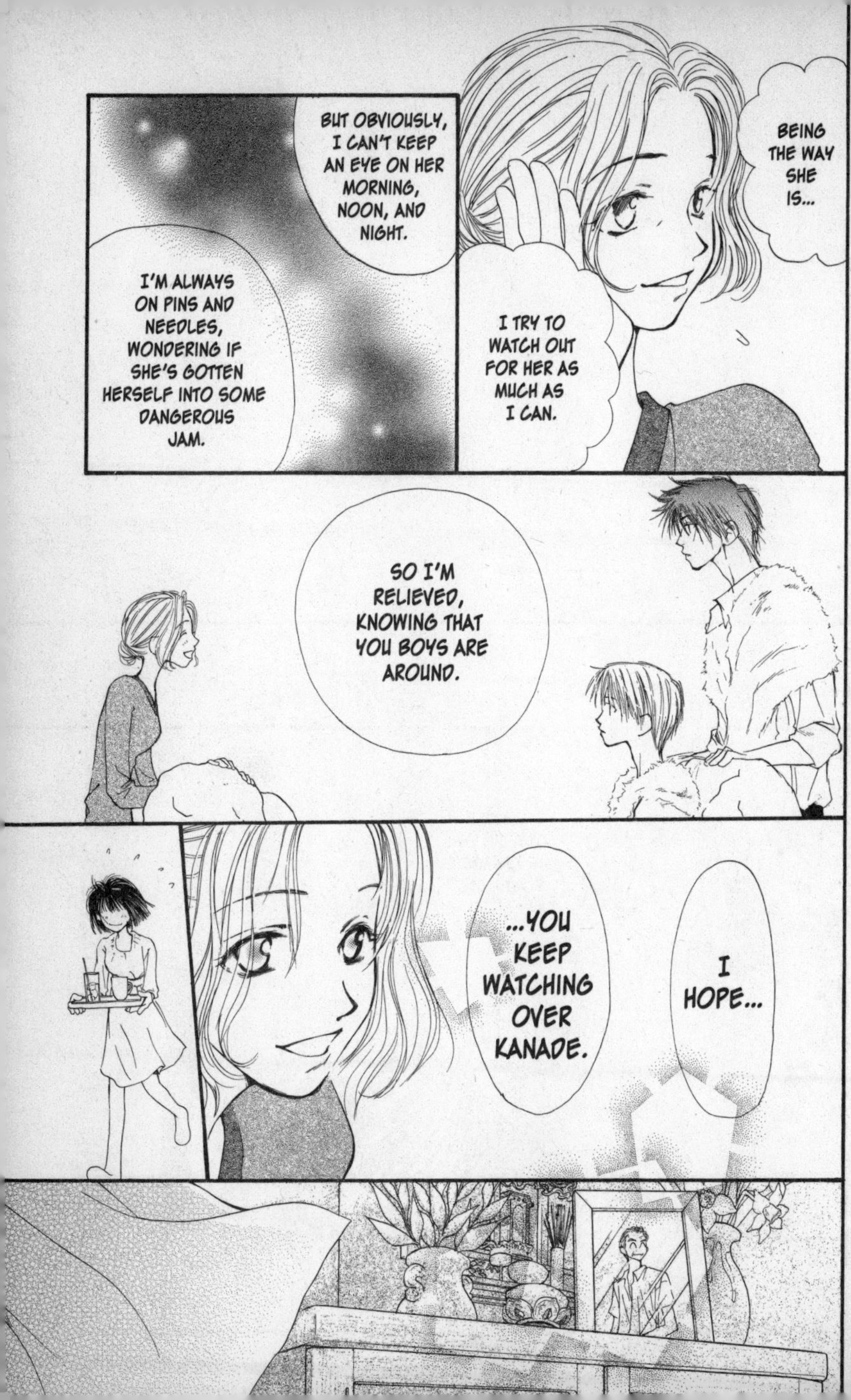
BEING THE WAY SHE IS...
I TRY TO WATCH OUT FOR HER AS MUCH AS I CAN.
BUT OBVIOUSLY, I CAN'T KEEP AN EYE ON HER MORNING, NOON, AND NIGHT.
I'M ALWAYS ON PINS AND NEEDLES, WONDERING IF SHE'S GOTTEN HERSELF INTO SOME DANGEROUS JAM.
SO I'M RELIEVED, KNOWING THAT YOU BOYS ARE AROUND.
I HOPE...
...YOU KEEP WATCHING OVER KANADE.

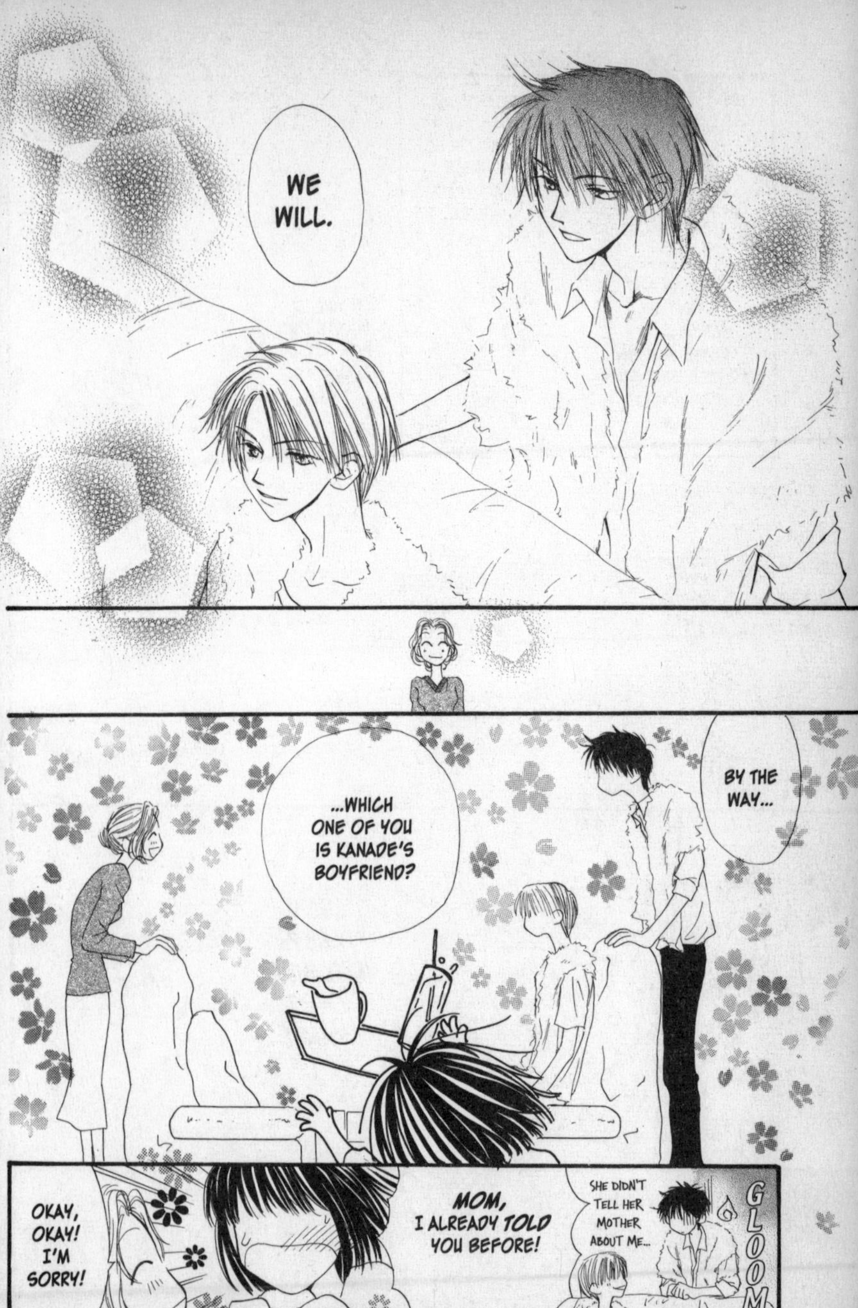
WE WILL.
BY THE WAY...
...WHICH ONE OF YOU IS KANADE'S BOYFRIEND?
GLOOM
SHE DIDN'T TELL HER MOTHER ABOUT ME...
MOM, I ALREADY TOLD YOU BEFORE!
OKAY, OKAY! I'M SORRY!

CHAPTER 7: END

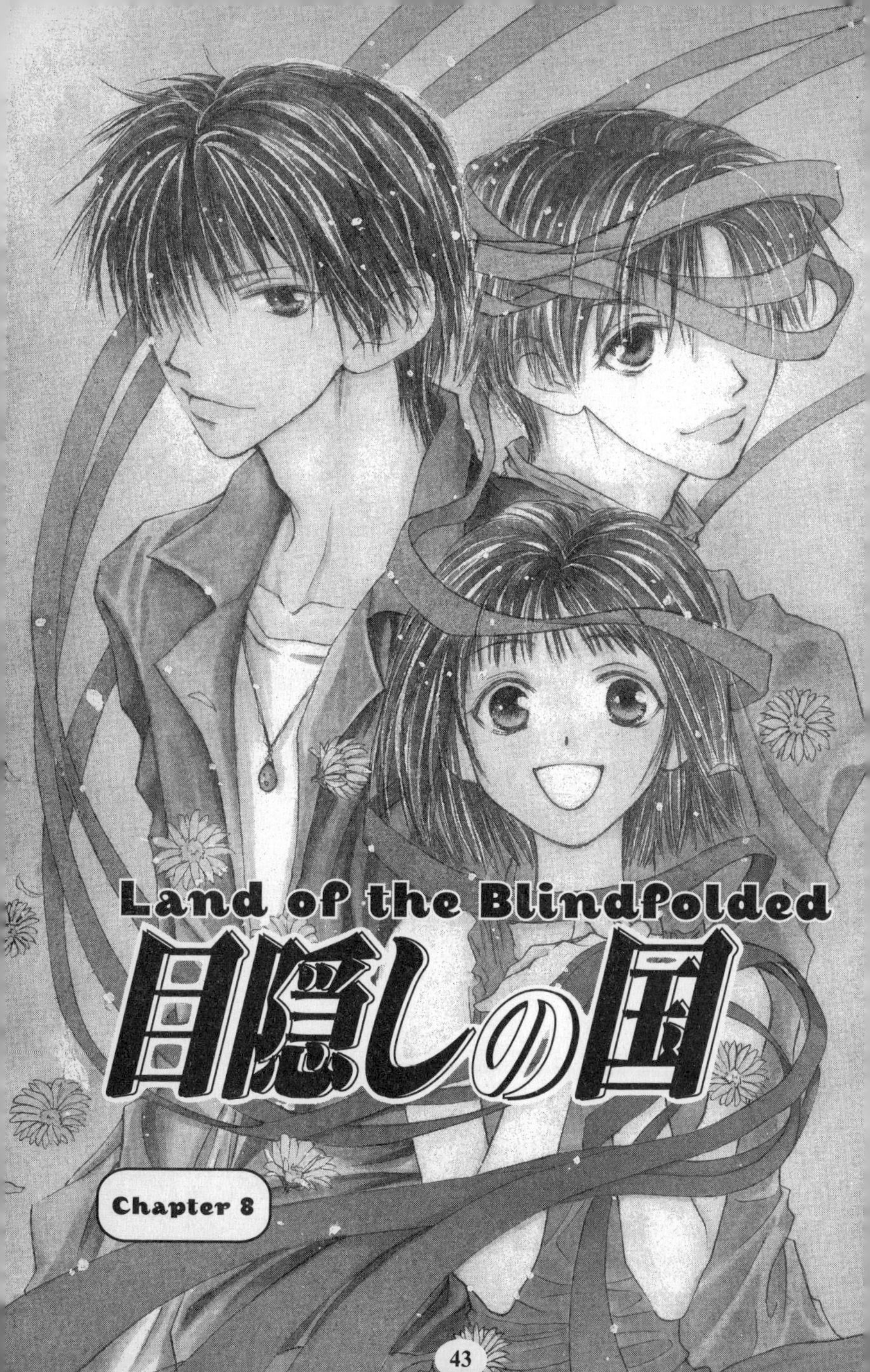
Land of the Blindfolded
目隠しの国
Chapter 8

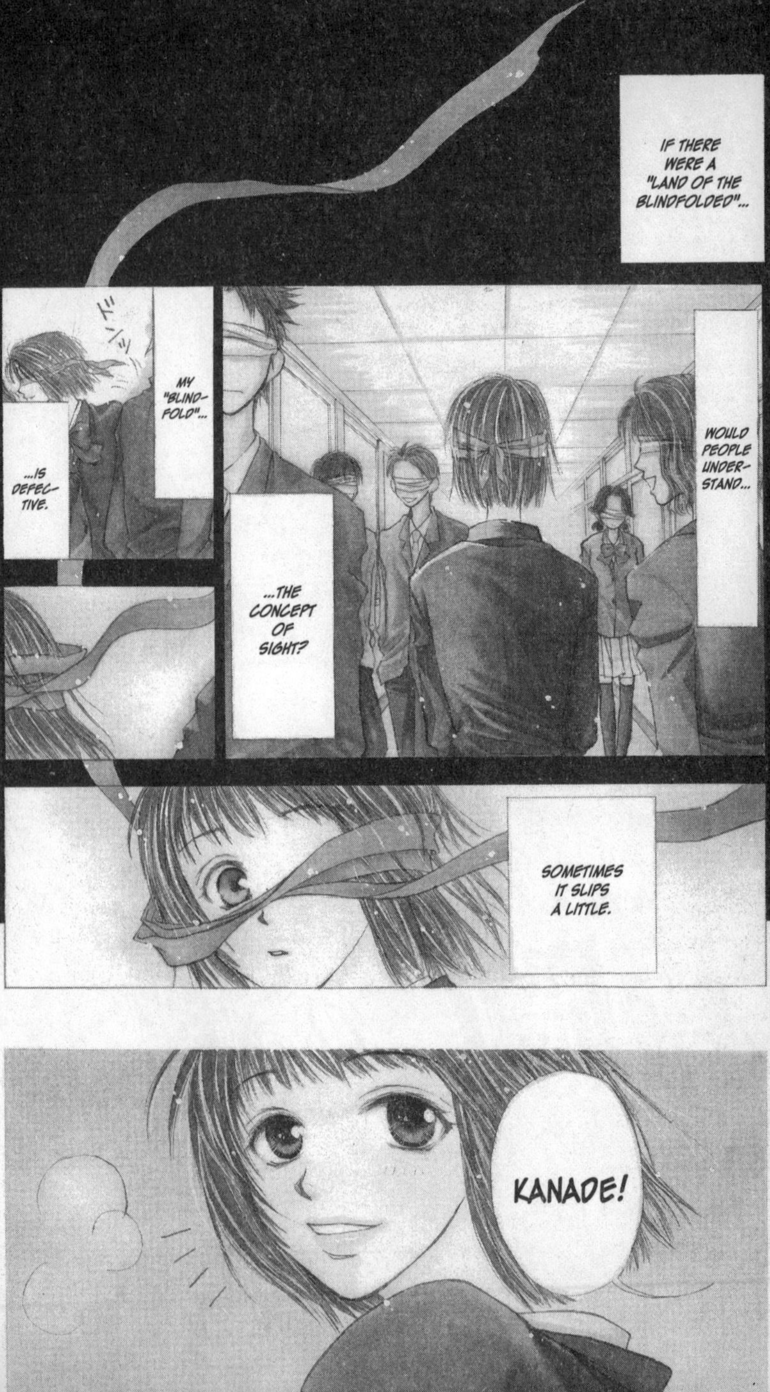
IF THERE WERE A "LAND OF THE BLINDFOLDED"...
WOULD PEOPLE UNDERSTAND...
...THE CONCEPT OF SIGHT?
MY "BLINDFOLD"...
...IS DEFECTIVE.
SOMETIMES IT SLIPS A LITTLE.
KANADE!

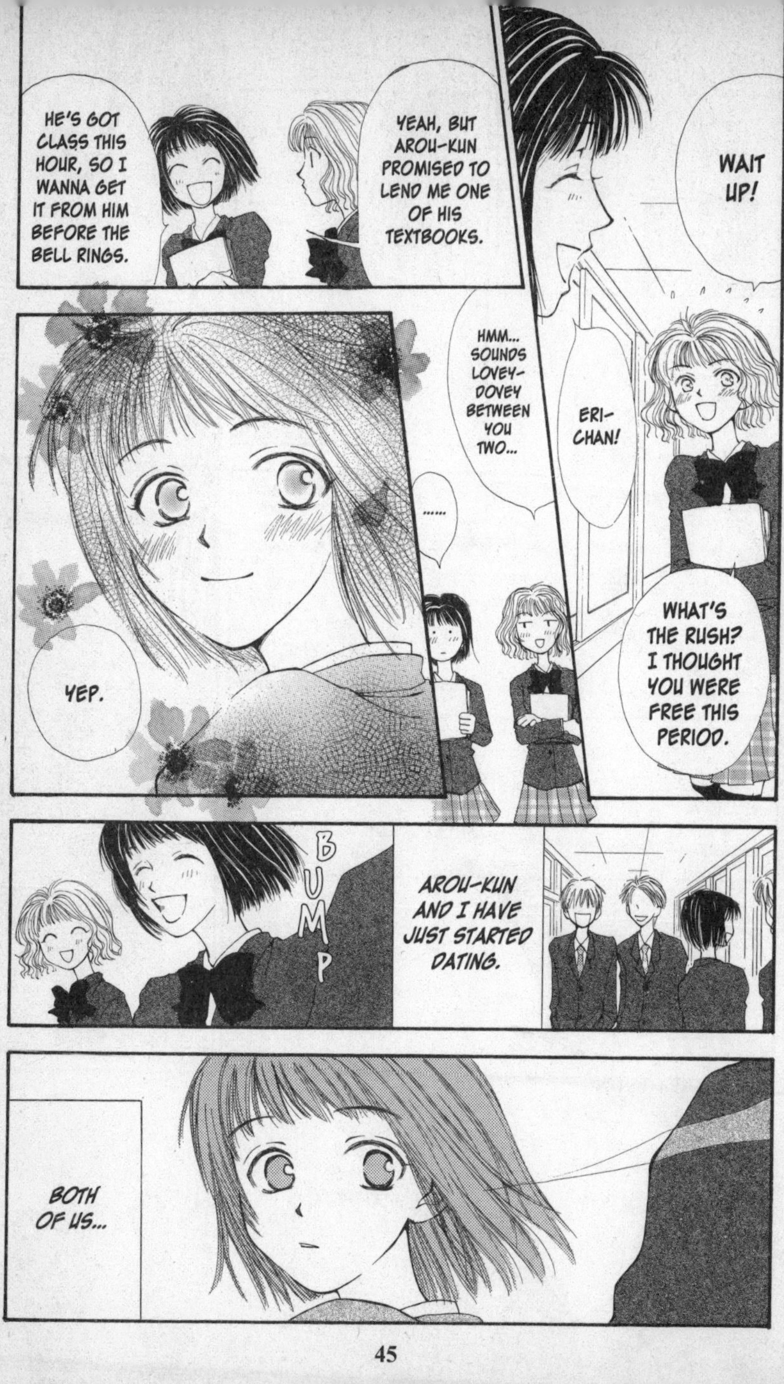
WAIT UP!
ERI-CHAN!
WHAT'S THE RUSH? I THOUGHT YOU WERE FREE THIS PERIOD.
YEAH, BUT AROU-KUN PROMISED TO LEND ME ONE OF HIS TEXTBOOKS.
HE'S GOT CLASS THIS HOUR, SO I WANNA GET IT FROM HIM BEFORE THE BELL RINGS.
HMM... SOUNDS LOVEY-DOVEY BETWEEN YOU TWO...
......
YEP.
AROU-KUN AND I HAVE JUST STARTED DATING.
BUMP
BOTH OF US...

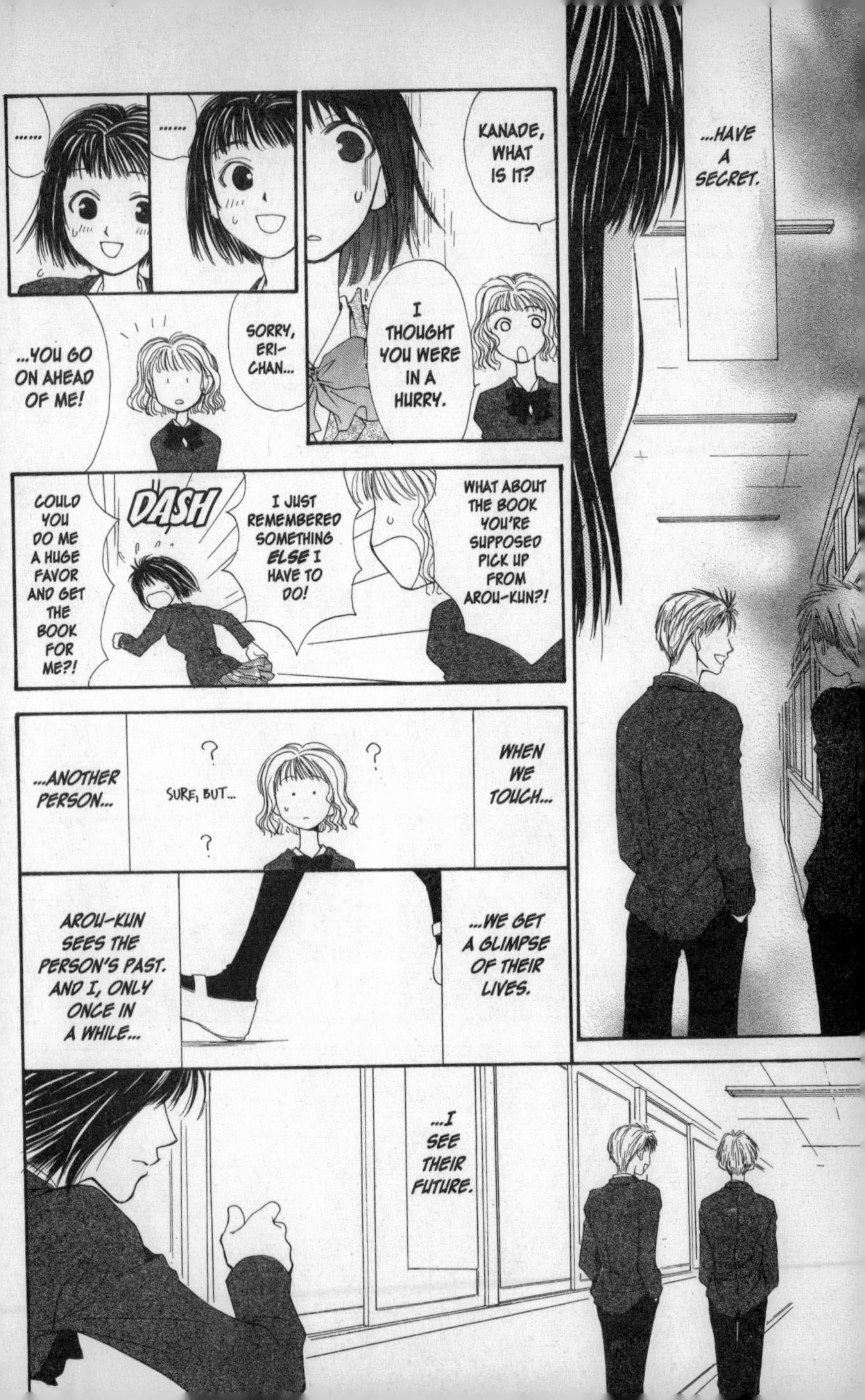
...HAVE A SECRET.
KANADE, WHAT IS IT?
I THOUGHT YOU WERE IN A HURRY.
......
......
SORRY, ERI-CHAN...
...YOU GO ON AHEAD OF ME!
WHAT ABOUT THE BOOK YOU'RE SUPPOSED PICK UP FROM AROU-KUN?!
I JUST REMEMBERED SOMETHING ELSE I HAVE TO DO!
DASH
COULD YOU DO ME A HUGE FAVOR AND GET THE BOOK FOR ME?!
WHEN WE TOUCH...
SURE, BUT...
...ANOTHER PERSON...
...WE GET A GLIMPSE OF THEIR LIVES.
AROU-KUN SEES THE PERSON'S PAST. AND I, ONLY ONCE IN A WHILE...
...I SEE THEIR FUTURE.

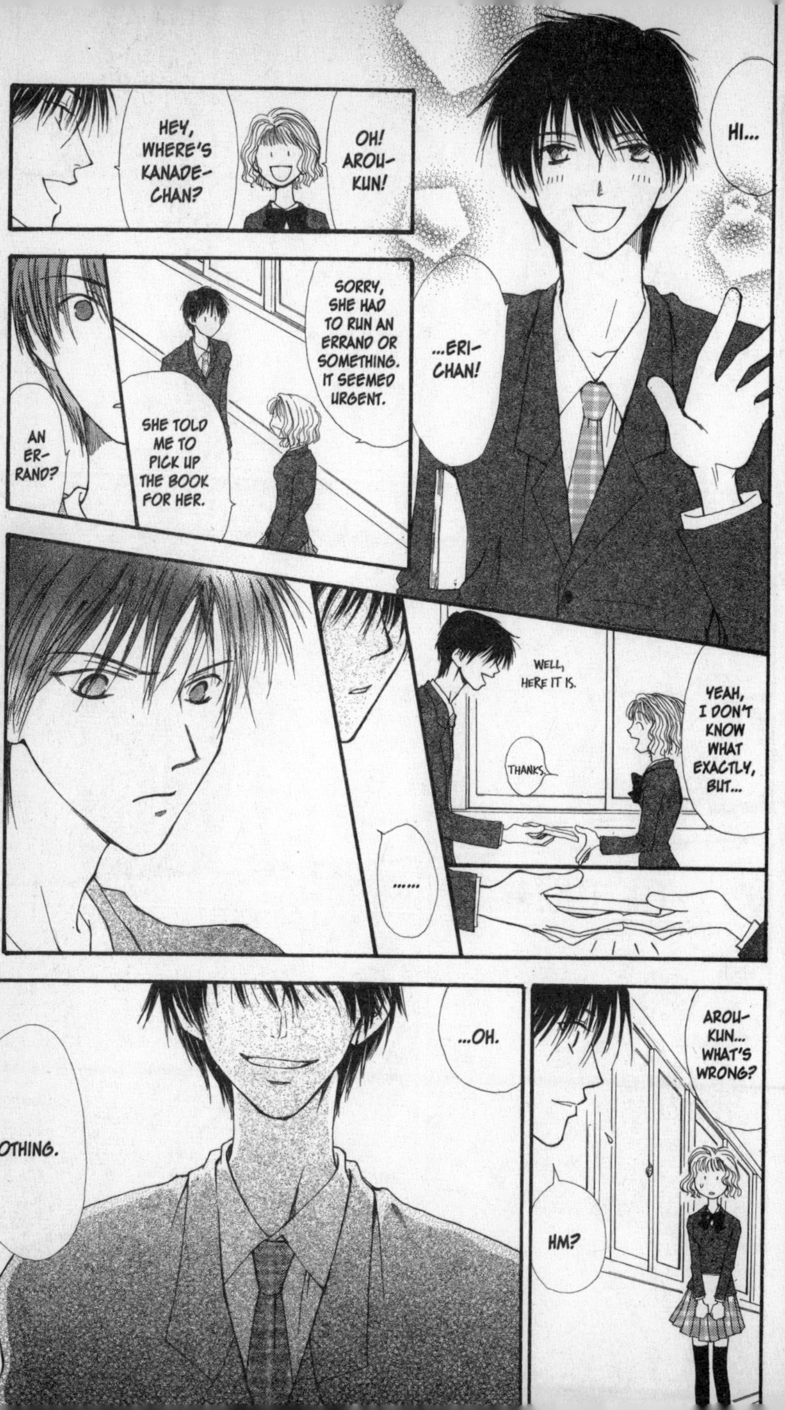
HI...
...ERI-CHAN!
OH! AROU-KUN!
HEY, WHERE'S KANADE-CHAN?
SORRY, SHE HAD TO RUN AN ERRAND OR SOMETHING. IT SEEMED URGENT.
SHE TOLD ME TO PICK UP THE BOOK FOR HER.
AN ER-RAND?
YEAH, I DON'T KNOW WHAT EXACTLY, BUT...
WELL, HERE IT IS.
THANKS.
......
AROU-KUN... WHAT'S WRONG?
HM?
...OH.
NOTHING.

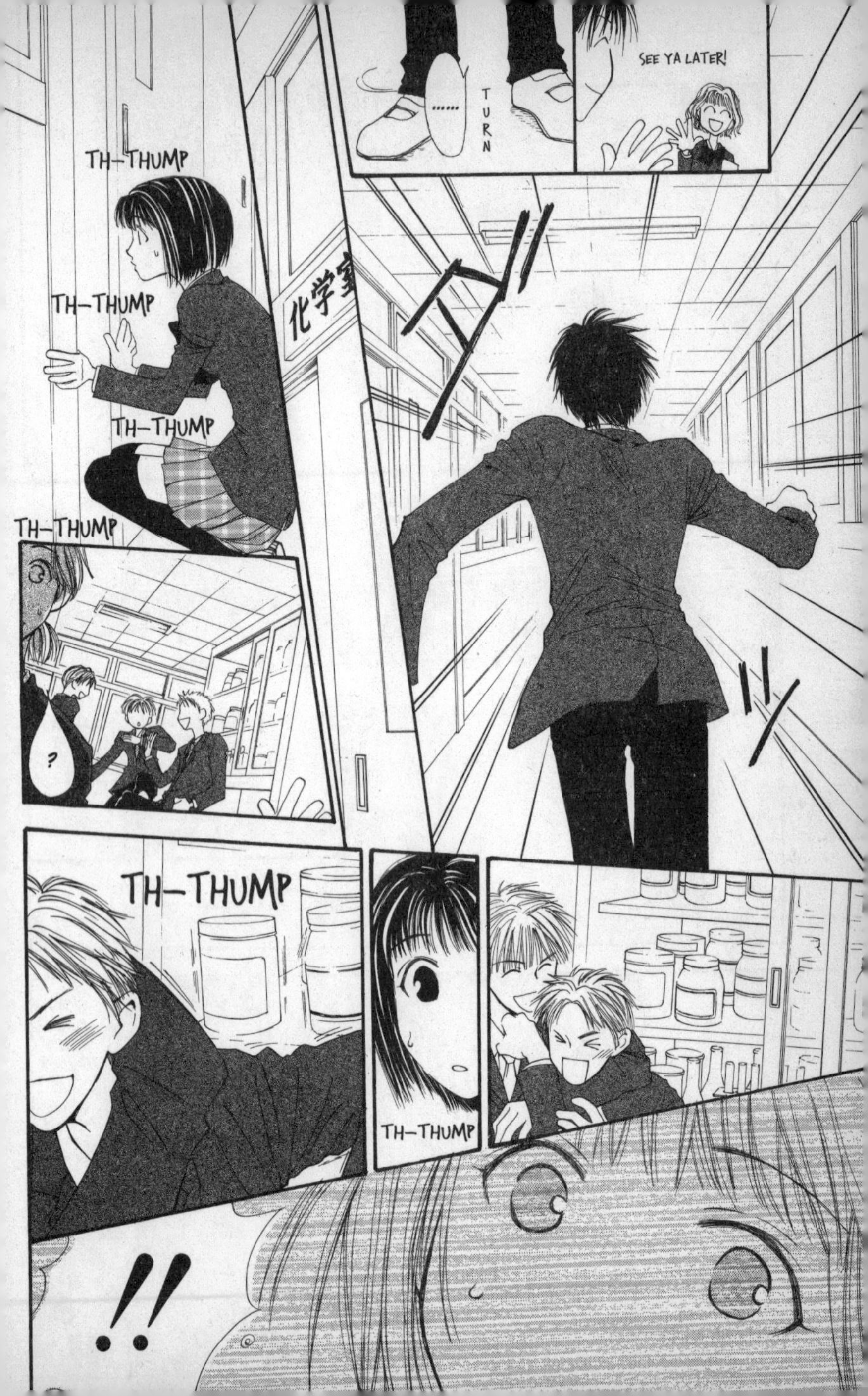

SEE YA LATER!
......
TURN
化学室
TH-THUMP
TH-THUMP
TH-THUMP
TH-THUMP
?
TH-THUMP
TH-THUMP
!!

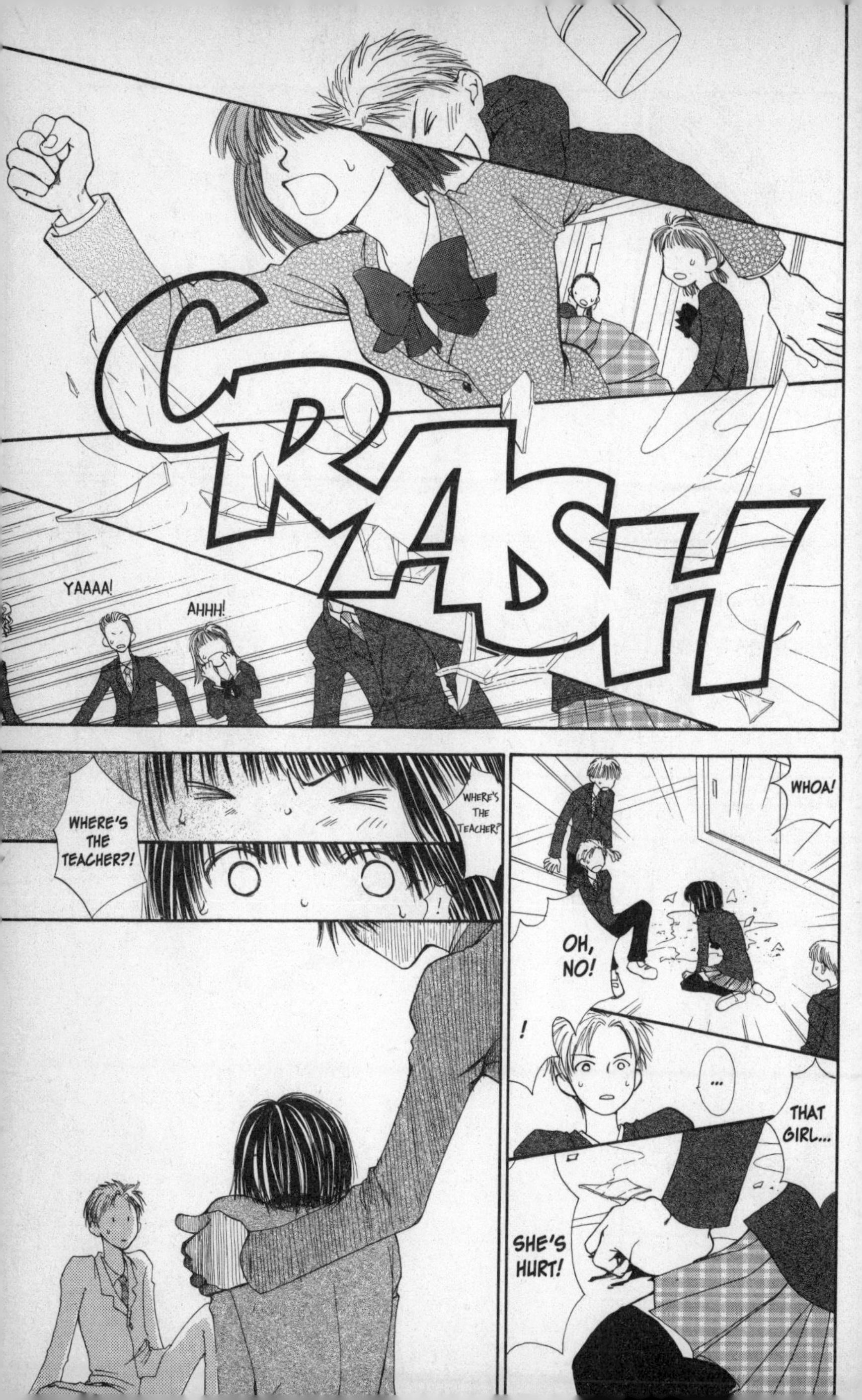
CRASH
AHHH!
YAAAA!
WHOA!
OH, NO!
THAT GIRL...
...
!
SHE'S HURT!
WHERE'S THE TEACHER?
WHERE'S THE TEACHER?!
!

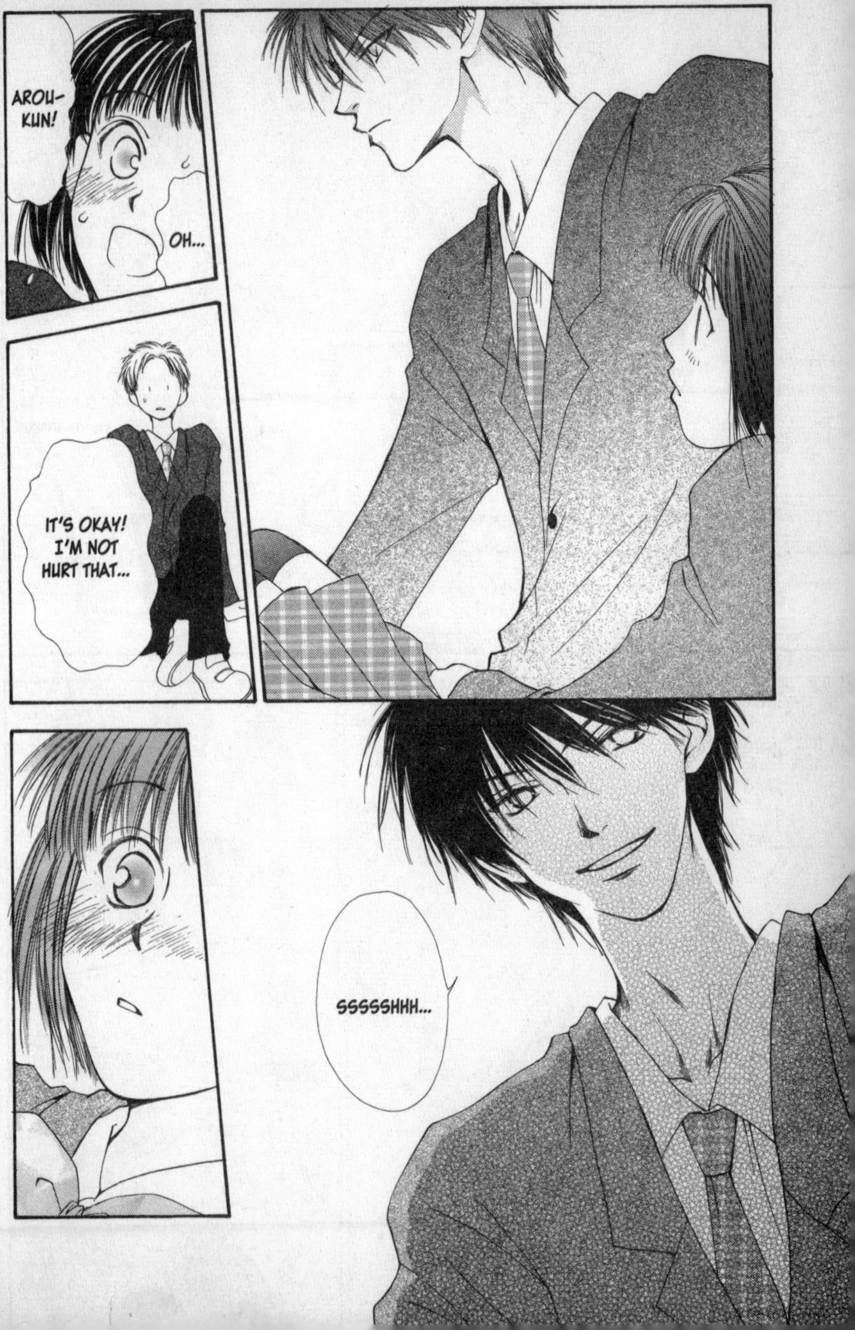
AROU-KUN!
OH...
IT'S OKAY! I'M NOT HURT THAT...
SSSSSHHH...

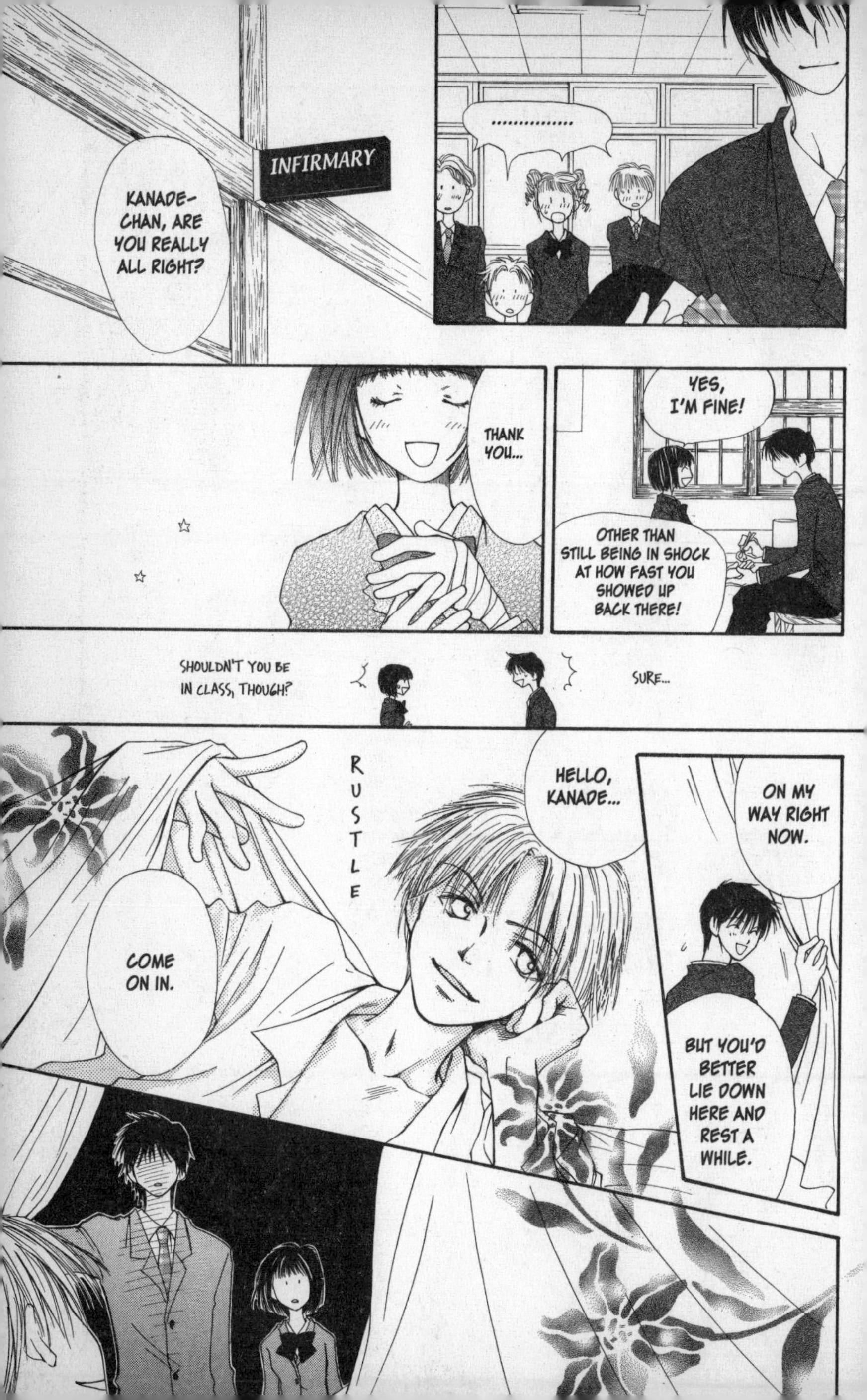
....
INFIRMARY
KANADE-CHAN, ARE YOU REALLY ALL RIGHT?
YES, I'M FINE!
OTHER THAN STILL BEING IN SHOCK AT HOW FAST YOU SHOWED UP BACK THERE!
THANK YOU...
SURE...
SHOULDN'T YOU BE IN CLASS, THOUGH?
ON MY WAY RIGHT NOW.
BUT YOU'D BETTER LIE DOWN HERE AND REST A WHILE.
HELLO, KANADE...
RUSTLE
COME ON IN.

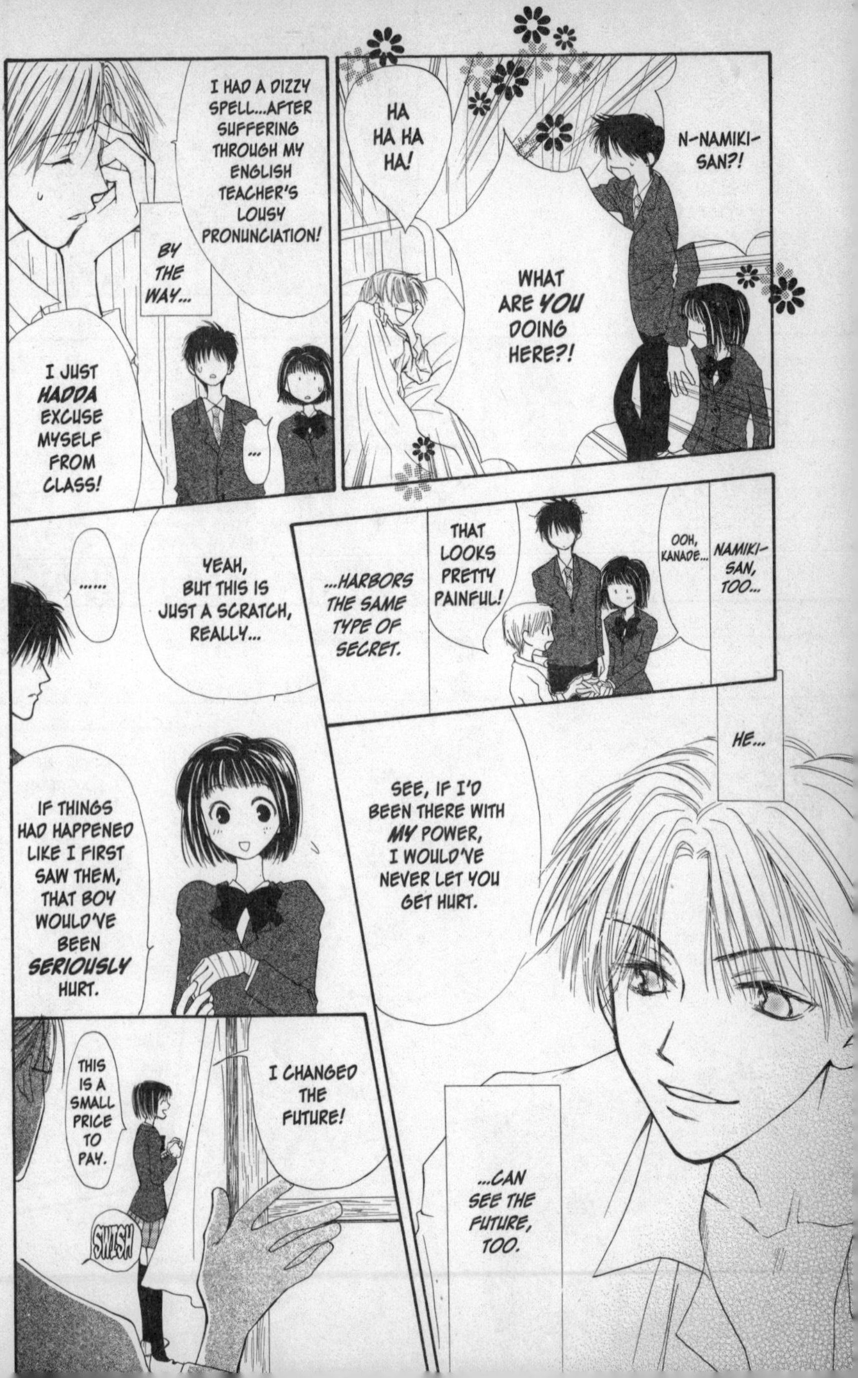
N-NAMIKI-SAN?!
HA HA HA HA!
WHAT ARE YOU DOING HERE?!
I HAD A DIZZY SPELL...AFTER SUFFERING THROUGH MY ENGLISH TEACHER'S LOUSY PRONUNCIATION!
BY THE WAY...
I JUST HADDA EXCUSE MYSELF FROM CLASS!
...
NAMIKI-SAN, TOO...
OOH, KANADE...
THAT LOOKS PRETTY PAINFUL!
...HARBORS THE SAME TYPE OF SECRET.
YEAH, BUT THIS IS JUST A SCRATCH, REALLY...
......
HE...
SEE, IF I'D BEEN THERE WITH MY POWER, I WOULD'VE NEVER LET YOU GET HURT.
...CAN SEE THE FUTURE, TOO.
IF THINGS HAD HAPPENED LIKE I FIRST SAW THEM, THAT BOY WOULD'VE BEEN SERIOUSLY HURT.
I CHANGED THE FUTURE!
THIS IS A SMALL PRICE TO PAY.
SWISH

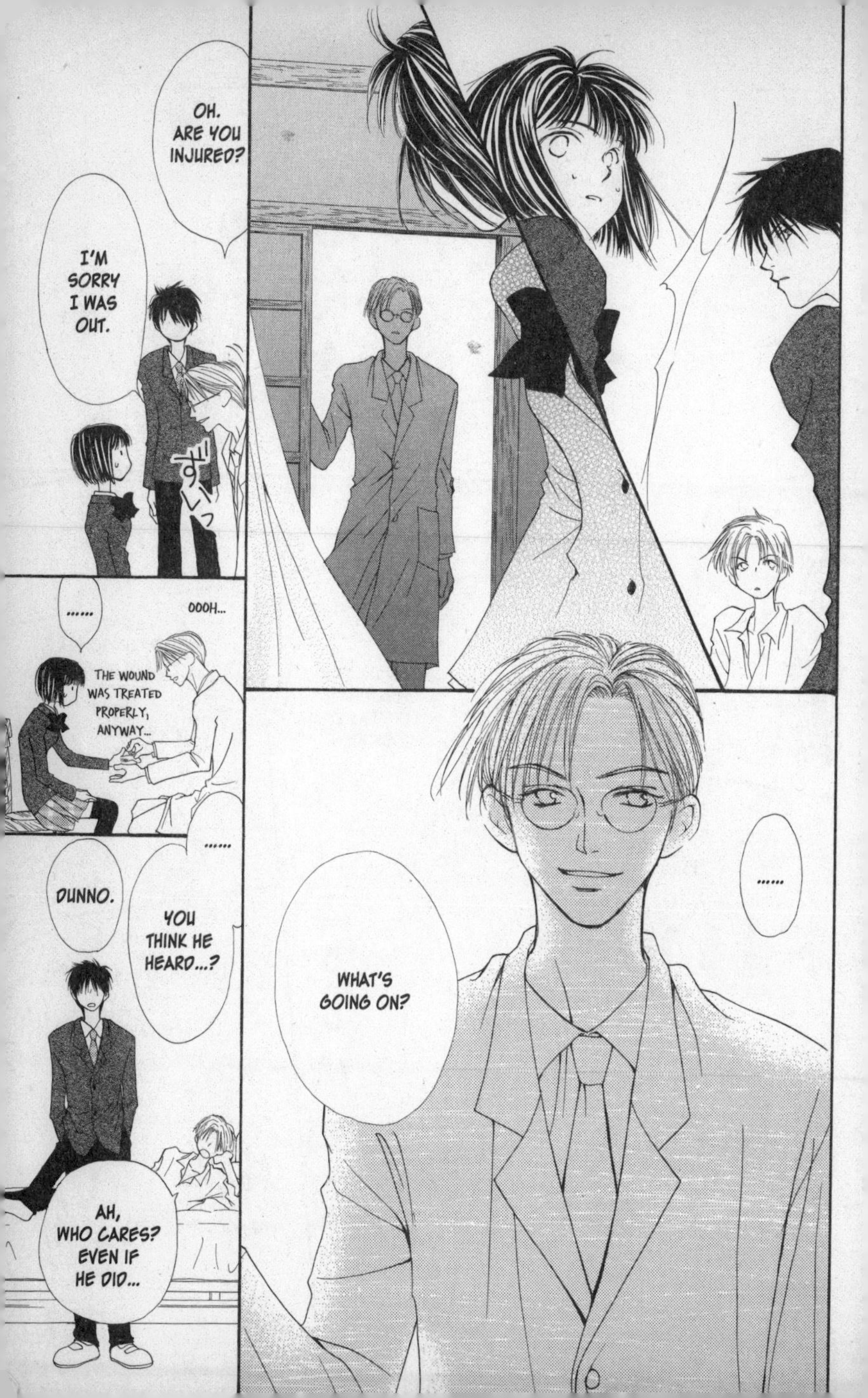
......
WHAT'S GOING ON?
OH. ARE YOU INJURED?
I'M SORRY I WAS OUT.
ずいっ
OOOH...
......
THE WOUND WAS TREATED PROPERLY, ANYWAY...
......
YOU THINK HE HEARD...?
DUNNO.
AH, WHO CARES? EVEN IF HE DID...

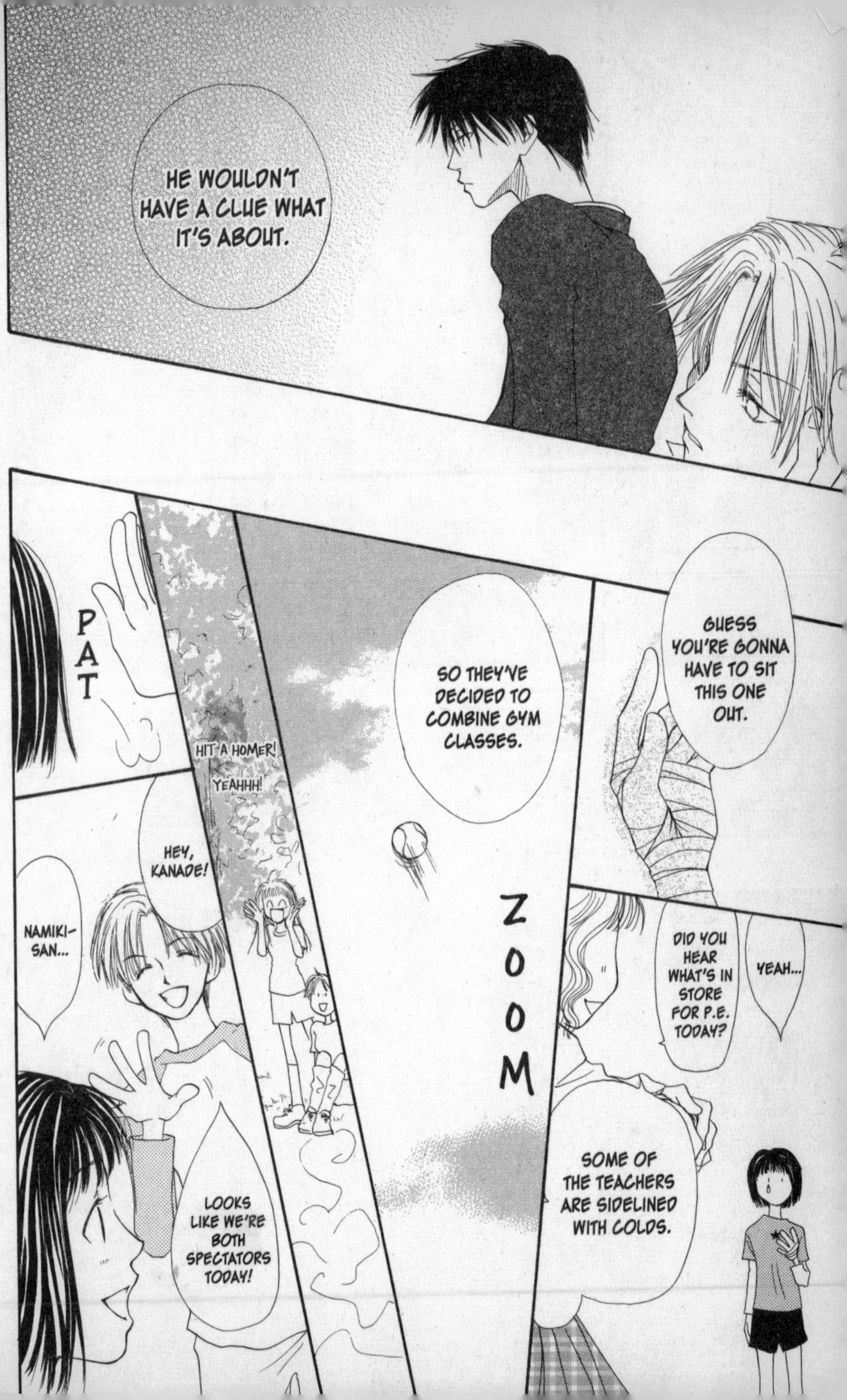
HE WOULDN'T HAVE A CLUE WHAT IT'S ABOUT.
GUESS YOU'RE GONNA HAVE TO SIT THIS ONE OUT.
DID YOU HEAR WHAT'S IN STORE FOR P.E. TODAY?
YEAH...
SOME OF THE TEACHERS ARE SIDELINED WITH COLDS.
SO THEY'VE DECIDED TO COMBINE GYM CLASSES.
ZOOM
HIT A HOMER!
YEAHHH!
PAT
HEY, KANADE!
NAMIKI-SAN...
LOOKS LIKE WE'RE BOTH SPECTATORS TODAY!

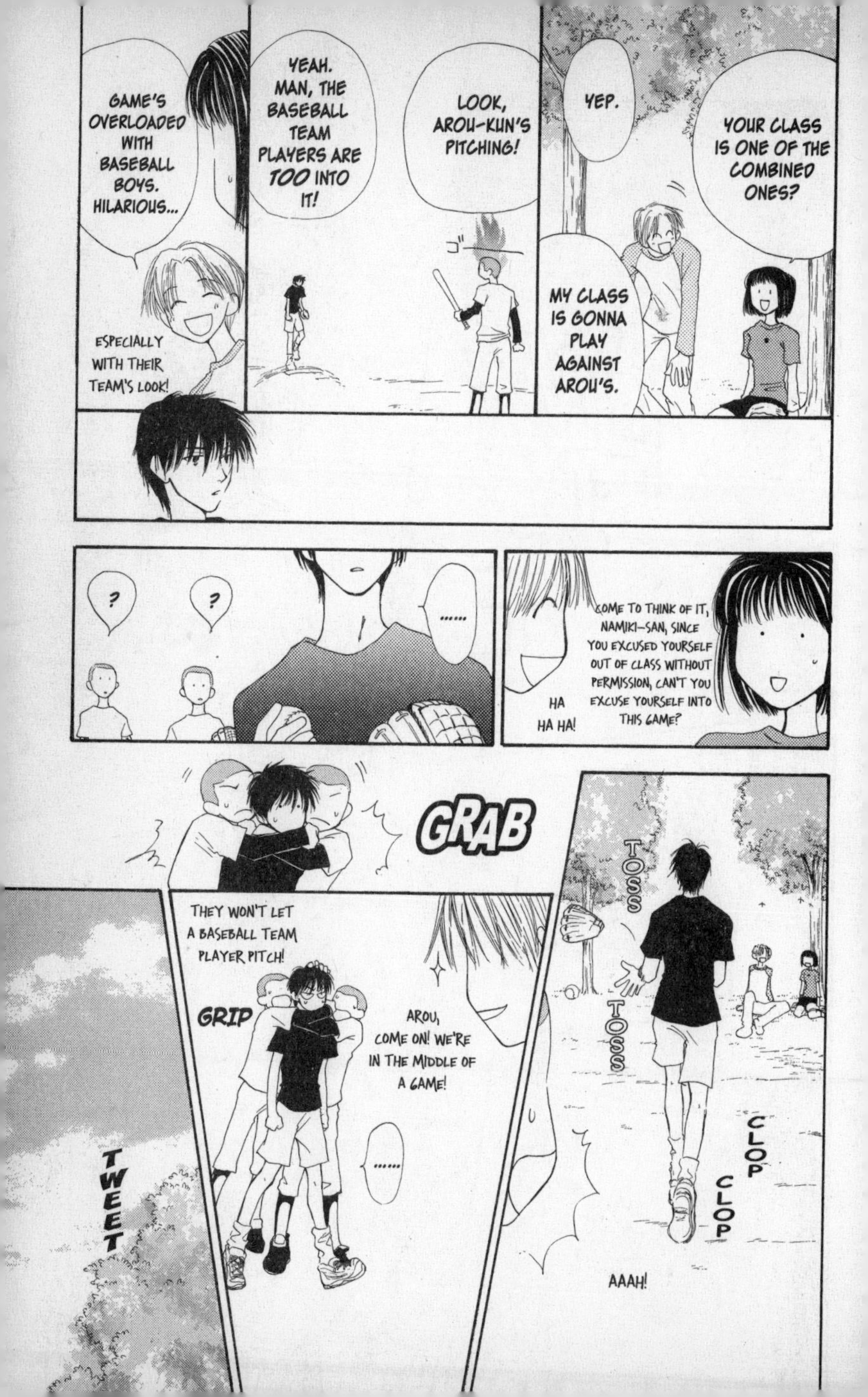
YOUR CLASS IS ONE OF THE COMBINED ONES?
YEP.
MY CLASS IS GONNA PLAY AGAINST AROU'S.
LOOK, AROU-KUN'S PITCHING!
YEAH. MAN, THE BASEBALL TEAM PLAYERS ARE *TOO* INTO IT!
GAME'S OVERLOADED WITH BASEBALL BOYS. HILARIOUS...
ESPECIALLY WITH THEIR TEAM'S LOOK!
COME TO THINK OF IT, NAMIKI-SAN, SINCE YOU EXCUSED YOURSELF OUT OF CLASS WITHOUT PERMISSION, CAN'T YOU EXCUSE YOURSELF INTO THIS GAME?
HA HA HA!
......
?
?
TOSS
TOSS
CLOP
CLOP
CLOP
CLOP
AAAH!
GRAB
THEY WON'T LET A BASEBALL TEAM PLAYER PITCH!
GRIP
AROU, COME ON! WE'RE IN THE MIDDLE OF A GAME!
......
TWEET

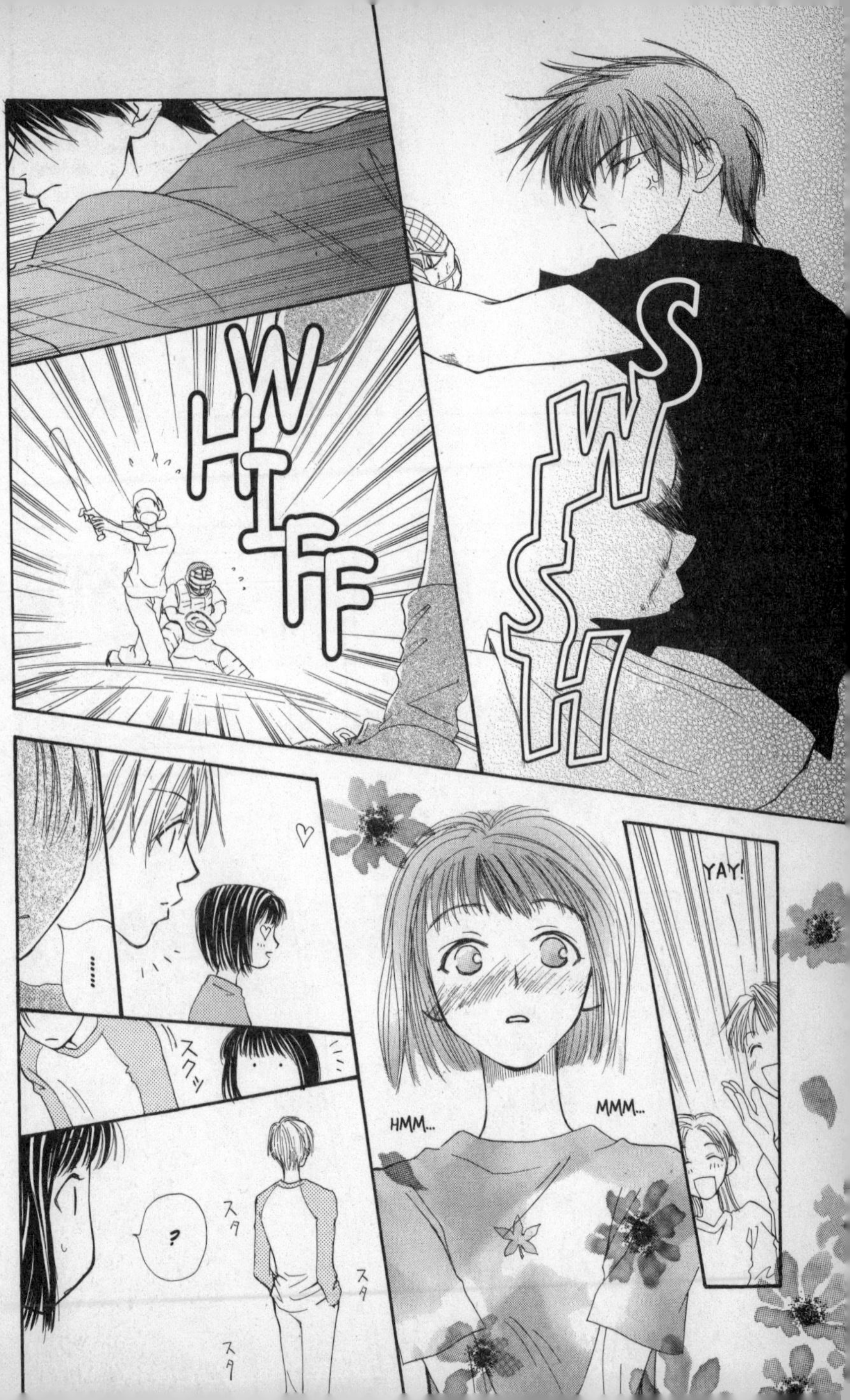
SWISH
WHIFF
YAY!
MMM...
HMM...
......
スクッ
?
スタ
スタ
スタ

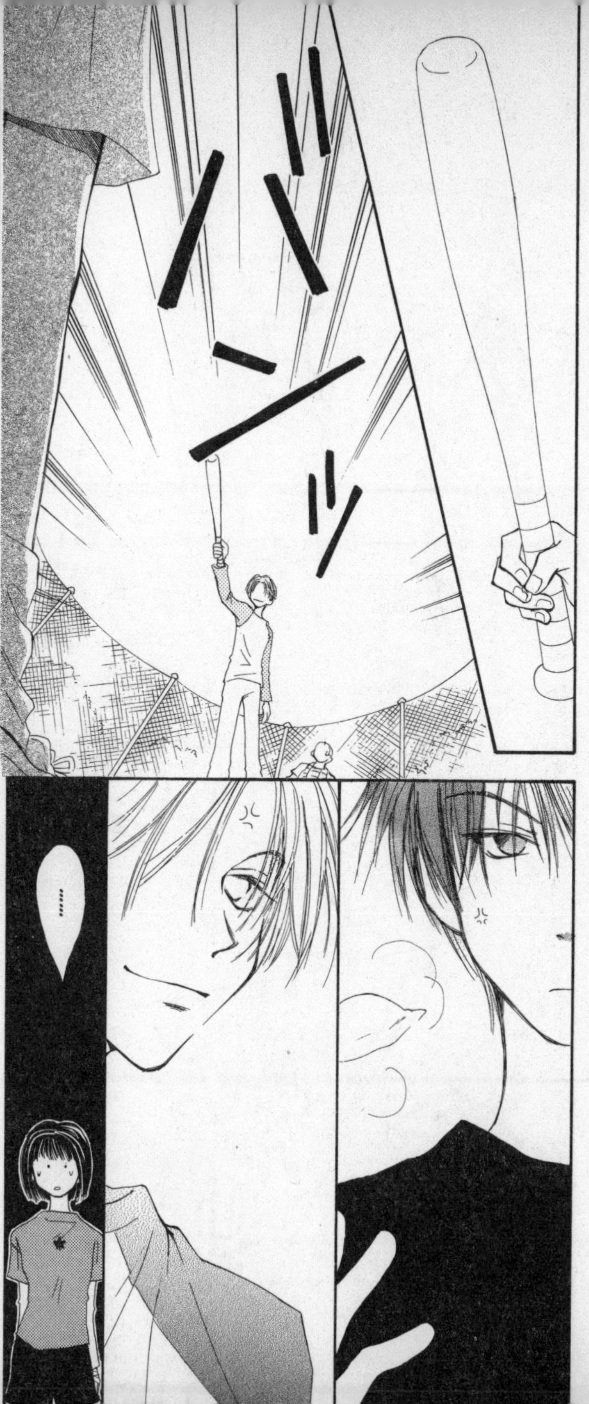
......

Sakura Mail

No. 2

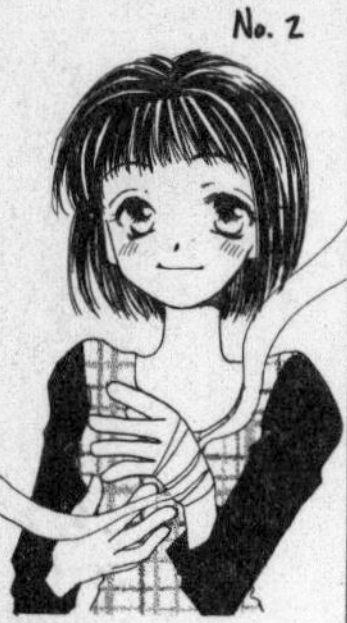

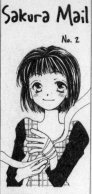

This story is the first of a three-part story arc, originally serialized in LaLa Magazine. But I only made it through my first stab at a multi-parter because of all the readers! I've said it before and I'll say it again. Thank you for all for your support! Although this is a three-part arc, the stories are only connected loosely. The hard part was finding the thread that would hold them together. I floundered for a while and got all nervous. But every time I work on a new story, I discover something new and overcome some wall, as well as become moved by the depth of the medium of manga. Someone out there right now is probably saying, "The god of manga is in the depth."

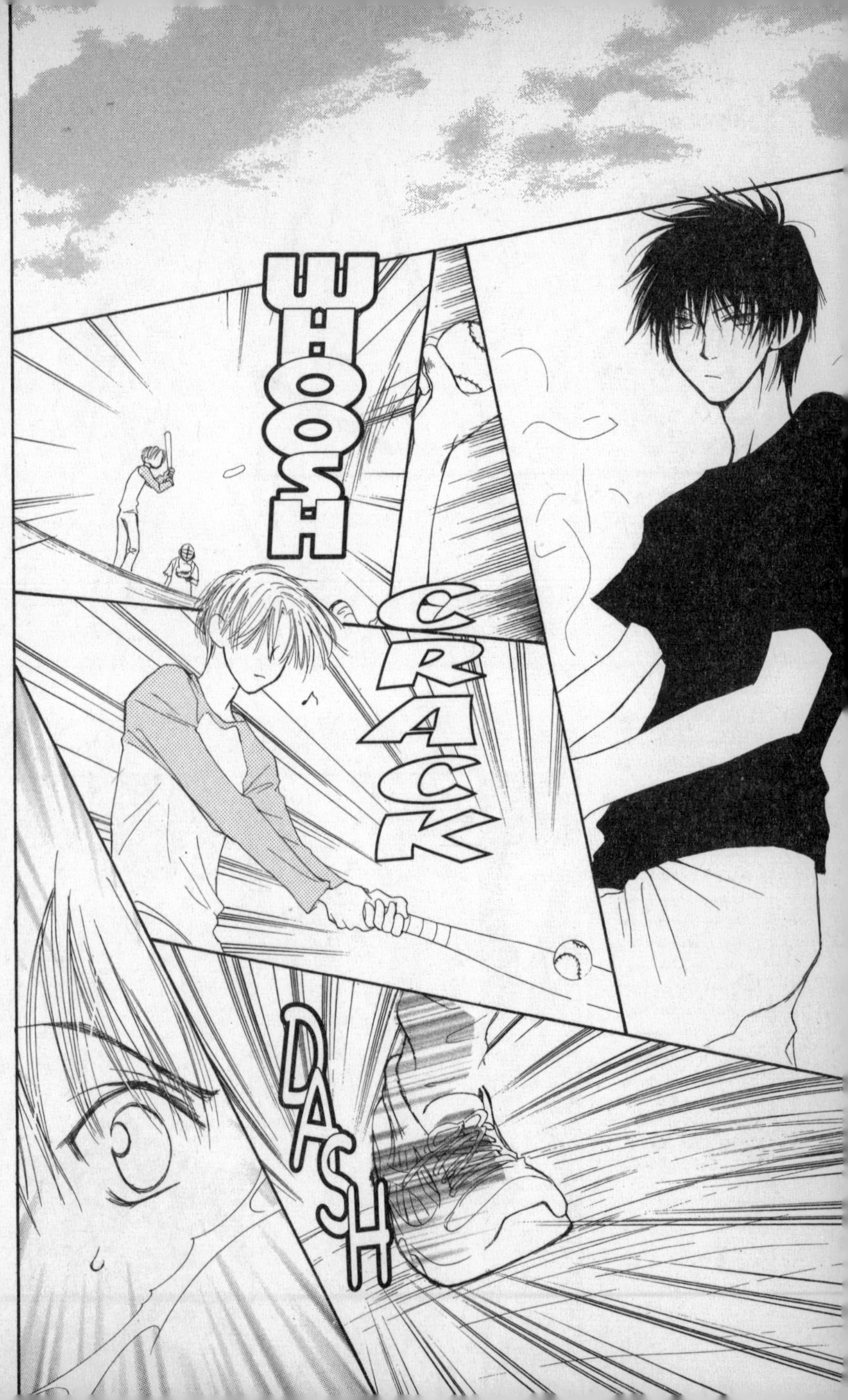
WHOOSH
CRACK
DASH

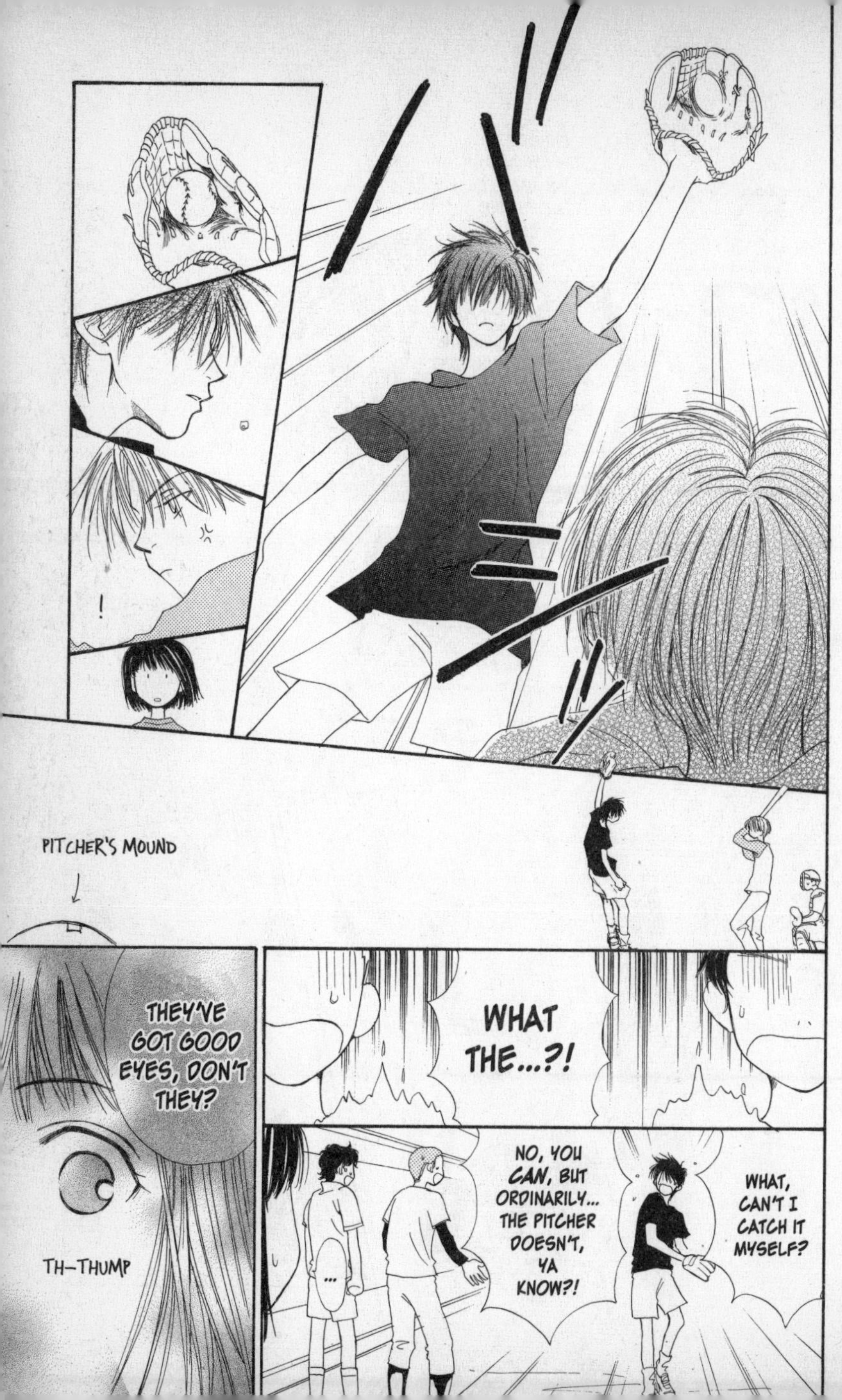
PITCHER'S MOUND
WHAT THE...?!
THEY'VE GOT GOOD EYES, DON'T THEY?
TH-THUMP
WHAT, CAN'T I CATCH IT MYSELF?
NO, YOU CAN, BUT ORDINARILY... THE PITCHER DOESN'T, YA KNOW?!
...

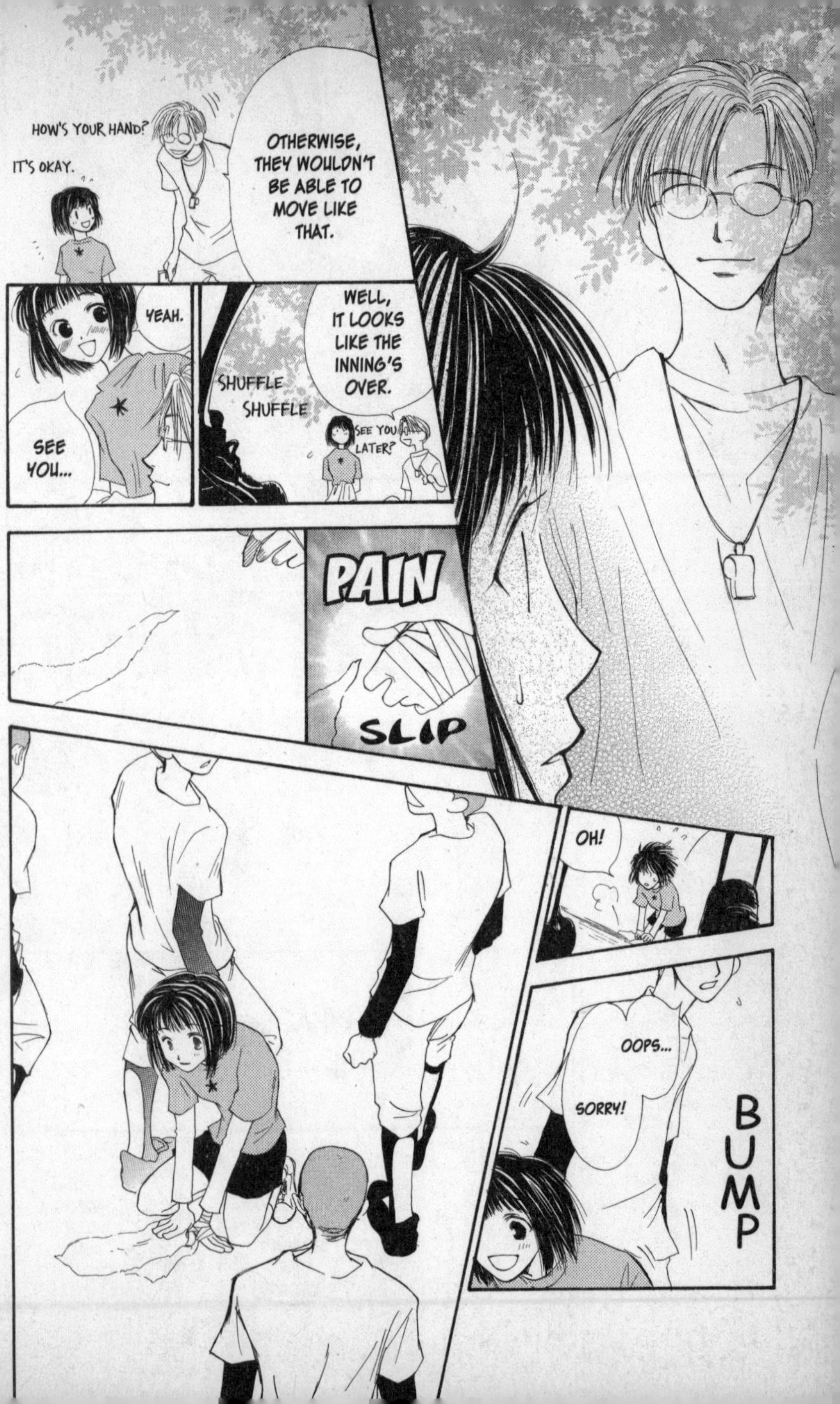
OTHERWISE, THEY WOULDN'T BE ABLE TO MOVE LIKE THAT.
HOW'S YOUR HAND?
IT'S OKAY.
WELL, IT LOOKS LIKE THE INNING'S OVER.
SHUFFLE SHUFFLE
SEE YOU LATER?
YEAH.
SEE YOU...
PAIN
SLIP
OH!
BUMP
OOPS...
SORRY!

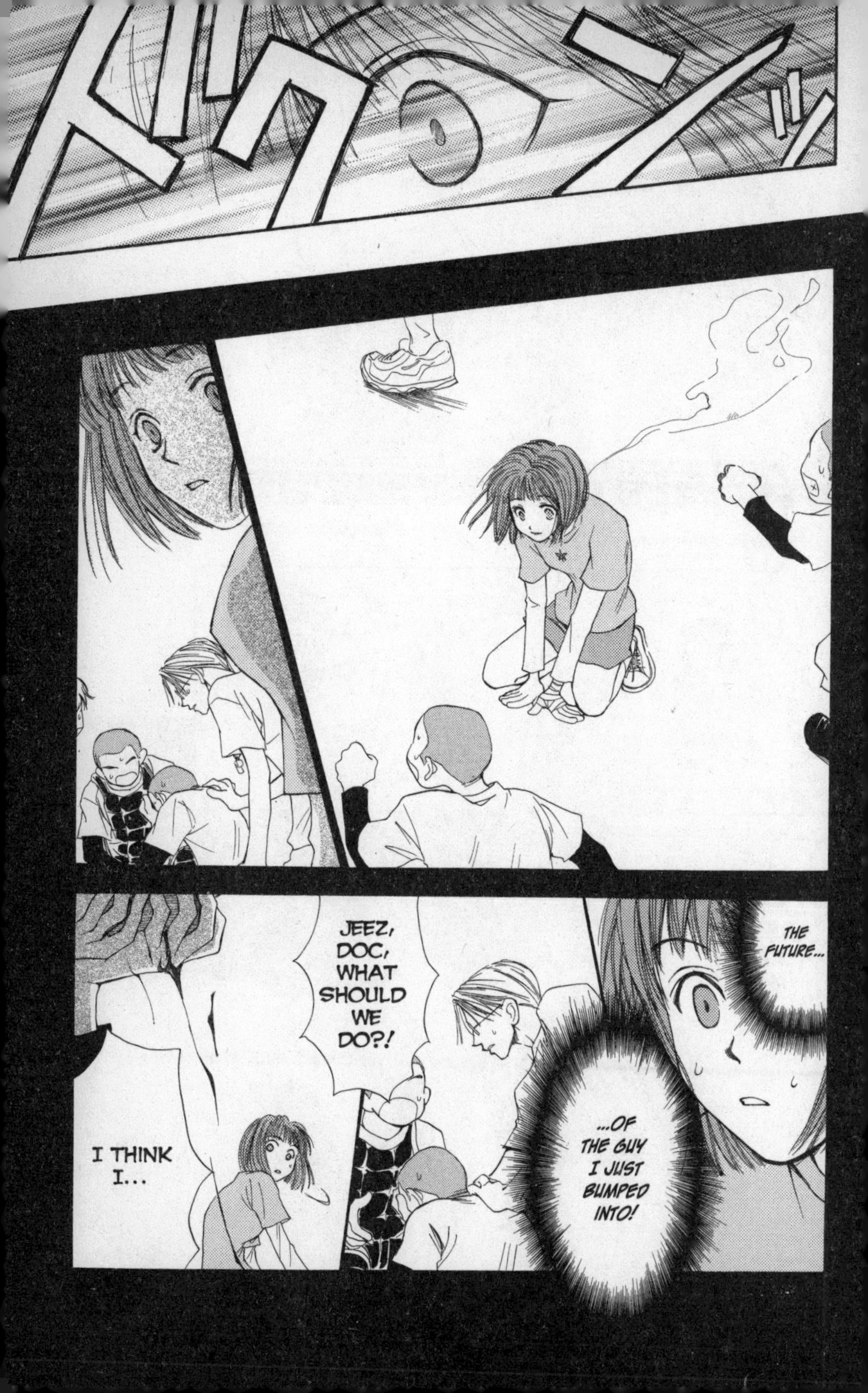
THE FUTURE...
...OF THE GUY I JUST BUMPED INTO!
JEEZ, DOC, WHAT SHOULD WE DO?!
I THINK I...

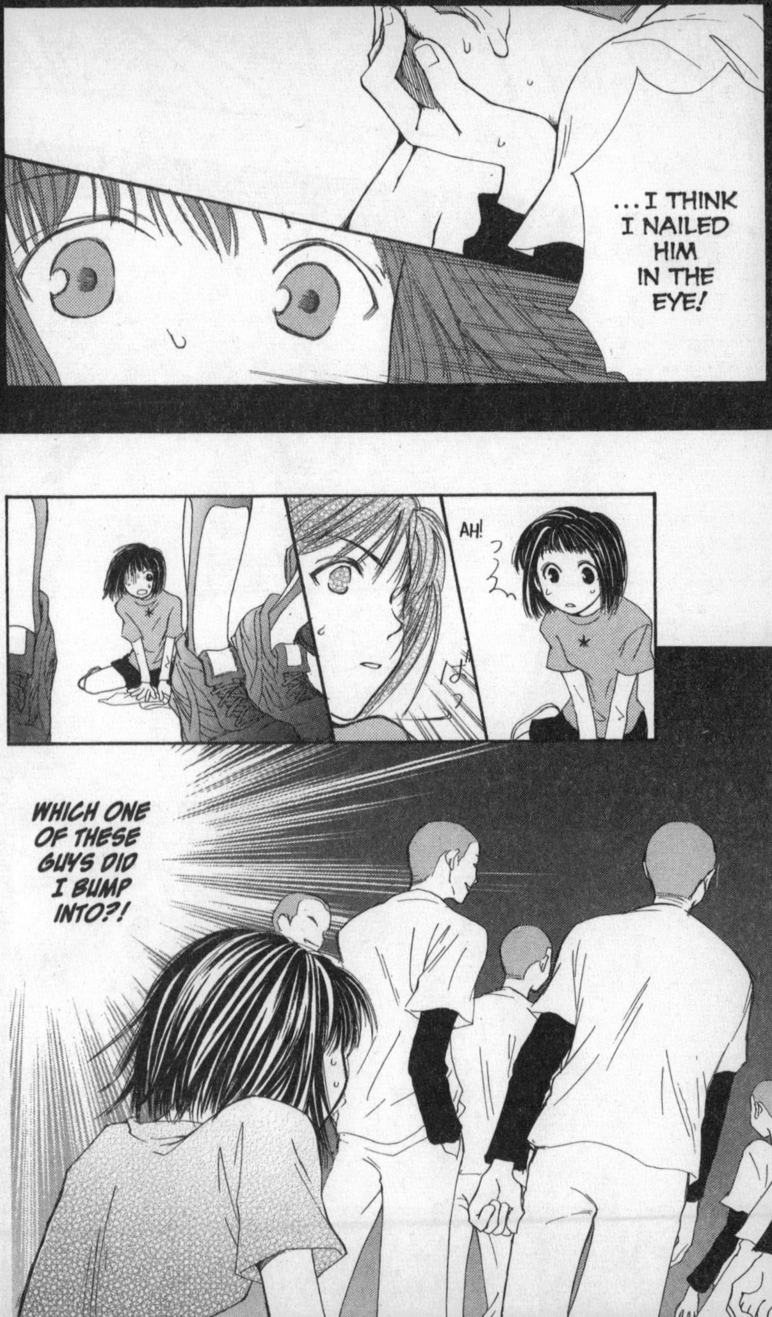
...I THINK I NAILED HIM IN THE EYE!
AH!
WHICH ONE OF THESE GUYS DID I BUMP INTO?!

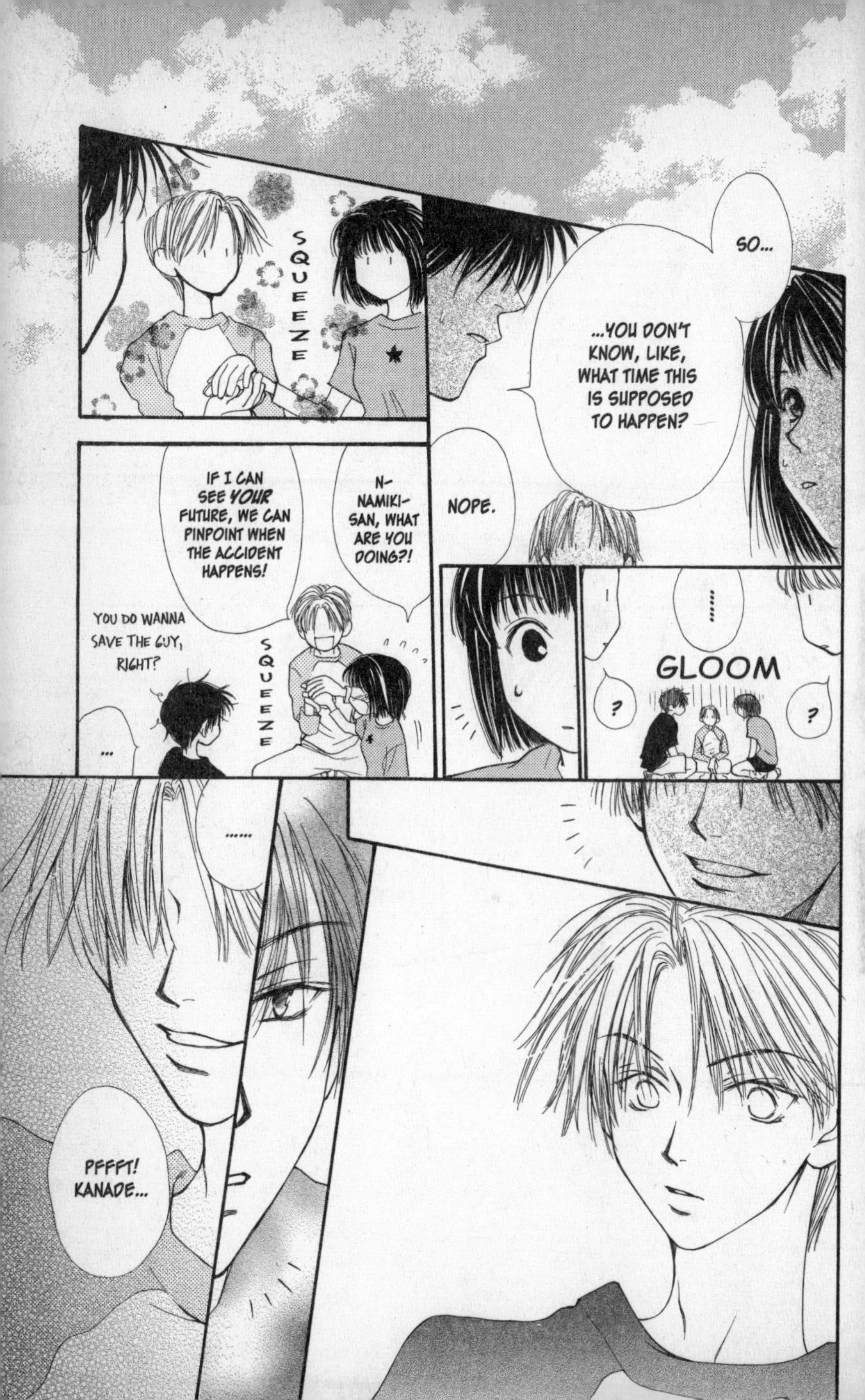
SO...
...YOU DON'T KNOW, LIKE, WHAT TIME THIS IS SUPPOSED TO HAPPEN?
NOPE.
SQUEEZE
!
......
!
GLOOM
?
?
N-NAMIKI-SAN, WHAT ARE YOU DOING?!
IF I CAN SEE YOUR FUTURE, WE CAN PINPOINT WHEN THE ACCIDENT HAPPENS!
YOU DO WANNA SAVE THE GUY, RIGHT?
SQUEEZE
...
......
PFFFT! KANADE...

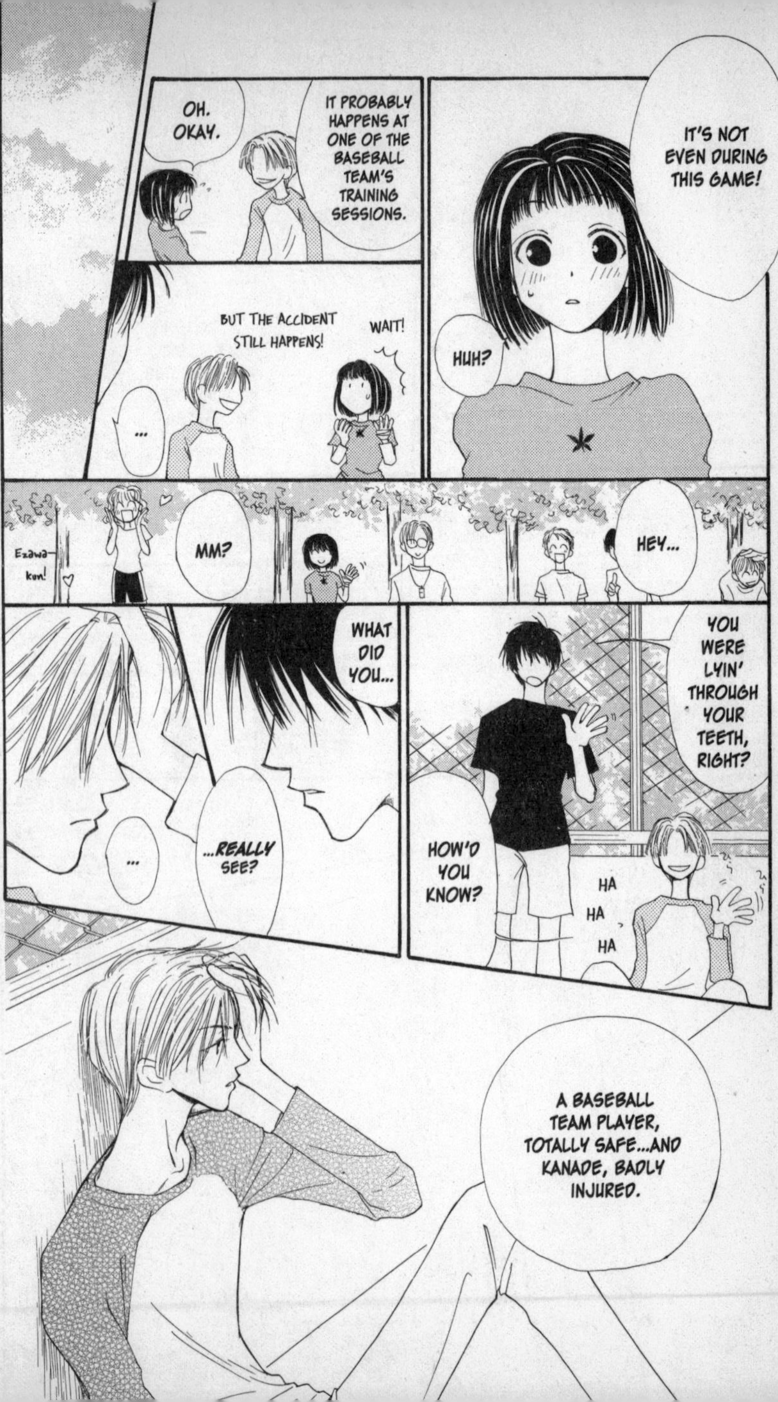
IT'S NOT EVEN DURING THIS GAME!
HUH?
IT PROBABLY HAPPENS AT ONE OF THE BASEBALL TEAM'S TRAINING SESSIONS.
OH. OKAY.
WAIT!
BUT THE ACCIDENT STILL HAPPENS!
...
HEY...
MM?
Ezawa-kun!
YOU WERE LYIN' THROUGH YOUR TEETH, RIGHT?
HOW'D YOU KNOW?
HA HA HA
WHAT DID YOU...
...REALLY SEE?
...
A BASEBALL TEAM PLAYER, TOTALLY SAFE...AND KANADE, BADLY INJURED.

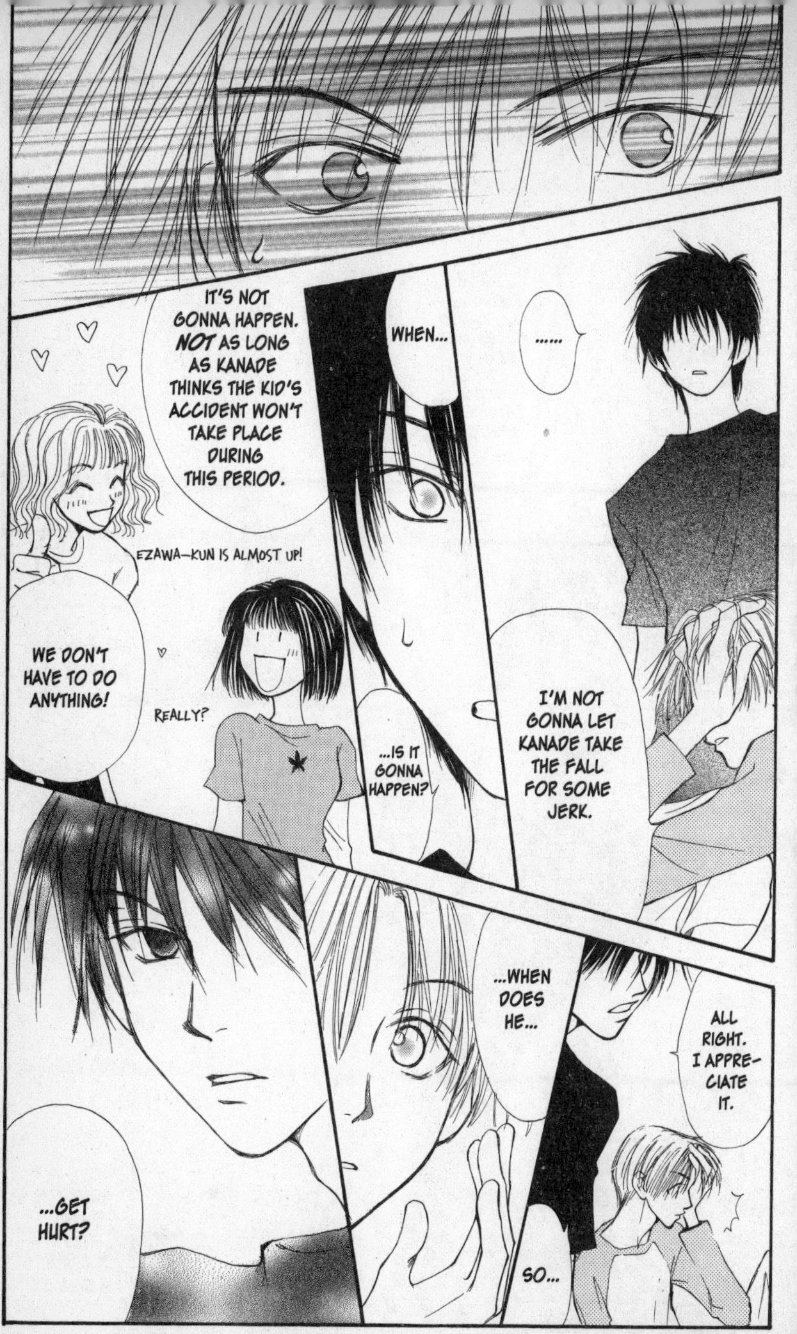
......
I'M NOT GONNA LET KANADE TAKE THE FALL FOR SOME JERK.
WHEN...
...IS IT GONNA HAPPEN?
IT'S NOT GONNA HAPPEN. NOT AS LONG AS KANADE THINKS THE KID'S ACCIDENT WON'T TAKE PLACE DURING THIS PERIOD.
EZAWA-KUN IS ALMOST UP!
WE DON'T HAVE TO DO ANYTHING!
REALLY?
ALL RIGHT. I APPRE-CIATE IT.
SO...
...WHEN DOES HE...
...GET HURT?

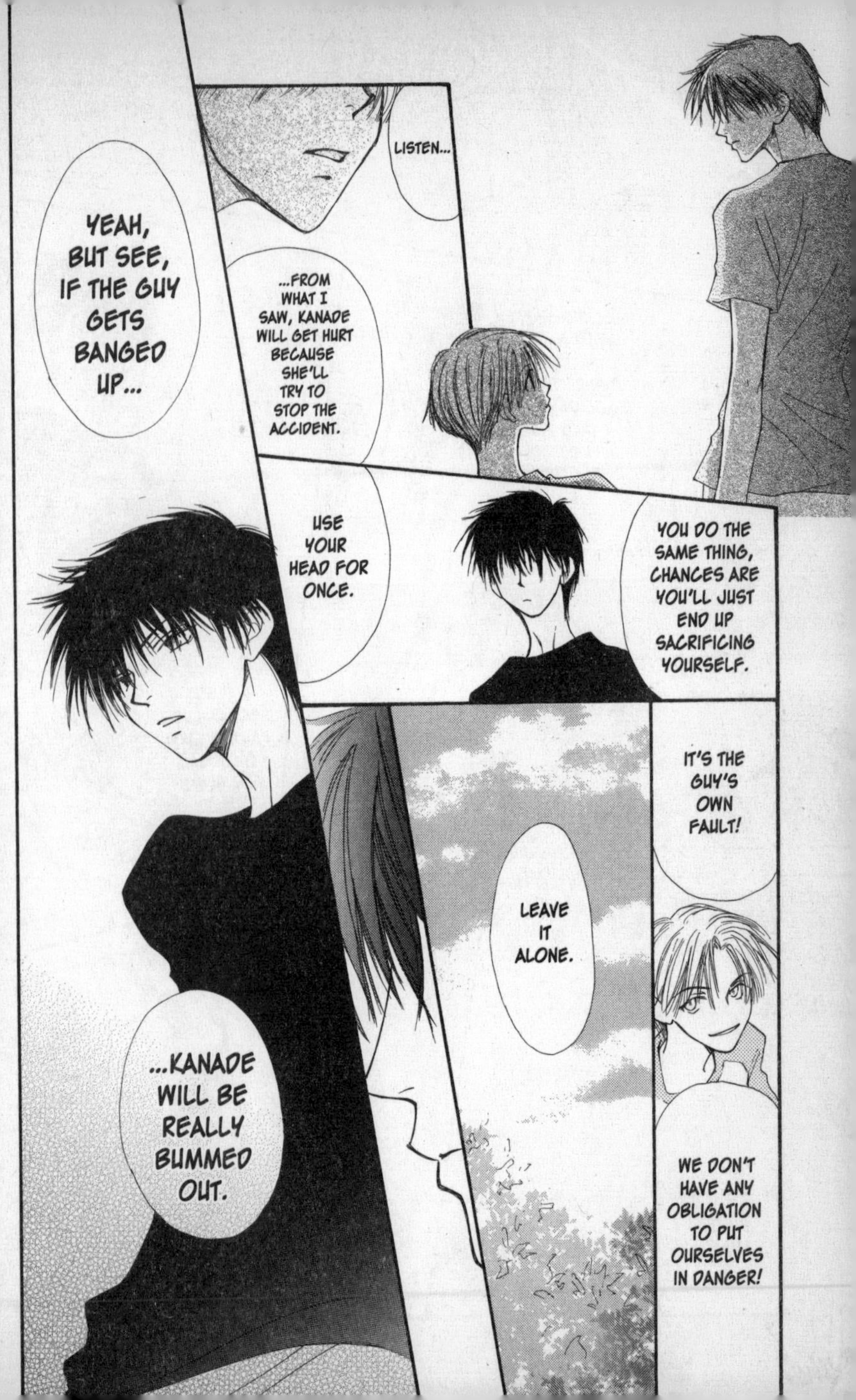
LISTEN...
...FROM WHAT I SAW, KANADE WILL GET HURT BECAUSE SHE'LL TRY TO STOP THE ACCIDENT.
YOU DO THE SAME THING, CHANCES ARE YOU'LL JUST END UP SACRIFICING YOURSELF.
USE YOUR HEAD FOR ONCE.
IT'S THE GUY'S OWN FAULT!
WE DON'T HAVE ANY OBLIGATION TO PUT OURSELVES IN DANGER!
LEAVE IT ALONE.
YEAH, BUT SEE, IF THE GUY GETS BANGED UP...
...KANADE WILL BE REALLY BUMMED OUT.

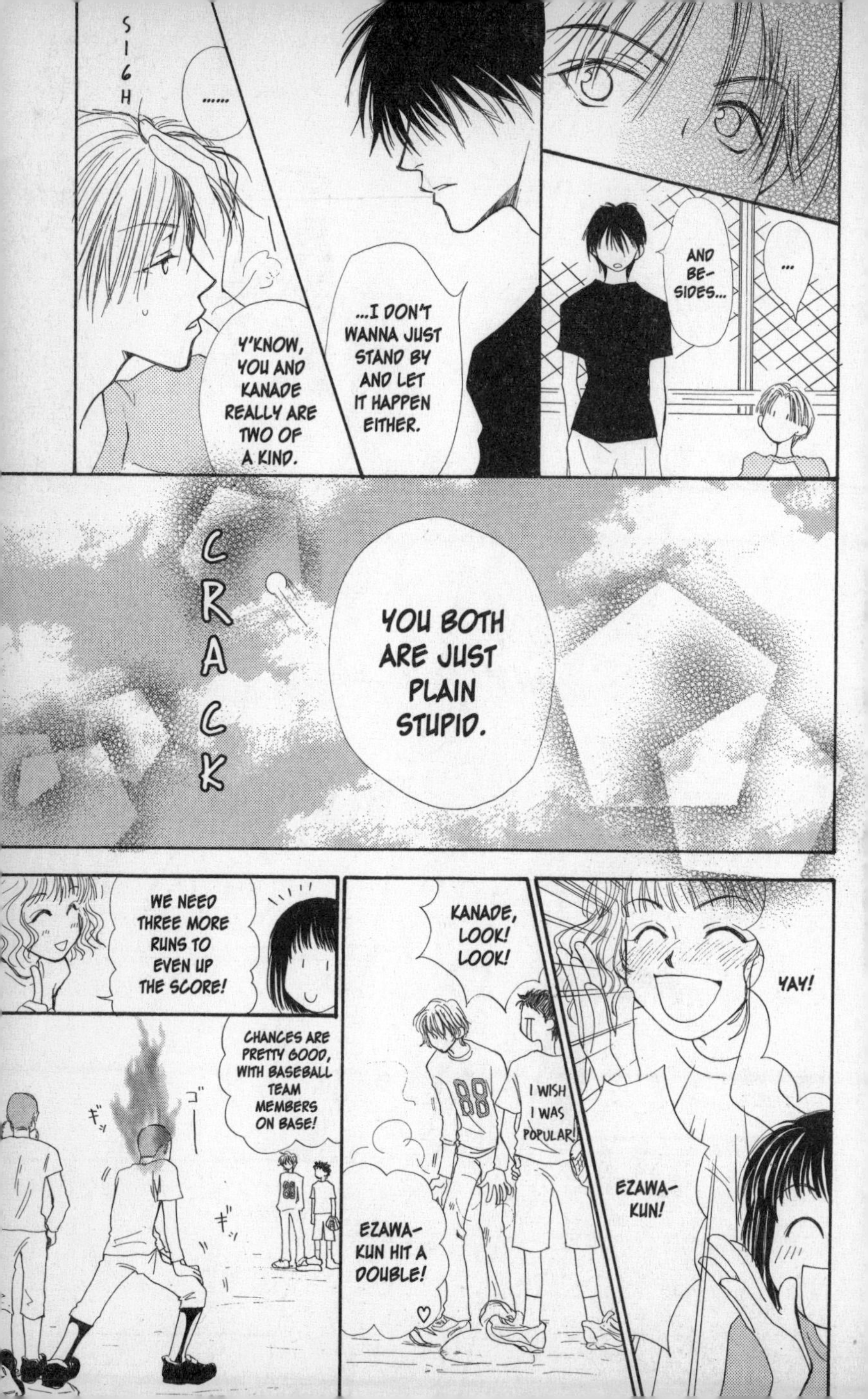
AND BE-SIDES...
...
...I DON'T WANNA JUST STAND BY AND LET IT HAPPEN EITHER.
SIGH
......
Y'KNOW, YOU AND KANADE REALLY ARE TWO OF A KIND.
CRACK
YOU BOTH ARE JUST PLAIN STUPID.
YAY!
EZAWA-KUN!
KANADE, LOOK! LOOK!
I WISH I WAS POPULAR!
EZAWA-KUN HIT A DOUBLE!
WE NEED THREE MORE RUNS TO EVEN UP THE SCORE!
CHANCES ARE PRETTY GOOD, WITH BASEBALL TEAM MEMBERS ON BASE!

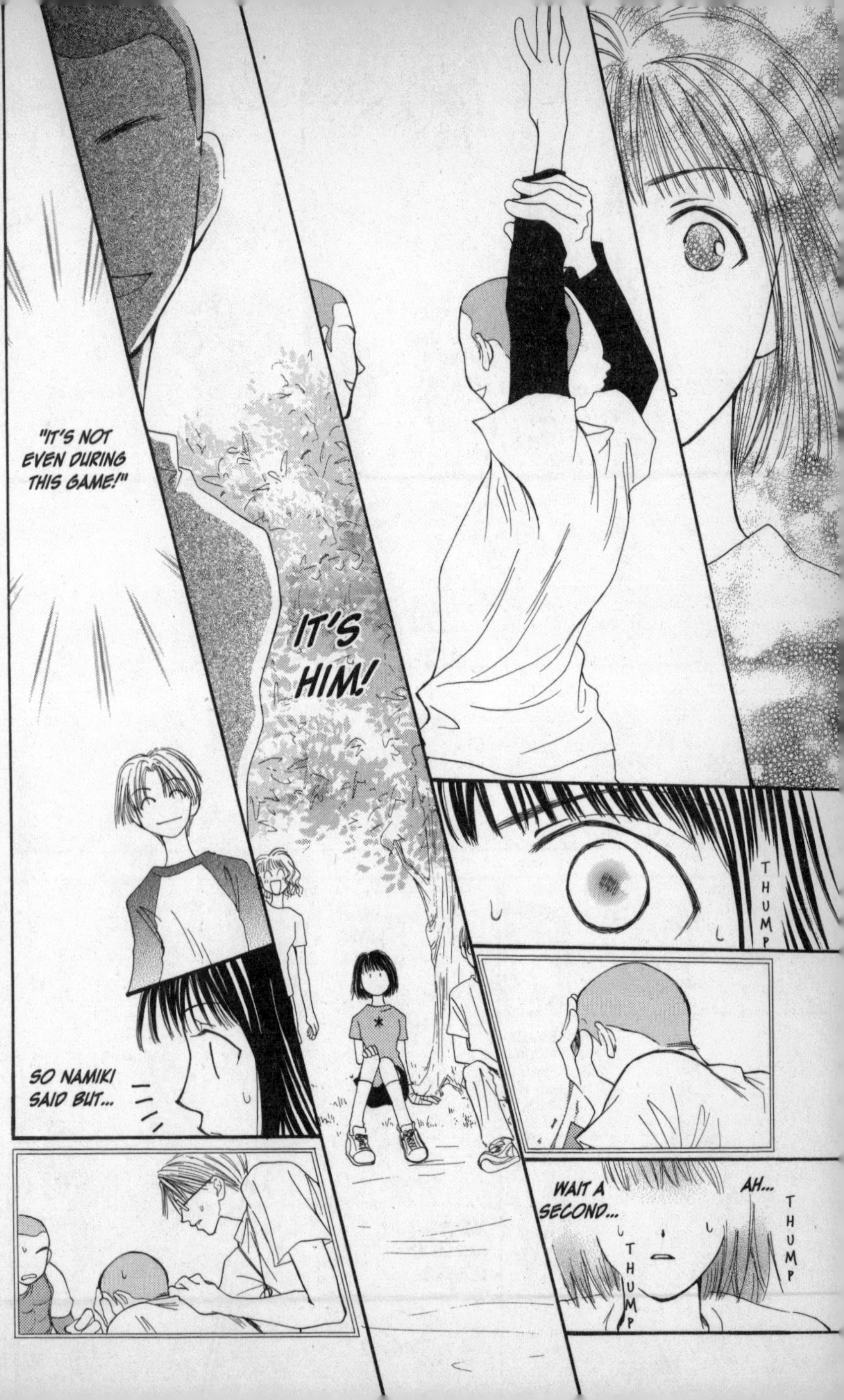
THUMP
AH...
THUMP
WAIT A SECOND...
THUMP
IT'S HIM!
"IT'S NOT EVEN DURING THIS GAME!"
SO NAMIKI SAID BUT...

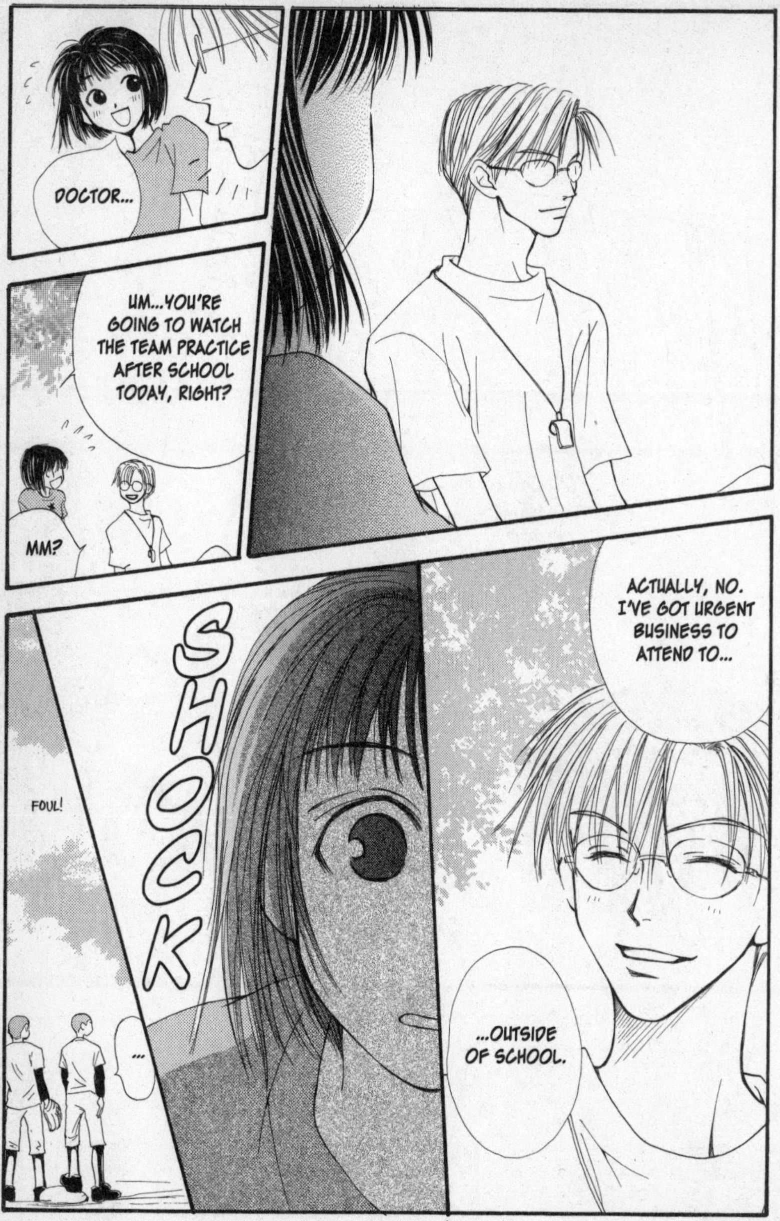
DOCTOR...
UM...YOU'RE GOING TO WATCH THE TEAM PRACTICE AFTER SCHOOL TODAY, RIGHT?
MM?
ACTUALLY, NO. I'VE GOT URGENT BUSINESS TO ATTEND TO...
...OUTSIDE OF SCHOOL.
SHOCK
FOUL!
...

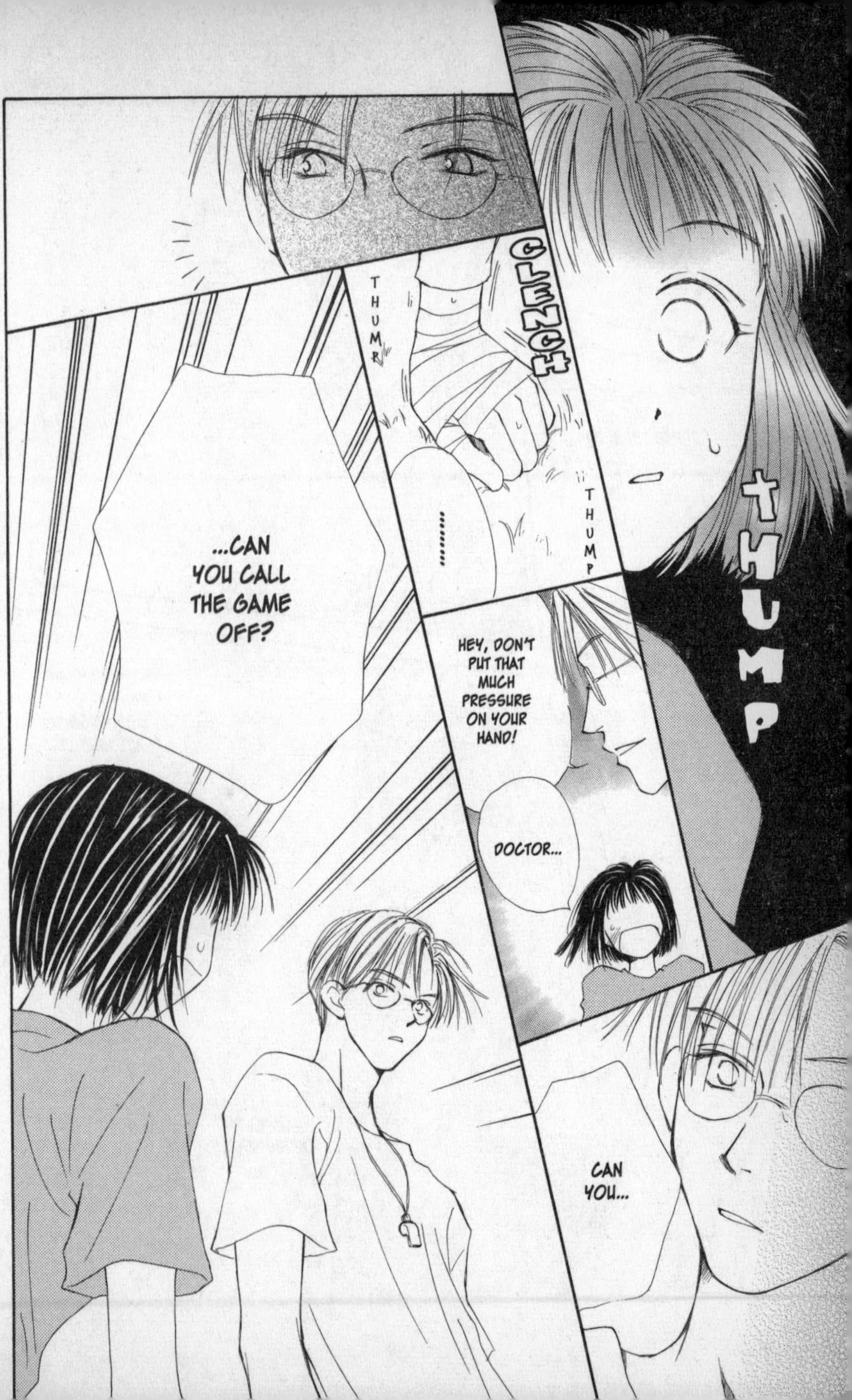
THUMP
CLENCH
THUMP
......
THUMP
HEY, DON'T PUT THAT MUCH PRESSURE ON YOUR HAND!
DOCTOR...
CAN YOU...
...CAN YOU CALL THE GAME OFF?

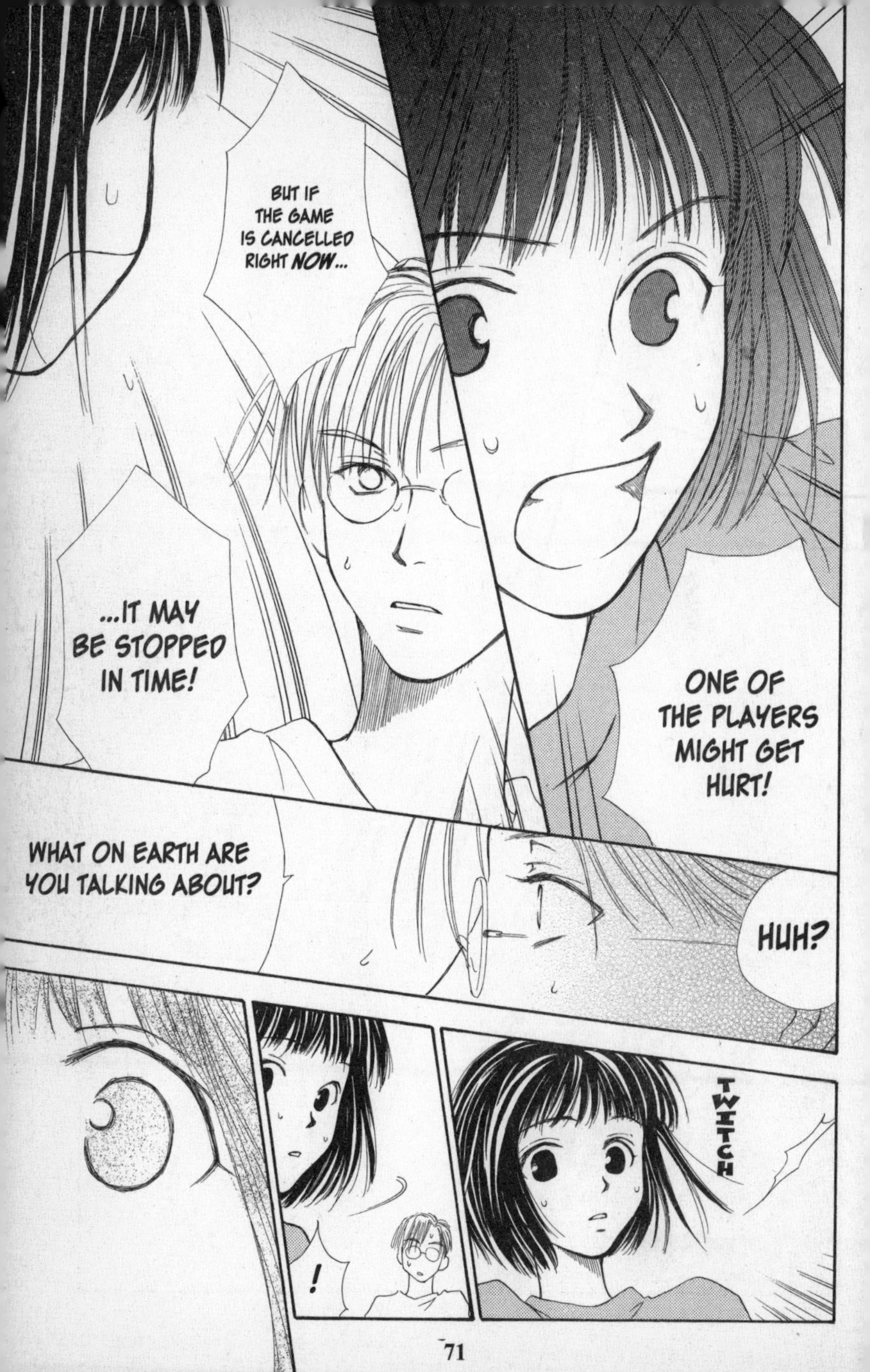
ONE OF THE PLAYERS MIGHT GET HURT!
BUT IF THE GAME IS CANCELLED RIGHT *NOW*...
...IT MAY BE STOPPED IN TIME!
HUH?
WHAT ON EARTH ARE YOU TALKING ABOUT?
TWITCH
!

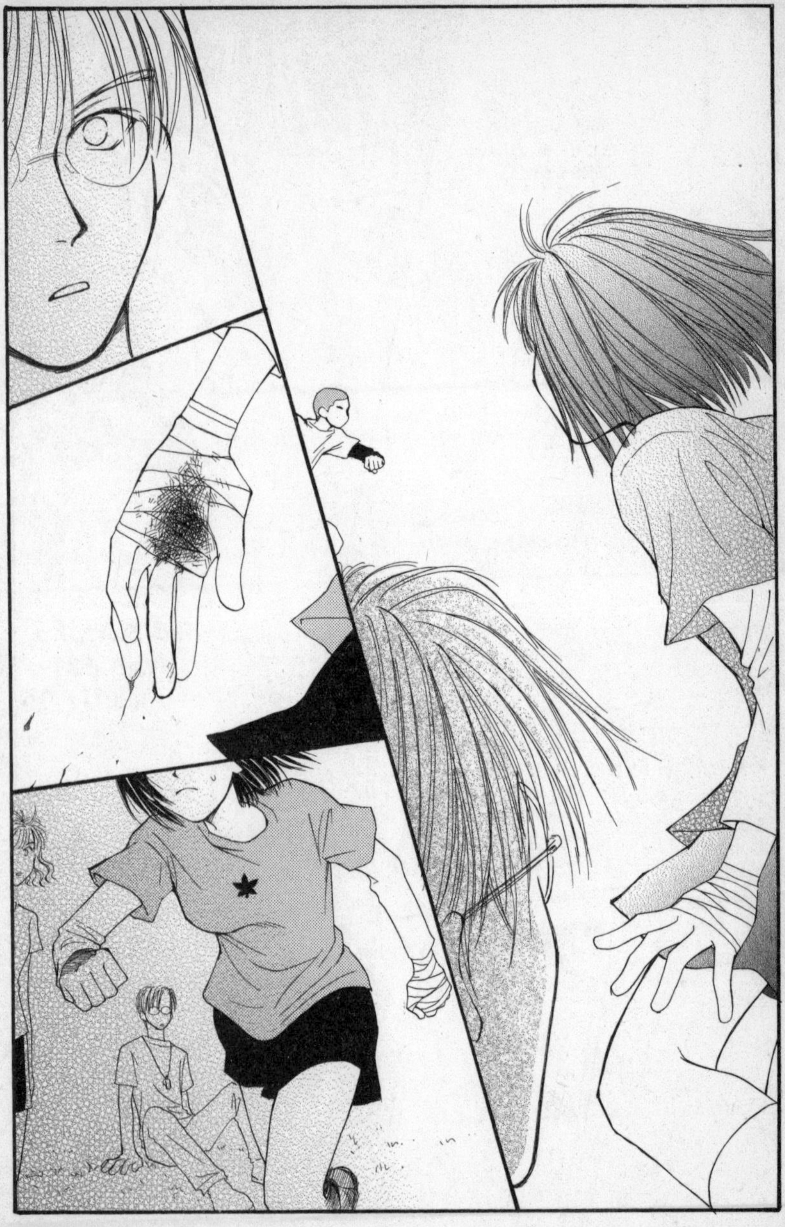

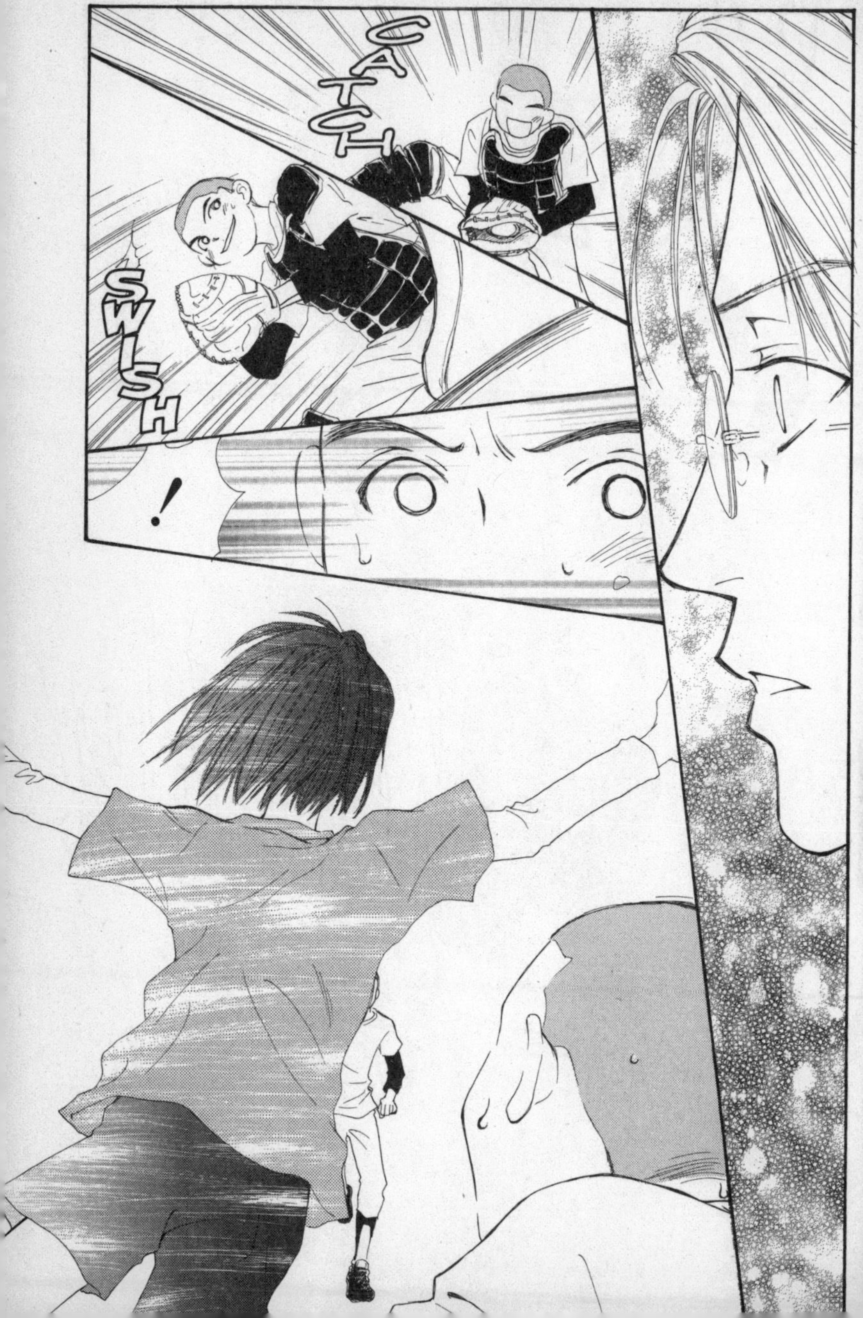
CATCH
SWISH
!

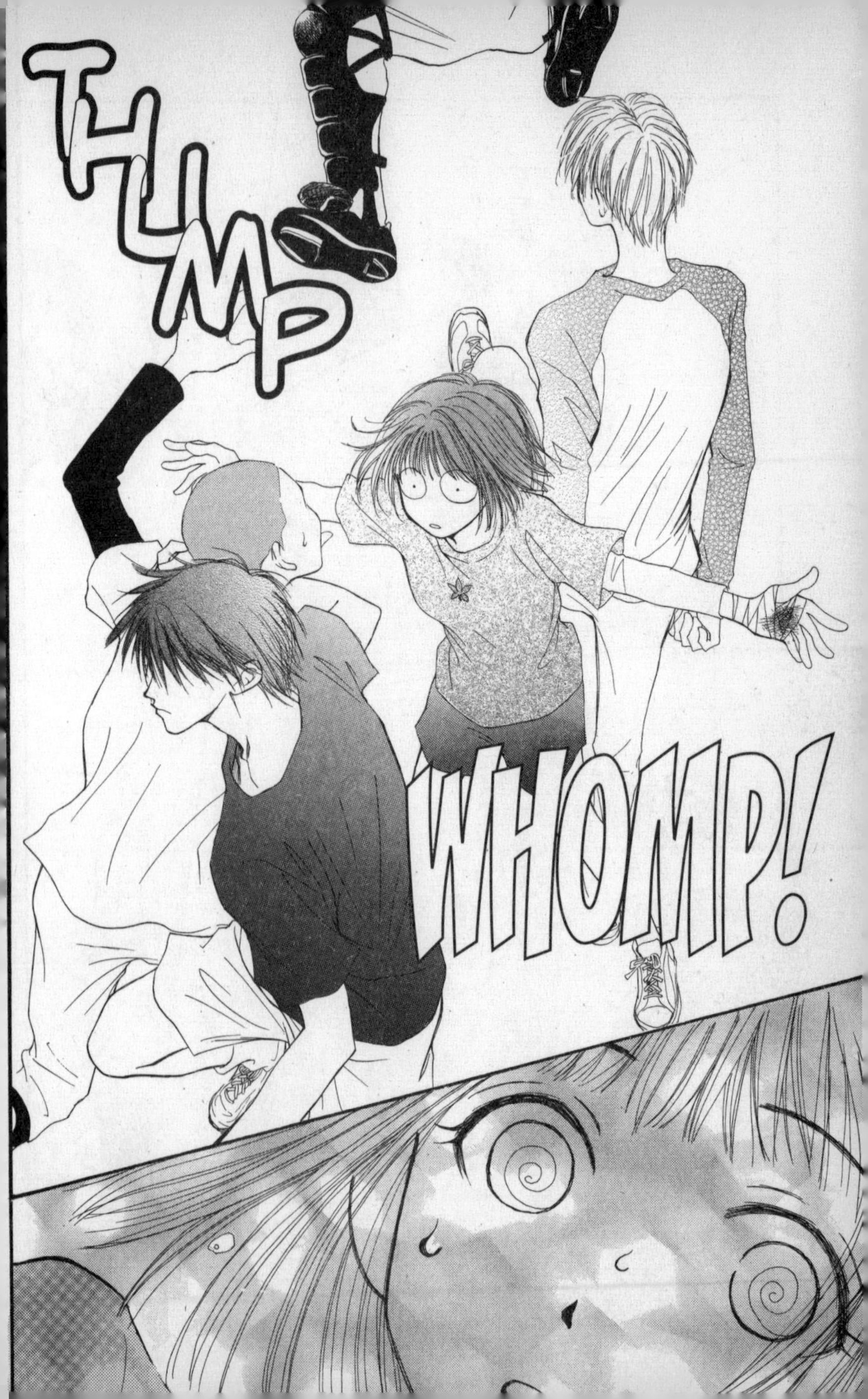
THUMP
WHOMP!

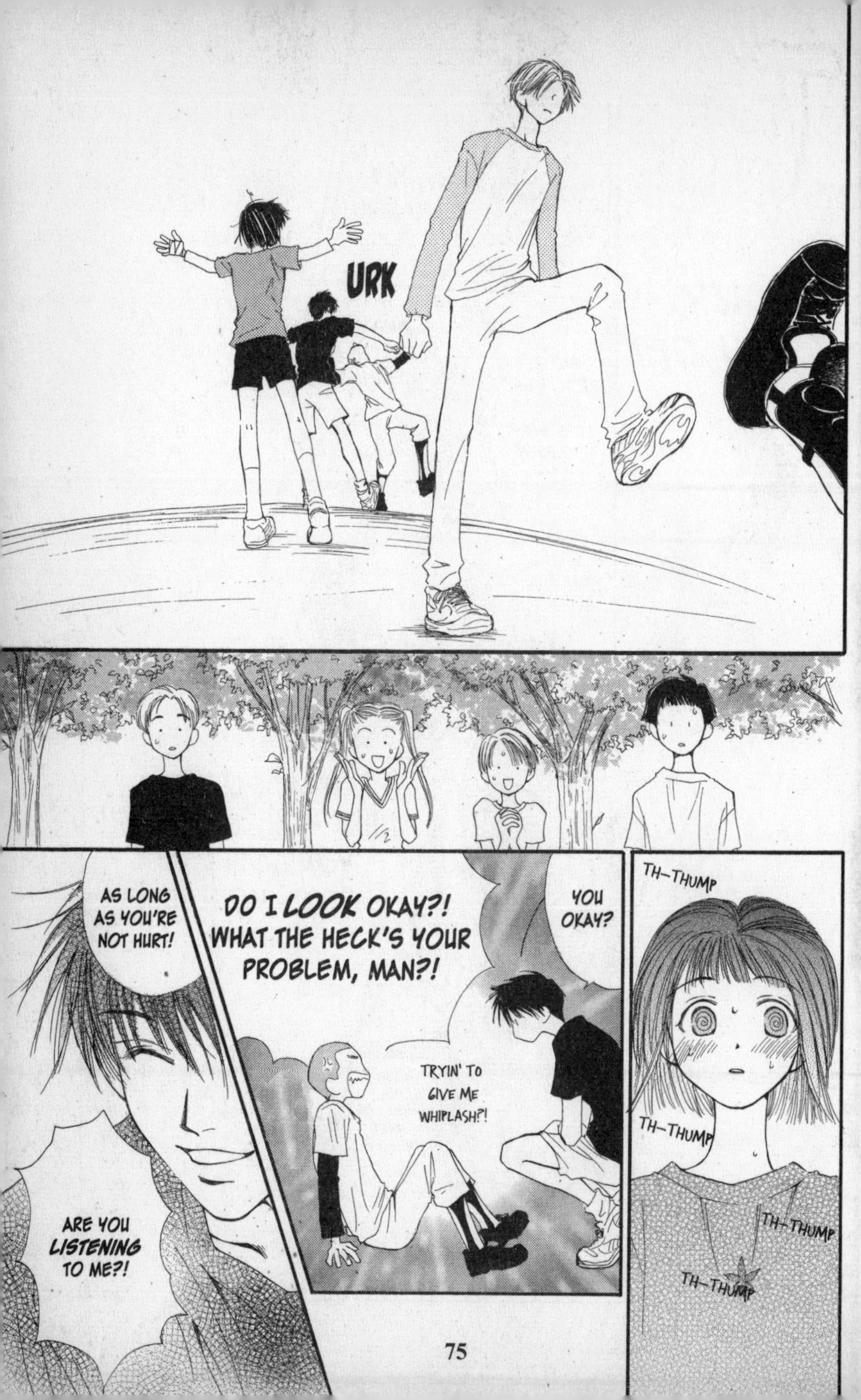
URK
TH-THUMP
TH-THUMP
TH-THUMP
TH-THUMP
YOU OKAY?
DO I LOOK OKAY?! WHAT THE HECK'S YOUR PROBLEM, MAN?!
TRYIN' TO GIVE ME WHIPLASH?!
AS LONG AS YOU'RE NOT HURT!
ARE YOU LISTENING TO ME?!

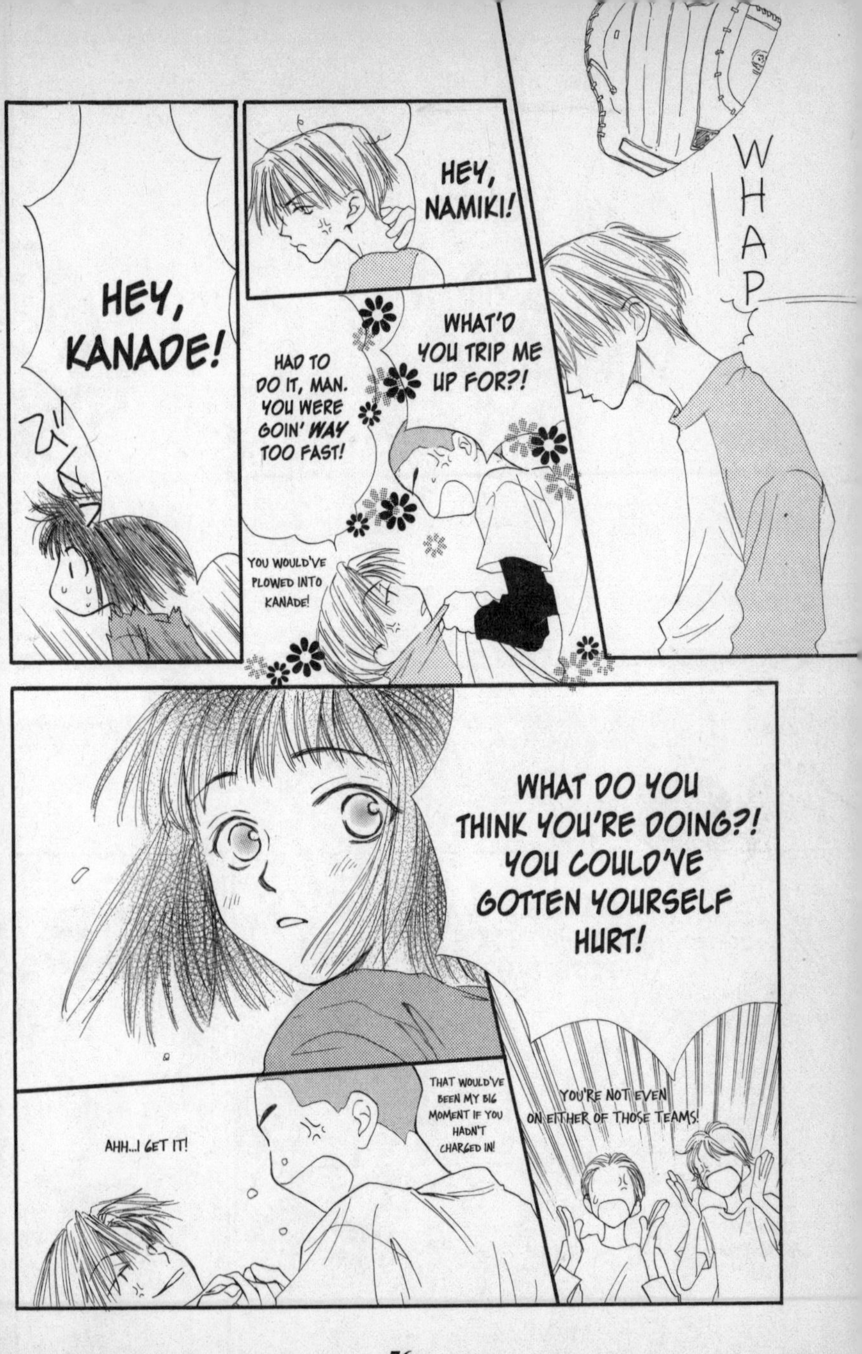
WHAP
HEY, NAMIKI!
WHAT'D YOU TRIP ME UP FOR?!
HAD TO DO IT, MAN. YOU WERE GOIN' WAY TOO FAST!
YOU WOULD'VE PLOWED INTO KANADE!
HEY, KANADE!
WHAT DO YOU THINK YOU'RE DOING?! YOU COULD'VE GOTTEN YOURSELF HURT!
YOU'RE NOT EVEN ON EITHER OF THOSE TEAMS!
THAT WOULD'VE BEEN MY BIG MOMENT IF YOU HADN'T CHARGED IN!
AHH...I GET IT!

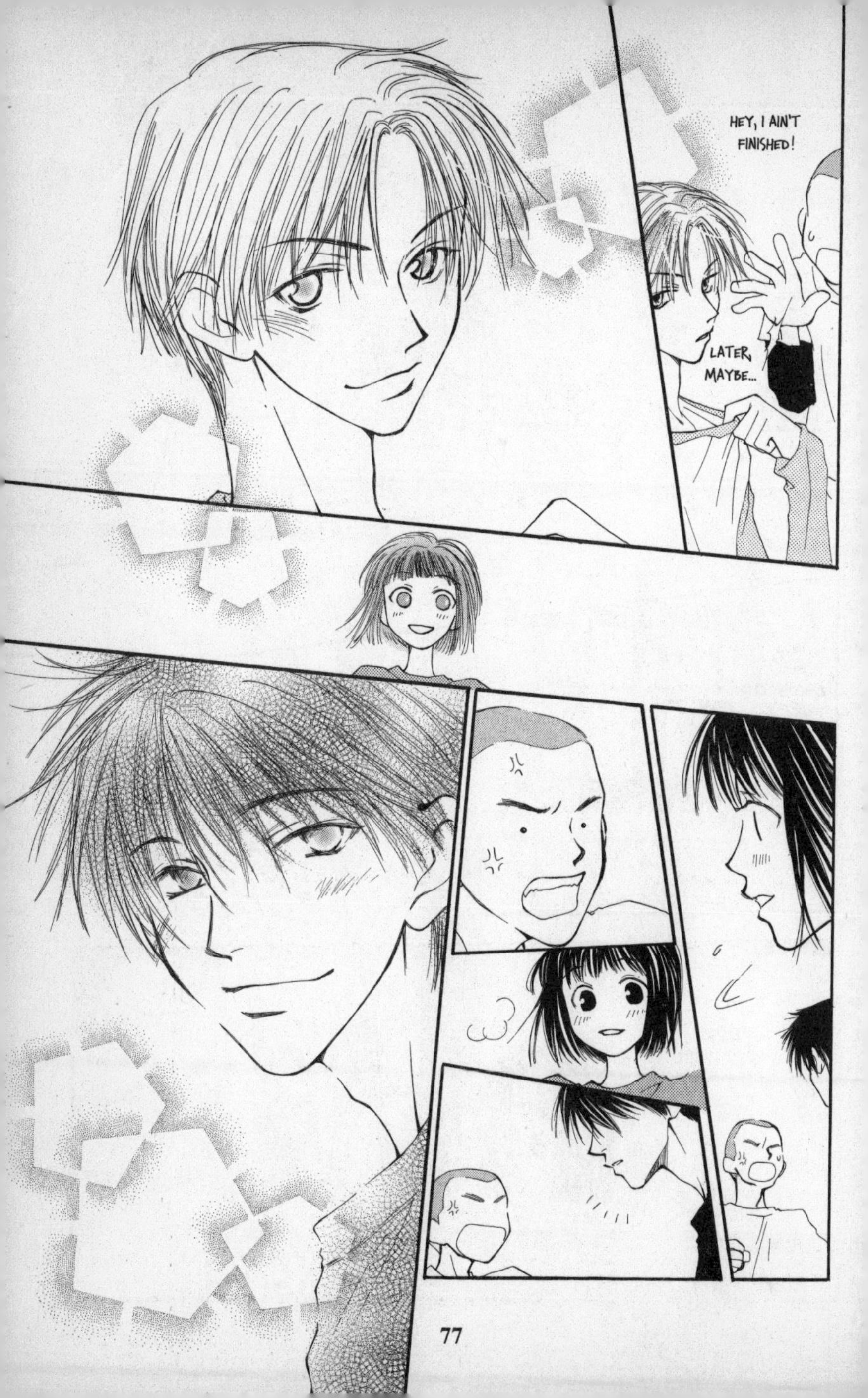
HEY, I AIN'T FINISHED!
LATER, MAYBE...

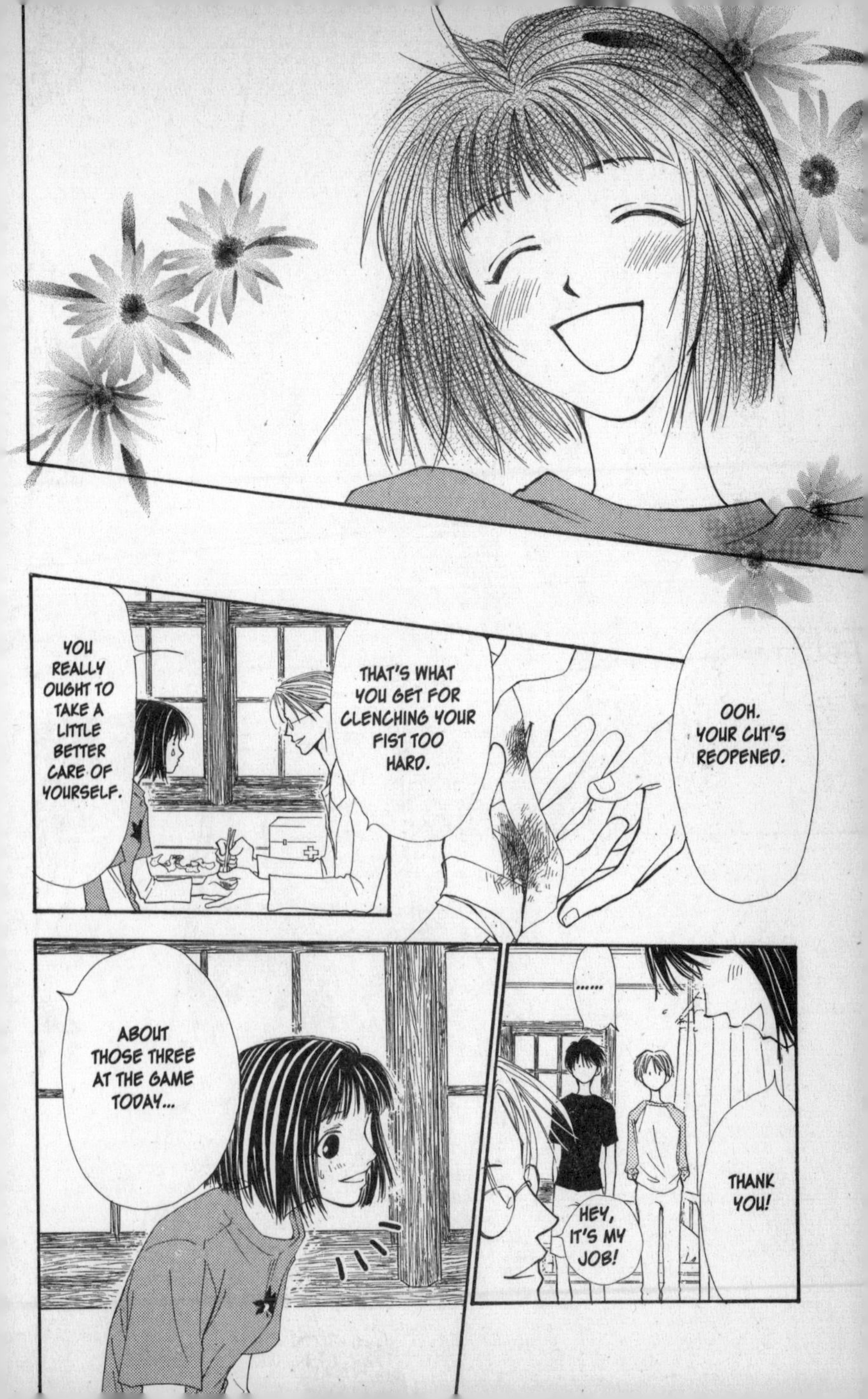
OOH. YOUR CUT'S REOPENED.
THAT'S WHAT YOU GET FOR CLENCHING YOUR FIST TOO HARD.
YOU REALLY OUGHT TO TAKE A LITTLE BETTER CARE OF YOURSELF.
THANK YOU!
HEY, IT'S MY JOB!
......
ABOUT THOSE THREE AT THE GAME TODAY...

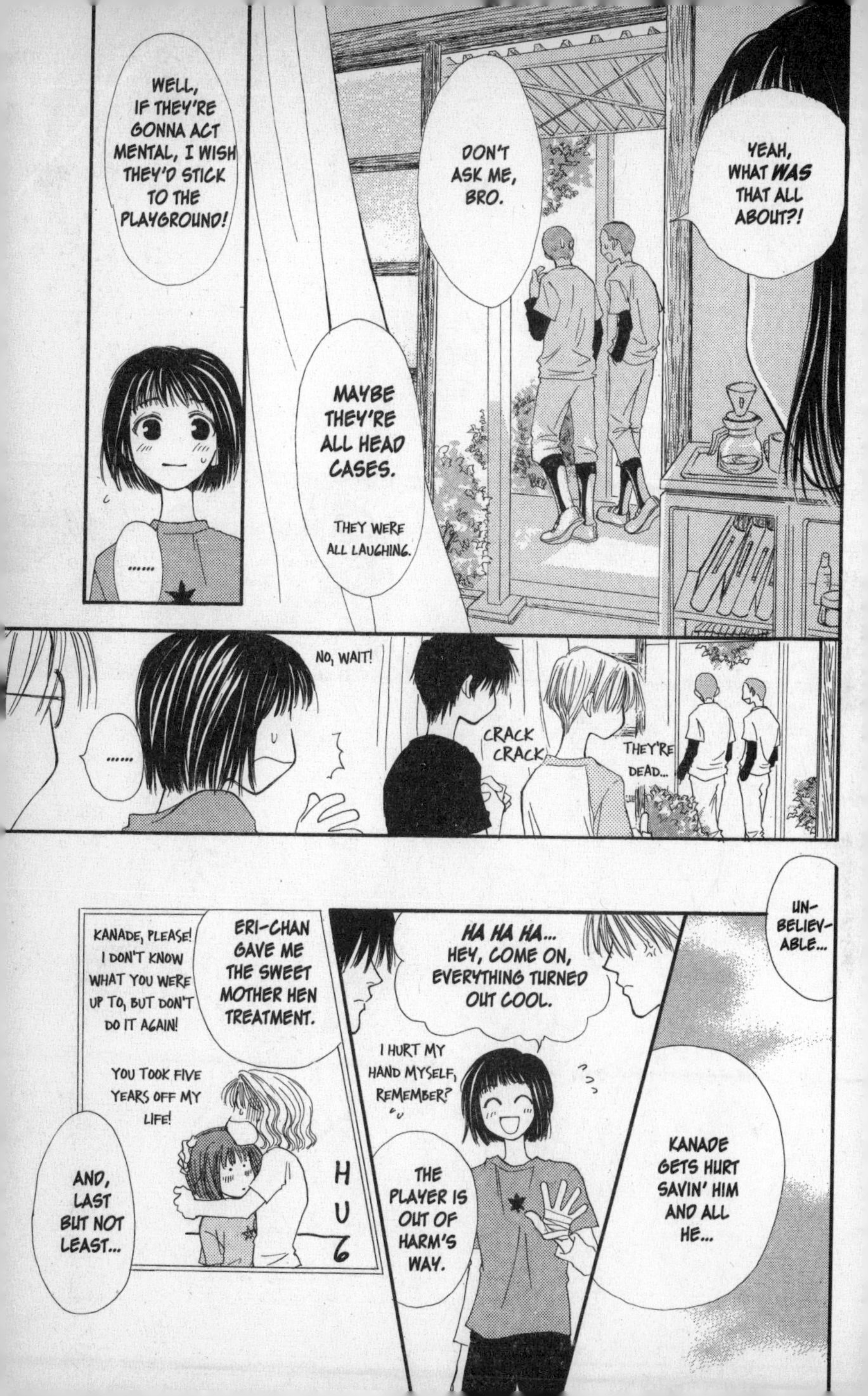
YEAH, WHAT WAS THAT ALL ABOUT?!
DON'T ASK ME, BRO.
MAYBE THEY'RE ALL HEAD CASES.
THEY WERE ALL LAUGHING.
WELL, IF THEY'RE GONNA ACT MENTAL, I WISH THEY'D STICK TO THE PLAYGROUND!
......
THEY'RE DEAD...
CRACK CRACK
NO, WAIT!
......
UN-BELIEV-ABLE...
KANADE GETS HURT SAVIN' HIM AND ALL HE...
HA HA HA... HEY, COME ON, EVERYTHING TURNED OUT COOL.
I HURT MY HAND MYSELF, REMEMBER?
THE PLAYER IS OUT OF HARM'S WAY.
ERI-CHAN GAVE ME THE SWEET MOTHER HEN TREATMENT.
KANADE, PLEASE! I DON'T KNOW WHAT YOU WERE UP TO, BUT DON'T DO IT AGAIN!
YOU TOOK FIVE YEARS OFF MY LIFE!
HUG
AND, LAST BUT NOT LEAST...

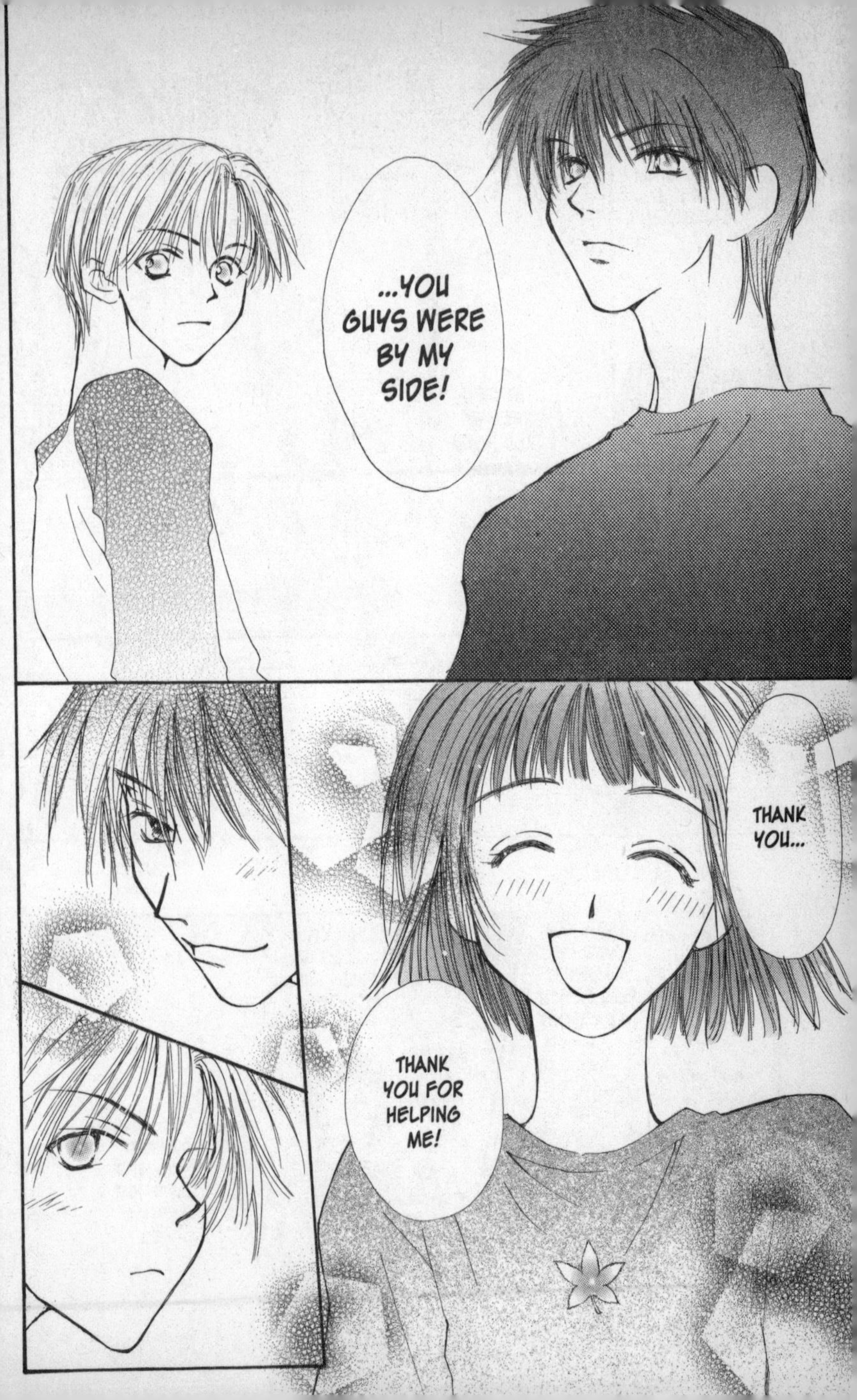
...YOU GUYS WERE BY MY SIDE!
THANK YOU...
THANK YOU FOR HELPING ME!

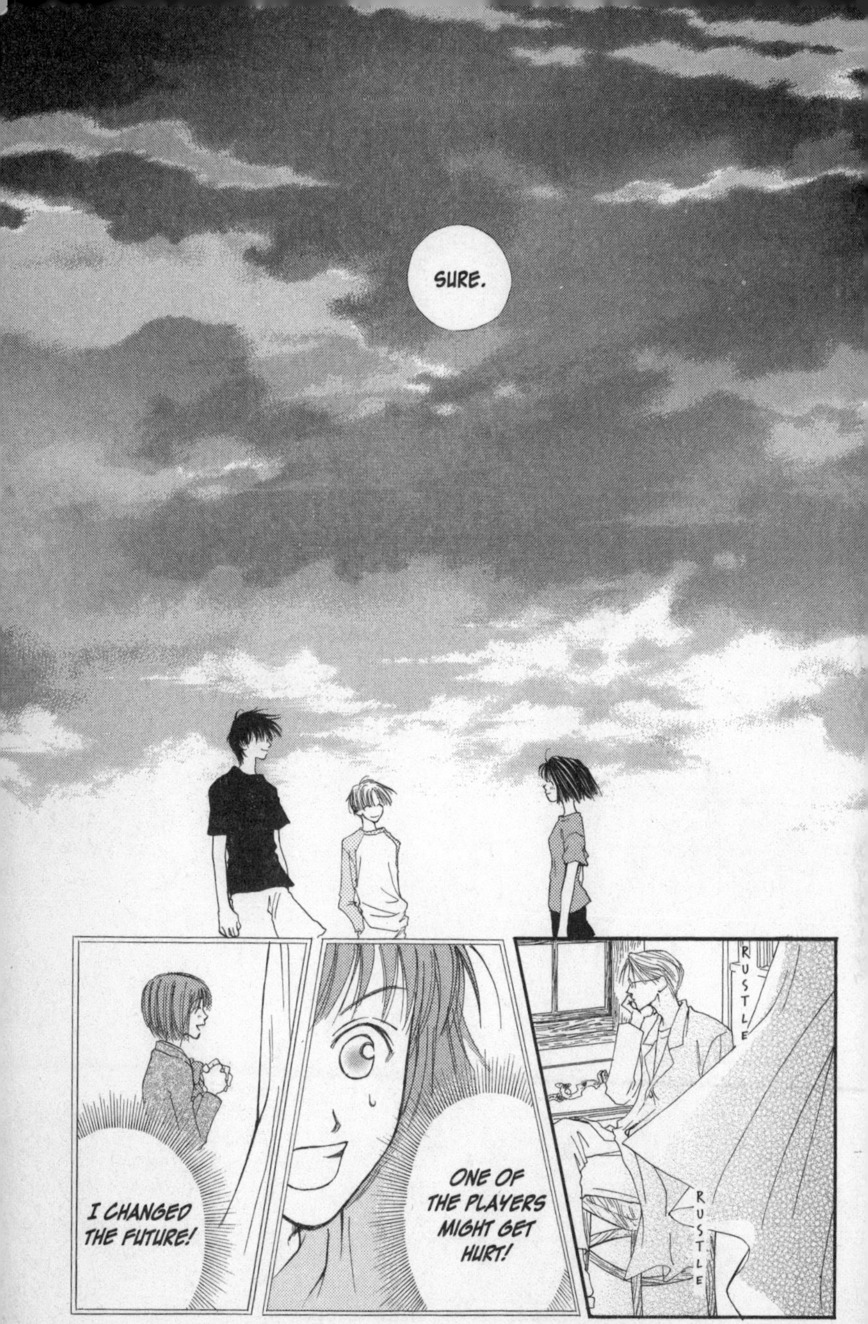
SURE.
RUSTLE
RUSTLE
ONE OF THE PLAYERS MIGHT GET HURT!
I CHANGED THE FUTURE!

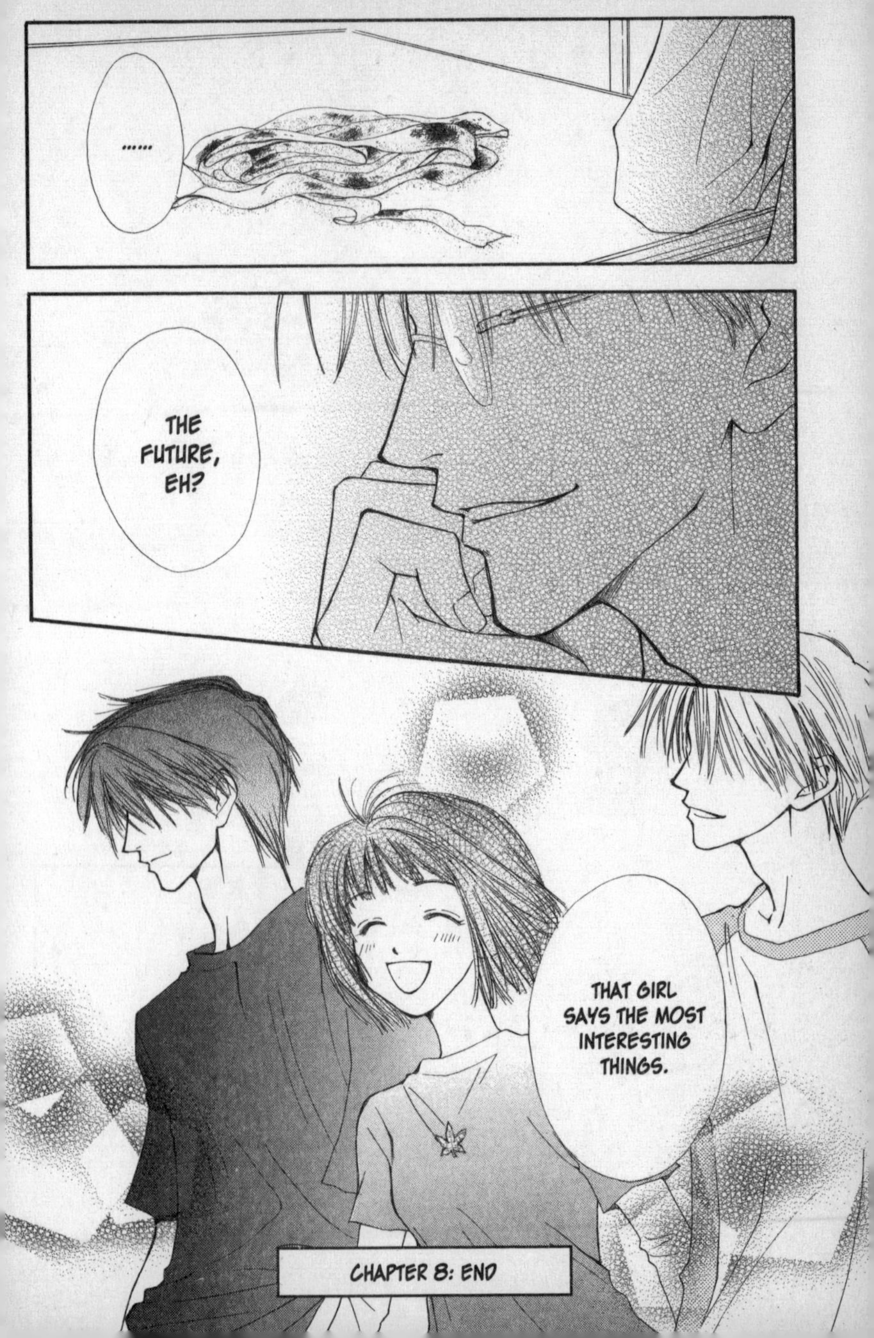
......
THE FUTURE, EH?
THAT GIRL SAYS THE MOST INTERESTING THINGS.
CHAPTER 8: END

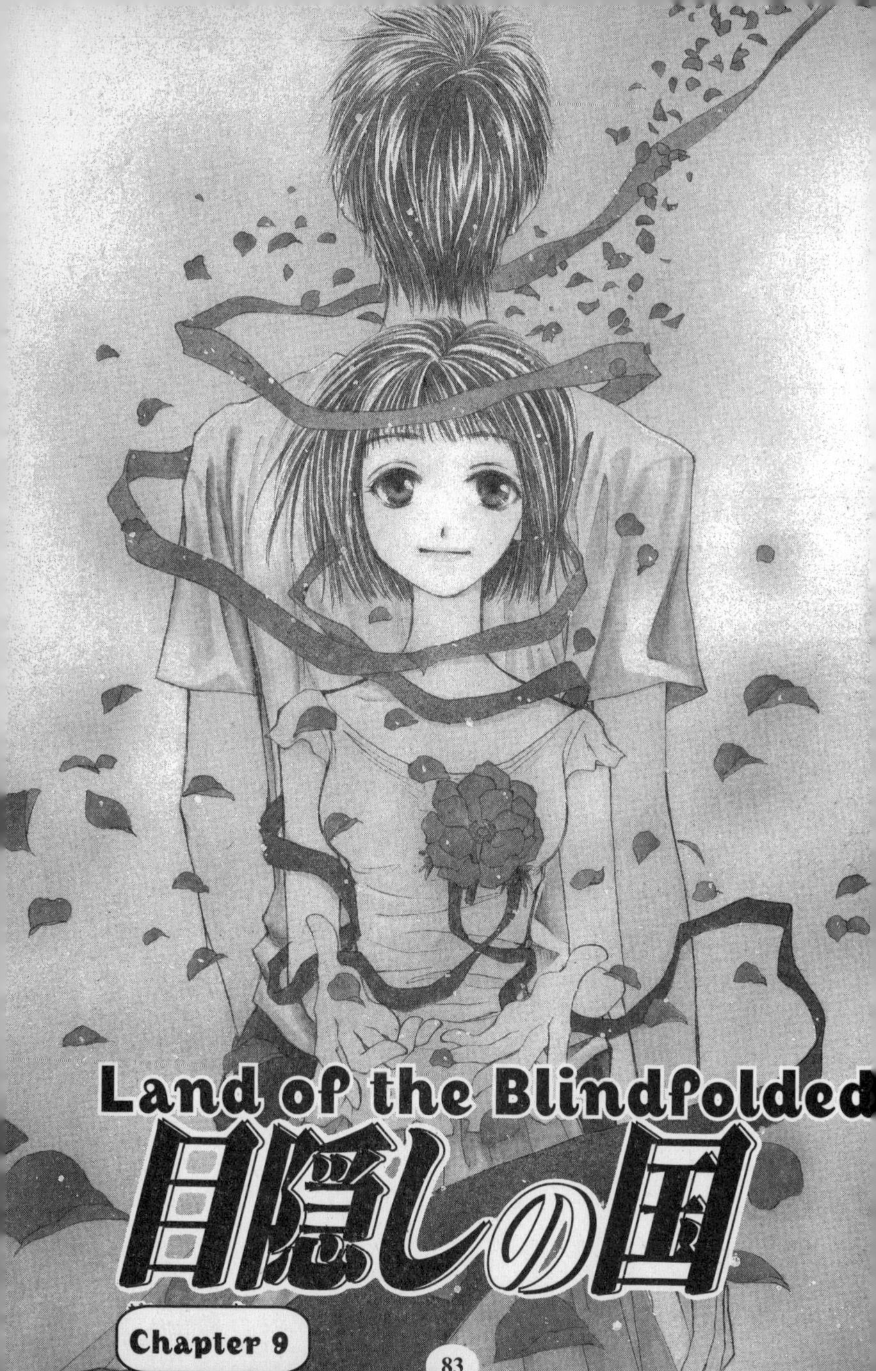
Land of the Blindfolded
目隠しの国
Chapter 9

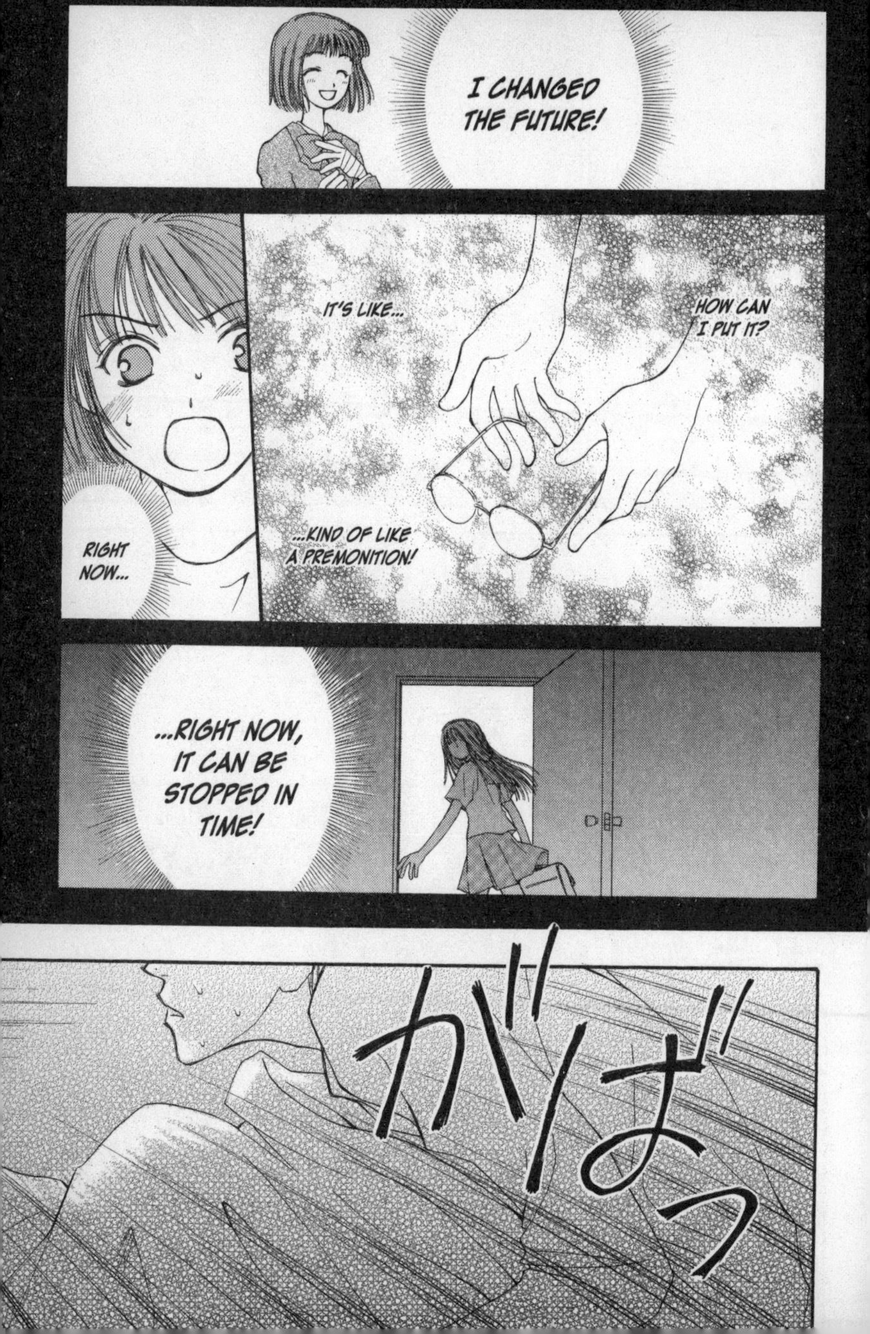
I CHANGED THE FUTURE!
HOW CAN I PUT IT?
IT'S LIKE...
...KIND OF LIKE A PREMONITION!
RIGHT NOW...
...RIGHT NOW, IT CAN BE STOPPED IN TIME!
がばっ

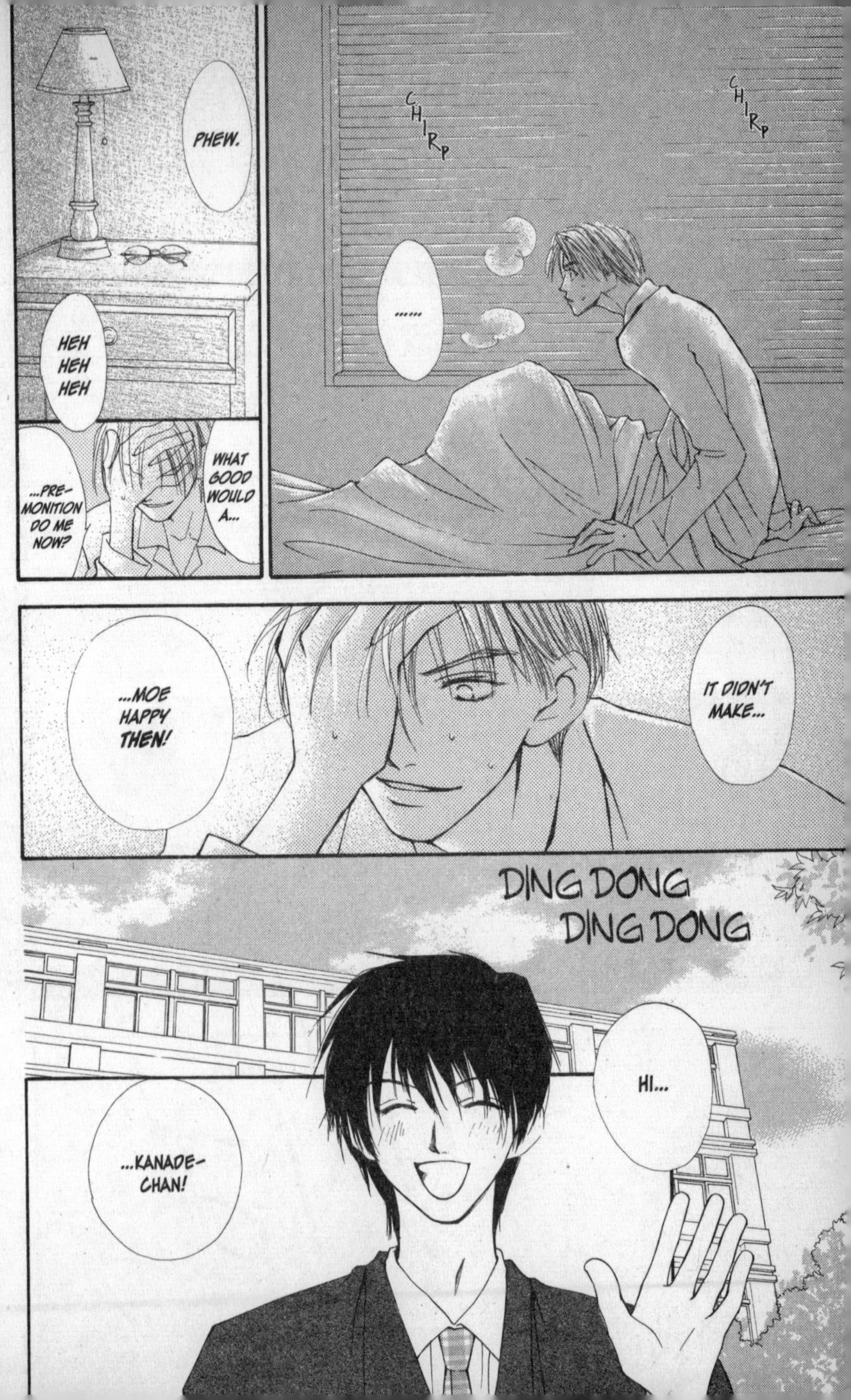
CHIRP
CHIRP
......
PHEW.
HEH HEH HEH
WHAT GOOD WOULD A...
...PRE-MONITION DO ME NOW?
IT DIDN'T MAKE...
...MOE HAPPY THEN!
DING DONG DING DONG
HI...
...KANADE-CHAN!

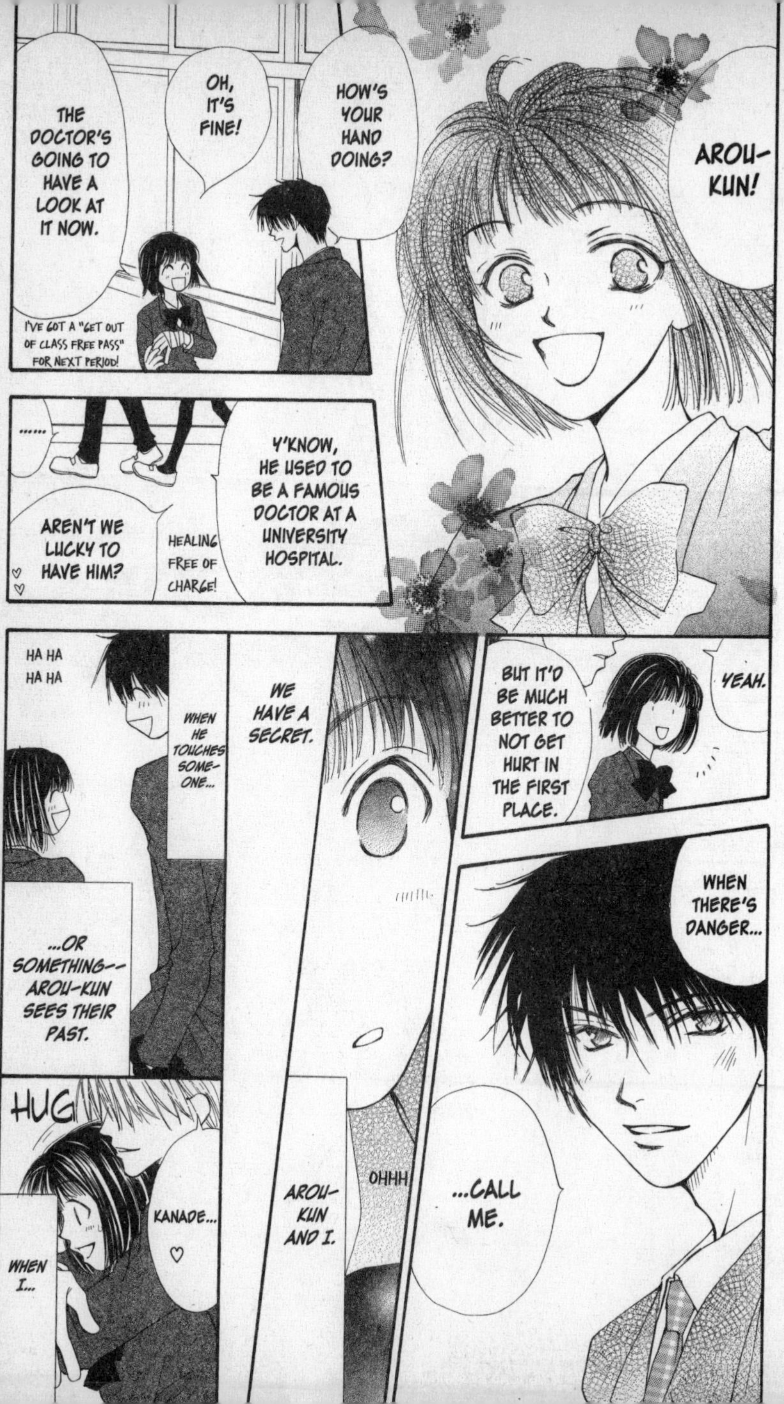
AROU-KUN!
HOW'S YOUR HAND DOING?
OH, IT'S FINE!
THE DOCTOR'S GOING TO HAVE A LOOK AT IT NOW.
I'VE GOT A "GET OUT OF CLASS FREE PASS" FOR NEXT PERIOD!
Y'KNOW, HE USED TO BE A FAMOUS DOCTOR AT A UNIVERSITY HOSPITAL.
......
HEALING FREE OF CHARGE!
AREN'T WE LUCKY TO HAVE HIM? ♡ ♡
YEAH.
BUT IT'D BE MUCH BETTER TO NOT GET HURT IN THE FIRST PLACE.
WHEN THERE'S DANGER...
...CALL ME.
WE HAVE A SECRET.
OHHH
AROU-KUN AND I.
HA HA HA HA
WHEN HE TOUCHES SOMEONE...
...OR SOMETHING--AROU-KUN SEES THEIR PAST.
HUG
KANADE... ♡
WHEN I...

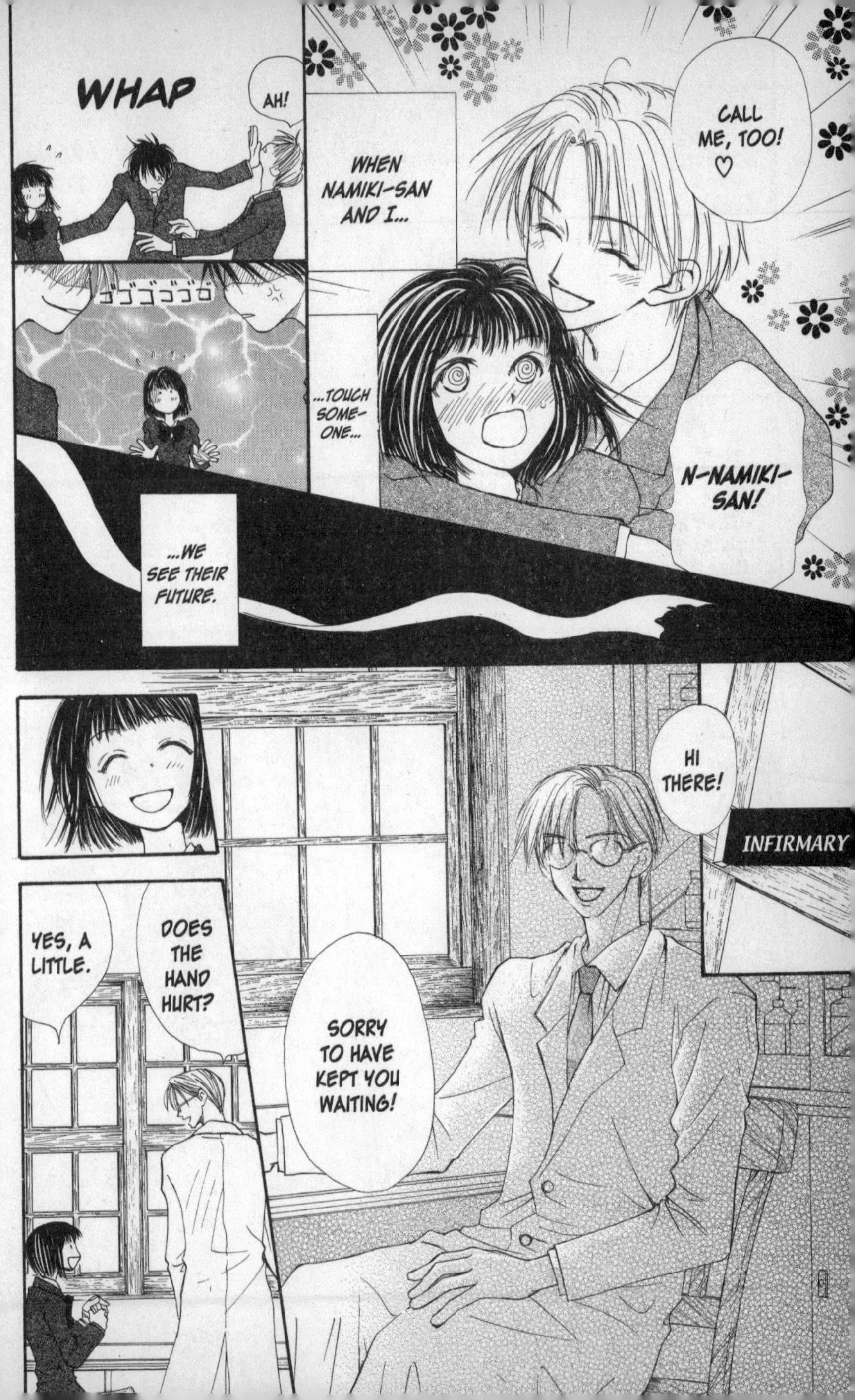
CALL ME, TOO! ♡
N-NAMIKI-SAN!
WHEN NAMIKI-SAN AND I...
...TOUCH SOME-ONE...
AH!
WHAP
ゴゴゴゴゴ
...WE SEE THEIR FUTURE.
INFIRMARY
HI THERE!
SORRY TO HAVE KEPT YOU WAITING!
DOES THE HAND HURT?
YES, A LITTLE.

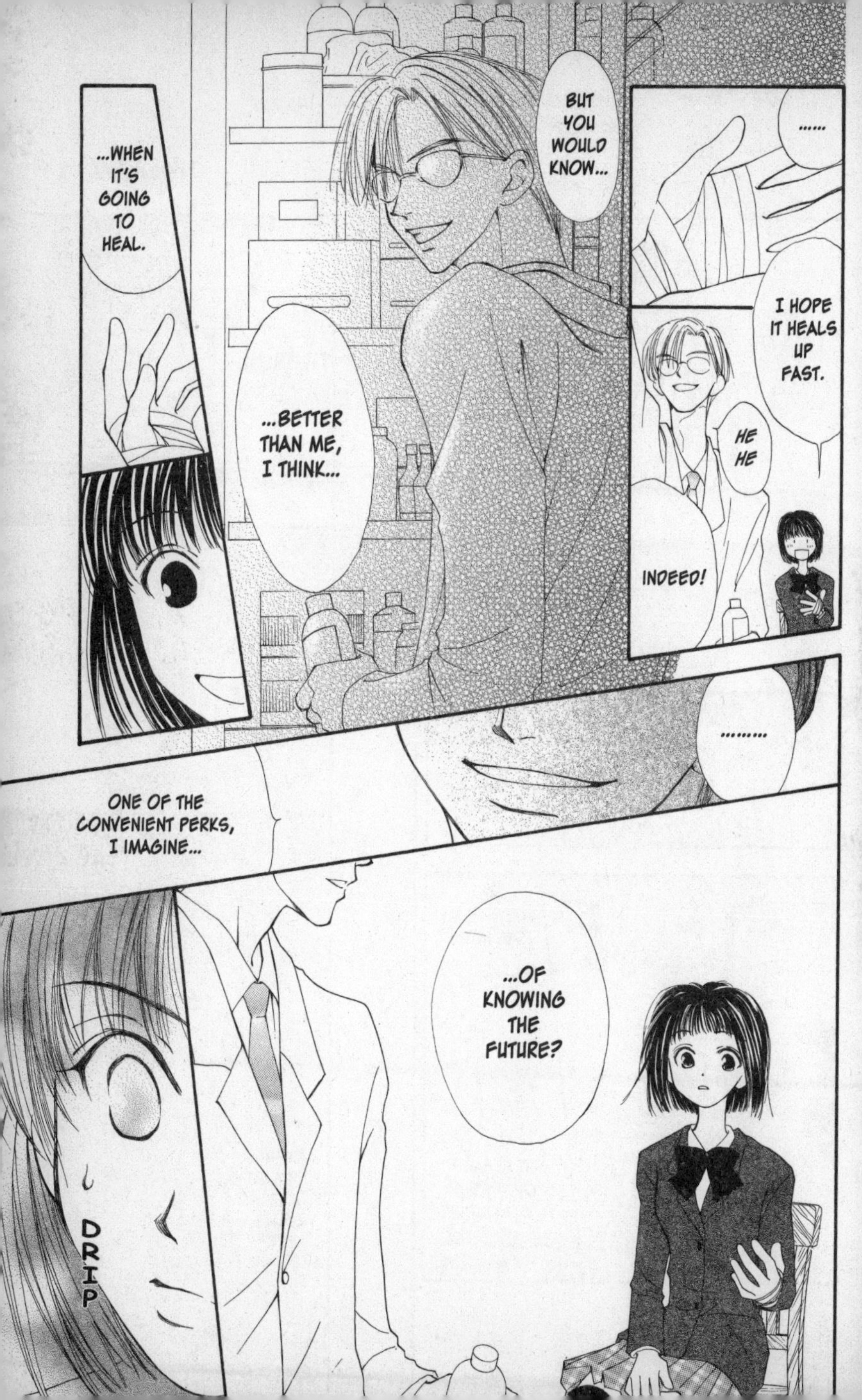
......
I HOPE IT HEALS UP FAST.
HE HE
INDEED!
BUT YOU WOULD KNOW...
...BETTER THAN ME, I THINK...
...WHEN IT'S GOING TO HEAL.
....
ONE OF THE CONVENIENT PERKS, I IMAGINE...
...OF KNOWING THE FUTURE?
DRIP

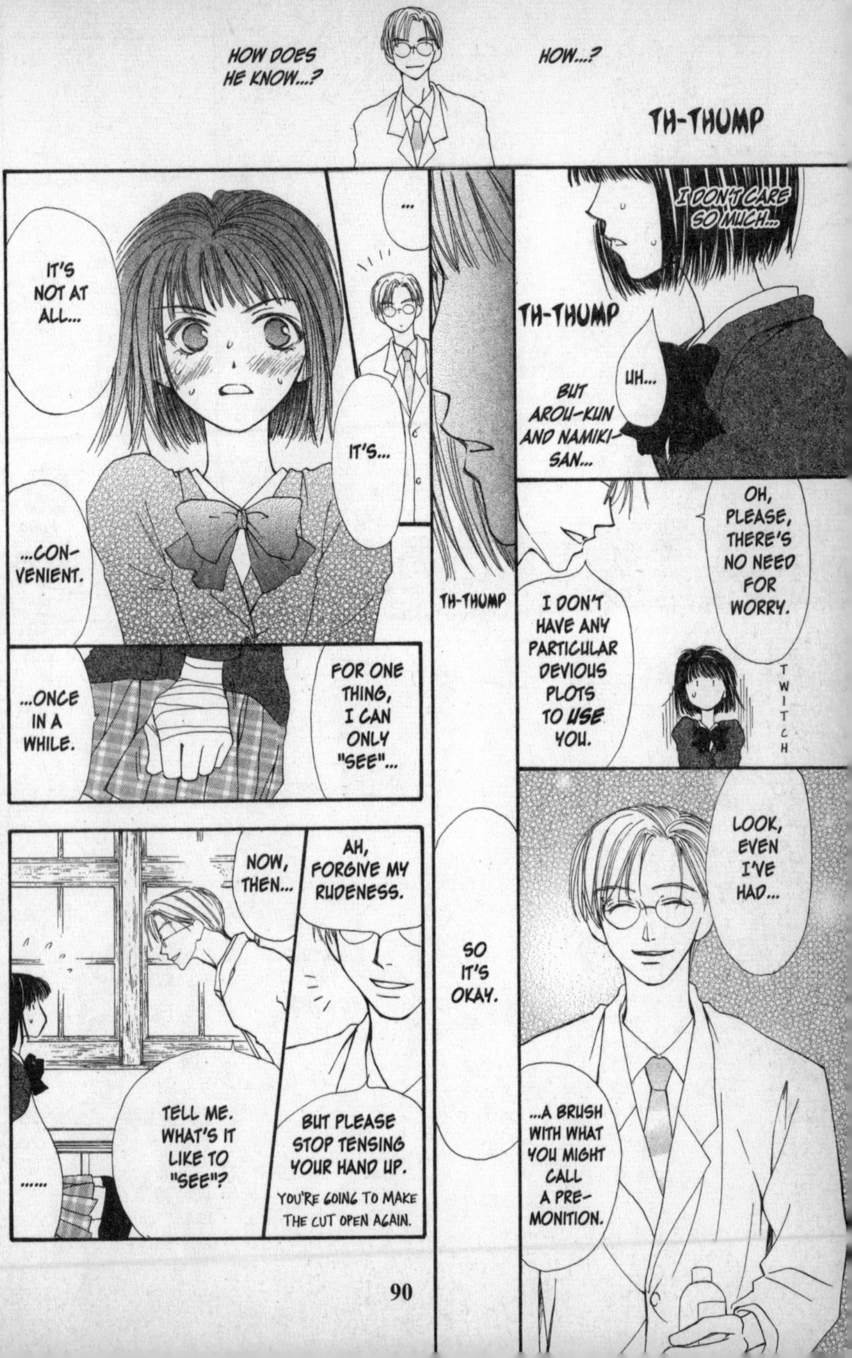
HOW...?
TH-THUMP
HOW DOES HE KNOW...?
I DON'T CARE SO MUCH...
TH-THUMP
UH...
BUT AROU-KUN AND NAMIKI-SAN...
OH, PLEASE, THERE'S NO NEED FOR WORRY.
I DON'T HAVE ANY PARTICULAR DEVIOUS PLOTS TO USE YOU.
TWITCH
LOOK, EVEN I'VE HAD...
...A BRUSH WITH WHAT YOU MIGHT CALL A PRE-MONITION.
TH-THUMP
SO IT'S OKAY.
...
IT'S...
IT'S NOT AT ALL...
...CON-VENIENT.
FOR ONE THING, I CAN ONLY "SEE"...
...ONCE IN A WHILE.
AH, FORGIVE MY RUDENESS.
BUT PLEASE STOP TENSING YOUR HAND UP.
YOU'RE GOING TO MAKE THE CUT OPEN AGAIN.
NOW, THEN...
TELL ME. WHAT'S IT LIKE TO "SEE"?
......

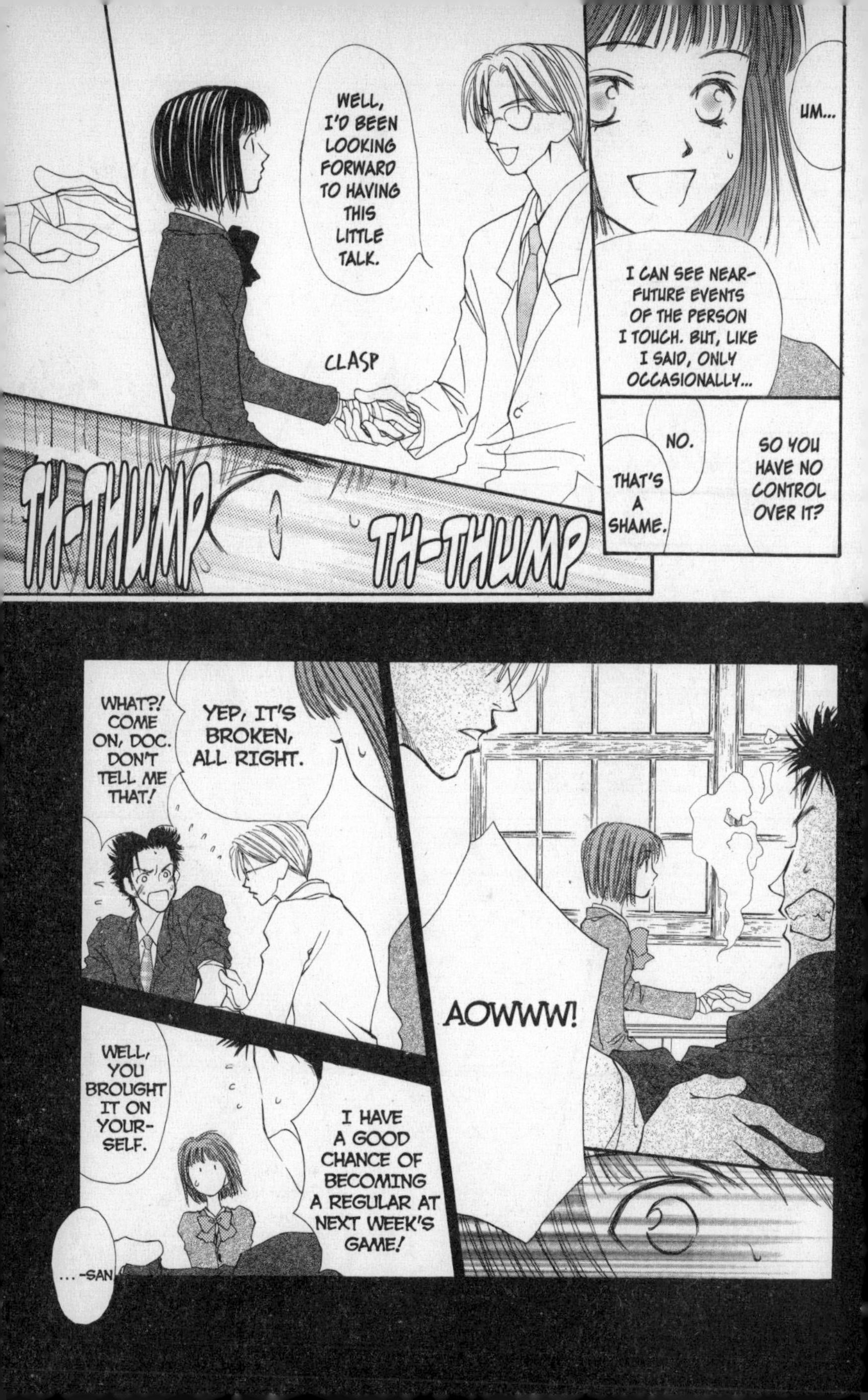
UM...
I CAN SEE NEAR-FUTURE EVENTS OF THE PERSON I TOUCH. BUT, LIKE I SAID, ONLY OCCASIONALLY...
SO YOU HAVE NO CONTROL OVER IT?
NO.
THAT'S A SHAME.
WELL, I'D BEEN LOOKING FORWARD TO HAVING THIS LITTLE TALK.
CLASP
TH-THUMP
TH-THUMP
AOWWW!
YEP, IT'S BROKEN, ALL RIGHT.
WHAT?! COME ON, DOC. DON'T TELL ME THAT!
I HAVE A GOOD CHANCE OF BECOMING A REGULAR AT NEXT WEEK'S GAME!
WELL, YOU BROUGHT IT ON YOURSELF.
... -SAN

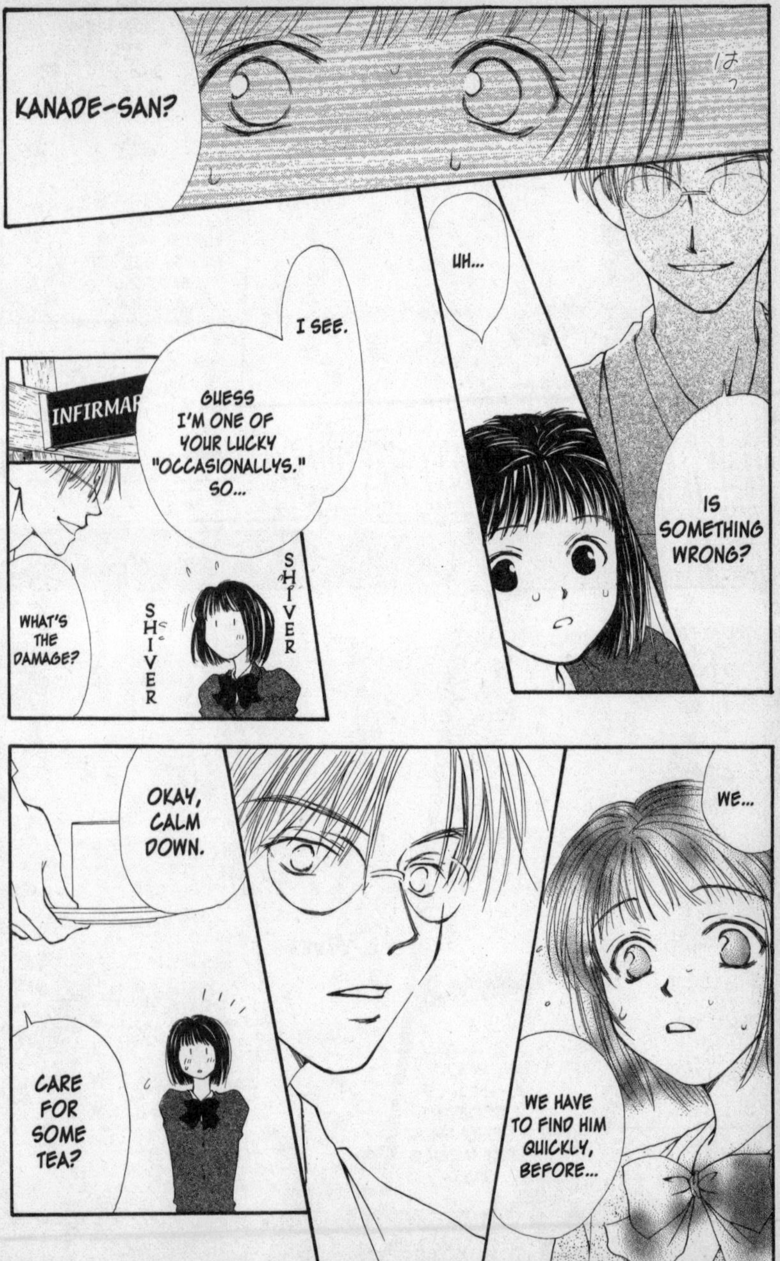
KANADE-SAN?
はっ
UH...
IS SOMETHING WRONG?
I SEE.
GUESS I'M ONE OF YOUR LUCKY "OCCASIONALLYS." SO...
INFIRMAR
SHIVER
SHIVER
WHAT'S THE DAMAGE?
WE...
WE HAVE TO FIND HIM QUICKLY, BEFORE...
OKAY, CALM DOWN.
CARE FOR SOME TEA?

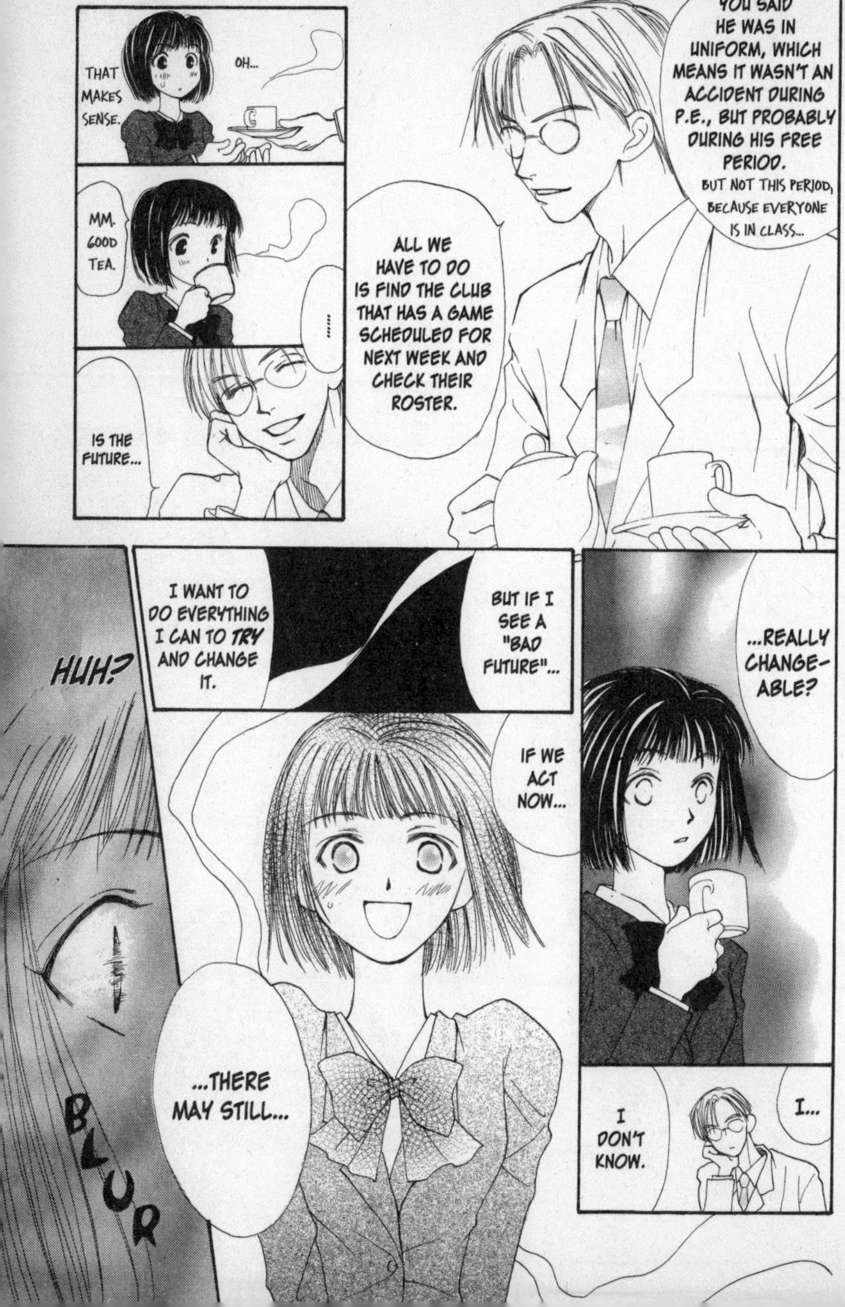
YOU SAID HE WAS IN UNIFORM, WHICH MEANS IT WASN'T AN ACCIDENT DURING P.E., BUT PROBABLY DURING HIS FREE PERIOD.
BUT NOT THIS PERIOD, BECAUSE EVERYONE IS IN CLASS...
ALL WE HAVE TO DO IS FIND THE CLUB THAT HAS A GAME SCHEDULED FOR NEXT WEEK AND CHECK THEIR ROSTER.
OH...
THAT MAKES SENSE.
MM. GOOD TEA.
......
IS THE FUTURE...
...REALLY CHANGE-ABLE?
I...
I DON'T KNOW.
BUT IF I SEE A "BAD FUTURE"...
I WANT TO DO EVERYTHING I CAN TO *TRY* AND CHANGE IT.
IF WE ACT NOW...
...THERE MAY STILL...
HUH?
BLUR

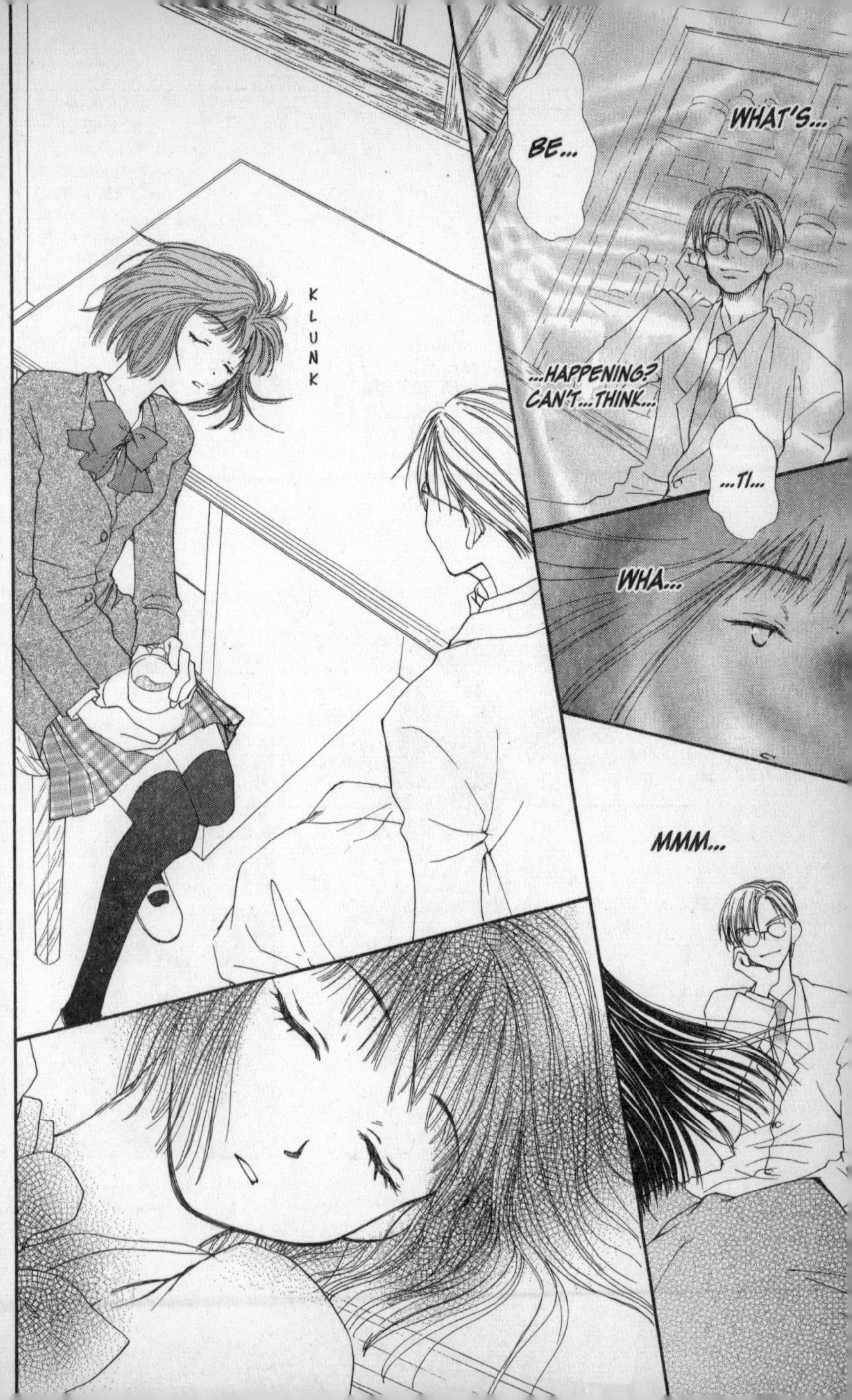
WHAT'S...
...HAPPENING?
CAN'T...THINK...
BE...
...TI...
WHA...
MMM...
KLUNK

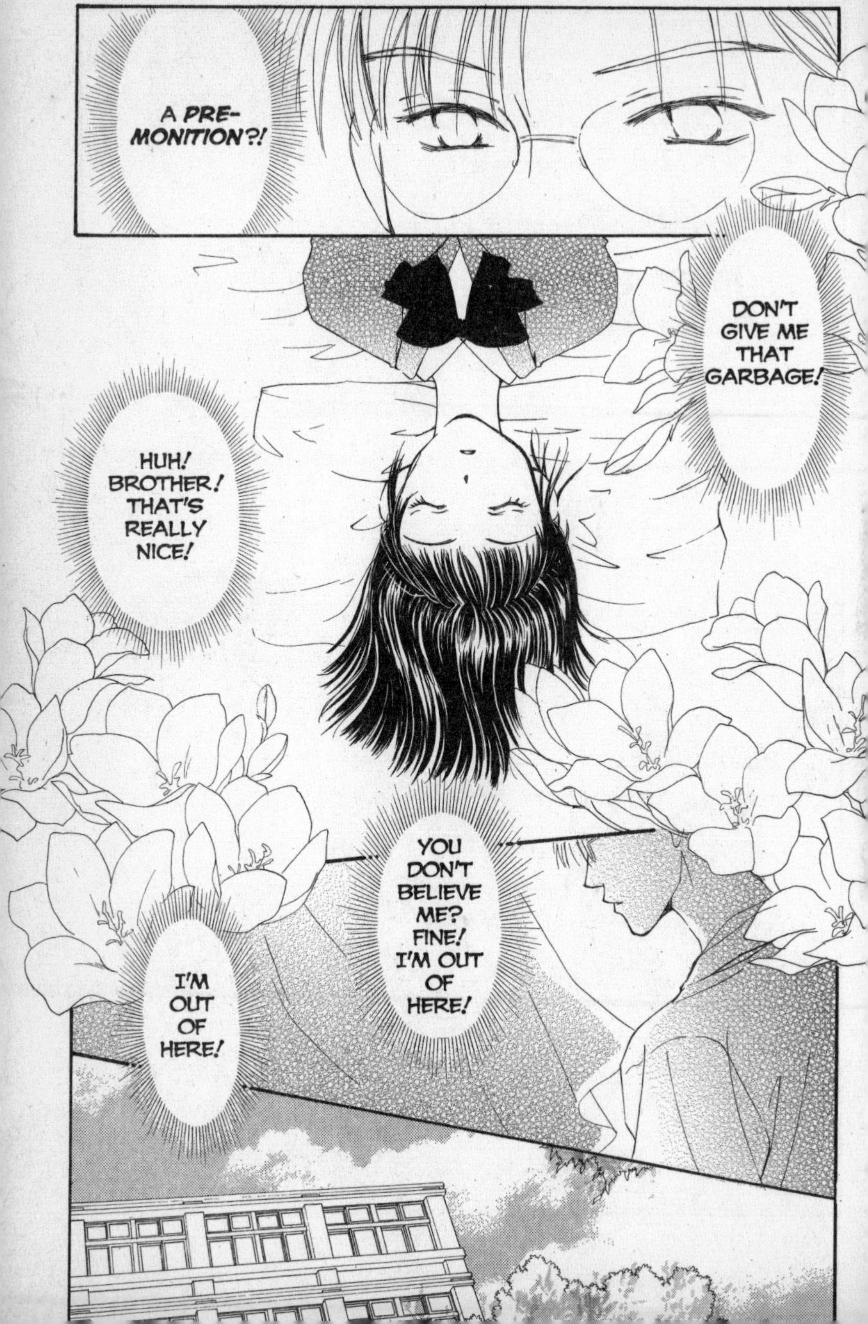
A PRE-MONITION?!
DON'T GIVE ME THAT GARBAGE!
HUH! BROTHER! THAT'S REALLY NICE!
YOU DON'T BELIEVE ME? FINE! I'M OUT OF HERE!
I'M OUT OF HERE!

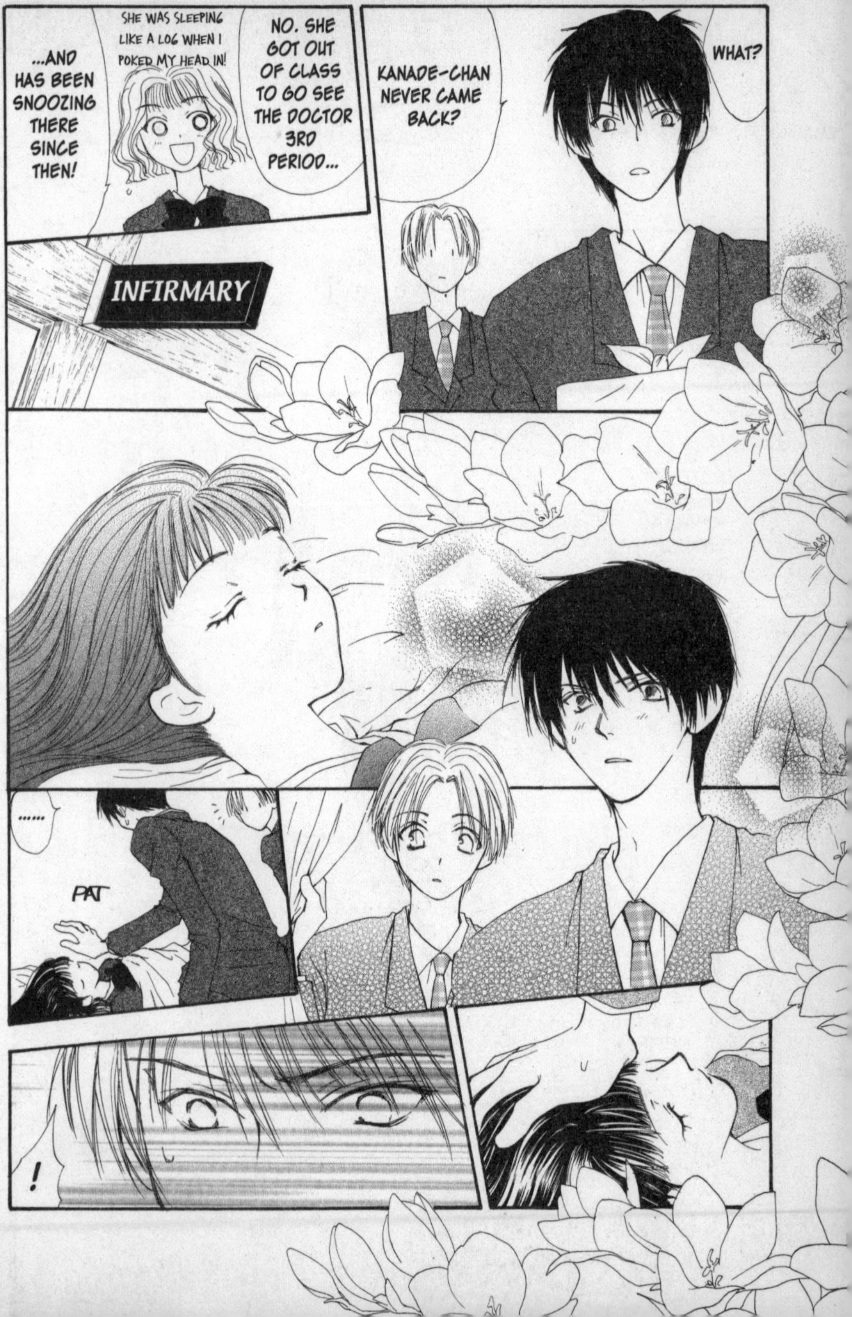
WHAT?
KANADE-CHAN NEVER CAME BACK?
NO. SHE GOT OUT OF CLASS TO GO SEE THE DOCTOR 3RD PERIOD...
SHE WAS SLEEPING LIKE A LOG WHEN I POKED MY HEAD IN!
...AND HAS BEEN SNOOZING THERE SINCE THEN!
INFIRMARY
......
PAT
!

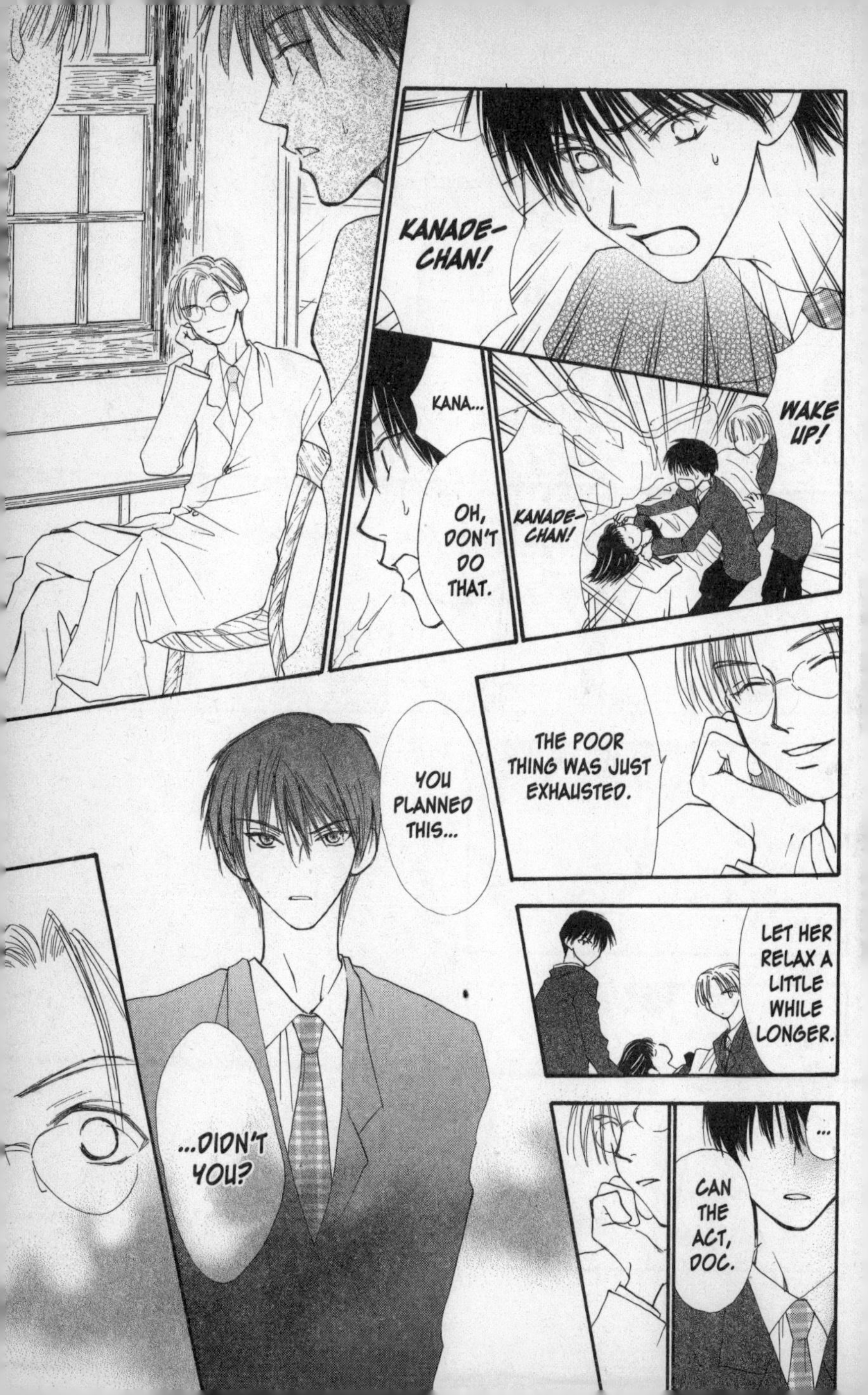
KANADE-CHAN!
WAKE UP!
KANADE-CHAN!
KANA...
OH, DON'T DO THAT.
THE POOR THING WAS JUST EXHAUSTED.
LET HER RELAX A LITTLE WHILE LONGER.
...
CAN THE ACT, DOC.
YOU PLANNED THIS...
...DIDN'T YOU?

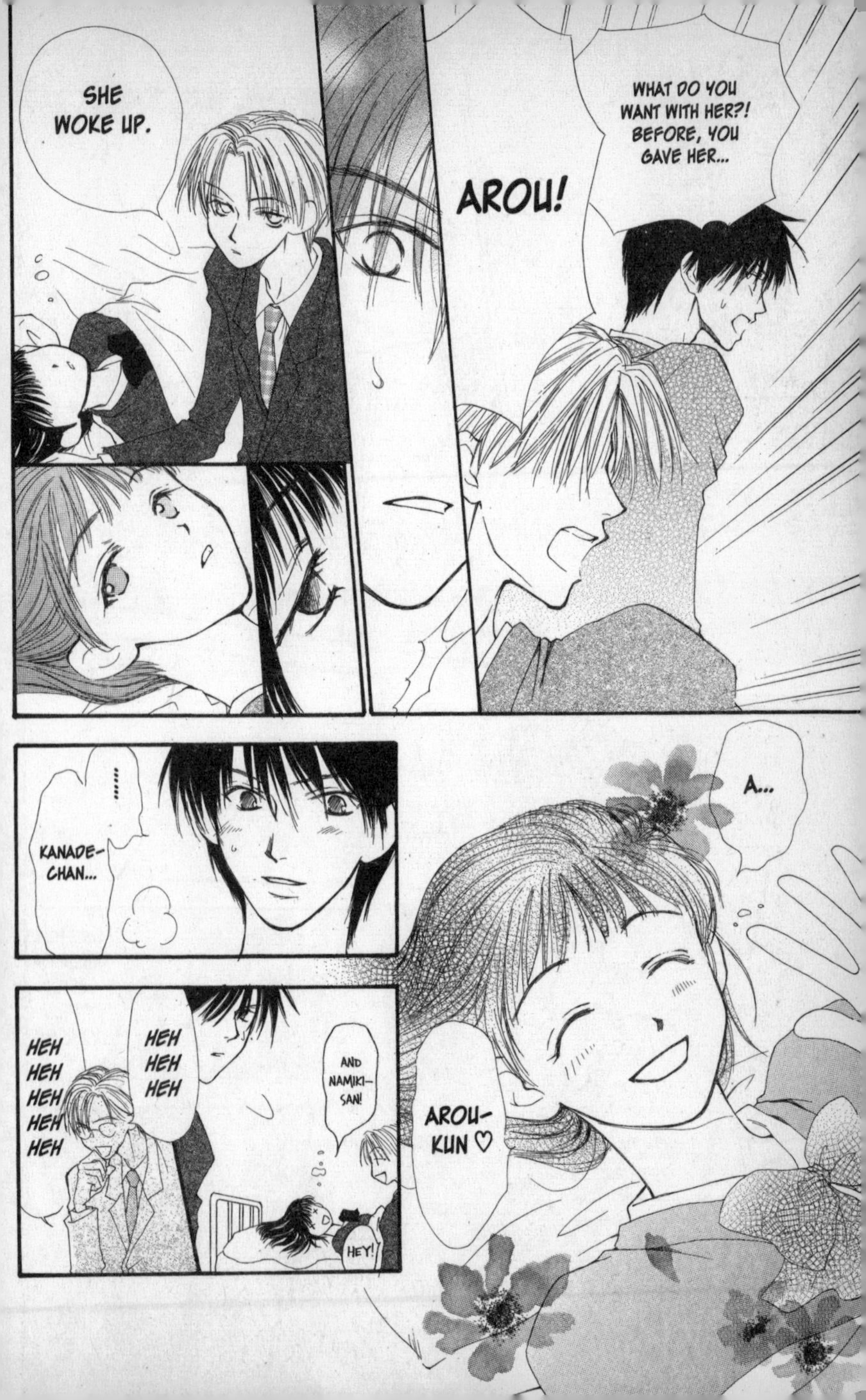
WHAT DO YOU WANT WITH HER?! BEFORE, YOU GAVE HER...
AROU!
SHE WOKE UP.
A...
AROU-KUN ♡
......
KANADE-CHAN...
AND NAMIKI-SAN!
HEH HEH HEH
HEY!
HEH HEH HEH HEH HEH

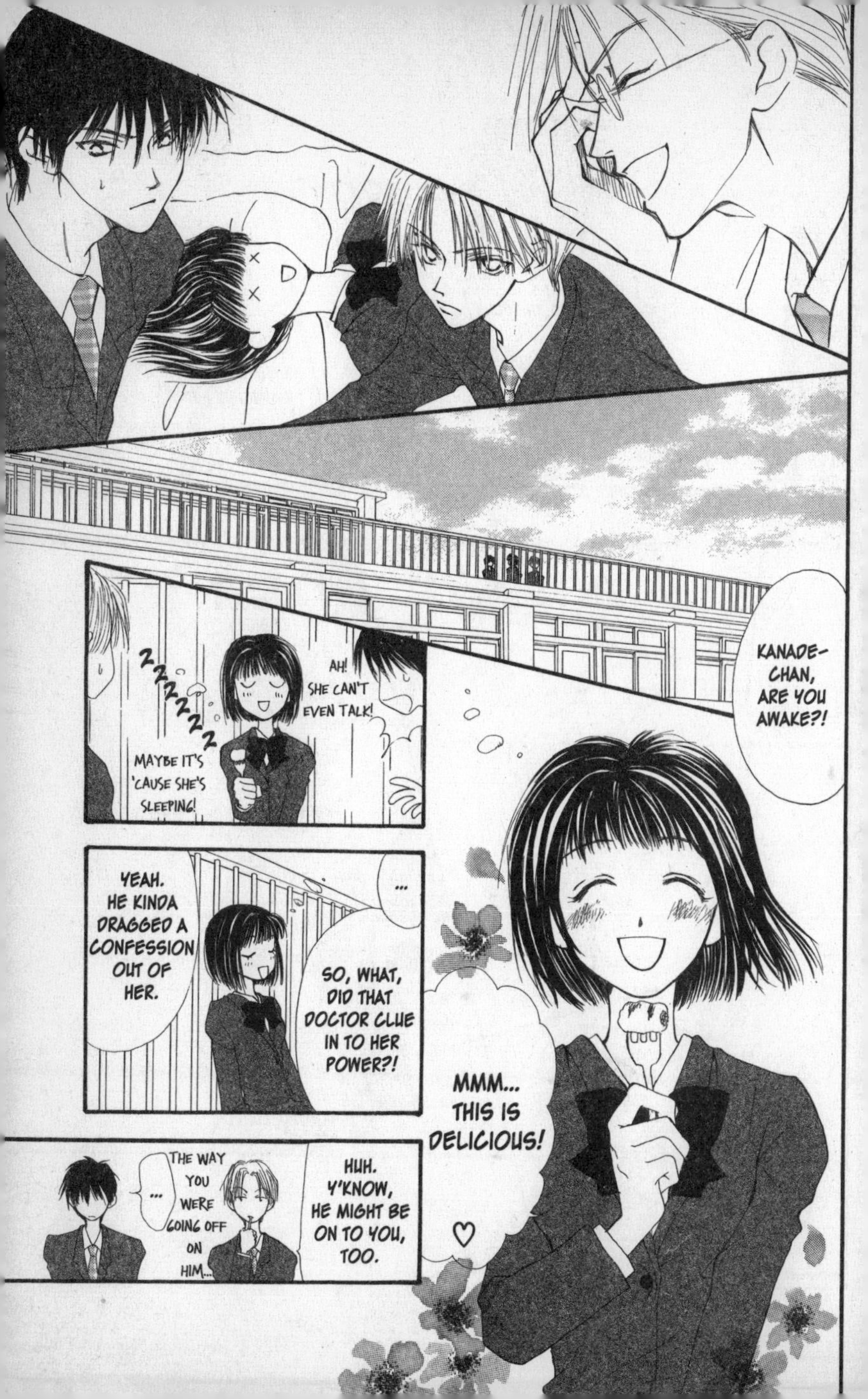
KANADE-CHAN, ARE YOU AWAKE?!
MMM... THIS IS DELICIOUS!
AH! SHE CAN'T EVEN TALK!
ZZZZZZZ
MAYBE IT'S 'CAUSE SHE'S SLEEPING!
...
SO, WHAT, DID THAT DOCTOR CLUE IN TO HER POWER?!
YEAH. HE KINDA DRAGGED A CONFESSION OUT OF HER.
HUH. Y'KNOW, HE MIGHT BE ON TO YOU, TOO.
...
THE WAY YOU WERE GOING OFF ON HIM...

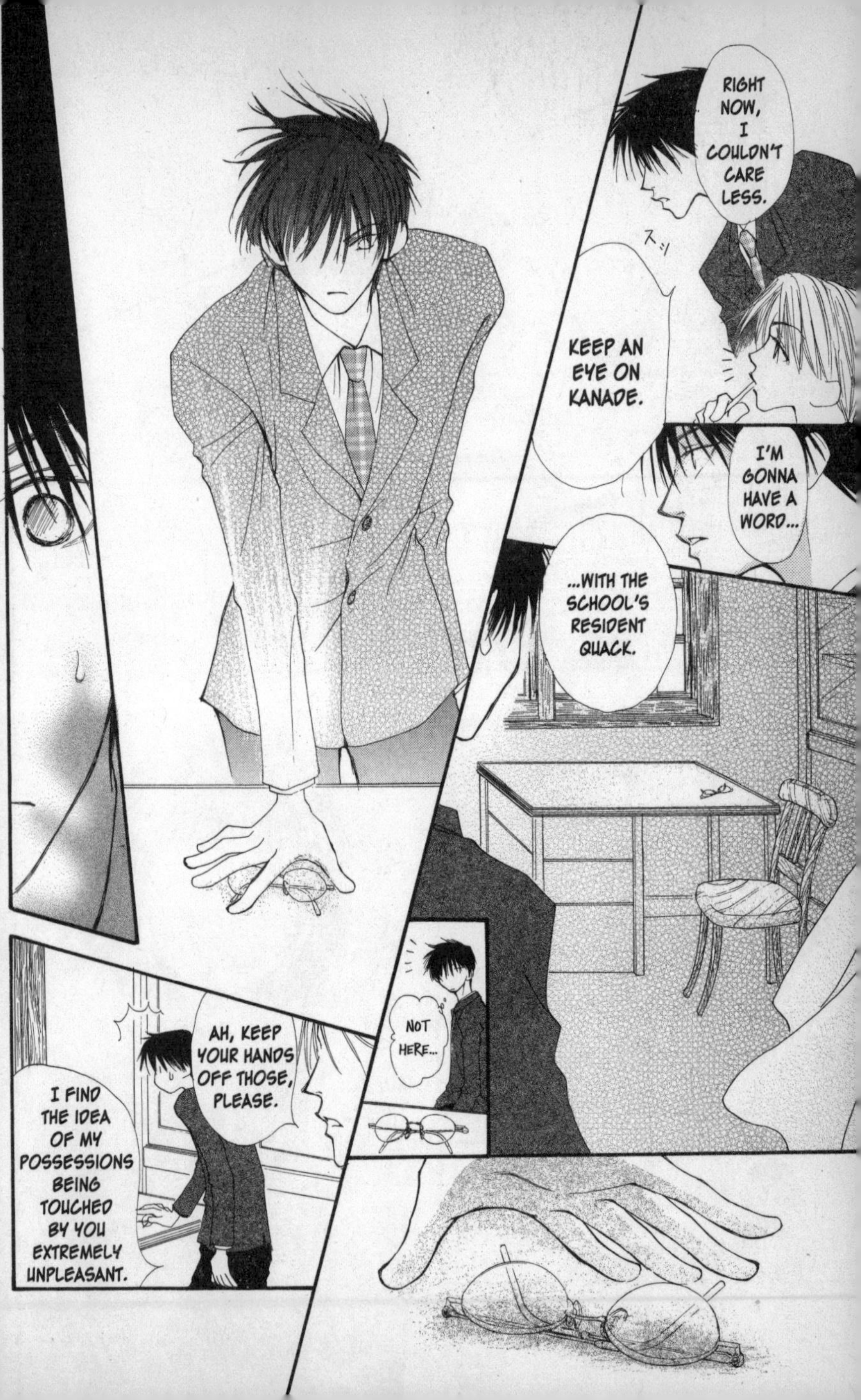
RIGHT NOW, I COULDN'T CARE LESS.
KEEP AN EYE ON KANADE.
I'M GONNA HAVE A WORD...
...WITH THE SCHOOL'S RESIDENT QUACK.
NOT HERE...
AH, KEEP YOUR HANDS OFF THOSE, PLEASE.
I FIND THE IDEA OF MY POSSESSIONS BEING TOUCHED BY YOU EXTREMELY UNPLEASANT.

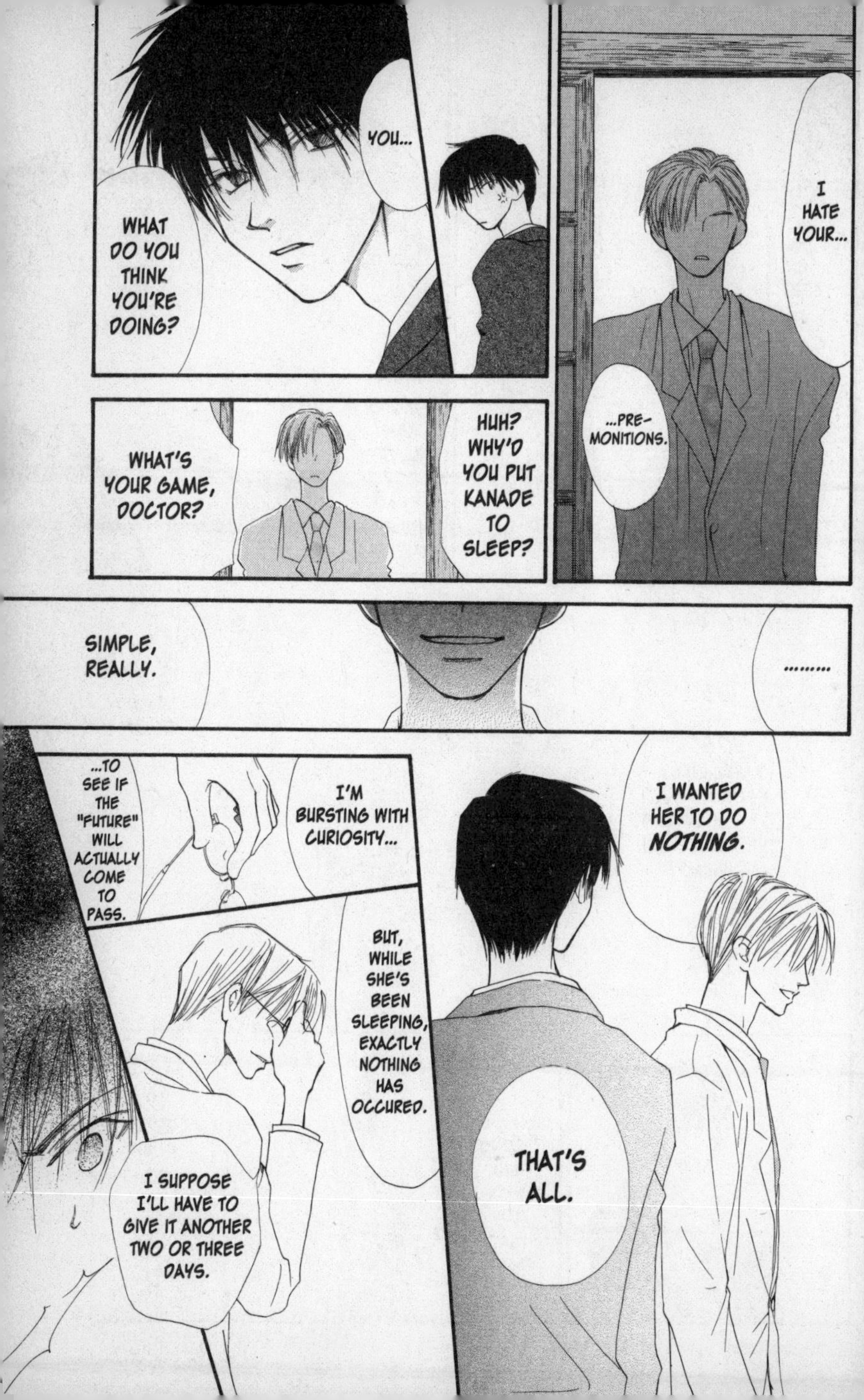
I HATE YOUR...
...PRE-MONITIONS.
YOU...
WHAT DO YOU THINK YOU'RE DOING?
HUH? WHY'D YOU PUT KANADE TO SLEEP?
WHAT'S YOUR GAME, DOCTOR?
....
SIMPLE, REALLY.
I WANTED HER TO DO *NOTHING*.
THAT'S ALL.
I'M BURSTING WITH CURIOSITY...
...TO SEE IF THE "FUTURE" WILL ACTUALLY COME TO PASS.
BUT, WHILE SHE'S BEEN SLEEPING, EXACTLY NOTHING HAS OCCURED.
I SUPPOSE I'LL HAVE TO GIVE IT ANOTHER TWO OR THREE DAYS.

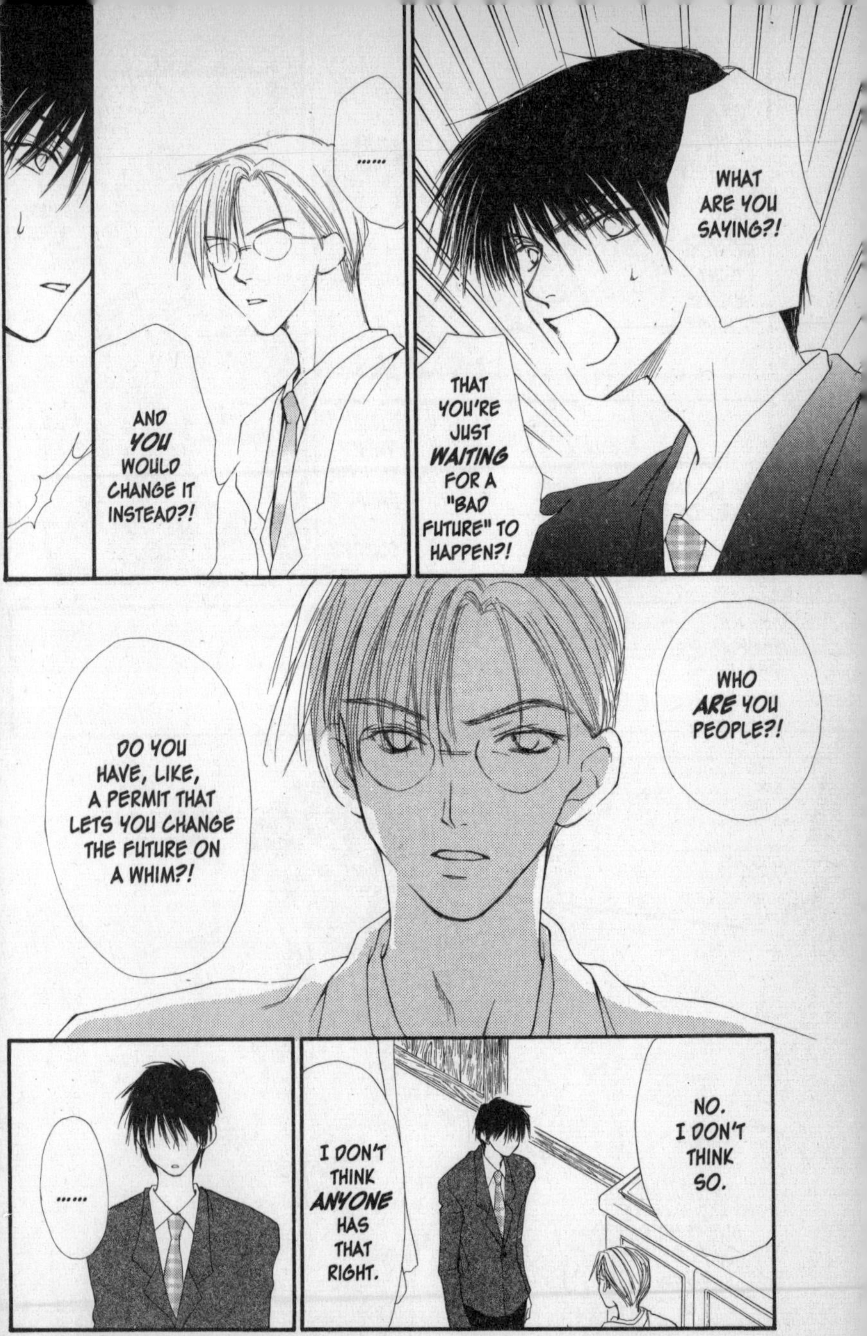
WHAT ARE YOU SAYING?!
THAT YOU'RE JUST WAITING FOR A "BAD FUTURE" TO HAPPEN?!
......
AND YOU WOULD CHANGE IT INSTEAD?!
WHO ARE YOU PEOPLE?!
DO YOU HAVE, LIKE, A PERMIT THAT LETS YOU CHANGE THE FUTURE ON A WHIM?!
NO. I DON'T THINK SO.
I DON'T THINK ANYONE HAS THAT RIGHT.
......

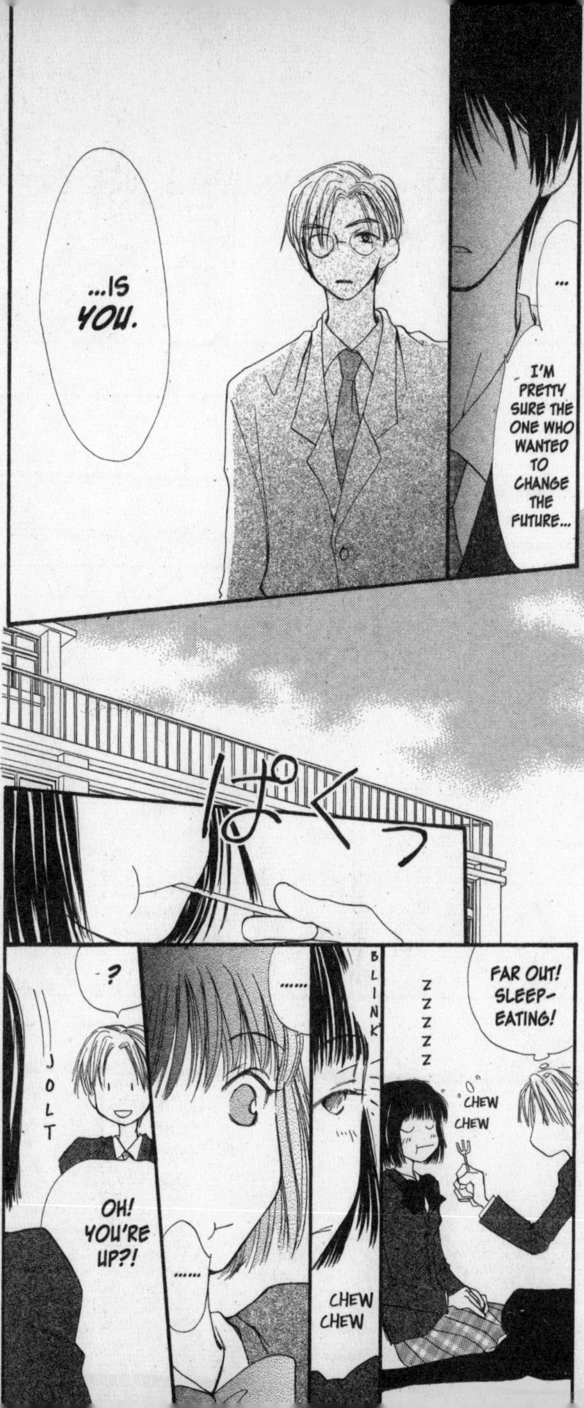
...
I'M PRETTY SURE THE ONE WHO WANTED TO CHANGE THE FUTURE...
...IS YOU.
ぱくっ
FAR OUT! SLEEP-EATING!
ZZZZZ
CHEW CHEW
BLINK
CHEW CHEW
......
?
JOLT
OH! YOU'RE UP?!
......

SAKURA MAIL

NO. 3

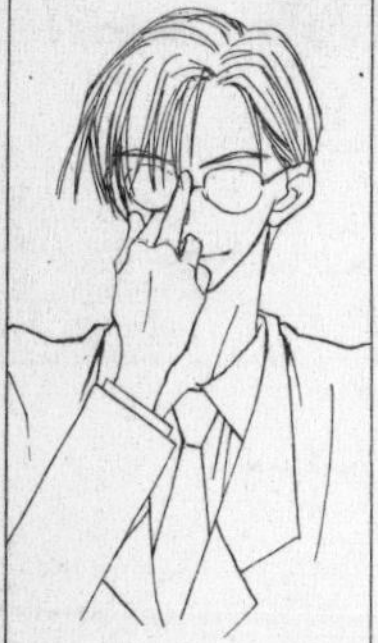

The school doctor takes center stage in this story. When you love someone intensely, both productive and destructive qualities can be stirred up. I combined that idea with my foolish fondness for characters who are socially backwards and this story was the result. By the way, Kanade sleeps through most of this story, leaving the other characters to carry the drama, and surprisingly, it became a fun story because of it. As always, but particularly with this episode, I couldn't have done it without my editor, whom I really, really appreciate!

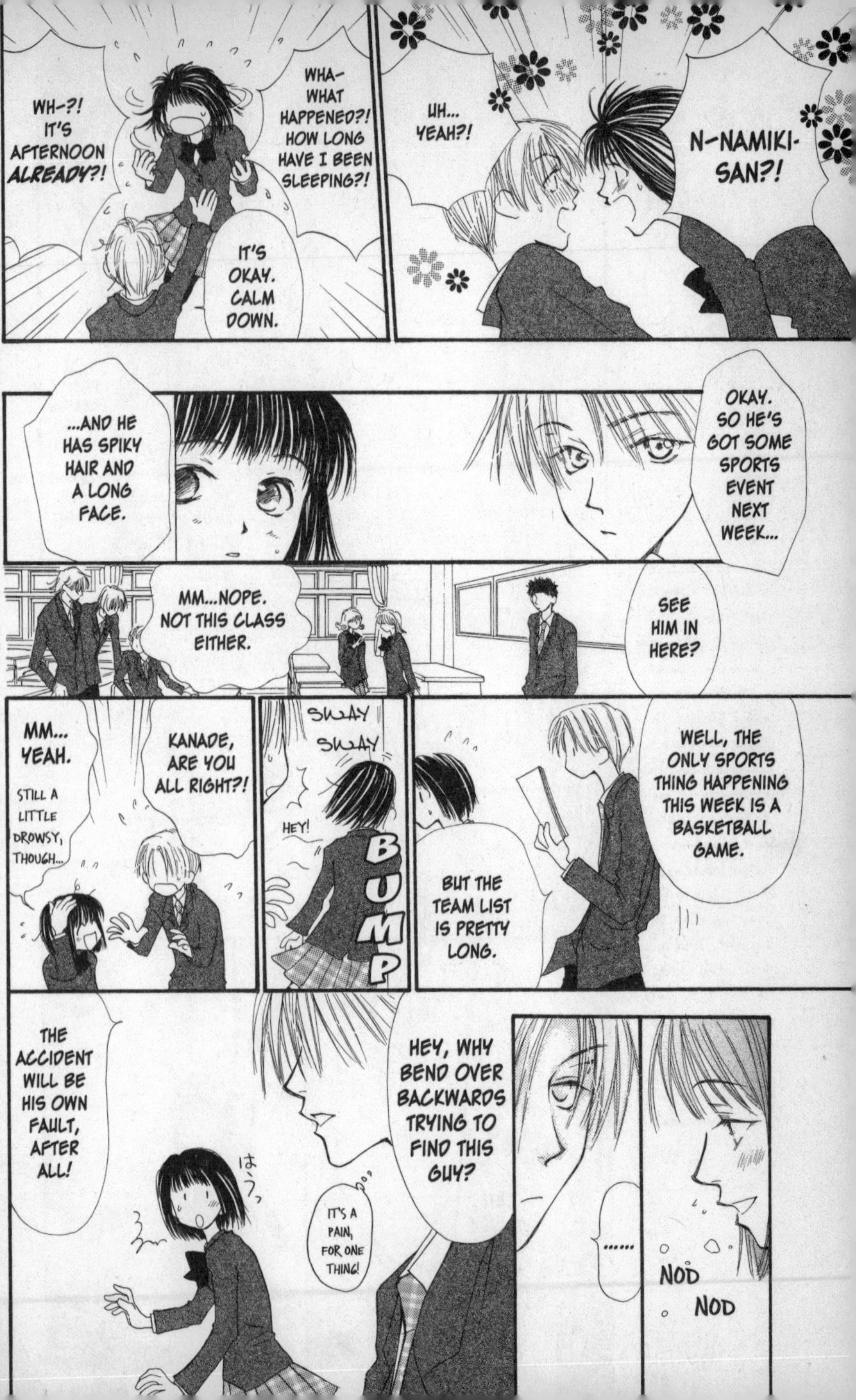

N-NAMIKI-SAN?!
UH... YEAH?!
WHA-WHAT HAPPENED?! HOW LONG HAVE I BEEN SLEEPING?!
WH-?! IT'S AFTERNOON ALREADY?!
IT'S OKAY. CALM DOWN.
OKAY. SO HE'S GOT SOME SPORTS EVENT NEXT WEEK...
...AND HE HAS SPIKY HAIR AND A LONG FACE.
SEE HIM IN HERE?
MM...NOPE. NOT THIS CLASS EITHER.
WELL, THE ONLY SPORTS THING HAPPENING THIS WEEK IS A BASKETBALL GAME.
BUT THE TEAM LIST IS PRETTY LONG.
SWAY SWAY
HEY!
BUMP
KANADE, ARE YOU ALL RIGHT?!
MM... YEAH.
STILL A LITTLE DROWSY, THOUGH...
NOD NOD
......
HEY, WHY BEND OVER BACKWARDS TRYING TO FIND THIS GUY?
IT'S A PAIN, FOR ONE THING!
THE ACCIDENT WILL BE HIS OWN FAULT, AFTER ALL!
はうっ

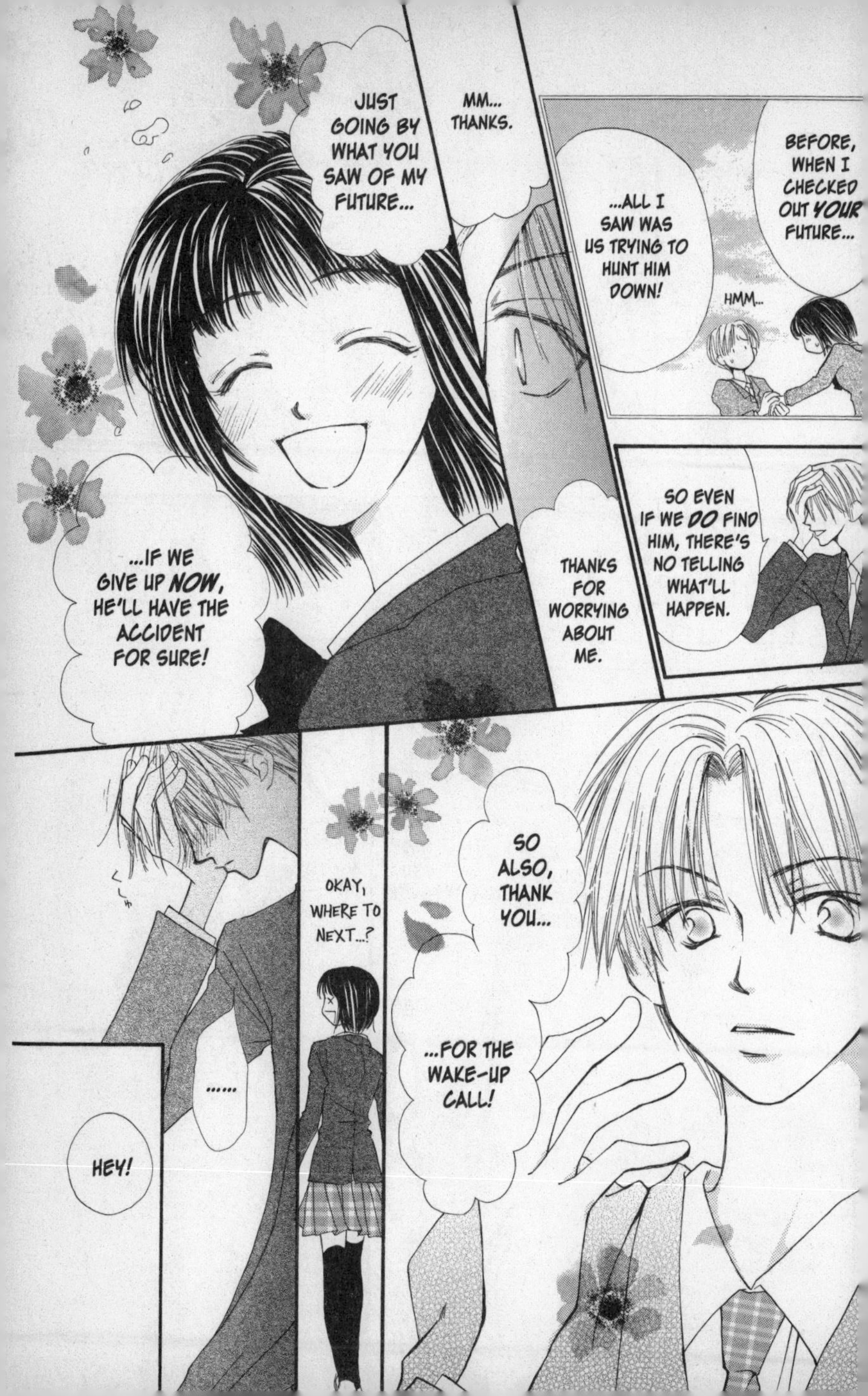
BEFORE, WHEN I CHECKED OUT YOUR FUTURE...
...ALL I SAW WAS US TRYING TO HUNT HIM DOWN!
HMM...
SO EVEN IF WE DO FIND HIM, THERE'S NO TELLING WHAT'LL HAPPEN.
THANKS FOR WORRYING ABOUT ME.
JUST GOING BY WHAT YOU SAW OF MY FUTURE...
...IF WE GIVE UP NOW, HE'LL HAVE THE ACCIDENT FOR SURE!
MM... THANKS.
SO ALSO, THANK YOU...
...FOR THE WAKE-UP CALL!
OKAY, WHERE TO NEXT...?
......
HEY!

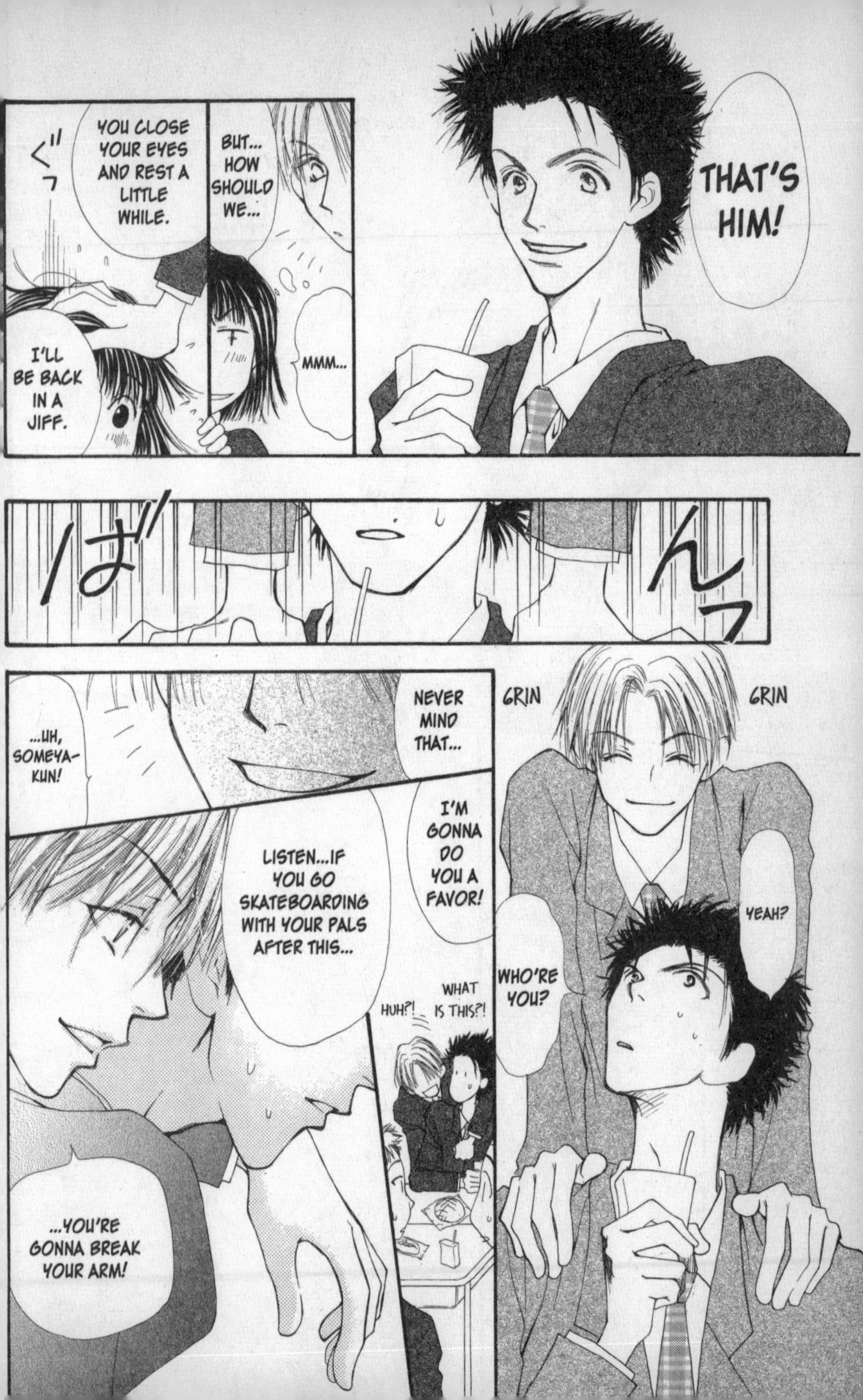
THAT'S HIM!
BUT... HOW SHOULD WE...
MMM...
ぐっ
YOU CLOSE YOUR EYES AND REST A LITTLE WHILE.
I'LL BE BACK IN A JIFF.
ばんっ
GRIN
GRIN
YEAH?
WHO'RE YOU?
NEVER MIND THAT...
...UH, SOMEYA-KUN!
I'M GONNA DO YOU A FAVOR!
WHAT IS THIS?!
HUH?!
LISTEN...IF YOU GO SKATEBOARDING WITH YOUR PALS AFTER THIS...
...YOU'RE GONNA BREAK YOUR ARM!

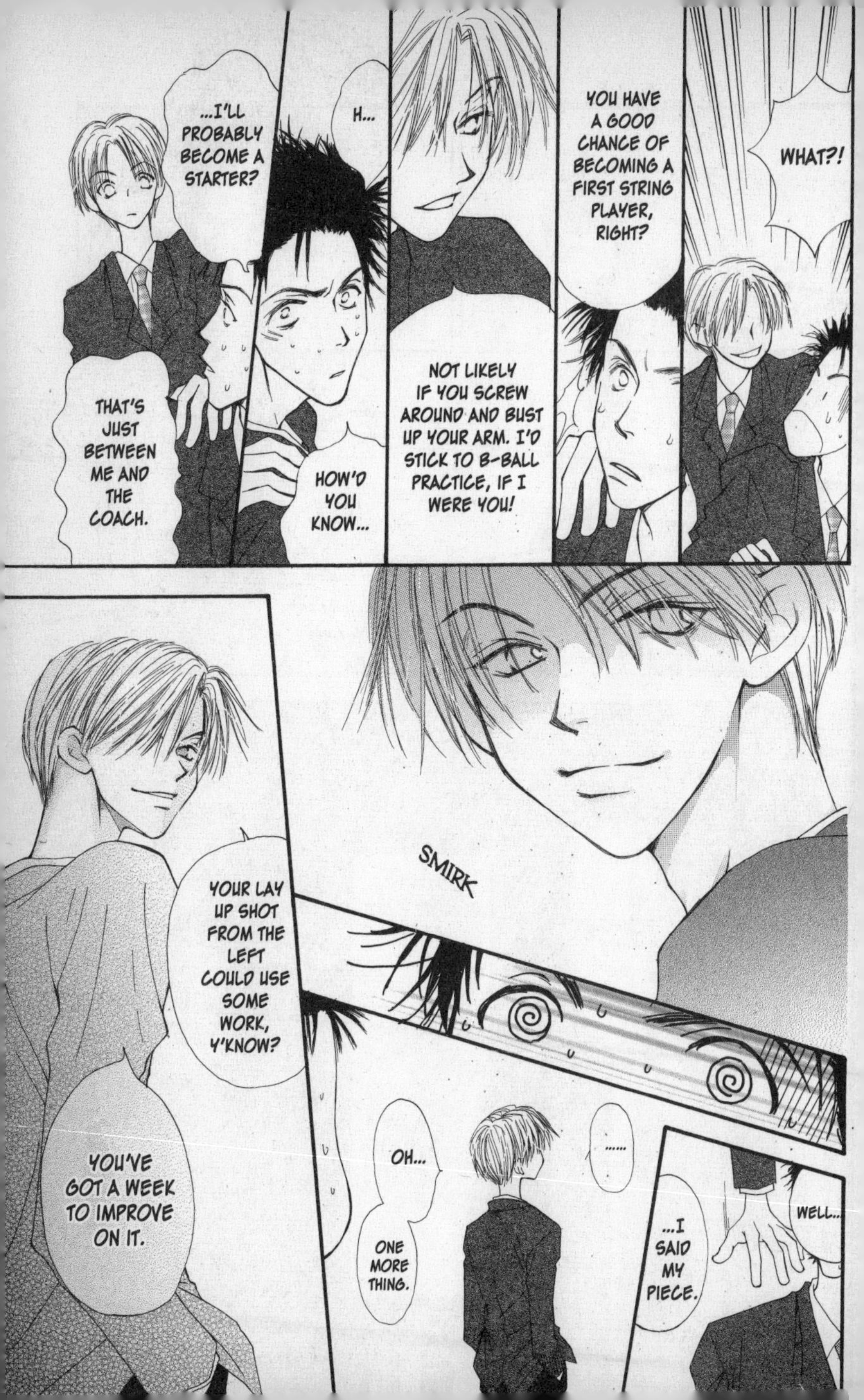
WHAT?!
YOU HAVE A GOOD CHANCE OF BECOMING A FIRST STRING PLAYER, RIGHT?
NOT LIKELY IF YOU SCREW AROUND AND BUST UP YOUR ARM. I'D STICK TO B-BALL PRACTICE, IF I WERE YOU!
H...
HOW'D YOU KNOW...
...I'LL PROBABLY BECOME A STARTER?
THAT'S JUST BETWEEN ME AND THE COACH.
SMIRK
YOUR LAY UP SHOT FROM THE LEFT COULD USE SOME WORK, Y'KNOW?
YOU'VE GOT A WEEK TO IMPROVE ON IT.
WELL...
...I SAID MY PIECE.
......
OH...
ONE MORE THING.

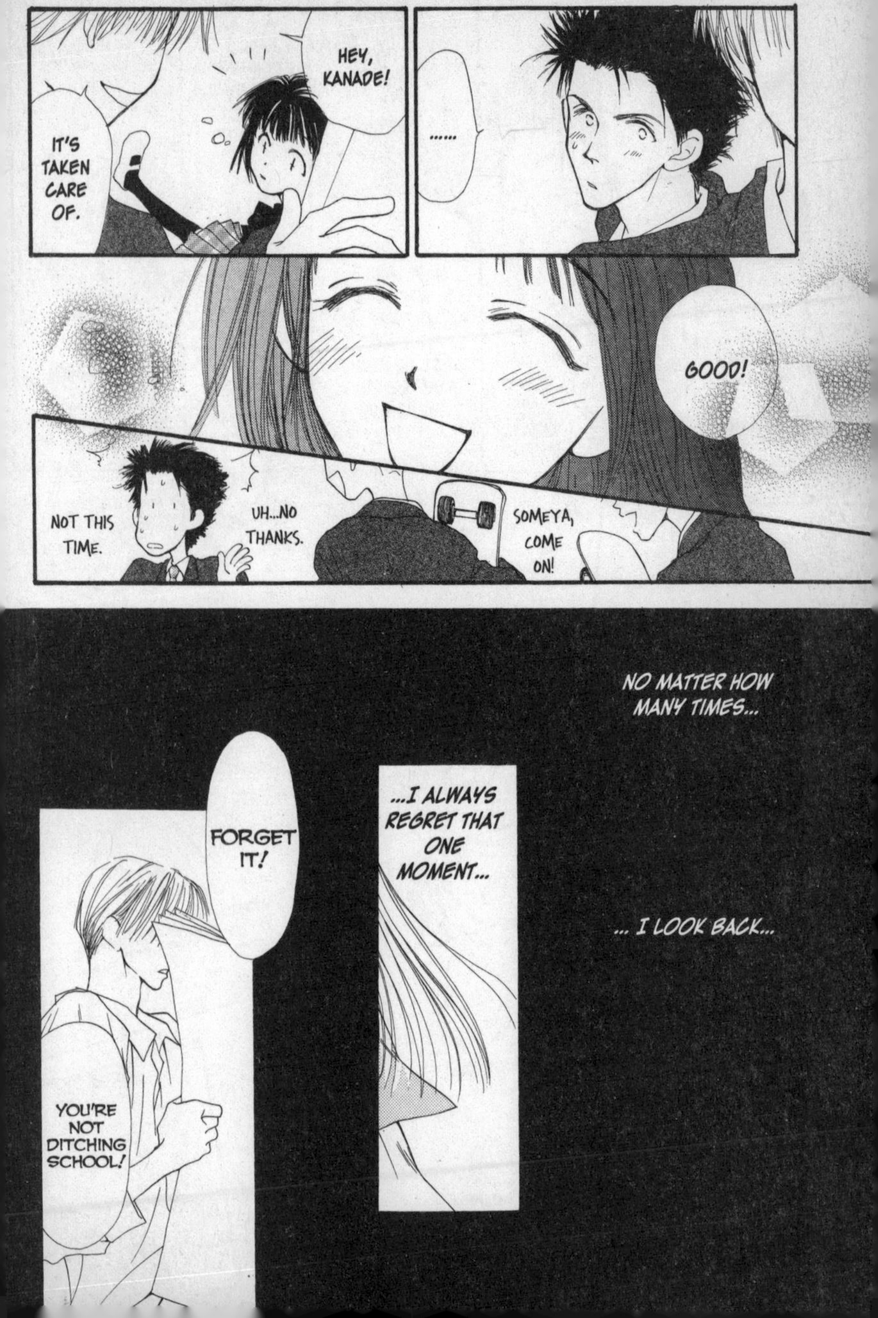
......
HEY, KANADE!
IT'S TAKEN CARE OF.
GOOD!
SOMEYA, COME ON!
UH...NO THANKS.
NOT THIS TIME.
NO MATTER HOW MANY TIMES...
... I LOOK BACK...
...I ALWAYS REGRET THAT ONE MOMENT...
FORGET IT!
YOU'RE NOT DITCHING SCHOOL!

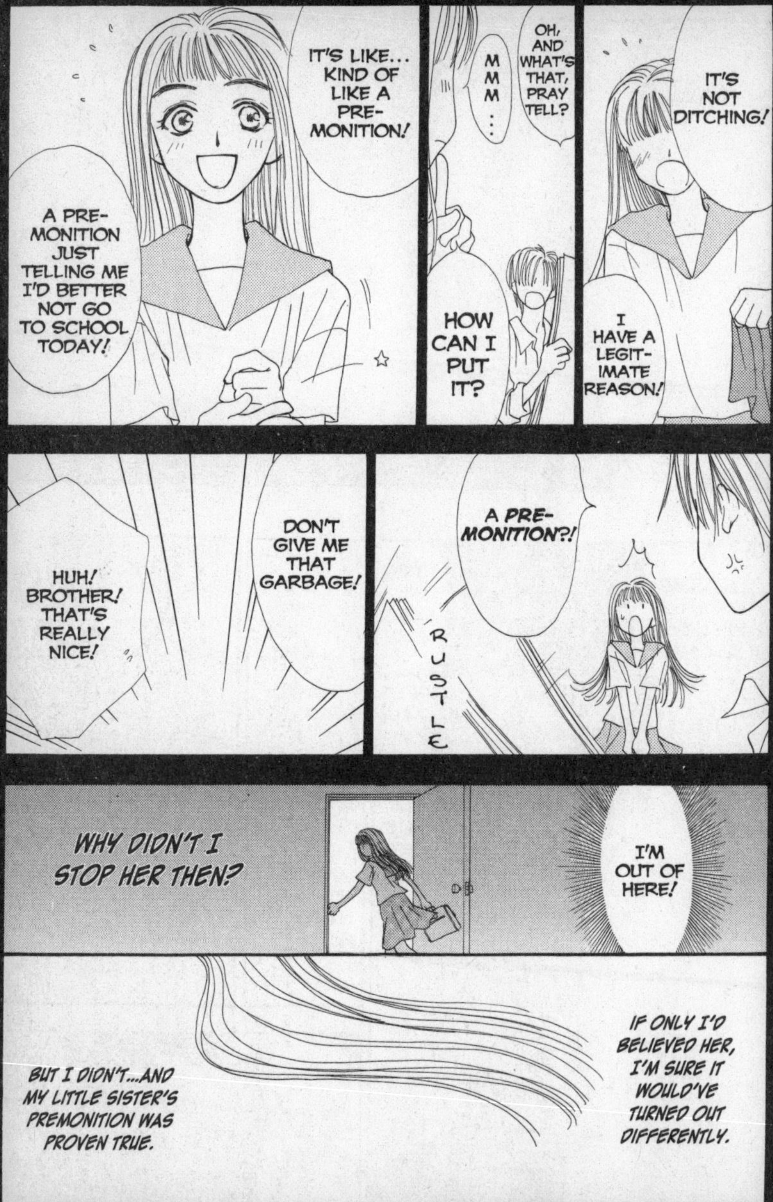
IT'S NOT DITCHING!
I HAVE A LEGITIMATE REASON!
OH, AND WHAT'S THAT, PRAY TELL?
MMM...
HOW CAN I PUT IT?
IT'S LIKE... KIND OF LIKE A PREMONITION!
A PREMONITION JUST TELLING ME I'D BETTER NOT GO TO SCHOOL TODAY!
A PREMONITION?!
RUSTLE
DON'T GIVE ME THAT GARBAGE!
HUH! BROTHER! THAT'S REALLY NICE!
I'M OUT OF HERE!
WHY DIDN'T I STOP HER THEN?
IF ONLY I'D BELIEVED HER, I'M SURE IT WOULD'VE TURNED OUT DIFFERENTLY.
BUT I DIDN'T...AND MY LITTLE SISTER'S PREMONITION WAS PROVEN TRUE.

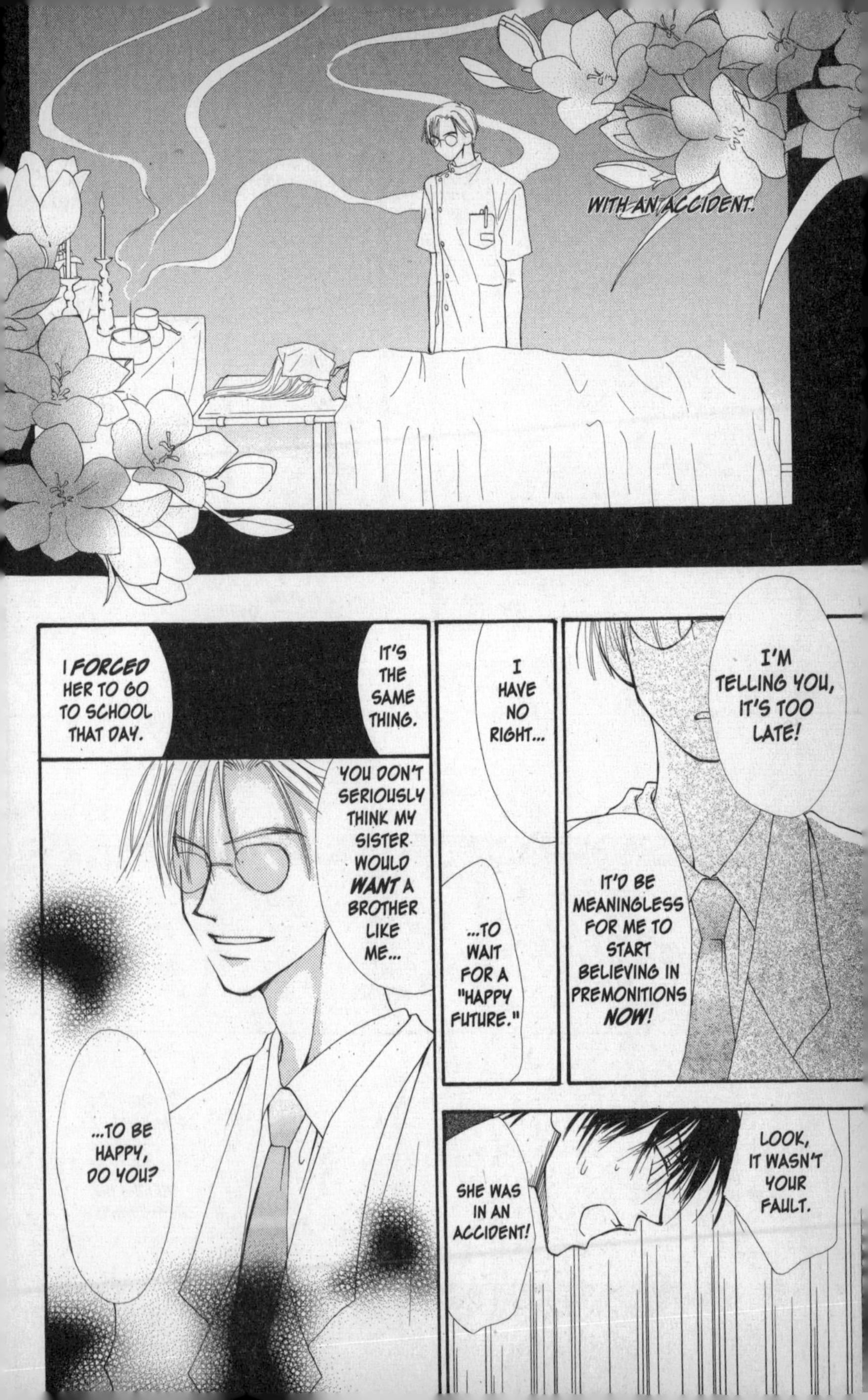
WITH AN ACCIDENT.
I'M TELLING YOU, IT'S TOO LATE!
IT'D BE MEANINGLESS FOR ME TO START BELIEVING IN PREMONITIONS NOW!
I HAVE NO RIGHT...
...TO WAIT FOR A "HAPPY FUTURE."
LOOK, IT WASN'T YOUR FAULT.
SHE WAS IN AN ACCIDENT!
IT'S THE SAME THING.
I FORCED HER TO GO TO SCHOOL THAT DAY.
YOU DON'T SERIOUSLY THINK MY SISTER WOULD WANT A BROTHER LIKE ME...
...TO BE HAPPY, DO YOU?

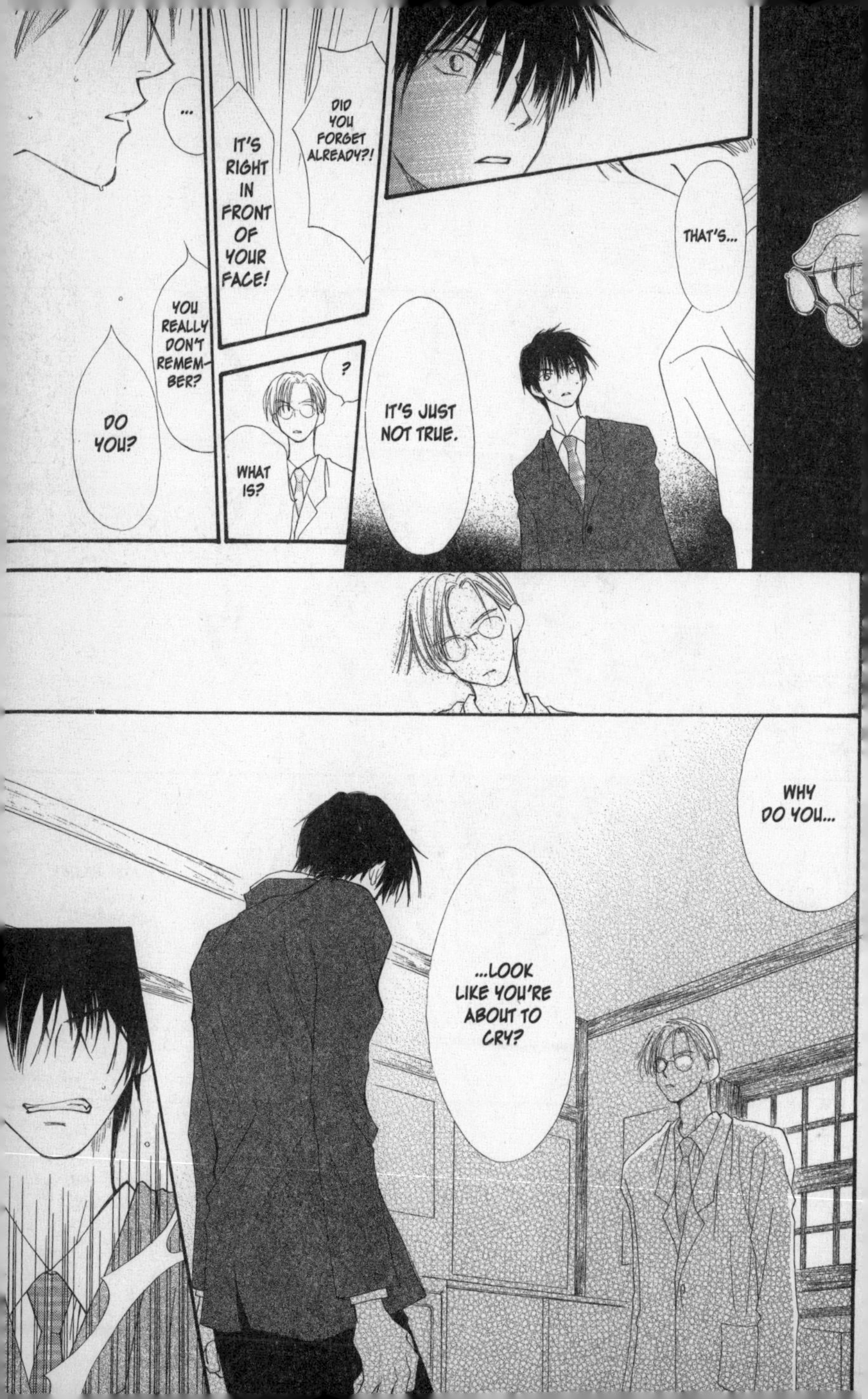
THAT'S...
IT'S JUST NOT TRUE.
DID YOU FORGET ALREADY?!
IT'S RIGHT IN FRONT OF YOUR FACE!
?
WHAT IS?
...
YOU REALLY DON'T REMEMBER?
DO YOU?
WHY DO YOU...
...LOOK LIKE YOU'RE ABOUT TO CRY?

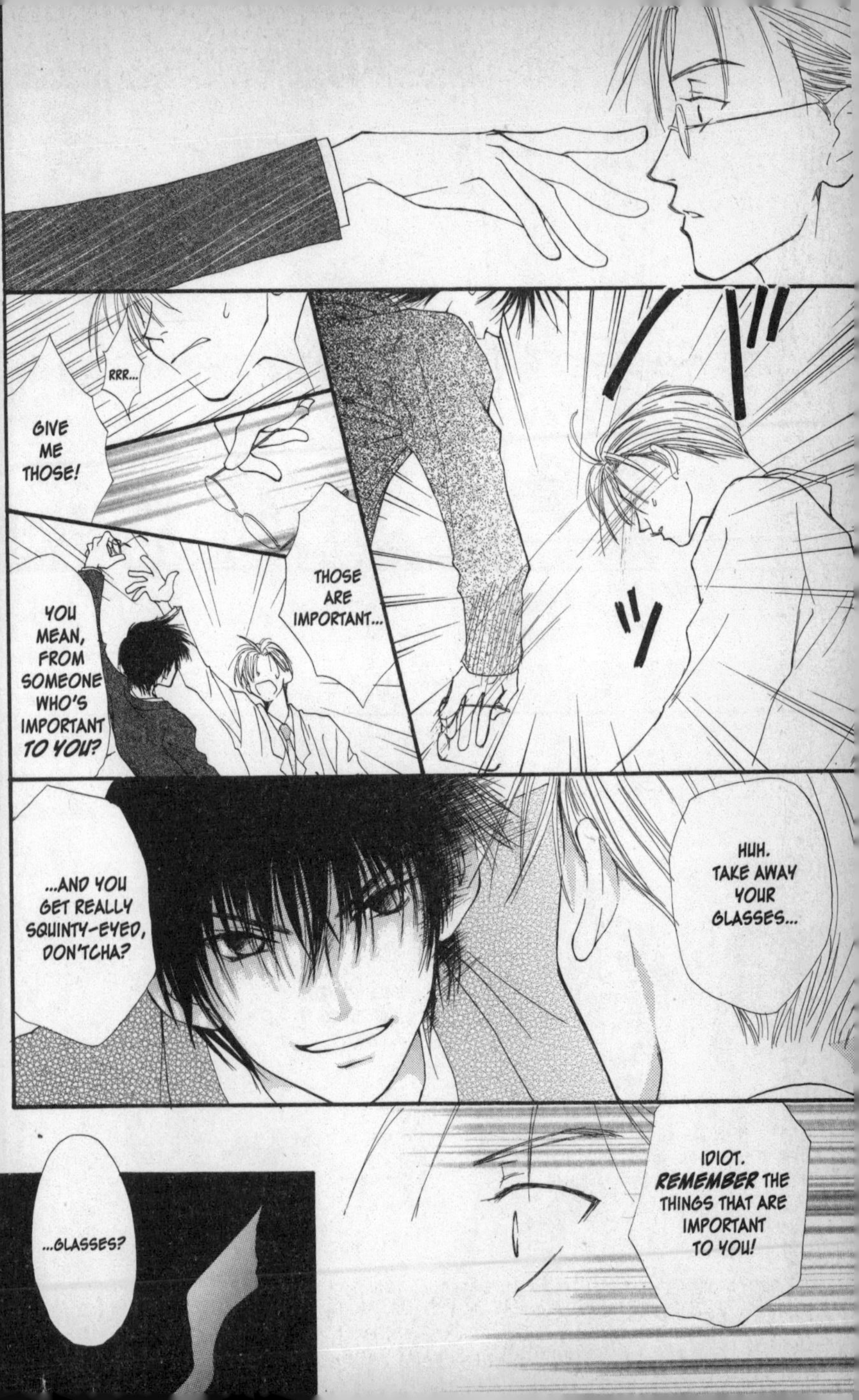
RRR...
GIVE ME THOSE!
THOSE ARE IMPORTANT...
YOU MEAN, FROM SOMEONE WHO'S IMPORTANT *TO YOU?*
HUH. TAKE AWAY YOUR GLASSES...
...AND YOU GET REALLY SQUINTY-EYED, DON'TCHA?
IDIOT. ***REMEMBER*** THE THINGS THAT ARE IMPORTANT TO YOU!
...GLASSES?

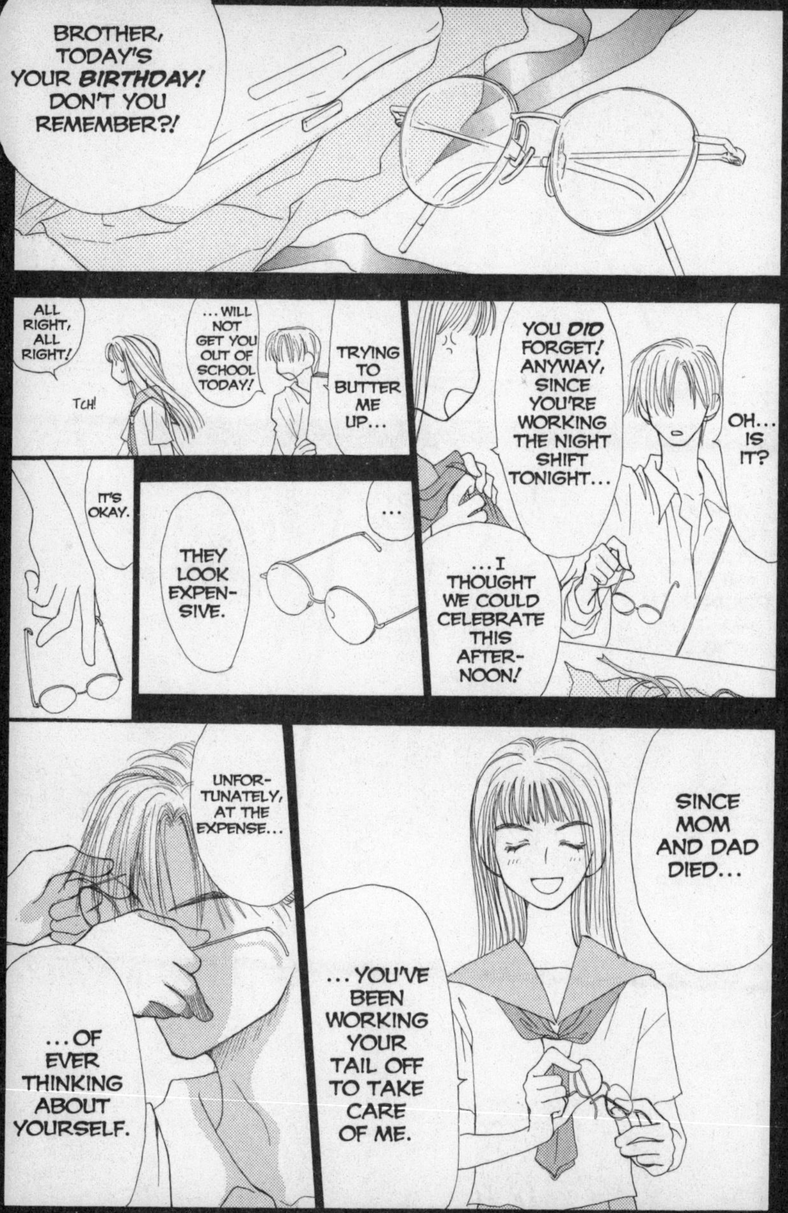
BROTHER, TODAY'S YOUR *BIRTHDAY!* DON'T YOU REMEMBER?!
OH... IS IT?
YOU *DID* FORGET! ANYWAY, SINCE YOU'RE WORKING THE NIGHT SHIFT TONIGHT...
...I THOUGHT WE COULD CELEBRATE THIS AFTERNOON!
TRYING TO BUTTER ME UP...
...WILL NOT GET YOU OUT OF SCHOOL TODAY!
ALL RIGHT, ALL RIGHT!
TCH!
...
THEY LOOK EXPENSIVE.
IT'S OKAY.
SINCE MOM AND DAD DIED...
...YOU'VE BEEN WORKING YOUR TAIL OFF TO TAKE CARE OF ME.
UNFORTUNATELY, AT THE EXPENSE...
...OF EVER THINKING ABOUT YOURSELF.

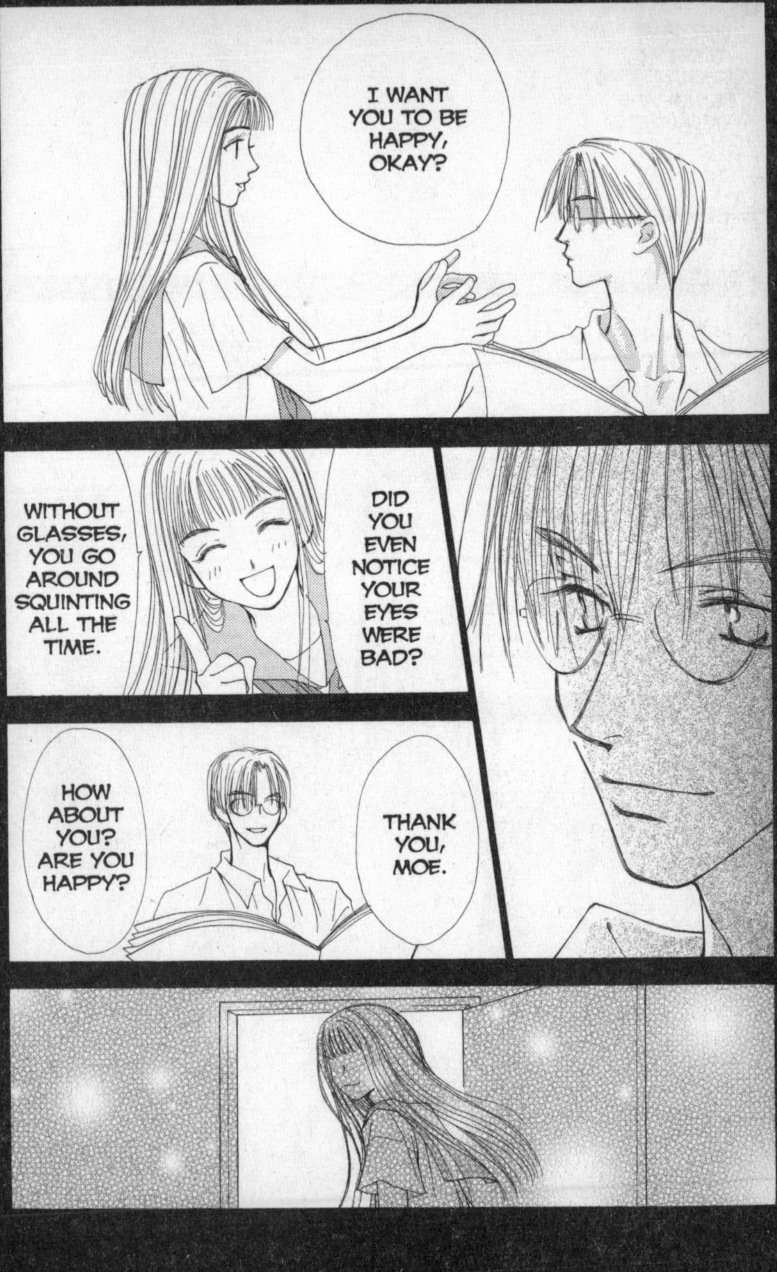
I WANT YOU TO BE HAPPY, OKAY?
DID YOU EVEN NOTICE YOUR EYES WERE BAD?
WITHOUT GLASSES, YOU GO AROUND SQUINTING ALL THE TIME.
THANK YOU, MOE.
HOW ABOUT YOU? ARE YOU HAPPY?

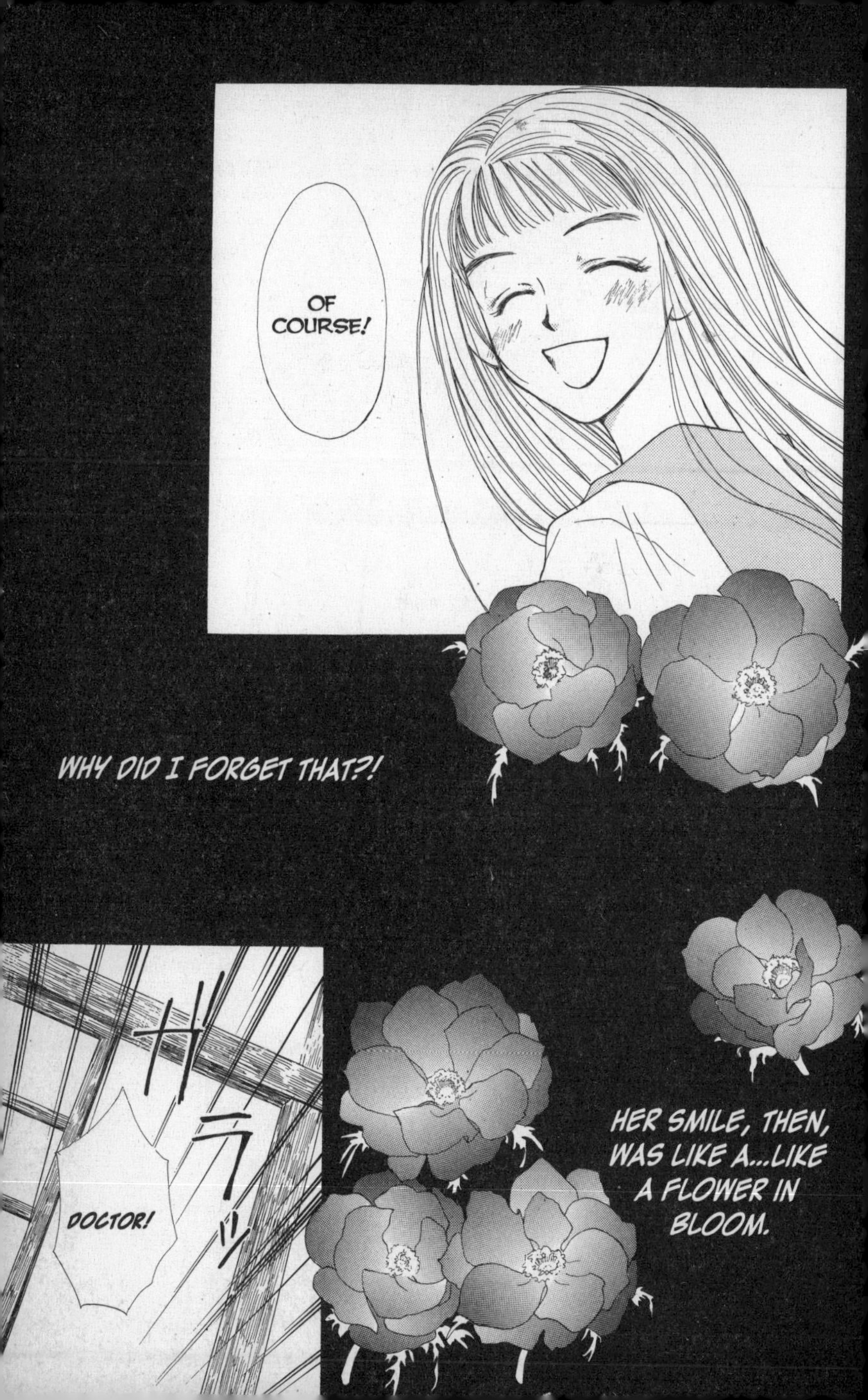
OF COURSE!
WHY DID I FORGET THAT?!
HER SMILE, THEN, WAS LIKE A...LIKE A FLOWER IN BLOOM.
ガラッ
DOCTOR!

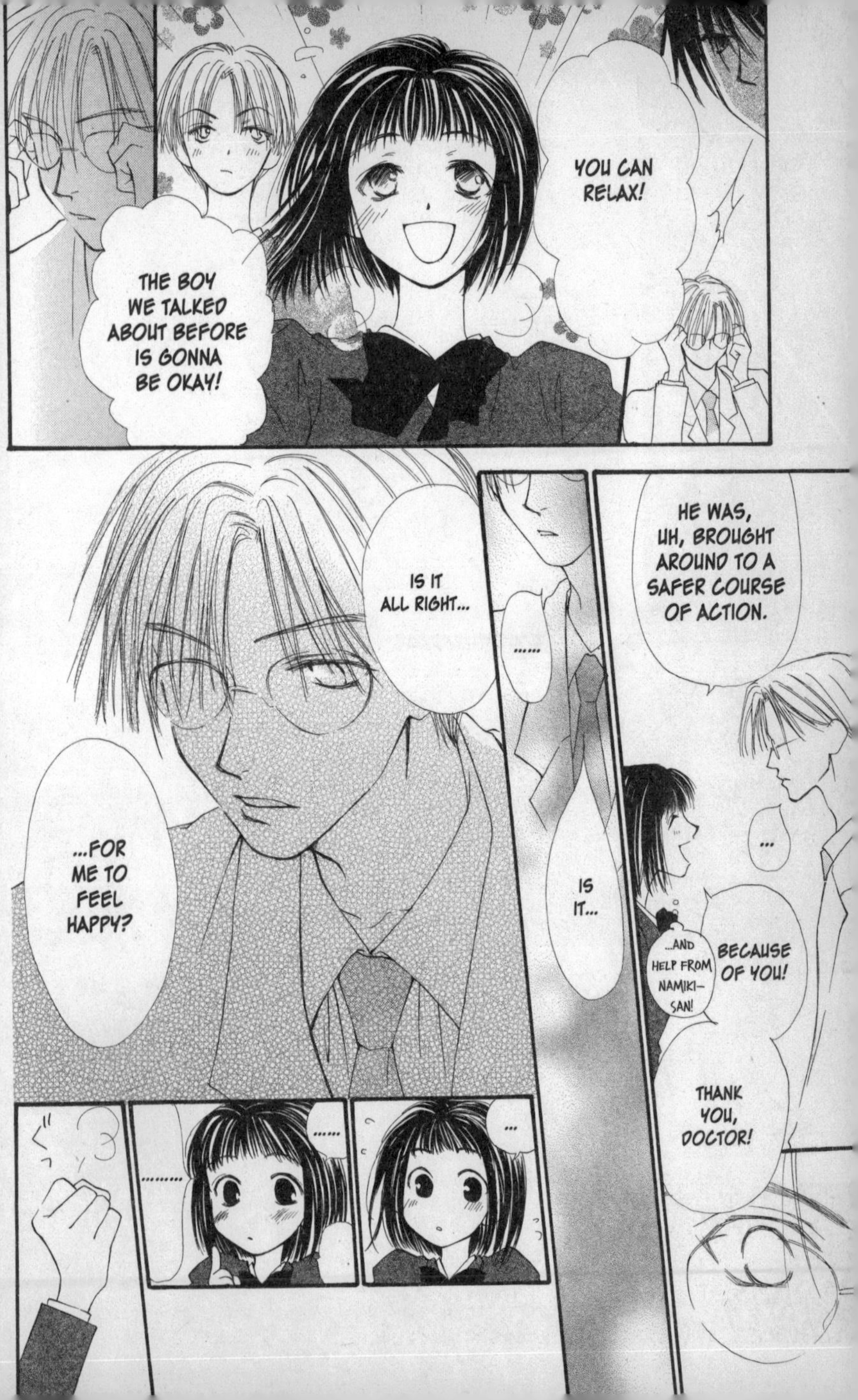
YOU CAN RELAX!
THE BOY WE TALKED ABOUT BEFORE IS GONNA BE OKAY!
HE WAS, UH, BROUGHT AROUND TO A SAFER COURSE OF ACTION.
...
BECAUSE OF YOU!
...AND HELP FROM NAMIKI-SAN!
THANK YOU, DOCTOR!
......
IS IT...
IS IT ALL RIGHT...
...FOR ME TO FEEL HAPPY?
...
......
....

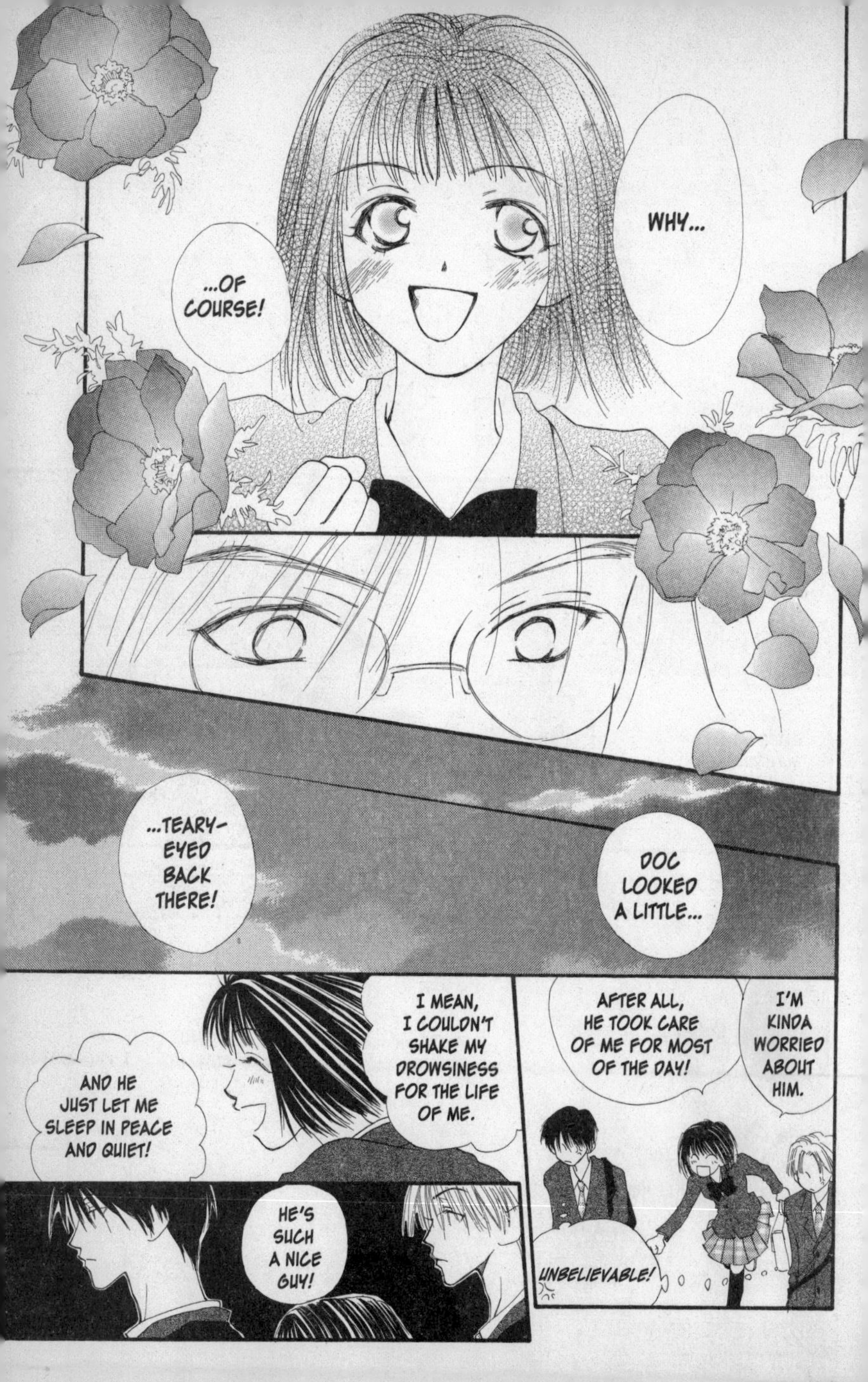
WHY...
...OF COURSE!
DOC LOOKED A LITTLE...
...TEARY-EYED BACK THERE!
I'M KINDA WORRIED ABOUT HIM.
AFTER ALL, HE TOOK CARE OF ME FOR MOST OF THE DAY!
UNBELIEVABLE!
I MEAN, I COULDN'T SHAKE MY DROWSINESS FOR THE LIFE OF ME.
AND HE JUST LET ME SLEEP IN PEACE AND QUIET!
HE'S SUCH A NICE GUY!

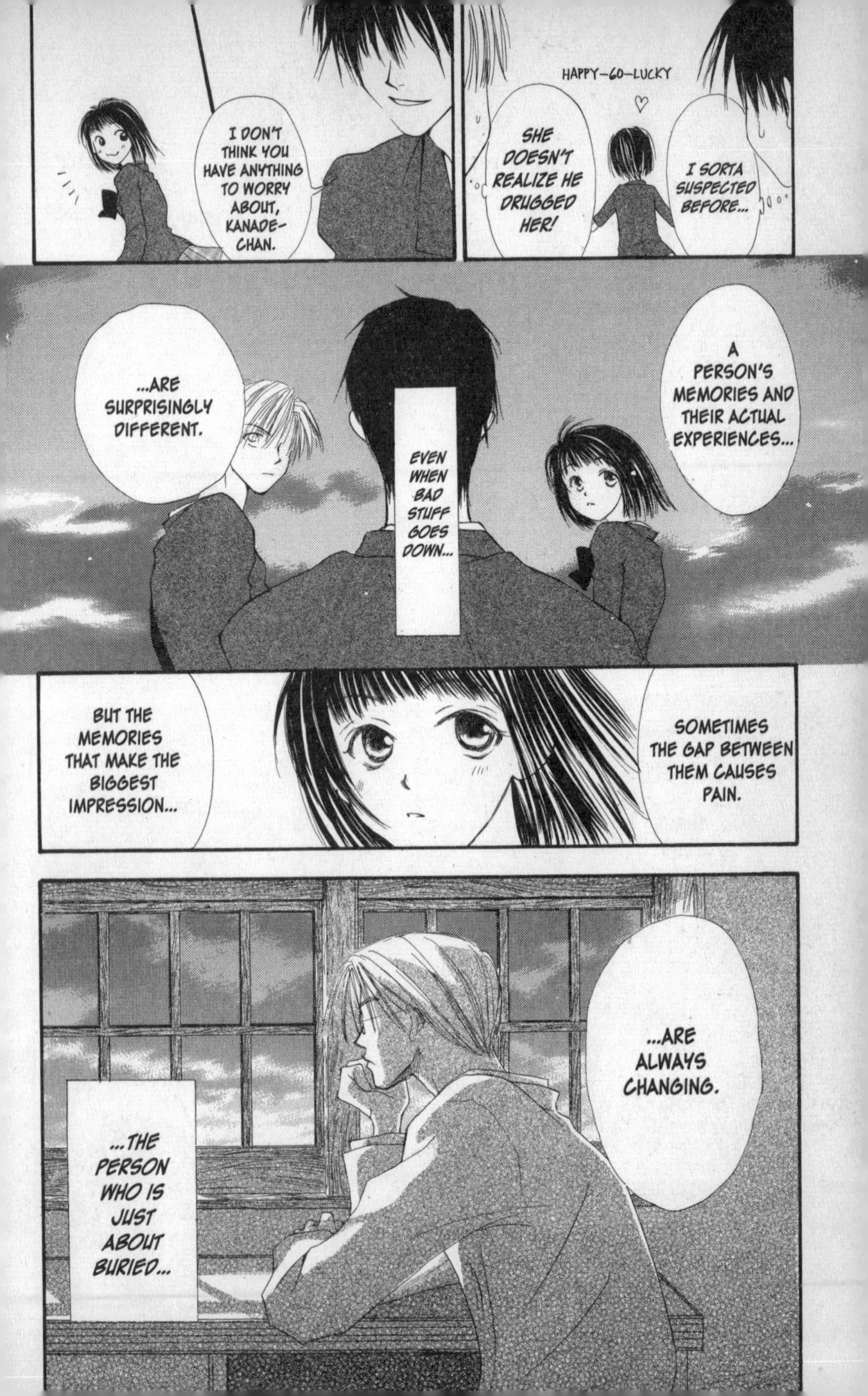
HAPPY-GO-LUCKY
I SORTA SUSPECTED BEFORE...
SHE DOESN'T REALIZE HE DRUGGED HER!
I DON'T THINK YOU HAVE ANYTHING TO WORRY ABOUT, KANADE-CHAN.
A PERSON'S MEMORIES AND THEIR ACTUAL EXPERIENCES...
EVEN WHEN BAD STUFF GOES DOWN...
...ARE SURPRISINGLY DIFFERENT.
SOMETIMES THE GAP BETWEEN THEM CAUSES PAIN.
BUT THE MEMORIES THAT MAKE THE BIGGEST IMPRESSION...
...ARE ALWAYS CHANGING.
...THE PERSON WHO IS JUST ABOUT BURIED...

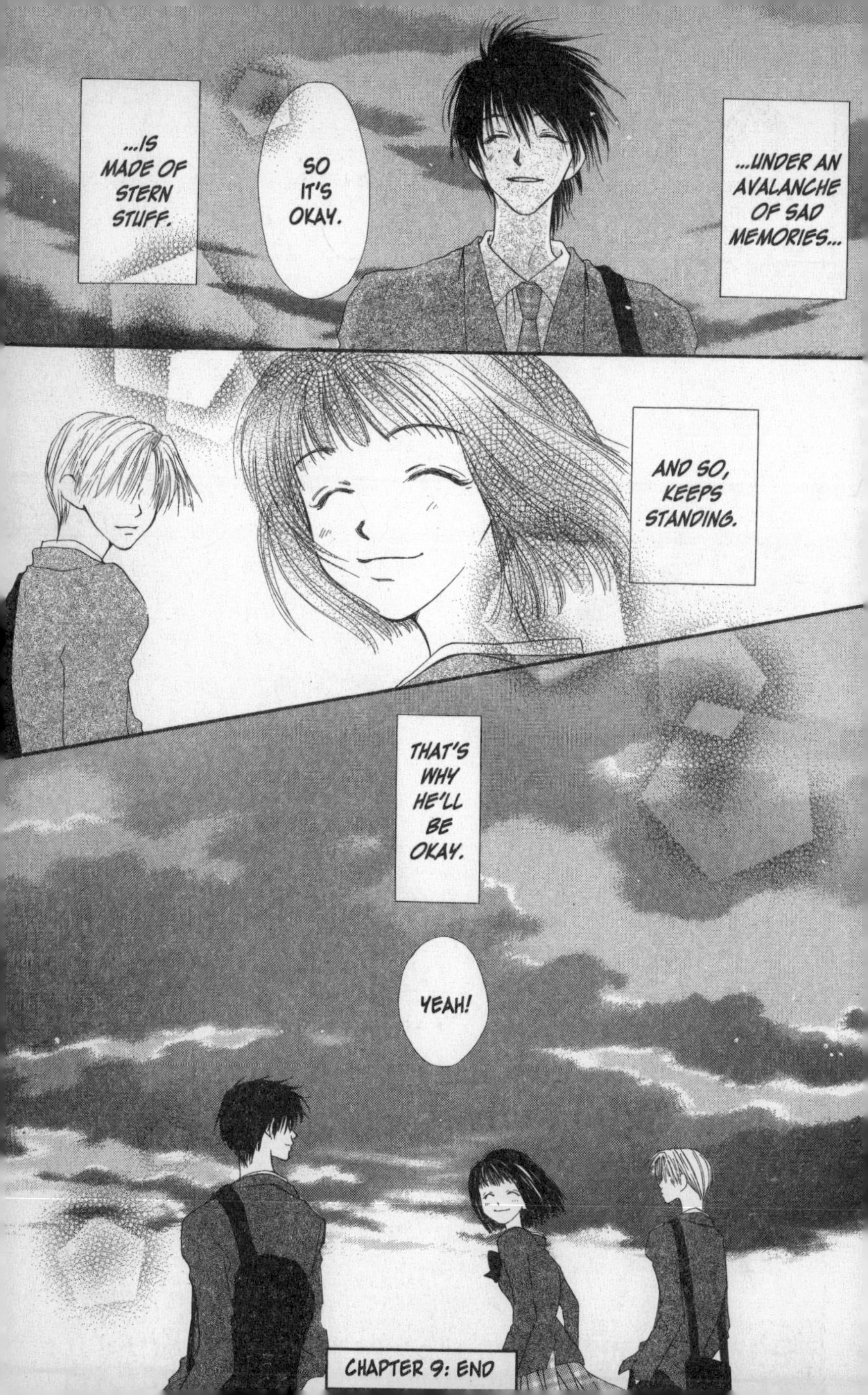
...UNDER AN AVALANCHE OF SAD MEMORIES...
SO IT'S OKAY.
...IS MADE OF STERN STUFF.
AND SO, KEEPS STANDING.
THAT'S WHY HE'LL BE OKAY.
YEAH!
CHAPTER 9: END

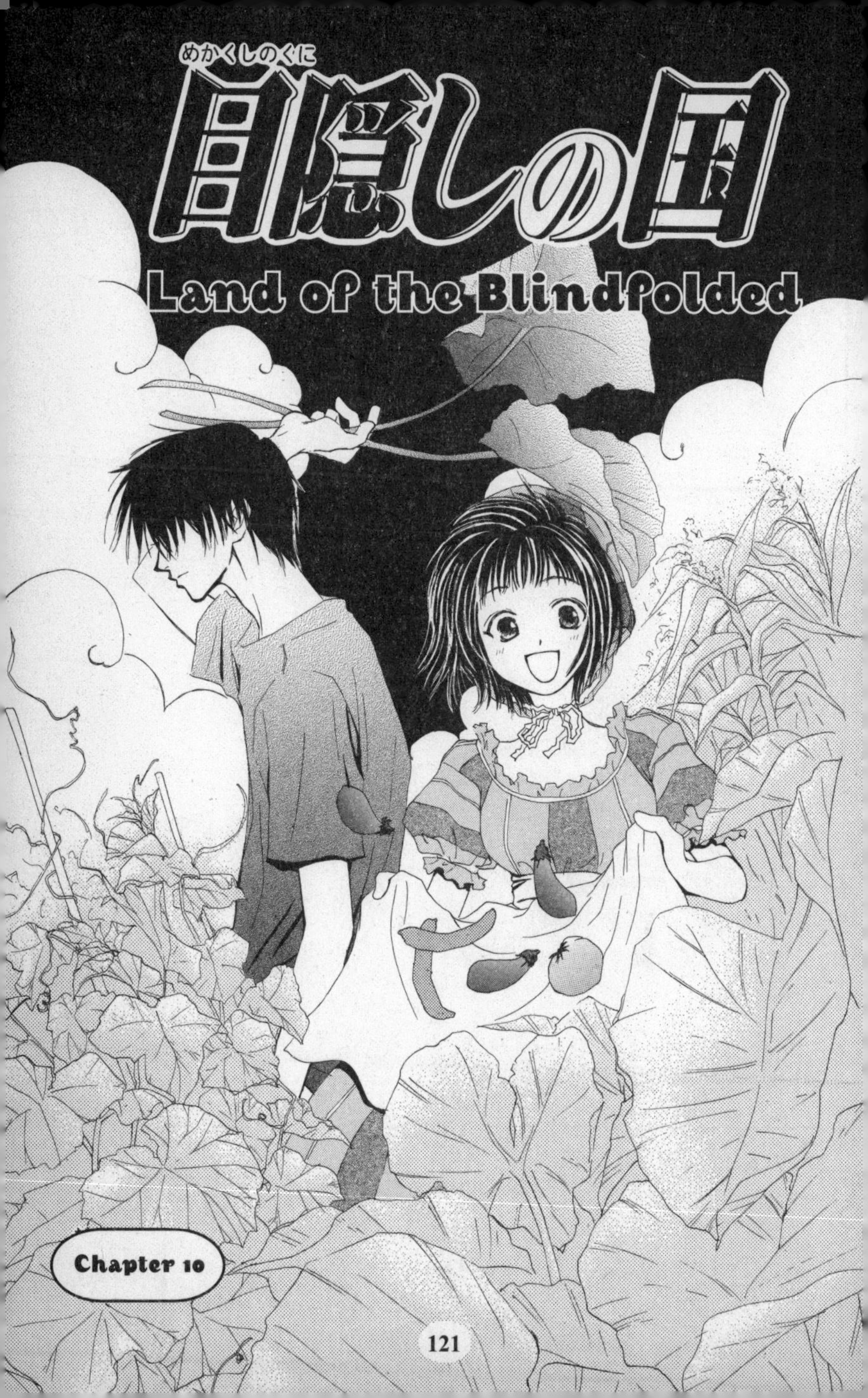
めかくしのくに
目隠しの国
Land of the Blindfolded
Chapter 10

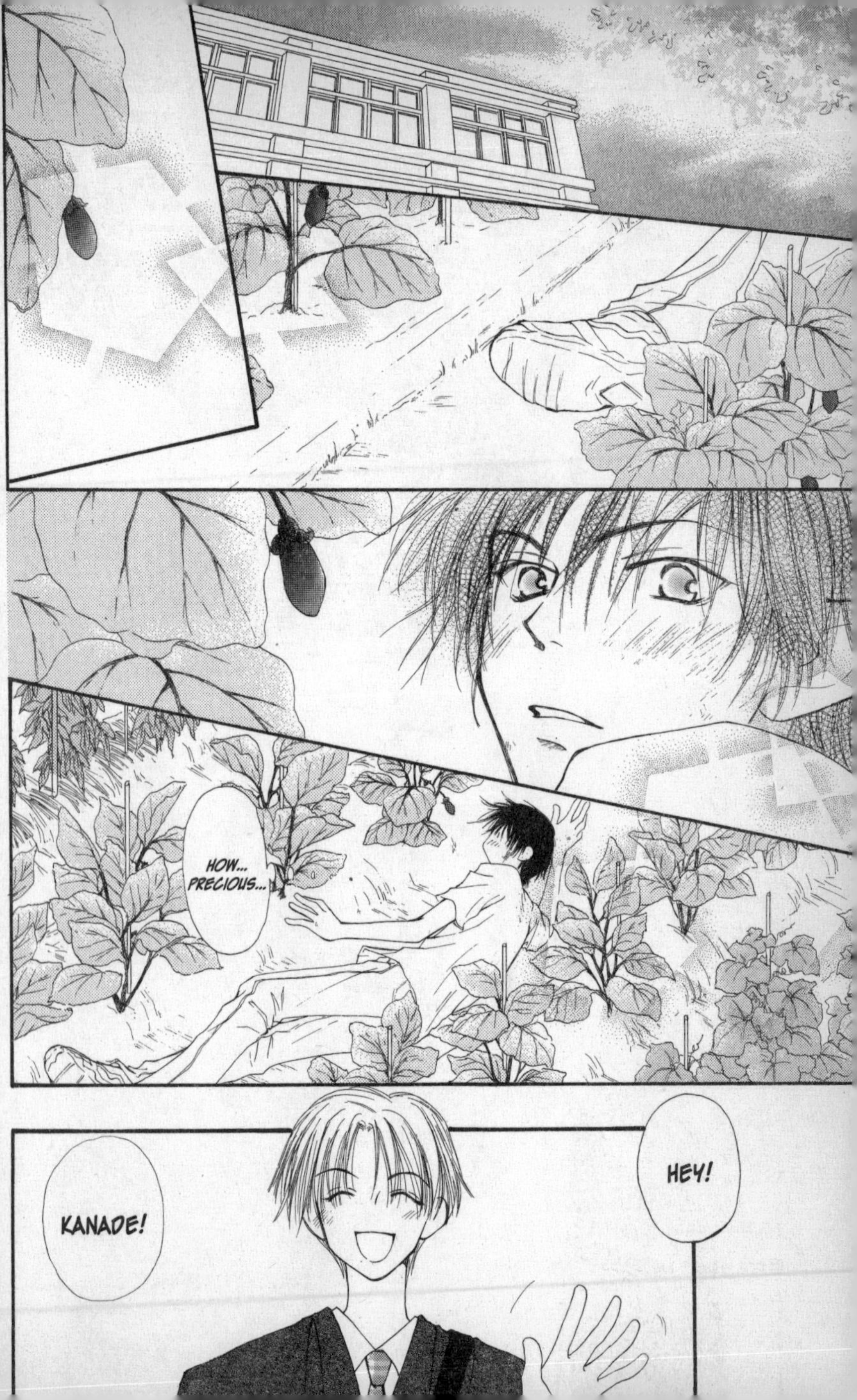
HOW... PRECIOUS...
HEY!
KANADE!

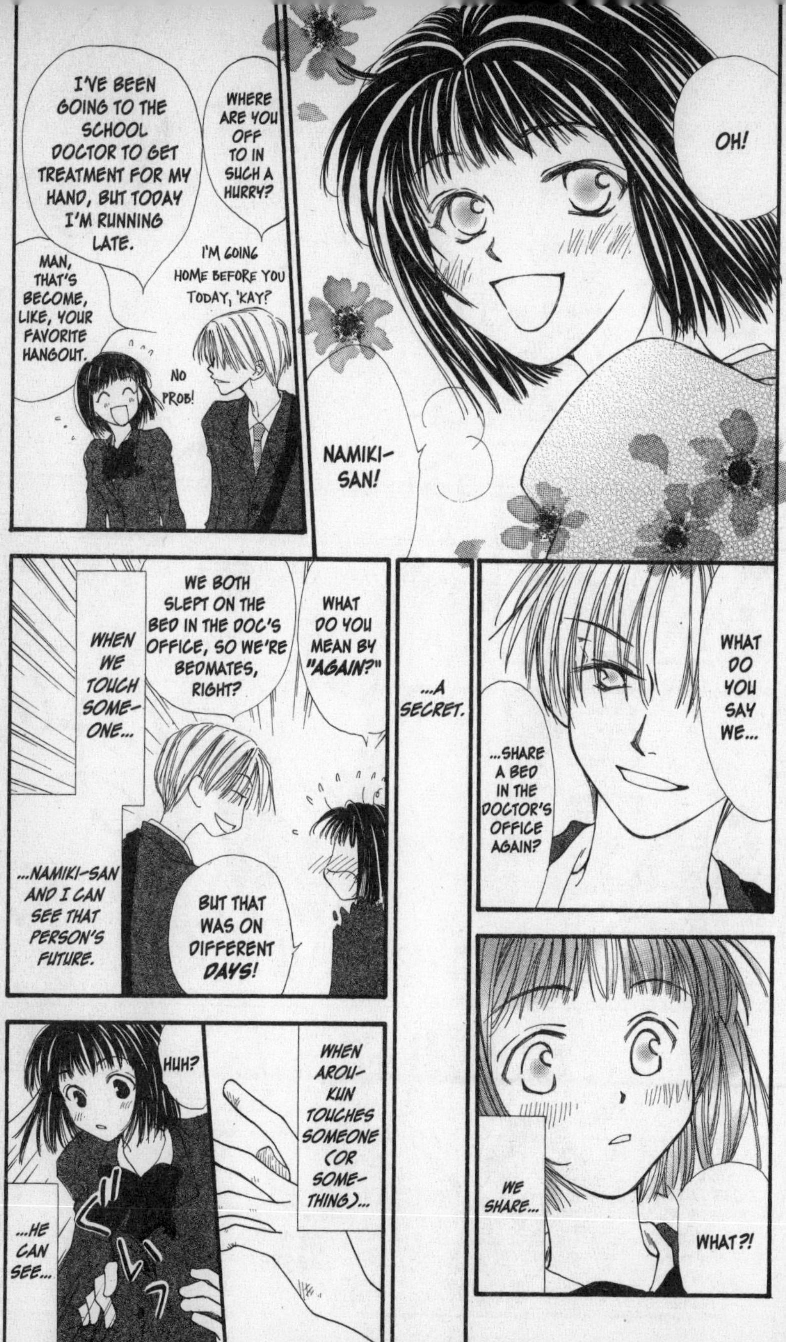
OH!
NAMIKI-SAN!
WHERE ARE YOU OFF TO IN SUCH A HURRY?
I'VE BEEN GOING TO THE SCHOOL DOCTOR TO GET TREATMENT FOR MY HAND, BUT TODAY I'M RUNNING LATE.
I'M GOING HOME BEFORE YOU TODAY, 'KAY?
MAN, THAT'S BECOME, LIKE, YOUR FAVORITE HANGOUT.
NO PROB!
WHAT DO YOU SAY WE...
...SHARE A BED IN THE DOCTOR'S OFFICE AGAIN?
WHAT?!
WE SHARE...
...A SECRET.
WHAT DO YOU MEAN BY "AGAIN?"
WE BOTH SLEPT ON THE BED IN THE DOC'S OFFICE, SO WE'RE BEDMATES, RIGHT?
WHEN WE TOUCH SOME-ONE...
BUT THAT WAS ON DIFFERENT DAYS!
...NAMIKI-SAN AND I CAN SEE THAT PERSON'S FUTURE.
WHEN AROU-KUN TOUCHES SOMEONE (OR SOME-THING)...
HUH?
...HE CAN SEE...

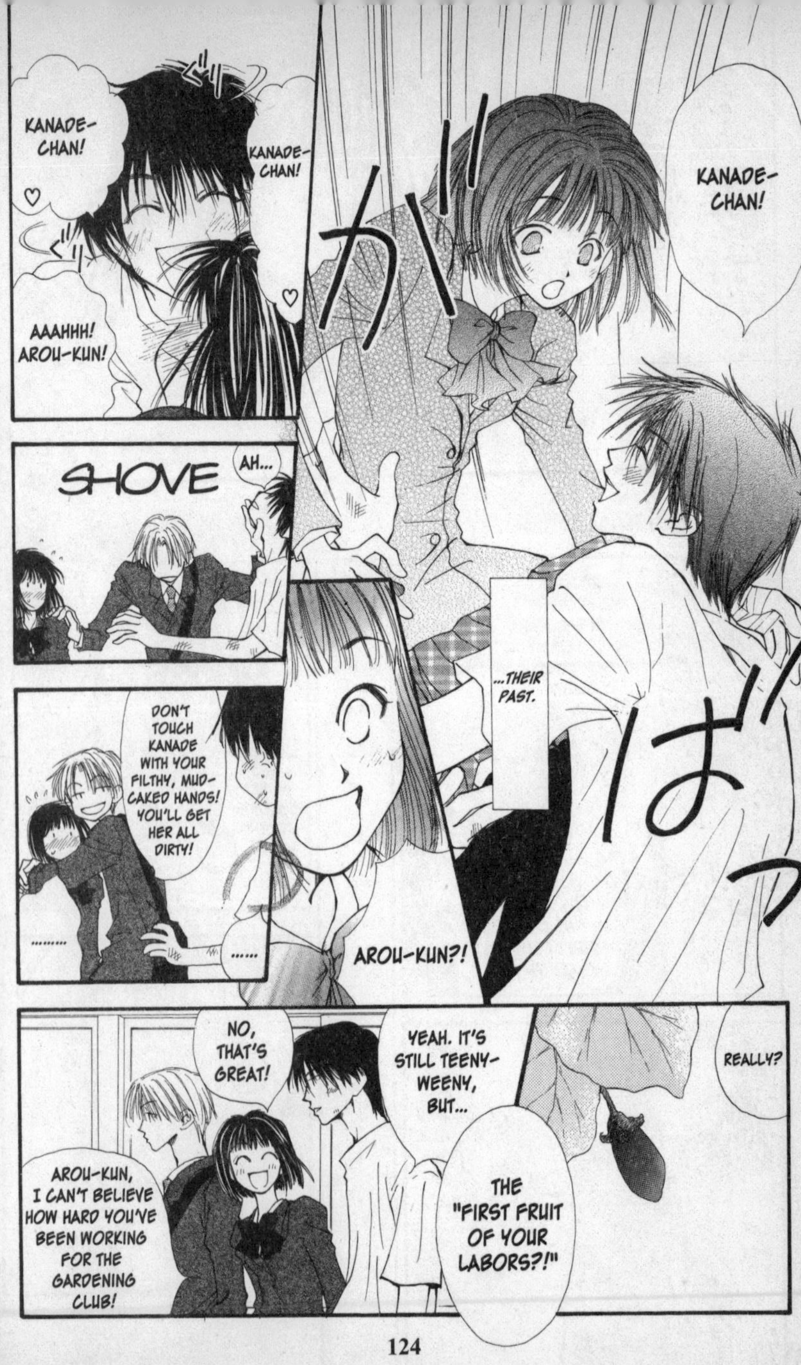
KANADE-CHAN!
...THEIR PAST.
AROU-KUN?!
KANADE-CHAN!
KANADE-CHAN!
AAAHHH! AROU-KUN!
SHOVE
AH...
DON'T TOUCH KANADE WITH YOUR FILTHY, MUD-CAKED HANDS! YOU'LL GET HER ALL DIRTY!
....
......
REALLY?
YEAH. IT'S STILL TEENY-WEENY, BUT...
THE "FIRST FRUIT OF YOUR LABORS?!"
NO, THAT'S GREAT!
AROU-KUN, I CAN'T BELIEVE HOW HARD YOU'VE BEEN WORKING FOR THE GARDENING CLUB!

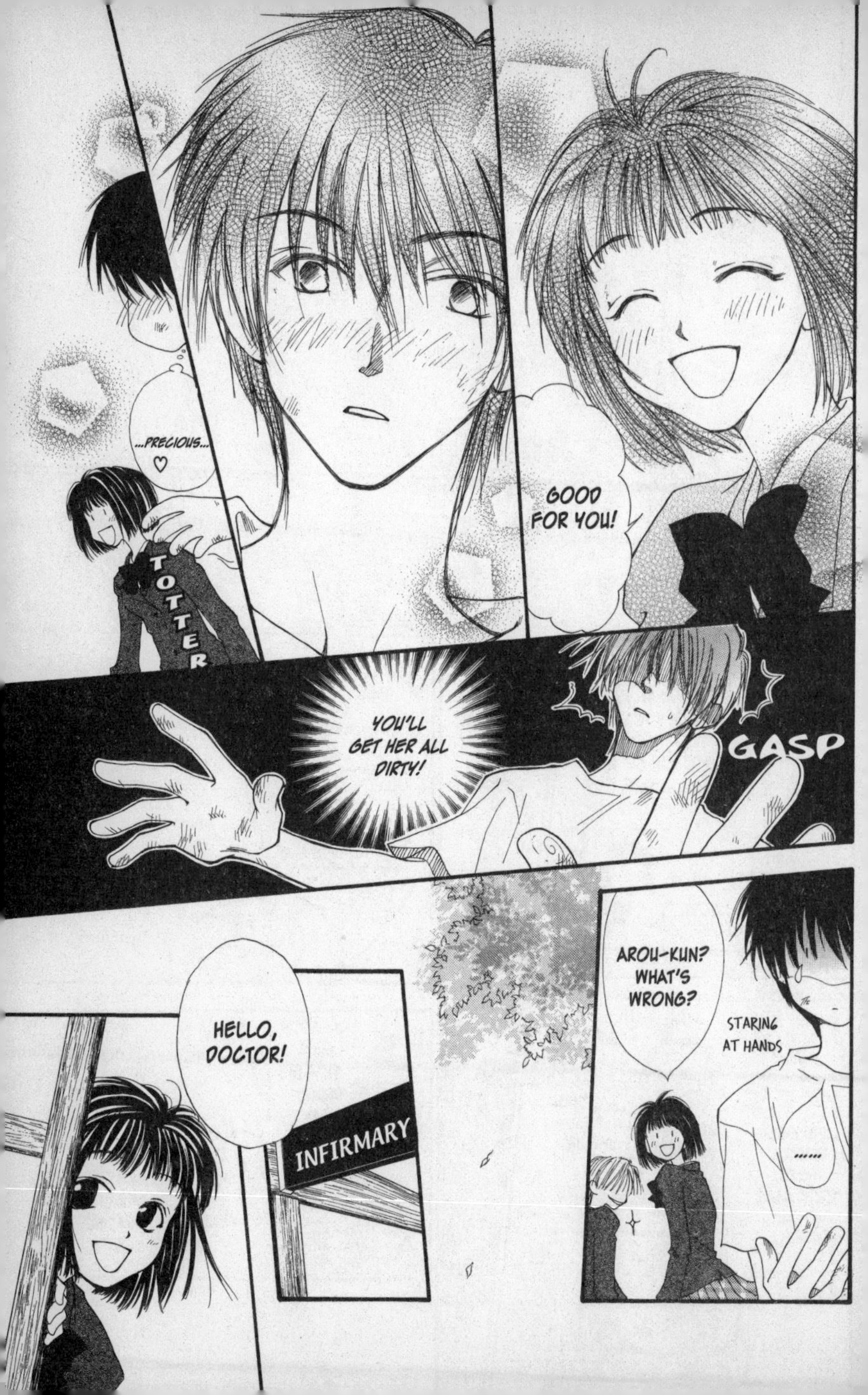
GOOD FOR YOU!
...PRECIOUS... ♡
TOTTER
GASP
YOU'LL GET HER ALL DIRTY!
AROU-KUN? WHAT'S WRONG?
STARING AT HANDS
......
HELLO, DOCTOR!
INFIRMARY

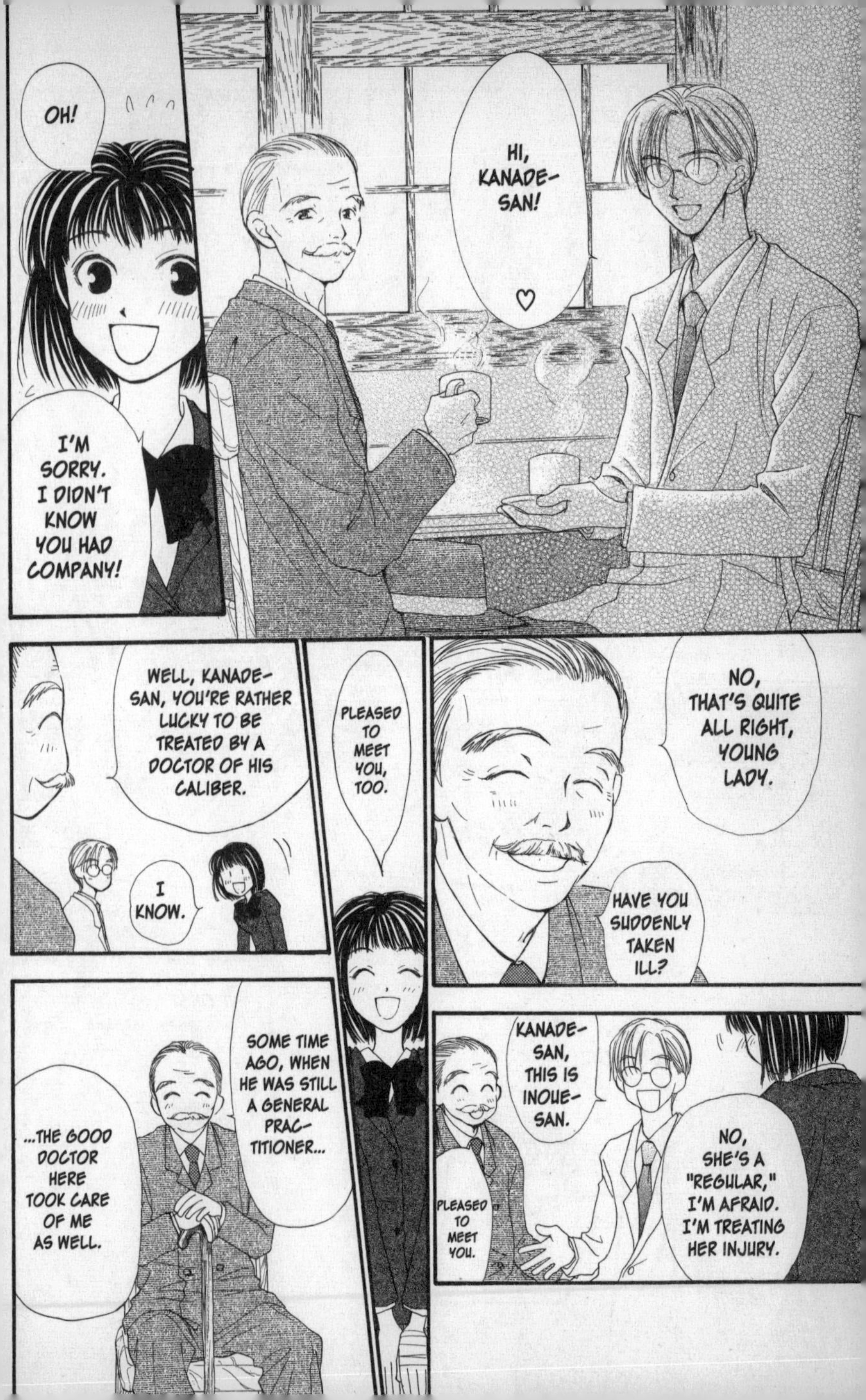
HI, KANADE-SAN! ♡
OH!
I'M SORRY. I DIDN'T KNOW YOU HAD COMPANY!
NO, THAT'S QUITE ALL RIGHT, YOUNG LADY.
HAVE YOU SUDDENLY TAKEN ILL?
NO, SHE'S A "REGULAR," I'M AFRAID. I'M TREATING HER INJURY.
KANADE-SAN, THIS IS INOUE-SAN.
PLEASED TO MEET YOU.
PLEASED TO MEET YOU, TOO.
WELL, KANADE-SAN, YOU'RE RATHER LUCKY TO BE TREATED BY A DOCTOR OF HIS CALIBER.
I KNOW.
SOME TIME AGO, WHEN HE WAS STILL A GENERAL PRAC-TITIONER...
...THE GOOD DOCTOR HERE TOOK CARE OF ME AS WELL.

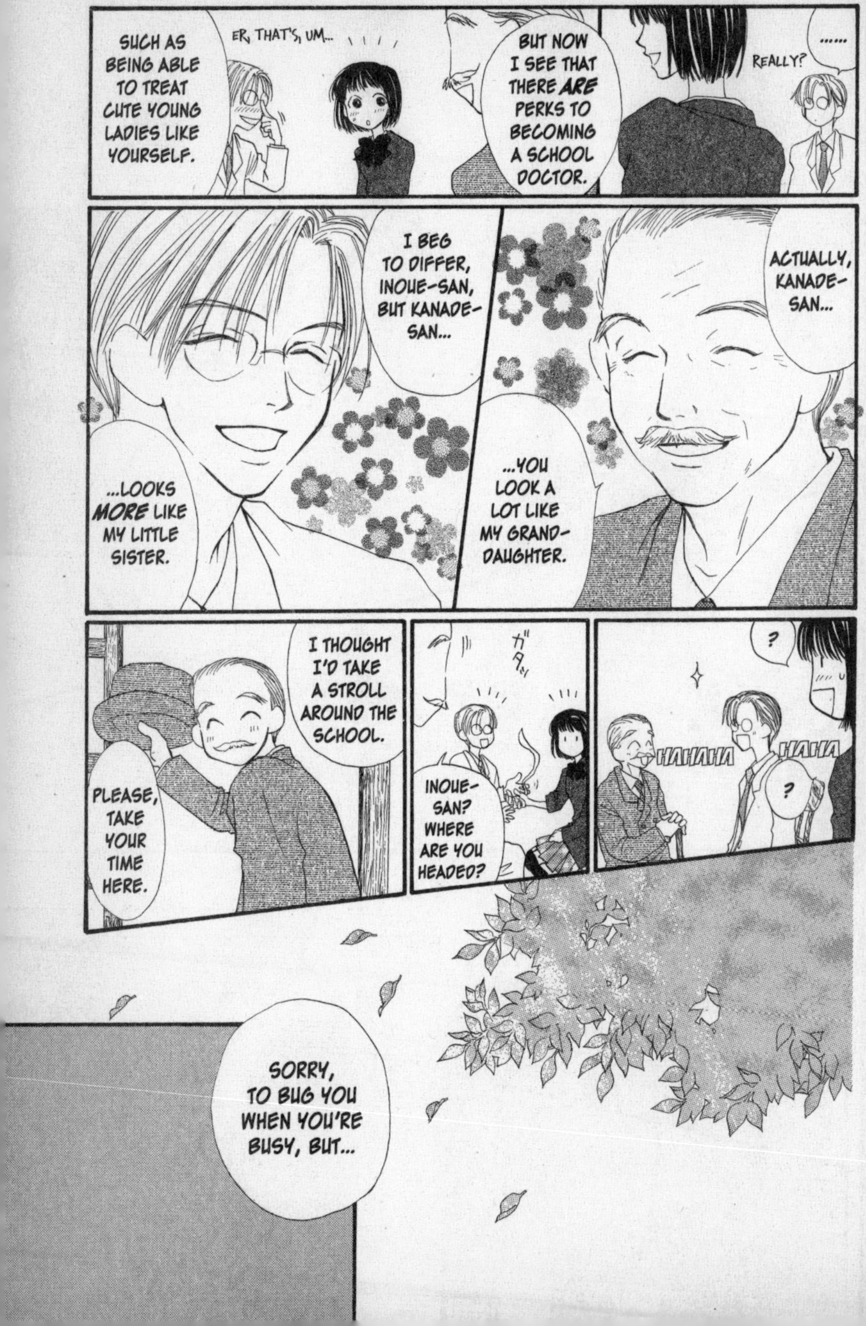
......
REALLY?
BUT NOW I SEE THAT THERE ARE PERKS TO BECOMING A SCHOOL DOCTOR.
SUCH AS BEING ABLE TO TREAT CUTE YOUNG LADIES LIKE YOURSELF.
ER, THAT'S, UM...
ACTUALLY, KANADE-SAN...
...YOU LOOK A LOT LIKE MY GRAND-DAUGHTER.
I BEG TO DIFFER, INOUE-SAN, BUT KANADE-SAN...
...LOOKS MORE LIKE MY LITTLE SISTER.
?
HAHAHA
HAHA
?
ガタ
INOUE-SAN? WHERE ARE YOU HEADED?
I THOUGHT I'D TAKE A STROLL AROUND THE SCHOOL.
PLEASE, TAKE YOUR TIME HERE.
SORRY, TO BUG YOU WHEN YOU'RE BUSY, BUT...

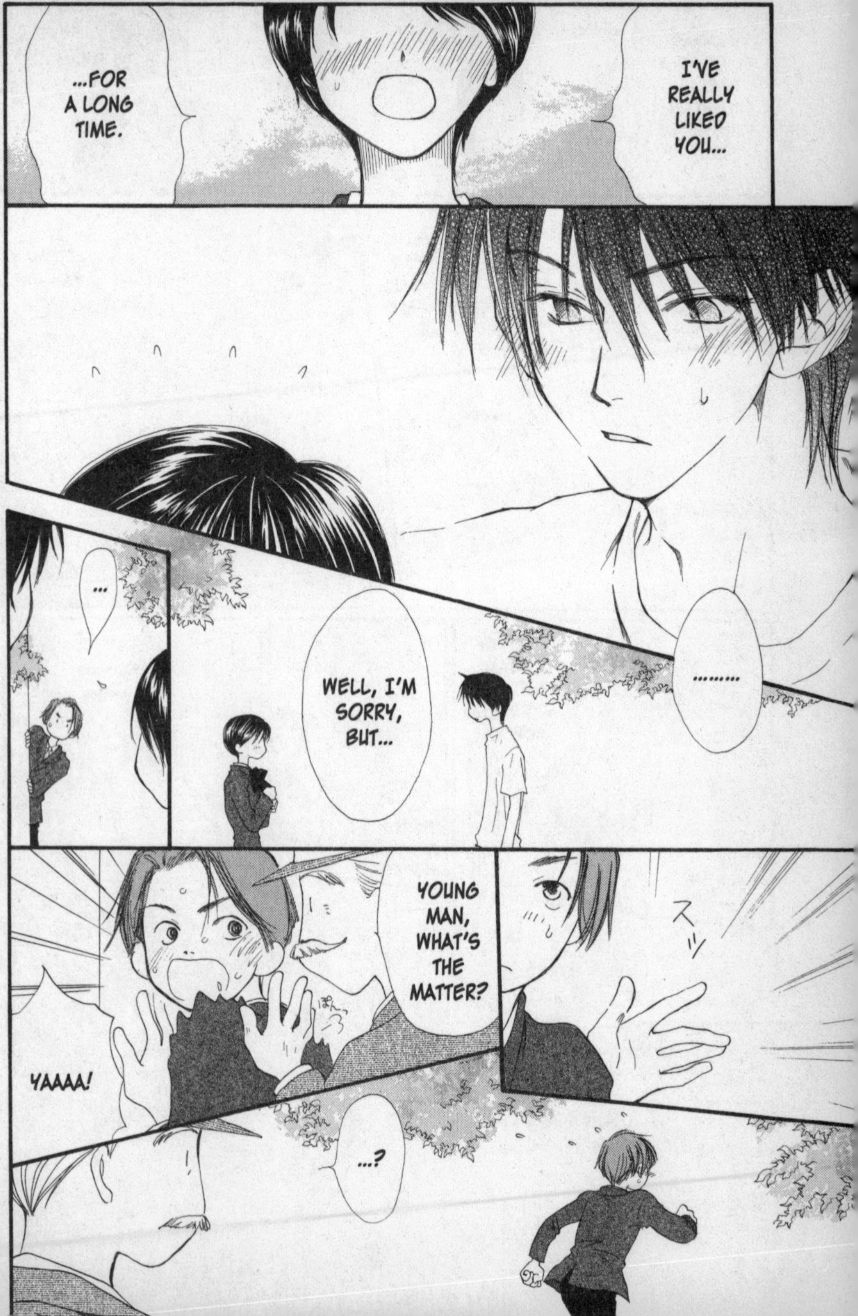
I'VE REALLY LIKED YOU...
...FOR A LONG TIME.
....
WELL, I'M SORRY, BUT...
...
スッ
YOUNG MAN, WHAT'S THE MATTER?
ぽんっ
YAAAA!
...?

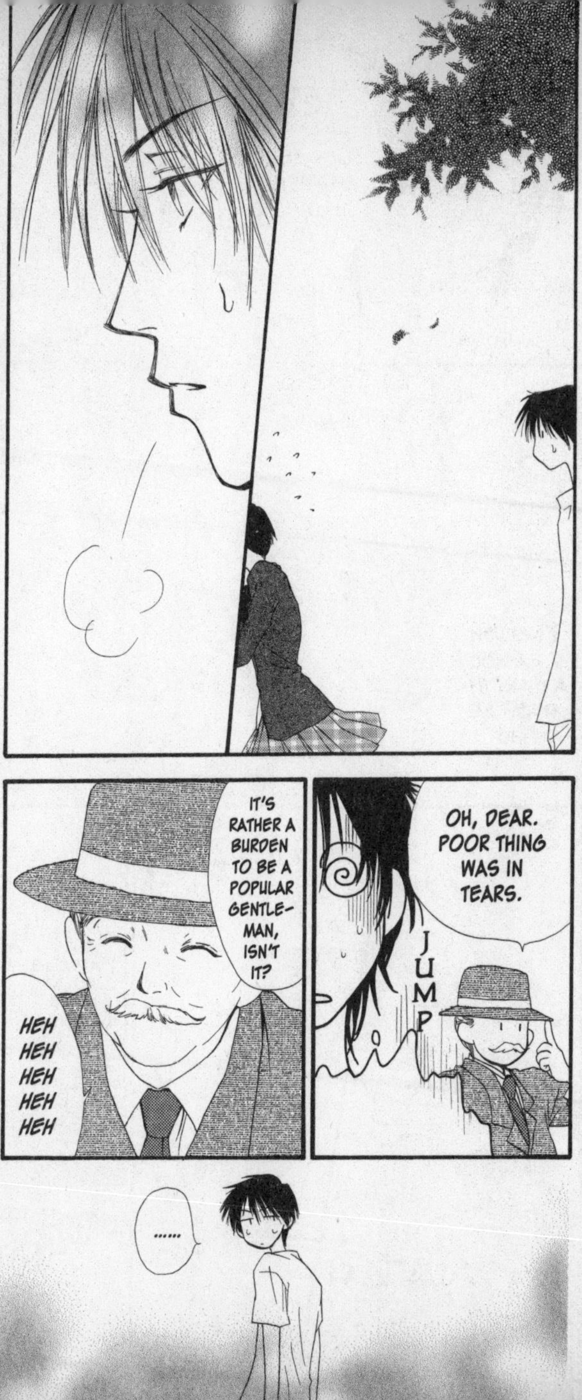
OH, DEAR. POOR THING WAS IN TEARS.
JUMP
IT'S RATHER A BURDEN TO BE A POPULAR GENTLE-MAN, ISN'T IT?
HEH HEH HEH HEH HEH
......

SAKURA MAIL

NO. 4

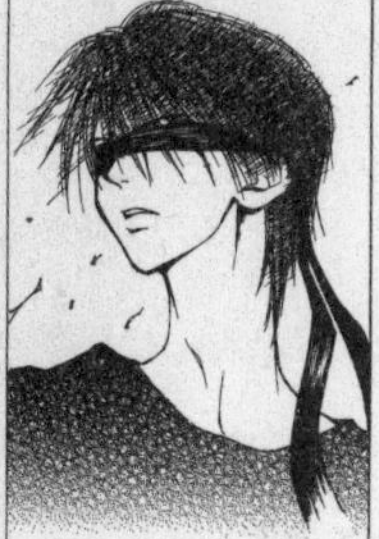

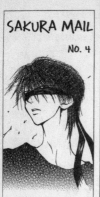

This is part of my three-part story arc. Aroo-kun takes the lead in this one. Since starting this series, I've wanted to do a no holds barred Aroo story, but when I finally got my chance, with this third part here, I couldn't think of a good story for the life of me and got all stressed out (in other words, the same old story). But I'm happy I finally nailed it! Even though I'm the author here, I'm in awe of Aroo's power, which has both the blessing and curse sides to it. When I really think of the "world" that he can see, a tear comes to my eye. But then I go and put the screws to his character... Sigh...What is this ambivalent feeling I have for my own character? I'd like to think it's love...

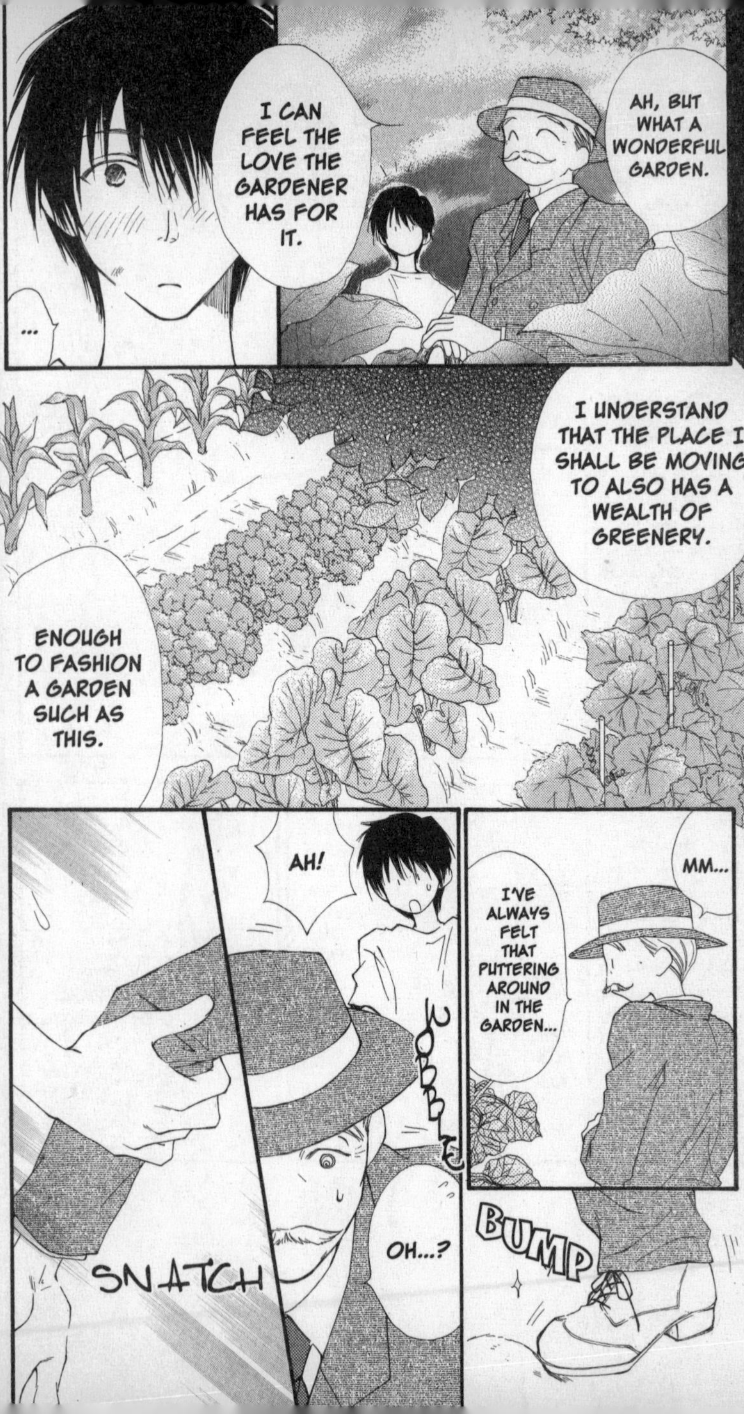
AH, BUT WHAT A WONDERFUL GARDEN.
I CAN FEEL THE LOVE THE GARDENER HAS FOR IT.
...
I UNDERSTAND THAT THE PLACE I SHALL BE MOVING TO ALSO HAS A WEALTH OF GREENERY.
ENOUGH TO FASHION A GARDEN SUCH AS THIS.
MM...
I'VE ALWAYS FELT THAT PUTTERING AROUND IN THE GARDEN...
BUMP
AH!
WOBBLE
OH...?
SNATCH

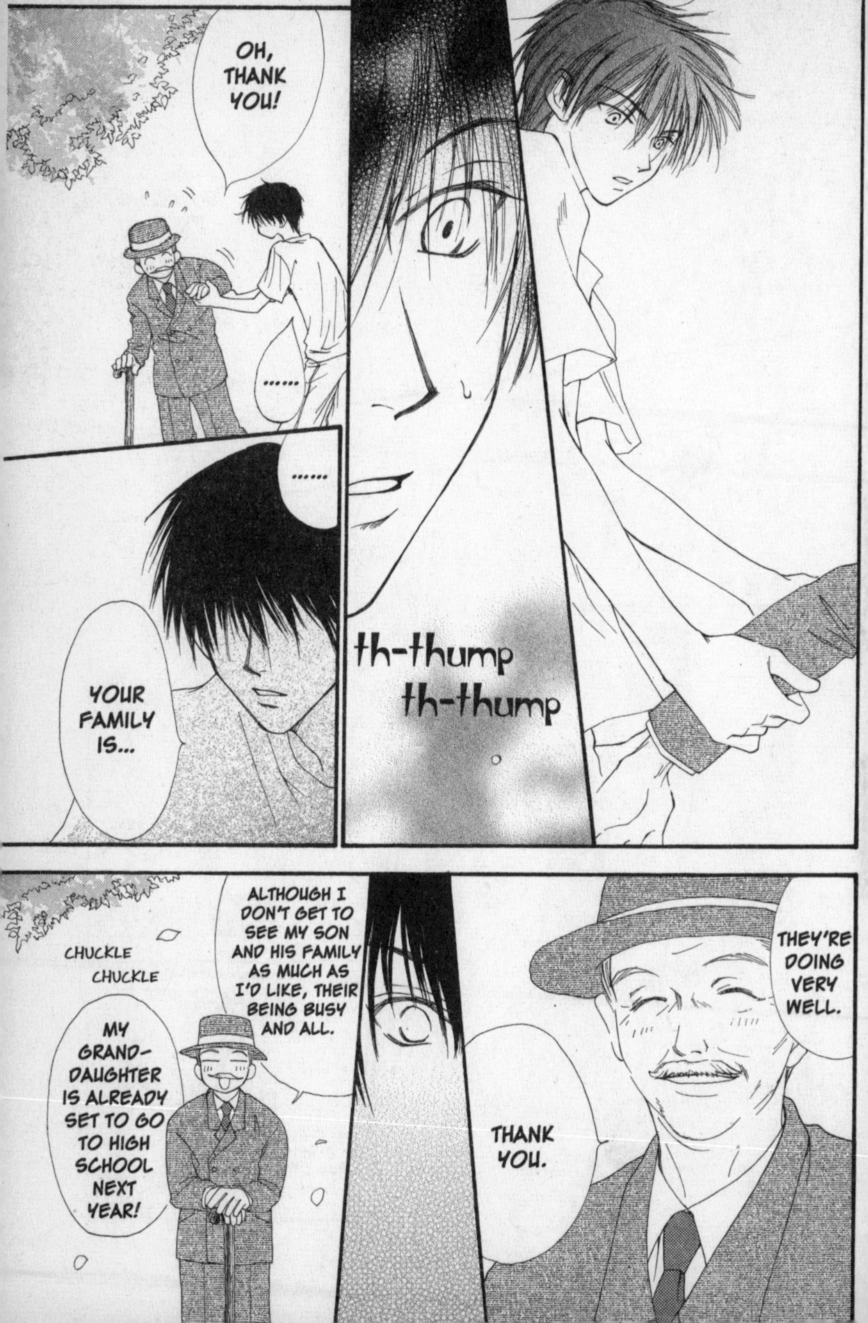
th-thump
th-thump
OH, THANK YOU!
......
......
YOUR FAMILY IS...
THEY'RE DOING VERY WELL.
THANK YOU.
ALTHOUGH I DON'T GET TO SEE MY SON AND HIS FAMILY AS MUCH AS I'D LIKE, THEIR BEING BUSY AND ALL.
CHUCKLE
CHUCKLE
MY GRAND-DAUGHTER IS ALREADY SET TO GO TO HIGH SCHOOL NEXT YEAR!

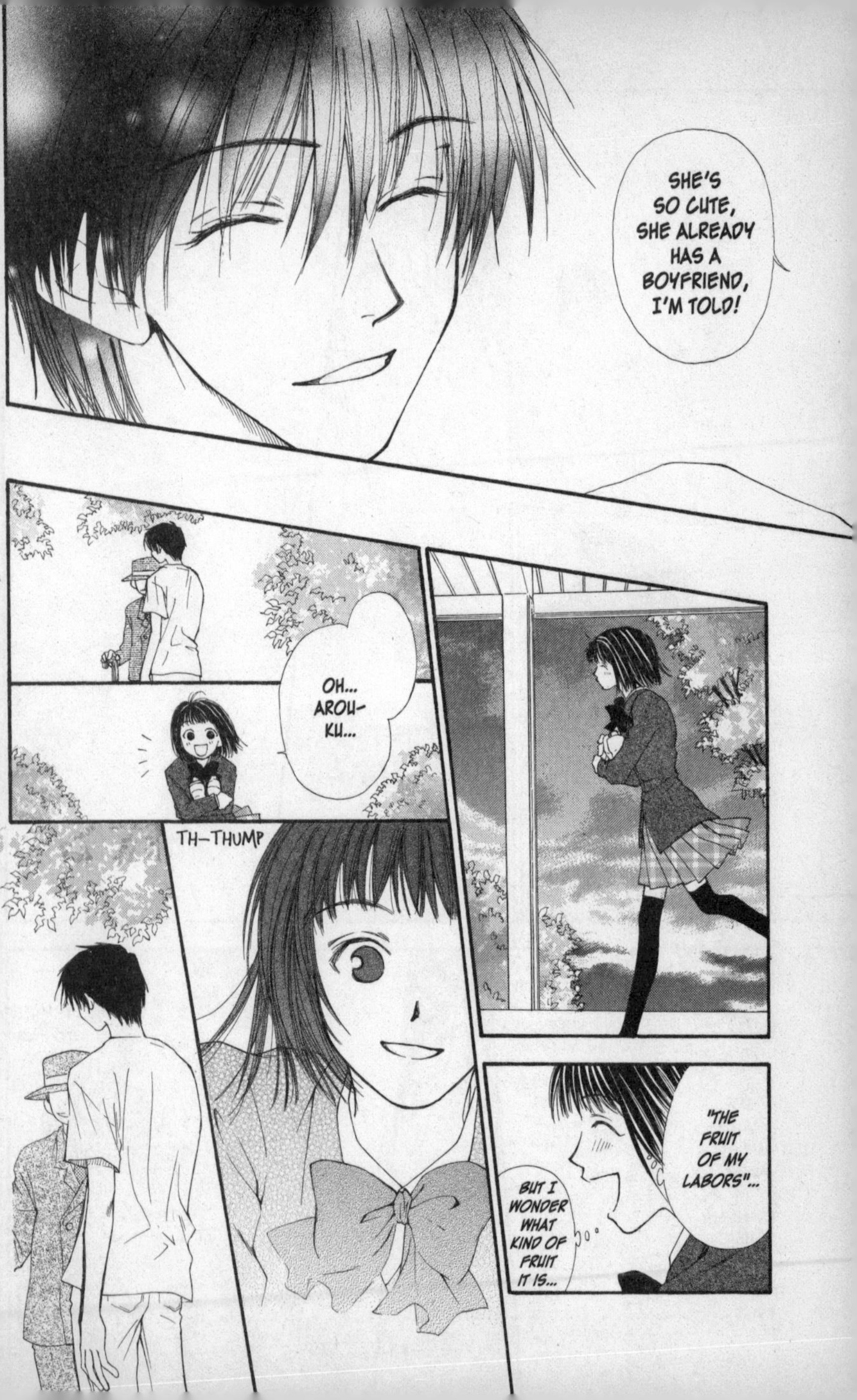
SHE'S SO CUTE, SHE ALREADY HAS A BOYFRIEND, I'M TOLD!
"THE FRUIT OF MY LABORS"...
BUT I WONDER WHAT KIND OF FRUIT IT IS...
OH... AROU-KU...
TH-THUMP

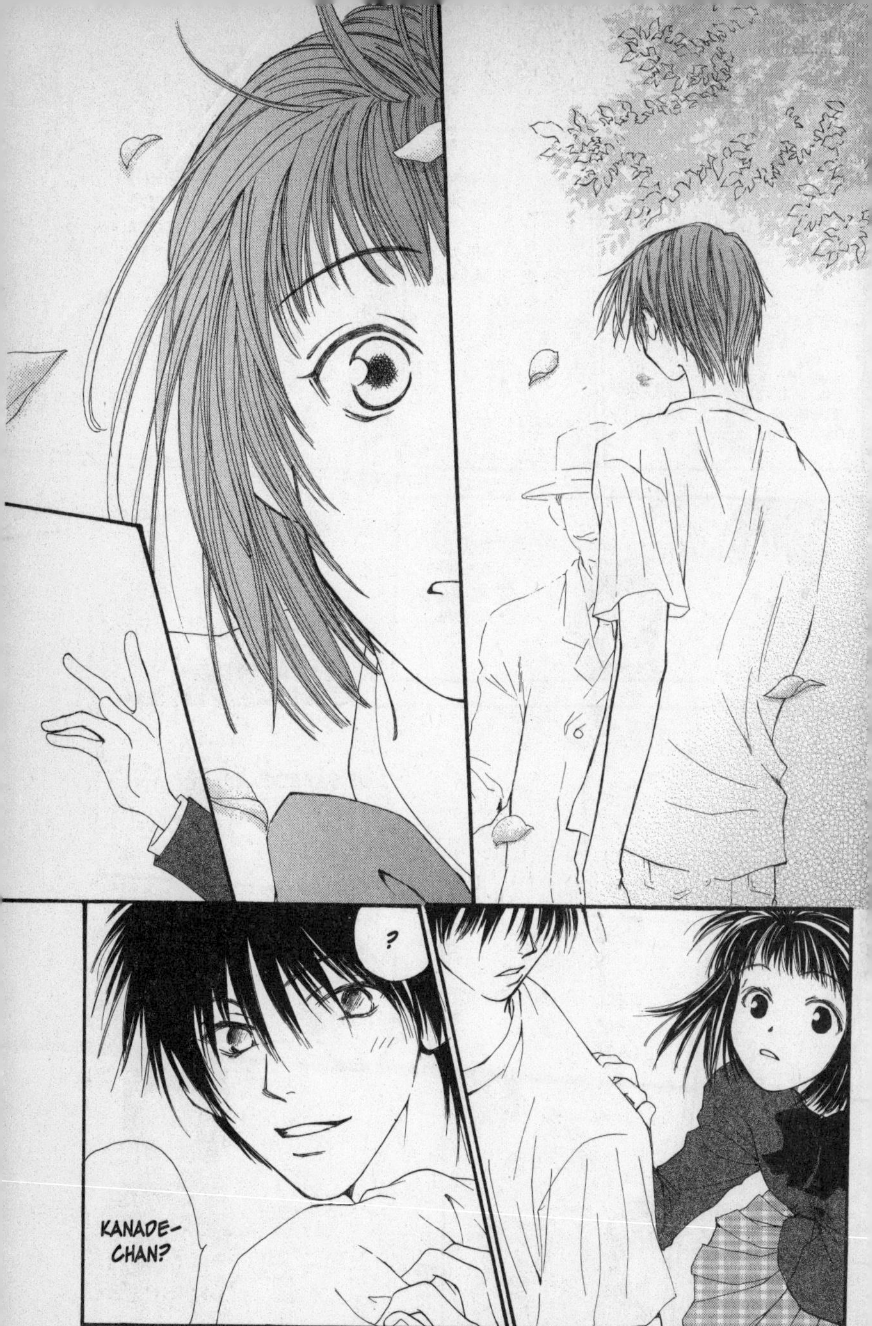
?
KANADE-CHAN?

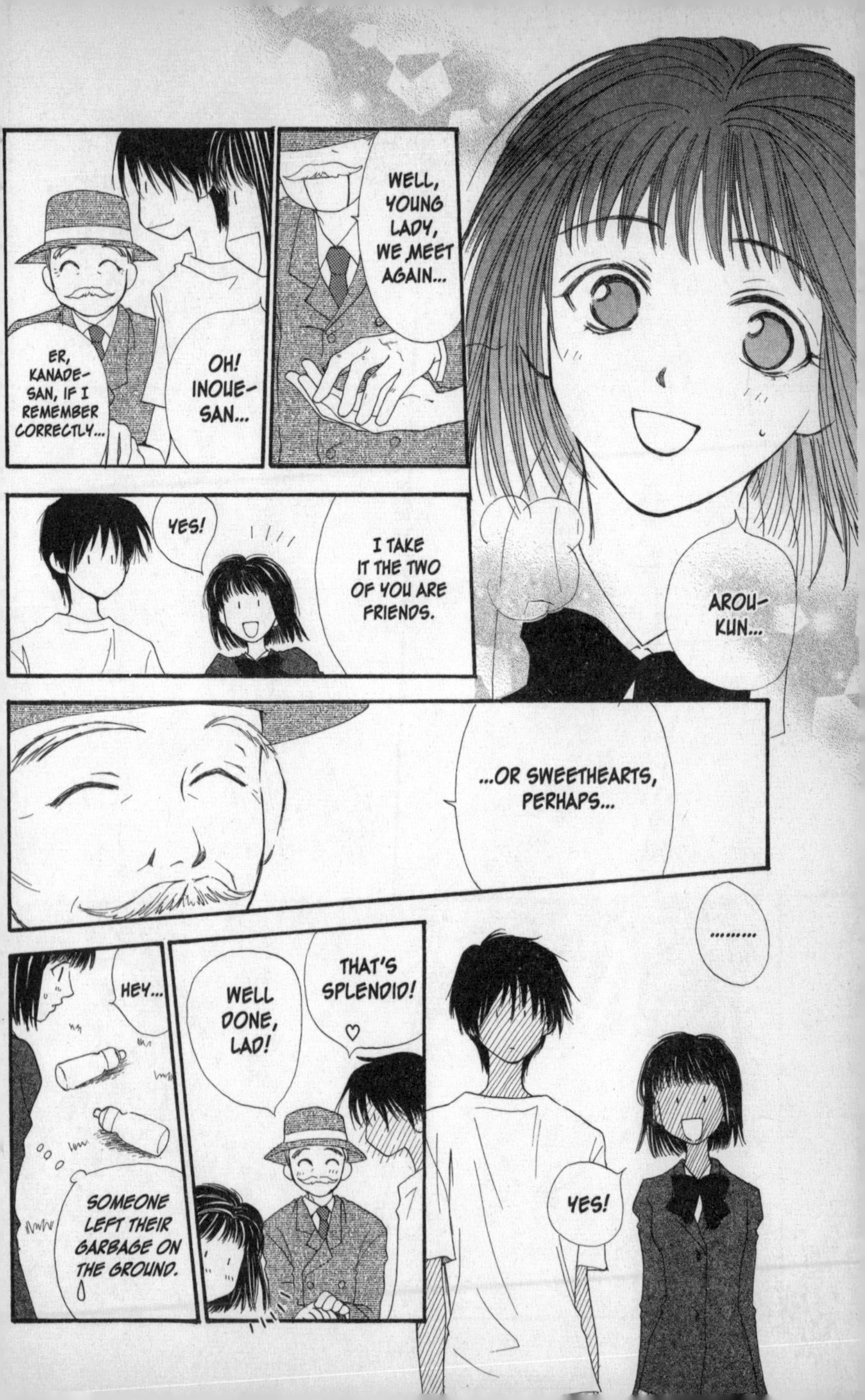
AROU-KUN...
WELL, YOUNG LADY, WE MEET AGAIN...
OH! INOUE-SAN...
ER, KANADE-SAN, IF I REMEMBER CORRECTLY...
I TAKE IT THE TWO OF YOU ARE FRIENDS.
YES!
...OR SWEETHEARTS, PERHAPS...
....
YES!
THAT'S SPLENDID!
WELL DONE, LAD!
HEY...
SOMEONE LEFT THEIR GARBAGE ON THE GROUND.

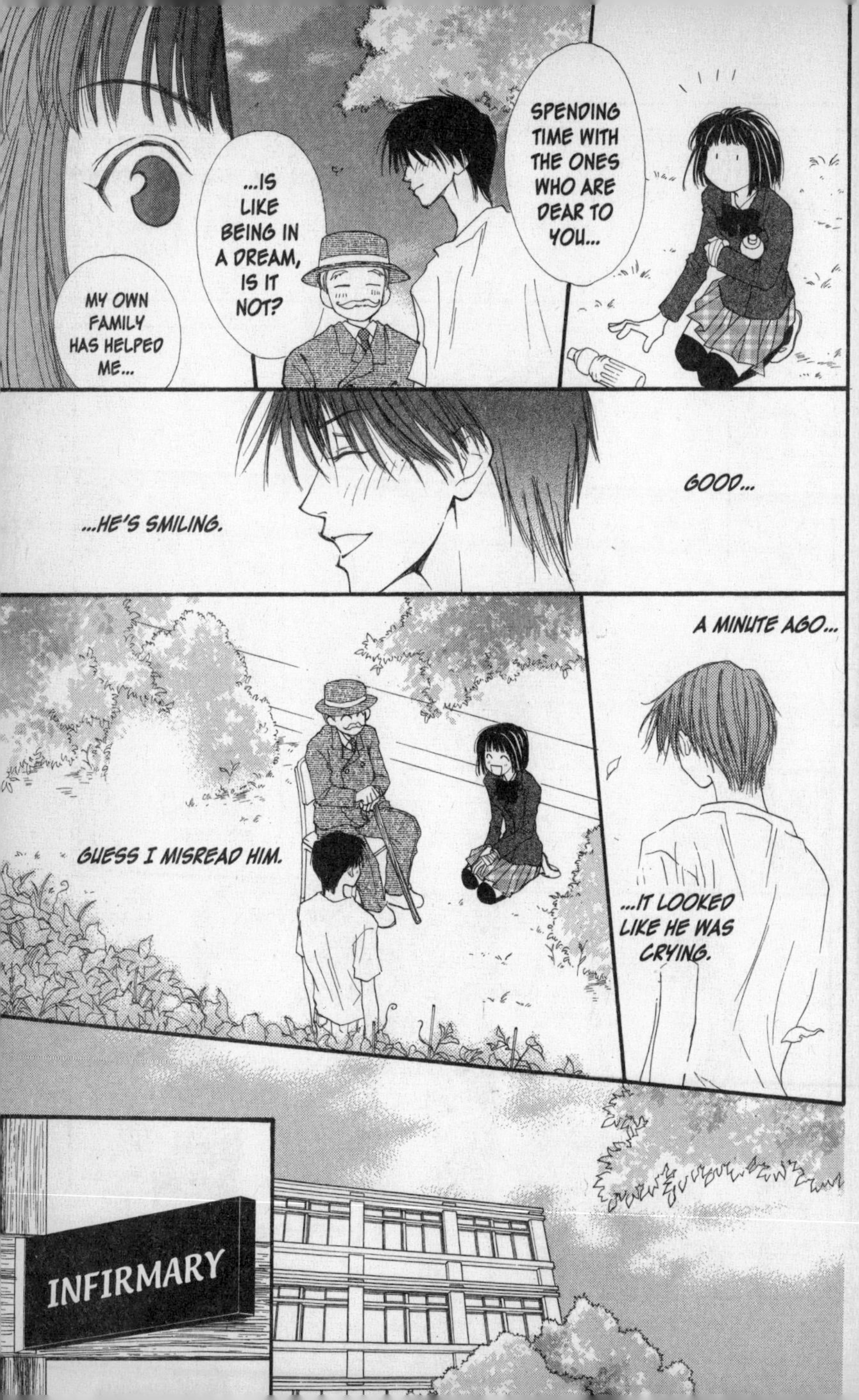
SPENDING TIME WITH THE ONES WHO ARE DEAR TO YOU...
...IS LIKE BEING IN A DREAM, IS IT NOT?
MY OWN FAMILY HAS HELPED ME...
GOOD...
...HE'S SMILING.
A MINUTE AGO...
...IT LOOKED LIKE HE WAS CRYING.
GUESS I MISREAD HIM.
INFIRMARY

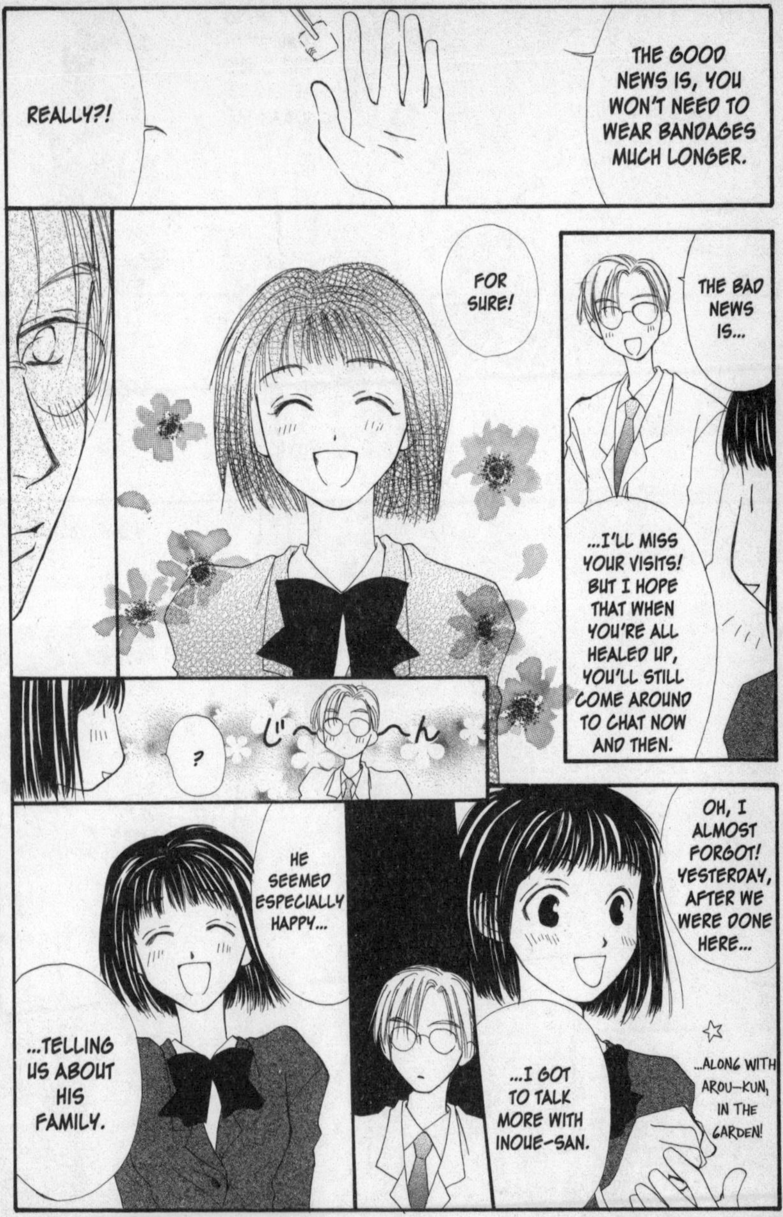
THE GOOD NEWS IS, YOU WON'T NEED TO WEAR BANDAGES MUCH LONGER.
REALLY?!
THE BAD NEWS IS...
...I'LL MISS YOUR VISITS! BUT I HOPE THAT WHEN YOU'RE ALL HEALED UP, YOU'LL STILL COME AROUND TO CHAT NOW AND THEN.
FOR SURE!
じ〜〜ん
?
OH, I ALMOST FORGOT! YESTERDAY, AFTER WE WERE DONE HERE...
...I GOT TO TALK MORE WITH INOUE-SAN.
...ALONG WITH AROU-KUN, IN THE GARDEN!
HE SEEMED ESPECIALLY HAPPY...
...TELLING US ABOUT HIS FAMILY.

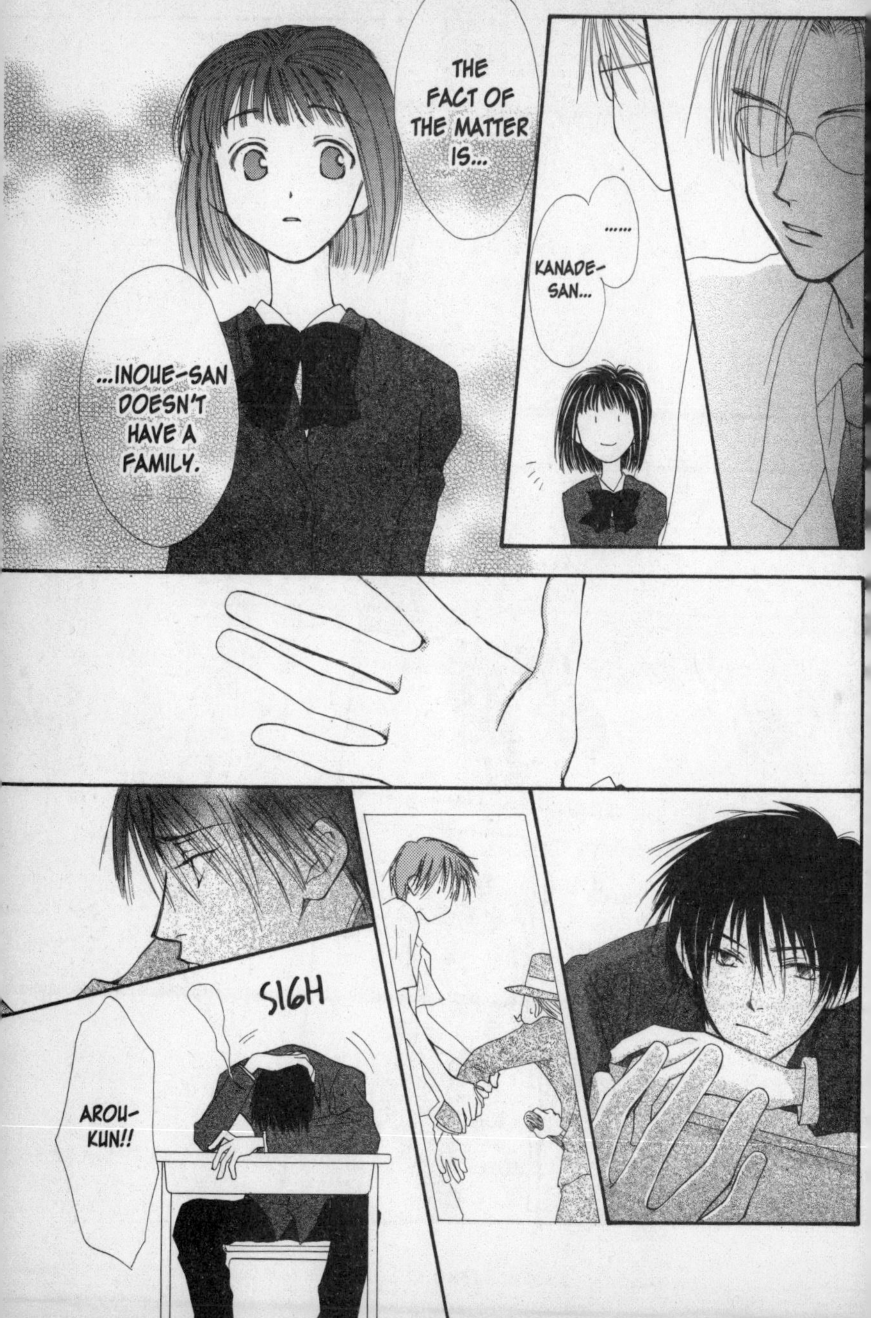
......
KANADE-SAN...
THE FACT OF THE MATTER IS...
...INOUE-SAN DOESN'T HAVE A FAMILY.
SIGH
AROU-KUN!!

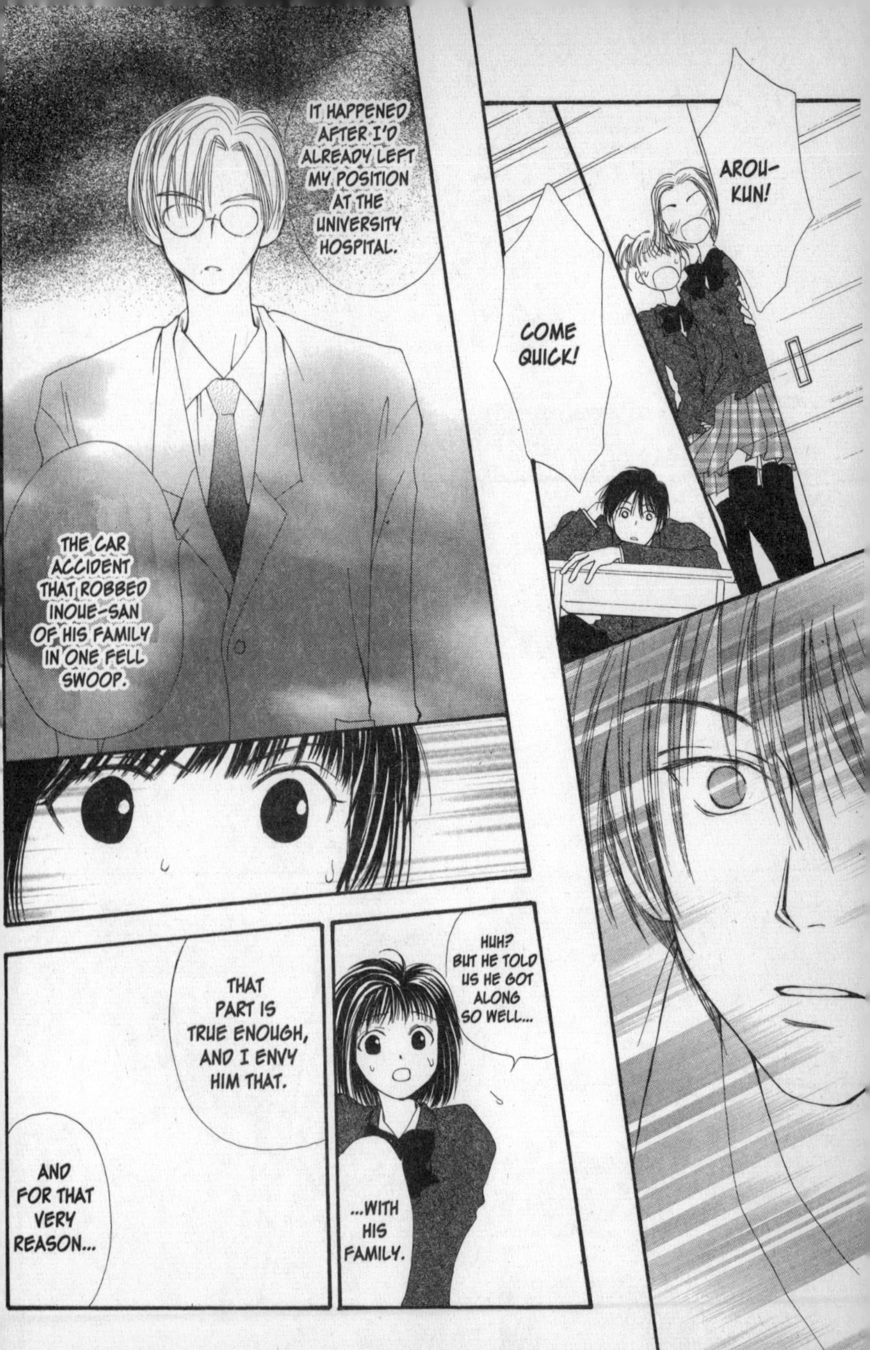
AROU-KUN!
COME QUICK!
IT HAPPENED AFTER I'D ALREADY LEFT MY POSITION AT THE UNIVERSITY HOSPITAL.
THE CAR ACCIDENT THAT ROBBED INOUE-SAN OF HIS FAMILY IN ONE FELL SWOOP.
HUH? BUT HE TOLD US HE GOT ALONG SO WELL...
...WITH HIS FAMILY.
THAT PART IS TRUE ENOUGH, AND I ENVY HIM THAT.
AND FOR THAT VERY REASON...

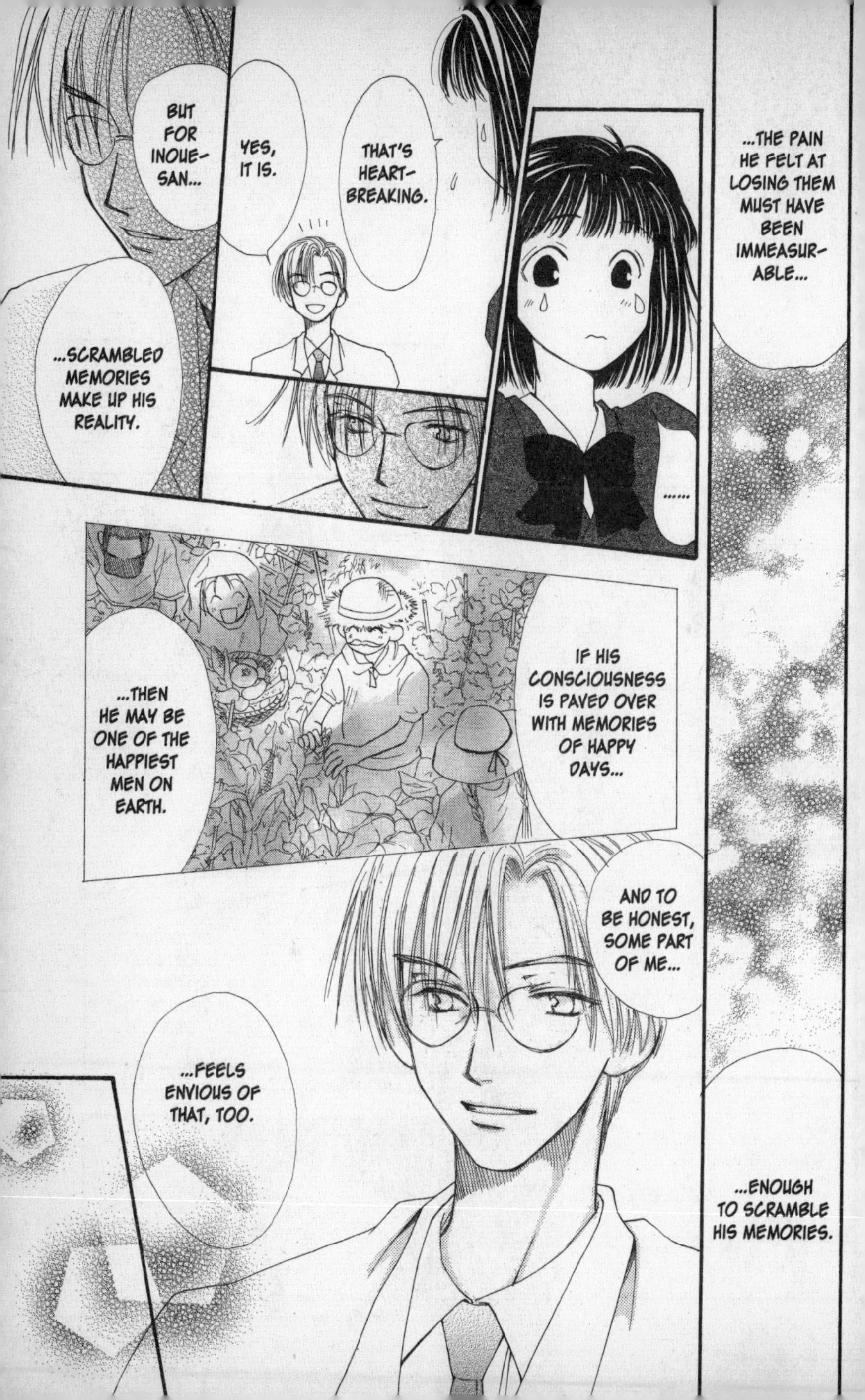
...THE PAIN HE FELT AT LOSING THEM MUST HAVE BEEN IMMEASURABLE...
...ENOUGH TO SCRAMBLE HIS MEMORIES.
......
THAT'S HEART-BREAKING.
YES, IT IS.
BUT FOR INOUE-SAN...
...SCRAMBLED MEMORIES MAKE UP HIS REALITY.
IF HIS CONSCIOUSNESS IS PAVED OVER WITH MEMORIES OF HAPPY DAYS...
...THEN HE MAY BE ONE OF THE HAPPIEST MEN ON EARTH.
AND TO BE HONEST, SOME PART OF ME...
...FEELS ENVIOUS OF THAT, TOO.

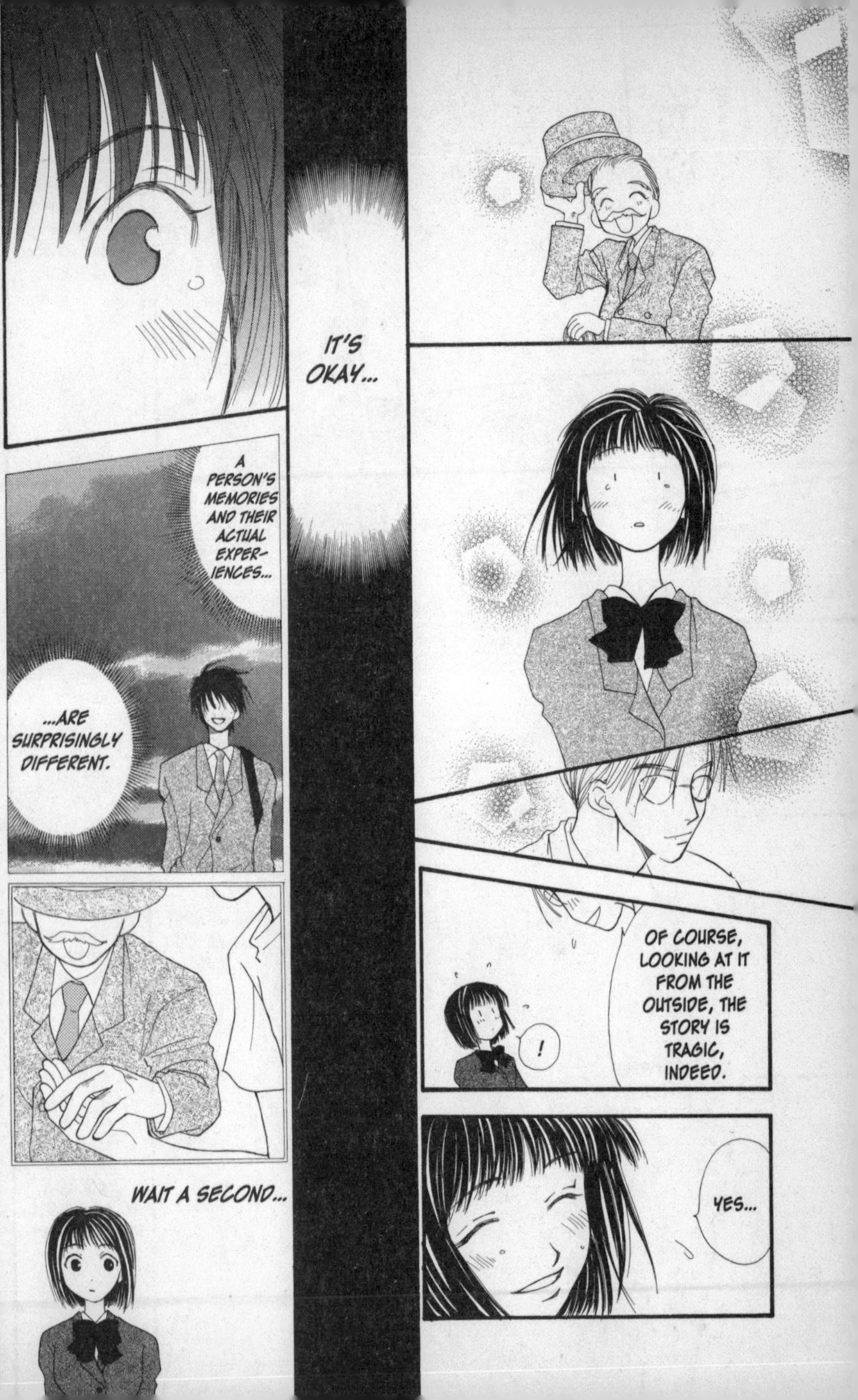

OF COURSE, LOOKING AT IT FROM THE OUTSIDE, THE STORY IS TRAGIC, INDEED.
!
YES...
IT'S OKAY...
A PERSON'S MEMORIES AND THEIR ACTUAL EXPERIENCES...
...ARE SURPRISINGLY DIFFERENT.
WAIT A SECOND...

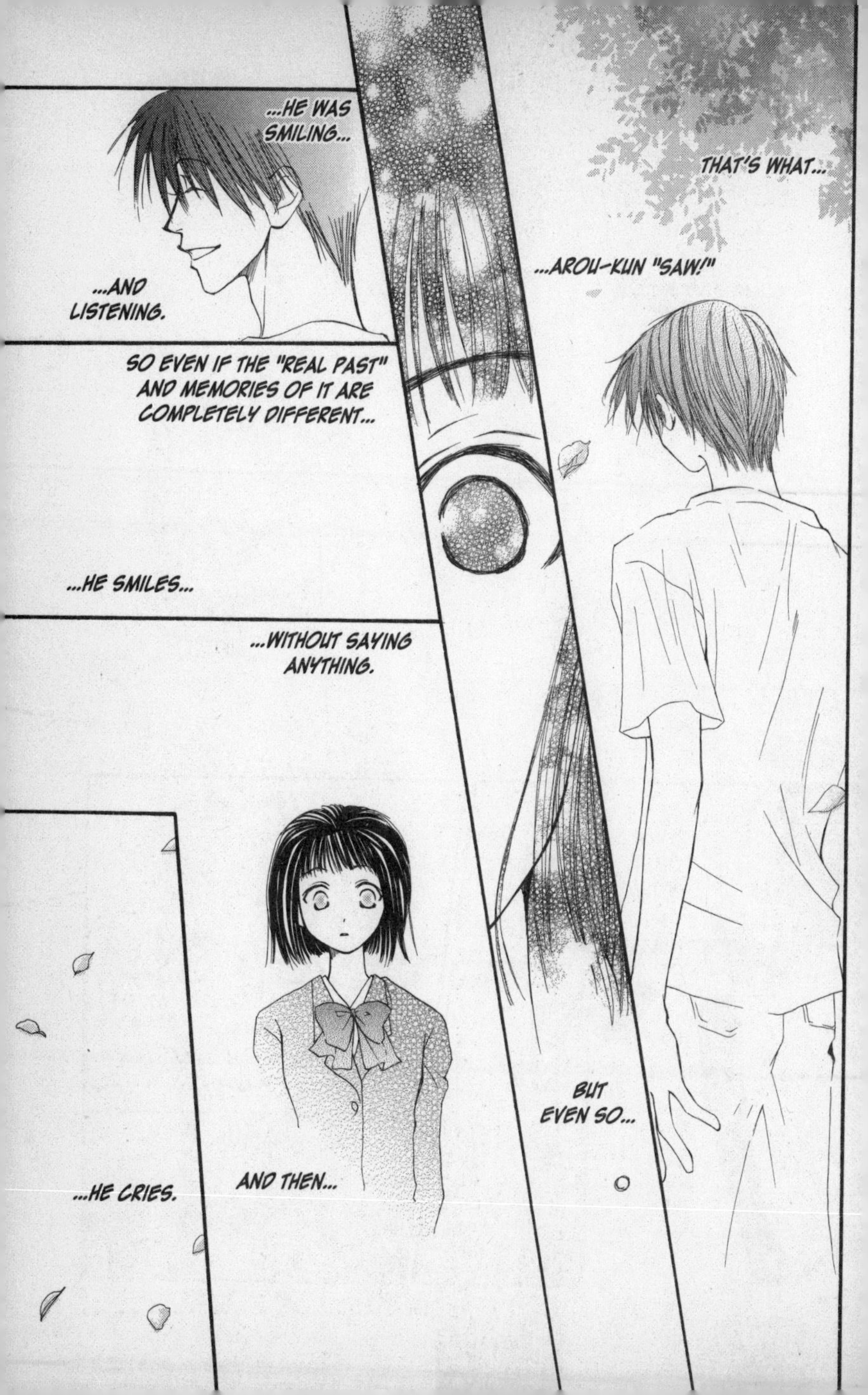
THAT'S WHAT...
...AROU-KUN "SAW!"
BUT EVEN SO...
...HE WAS SMILING...
...AND LISTENING.
SO EVEN IF THE "REAL PAST" AND MEMORIES OF IT ARE COMPLETELY DIFFERENT...
...HE SMILES...
...WITHOUT SAYING ANYTHING.
AND THEN...
...HE CRIES.

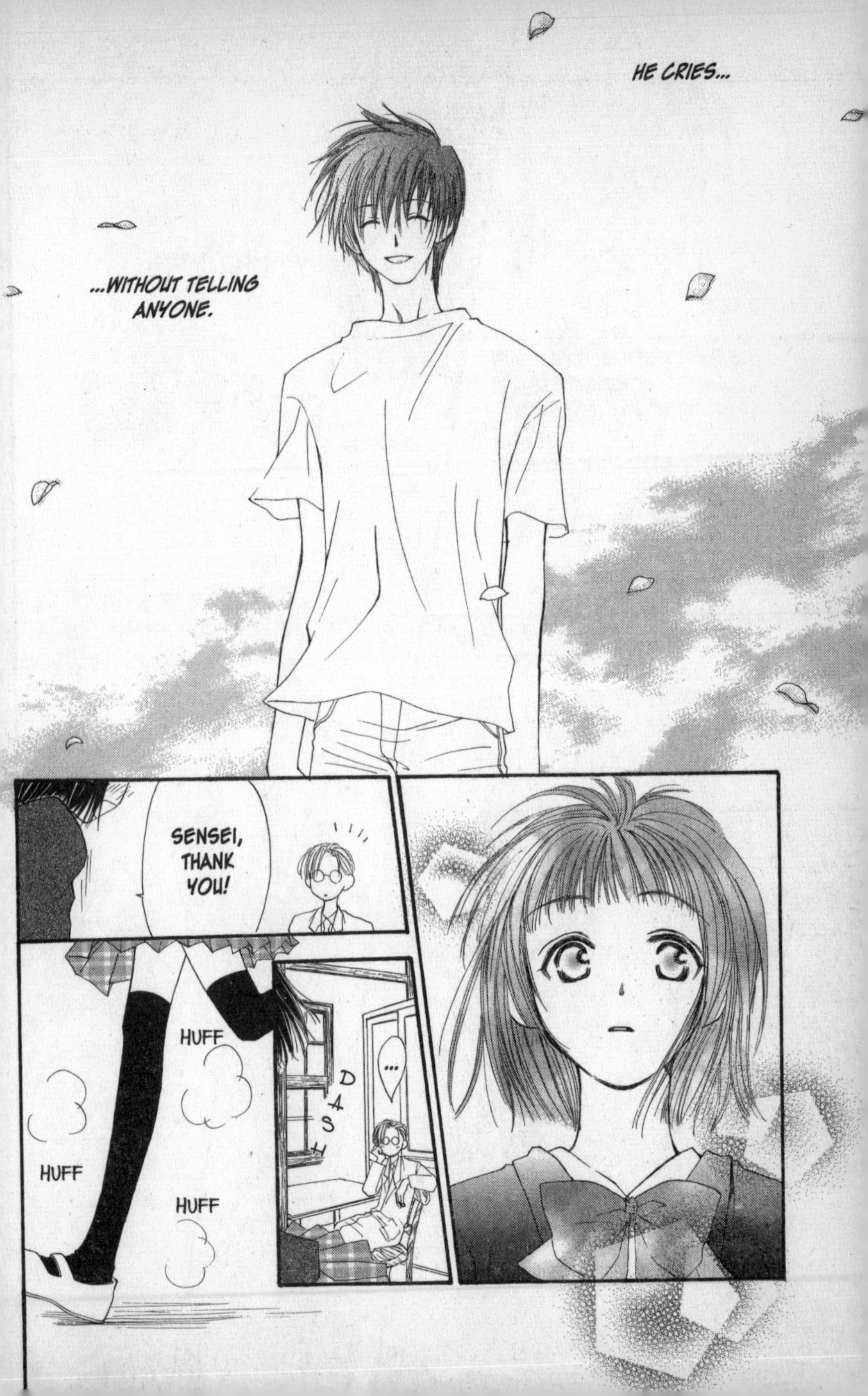
HE CRIES...
...WITHOUT TELLING ANYONE.
SENSEI, THANK YOU!
...
DASH
HUFF
HUFF
HUFF

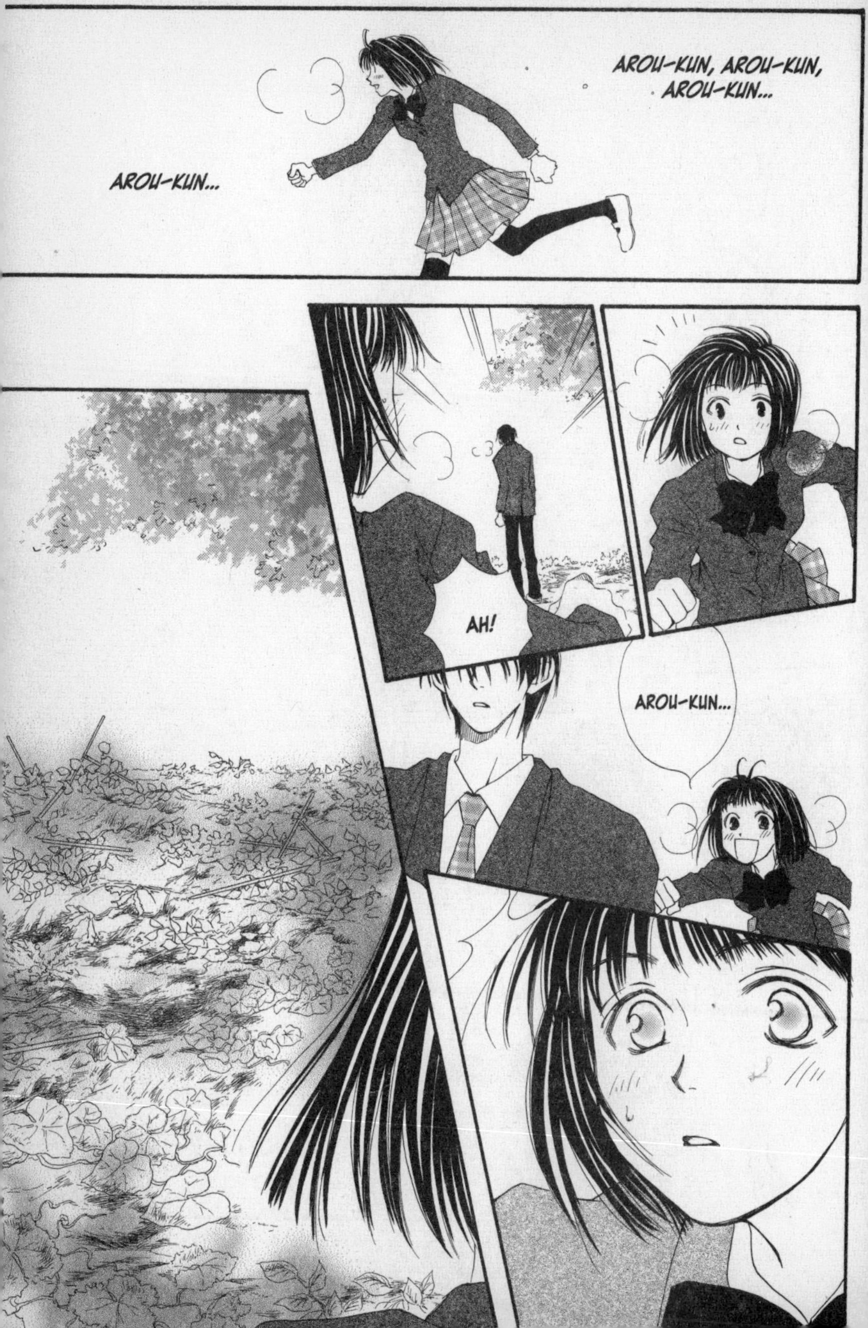
AROU-KUN, AROU-KUN, AROU-KUN...
AROU-KUN...
AH!
AROU-KUN...

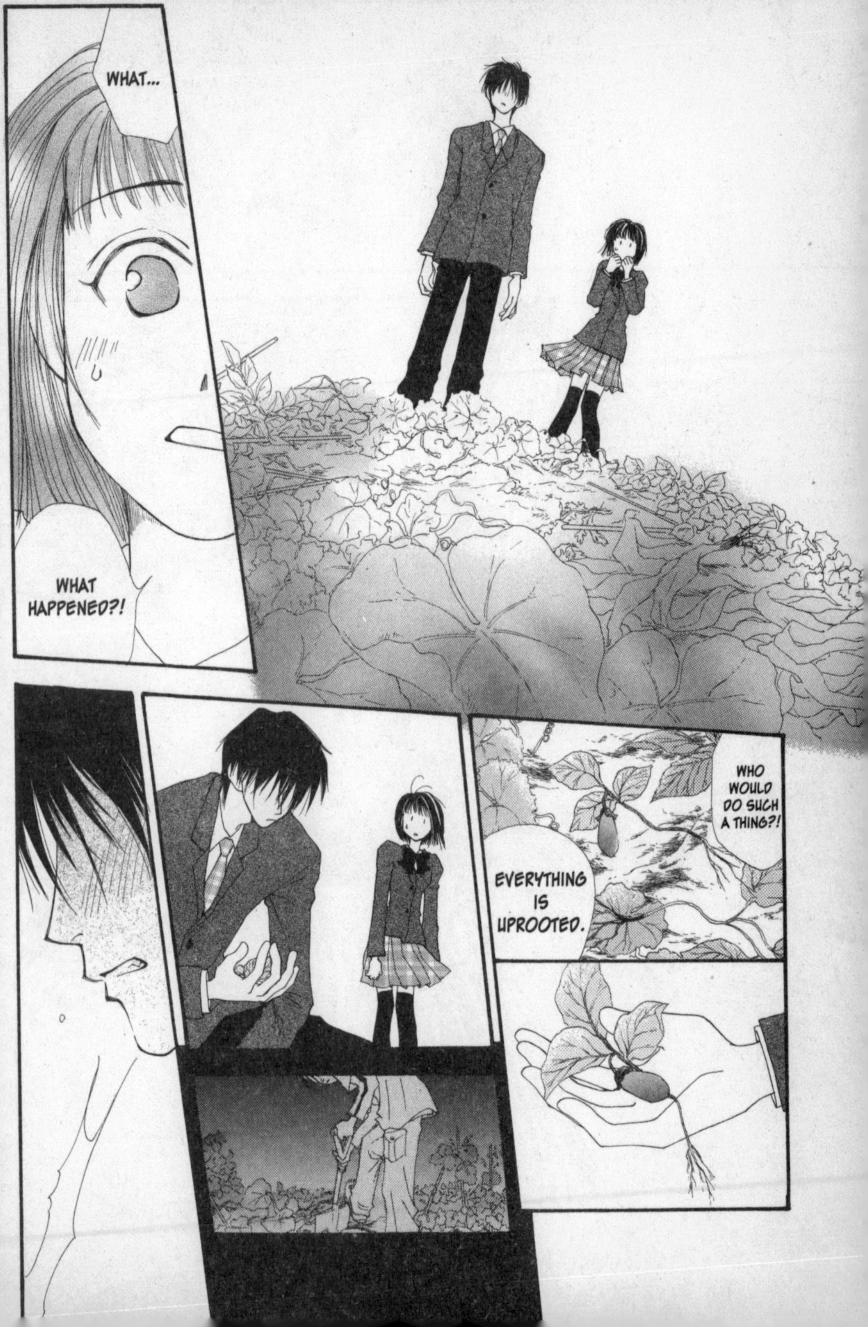
WHAT...
WHAT HAPPENED?!
WHO WOULD DO SUCH A THING?!
EVERYTHING IS UPROOTED.

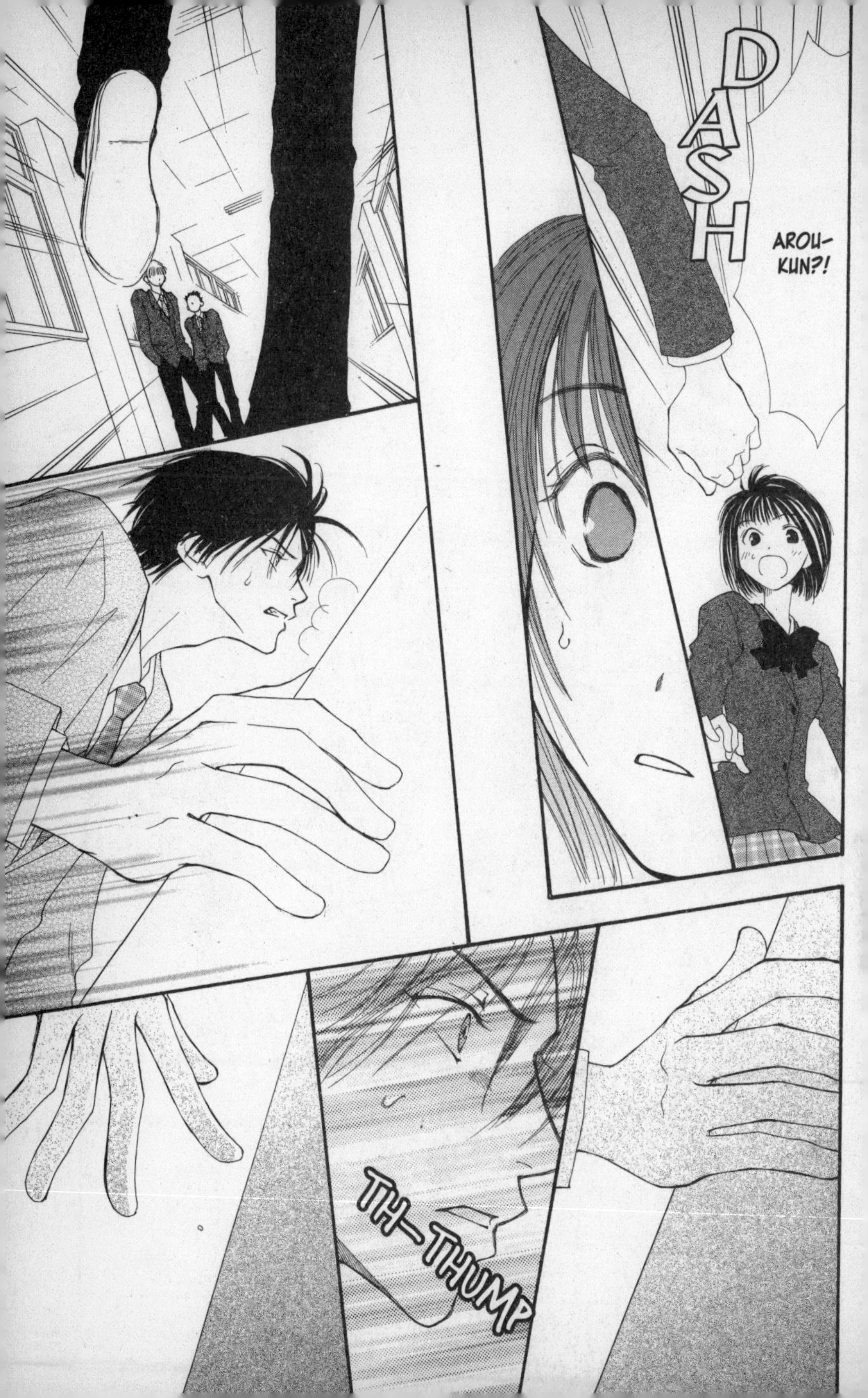
DASH
AROU-KUN?!
TH-THUMP

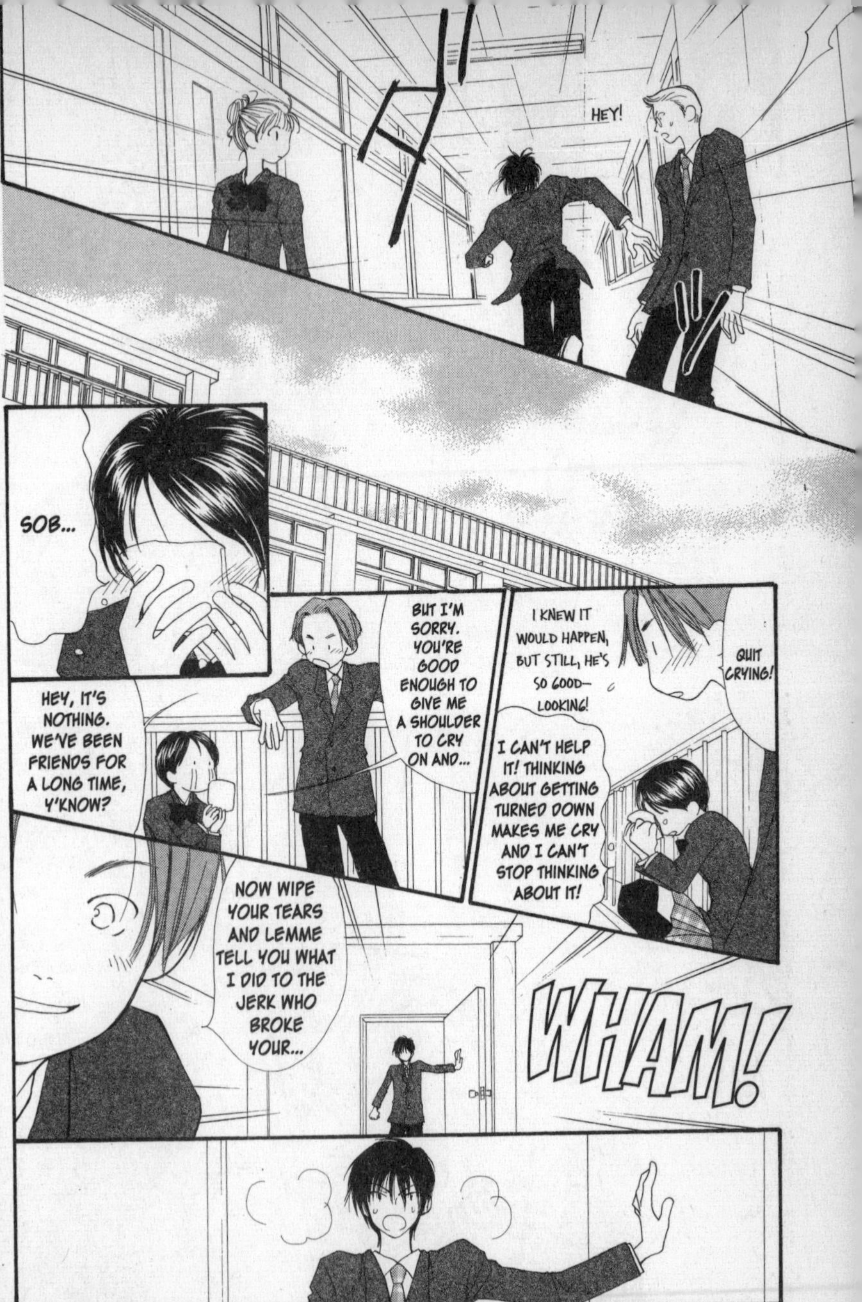
HEY!
SOB...
I KNEW IT WOULD HAPPEN, BUT STILL, HE'S SO GOOD-LOOKING!
QUIT CRYING!
I CAN'T HELP IT! THINKING ABOUT GETTING TURNED DOWN MAKES ME CRY AND I CAN'T STOP THINKING ABOUT IT!
BUT I'M SORRY. YOU'RE GOOD ENOUGH TO GIVE ME A SHOULDER TO CRY ON AND...
HEY, IT'S NOTHING. WE'VE BEEN FRIENDS FOR A LONG TIME, Y'KNOW?
NOW WIPE YOUR TEARS AND LEMME TELL YOU WHAT I DID TO THE JERK WHO BROKE YOUR...
WHAM!

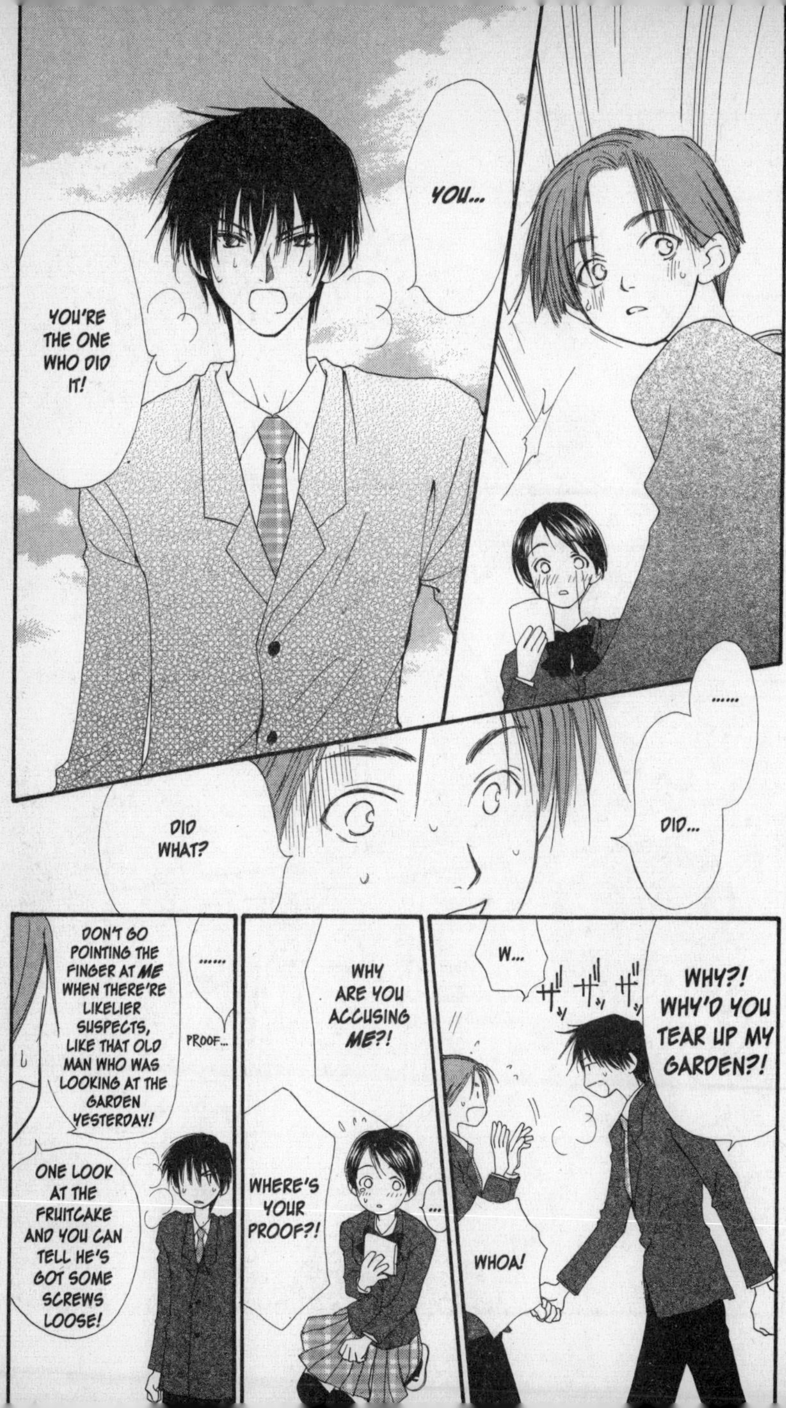
YOU...
YOU'RE THE ONE WHO DID IT!
......
DID...
DID WHAT?
WHY?! WHY'D YOU TEAR UP MY GARDEN?!
W...
ザッ ザッ ザッ
...
WHOA!
WHY ARE YOU ACCUSING *ME*?!
WHERE'S YOUR PROOF?!
......
PROOF...
DON'T GO POINTING THE FINGER AT *ME* WHEN THERE'RE LIKELIER SUSPECTS, LIKE THAT OLD MAN WHO WAS LOOKING AT THE GARDEN YESTERDAY!
ONE LOOK AT THE FRUITCAKE AND YOU CAN TELL HE'S GOT SOME SCREWS LOOSE!

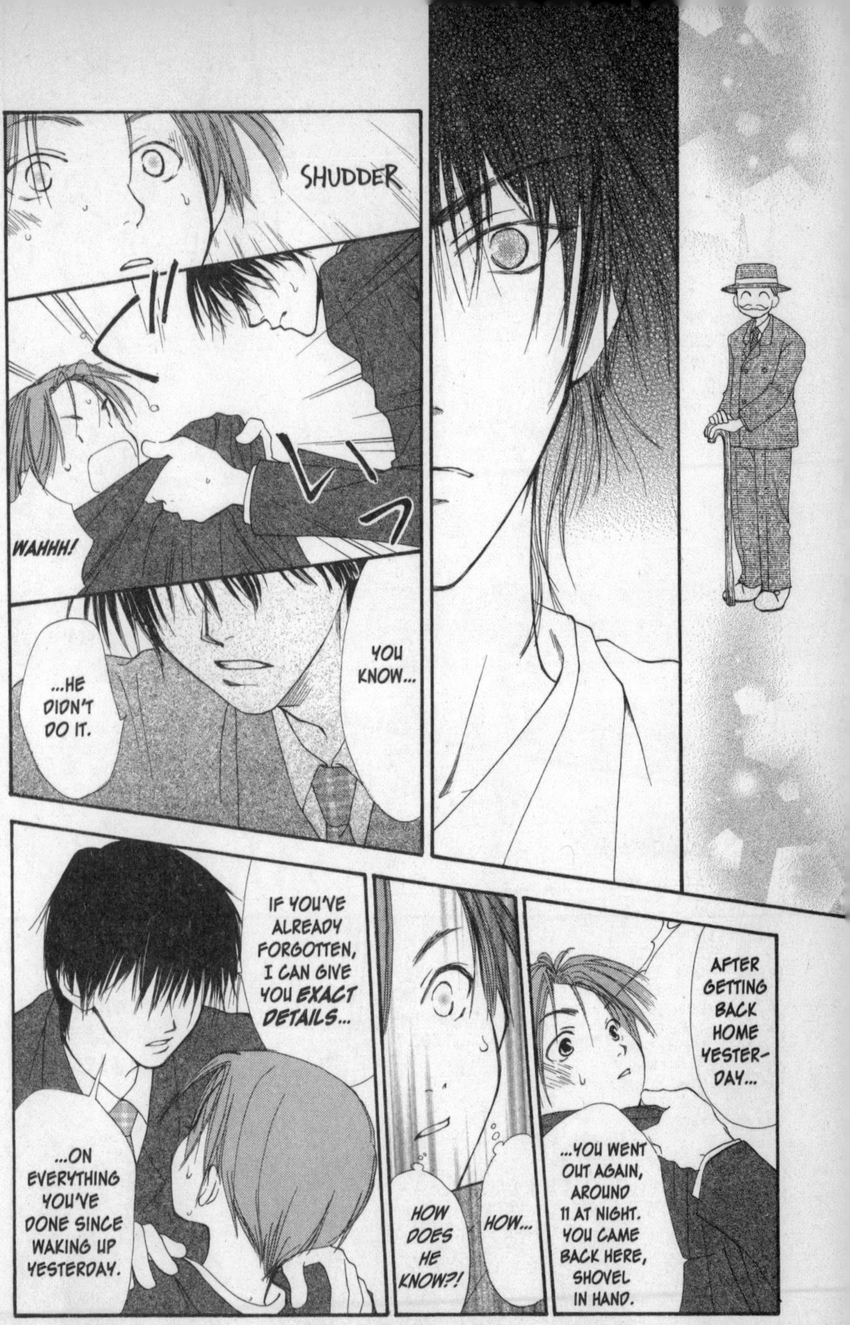
SHUDDER
WAHHH!
YOU KNOW...
...HE DIDN'T DO IT.
AFTER GETTING BACK HOME YESTERDAY...
...YOU WENT OUT AGAIN, AROUND 11 AT NIGHT. YOU CAME BACK HERE, SHOVEL IN HAND.
HOW...
HOW DOES HE KNOW?!
IF YOU'VE ALREADY FORGOTTEN, I CAN GIVE YOU *EXACT DETAILS*...
...ON EVERYTHING YOU'VE DONE SINCE WAKING UP YESTERDAY.

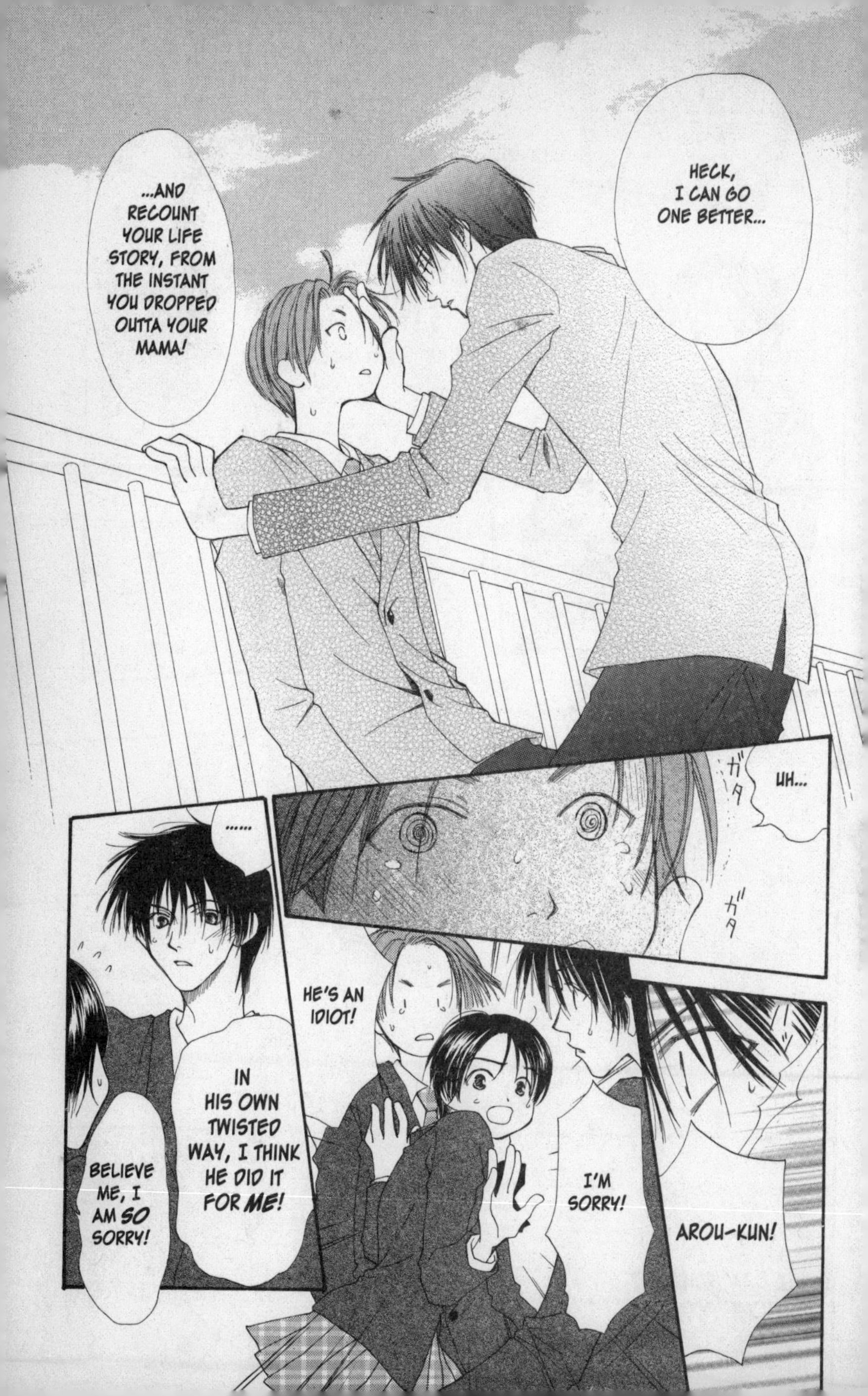
HECK, I CAN GO ONE BETTER...
...AND RECOUNT YOUR LIFE STORY, FROM THE INSTANT YOU DROPPED OUTTA YOUR MAMA!
ガタ
UH...
ガタ
AROU-KUN!
I'M SORRY!
HE'S AN IDIOT!
......
IN HIS OWN TWISTED WAY, I THINK HE DID IT FOR *ME*!
BELIEVE ME, I AM *SO* SORRY!

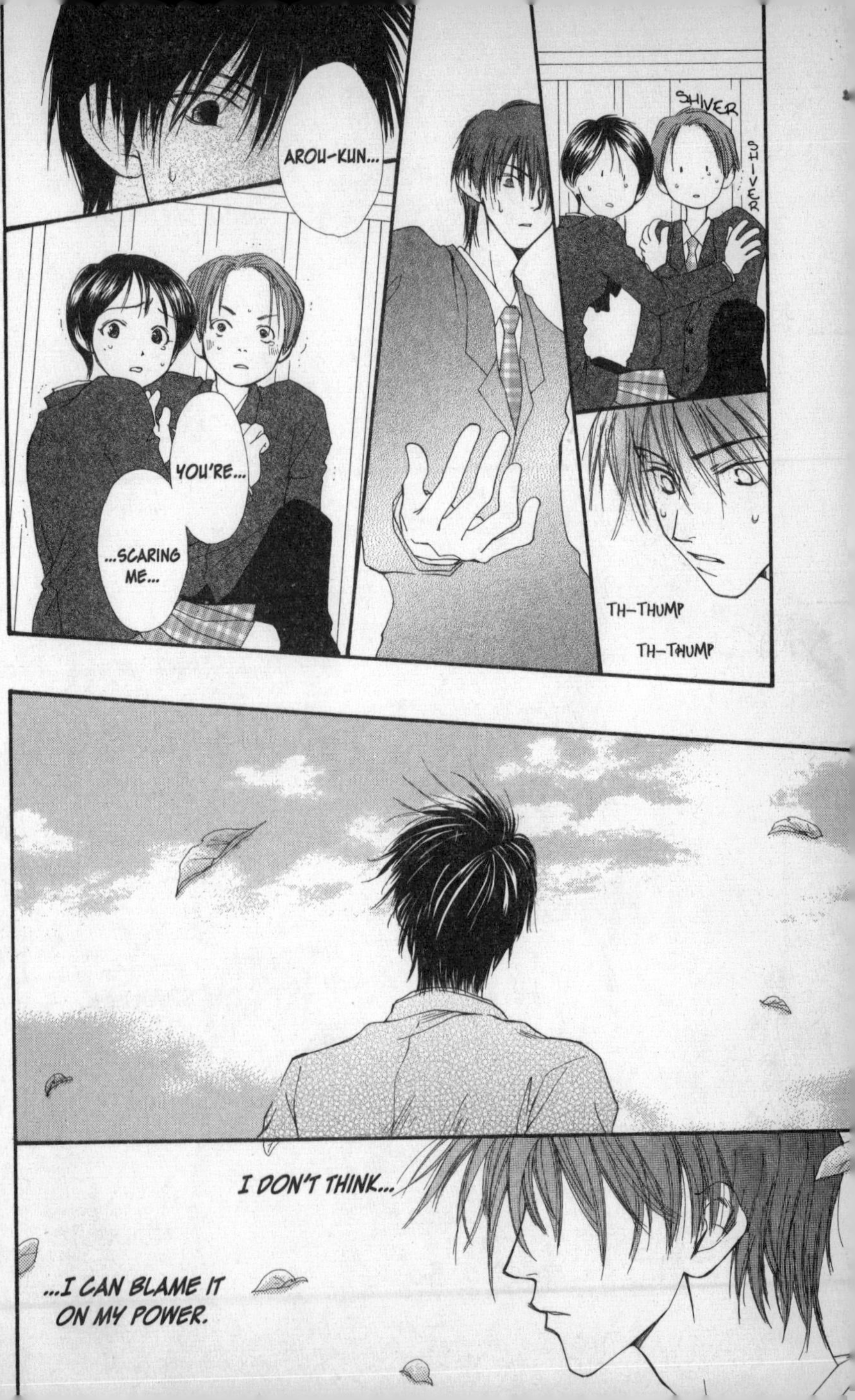
SHIVER
SHIVER
TH-THUMP
TH-THUMP
AROU-KUN...
YOU'RE...
...SCARING ME...
I DON'T THINK...
...I CAN BLAME IT ON MY POWER.

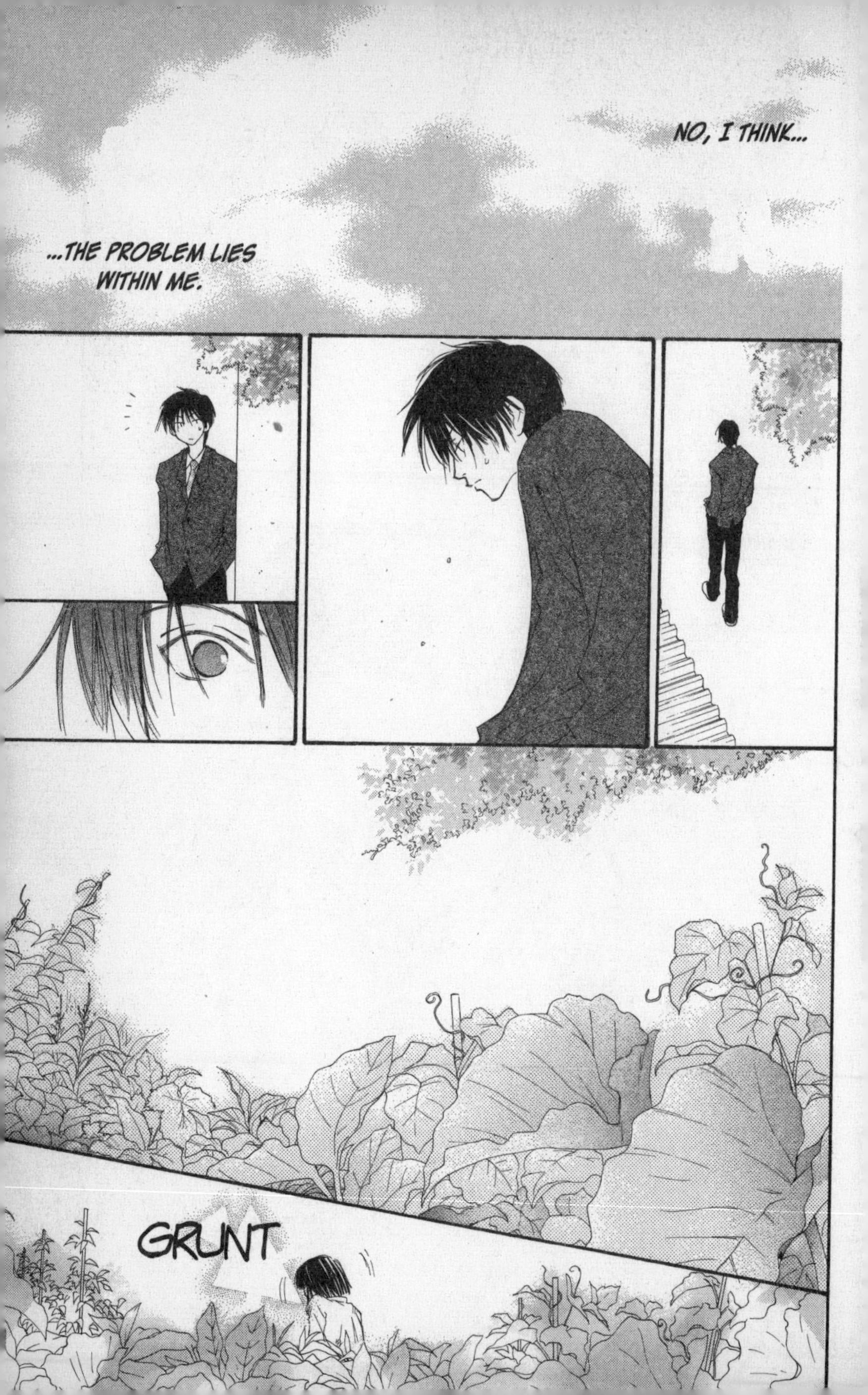
NO, I THINK...
...THE PROBLEM LIES WITHIN ME.
GRUNT

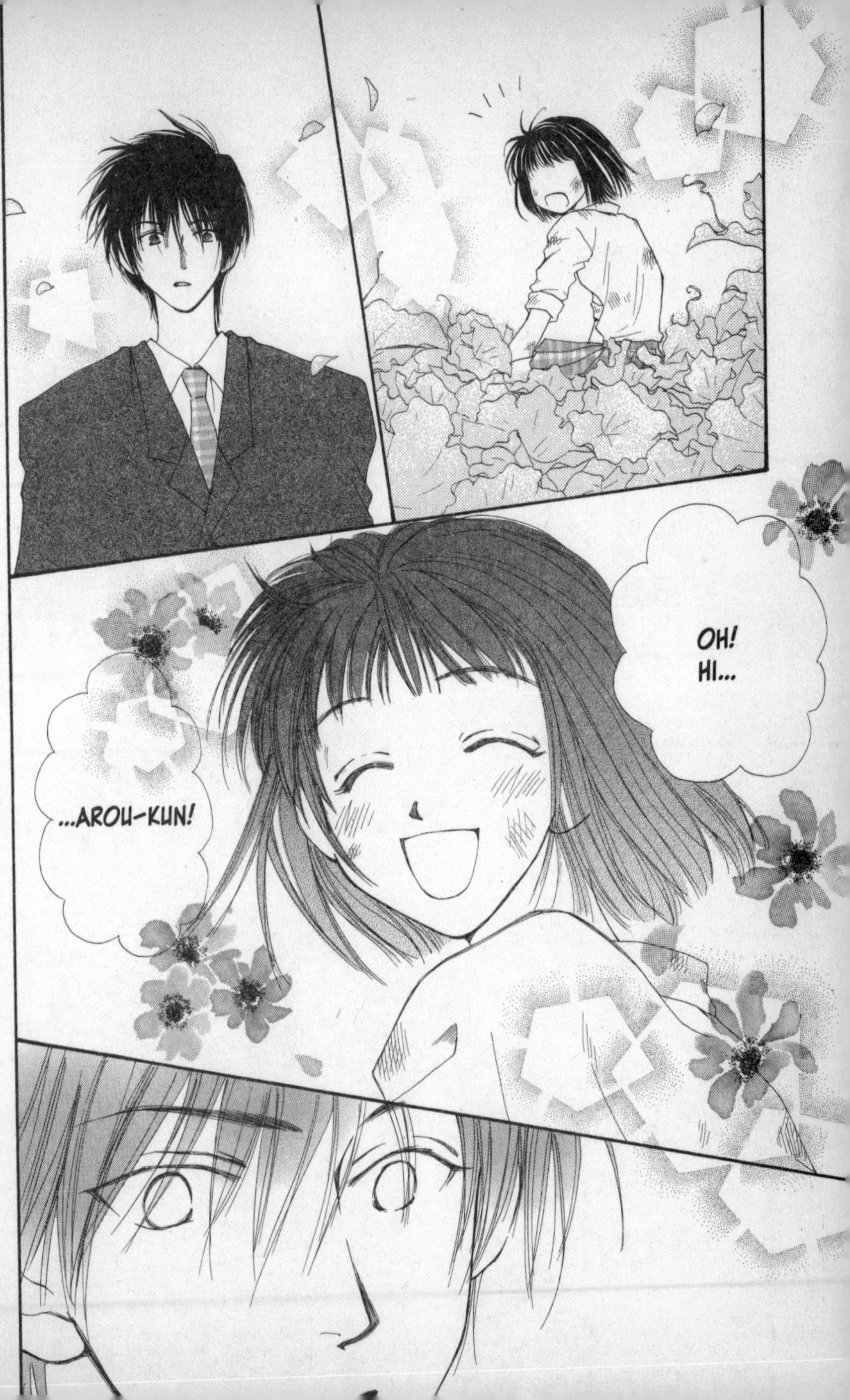
OH!
HI...
...AROU-KUN!

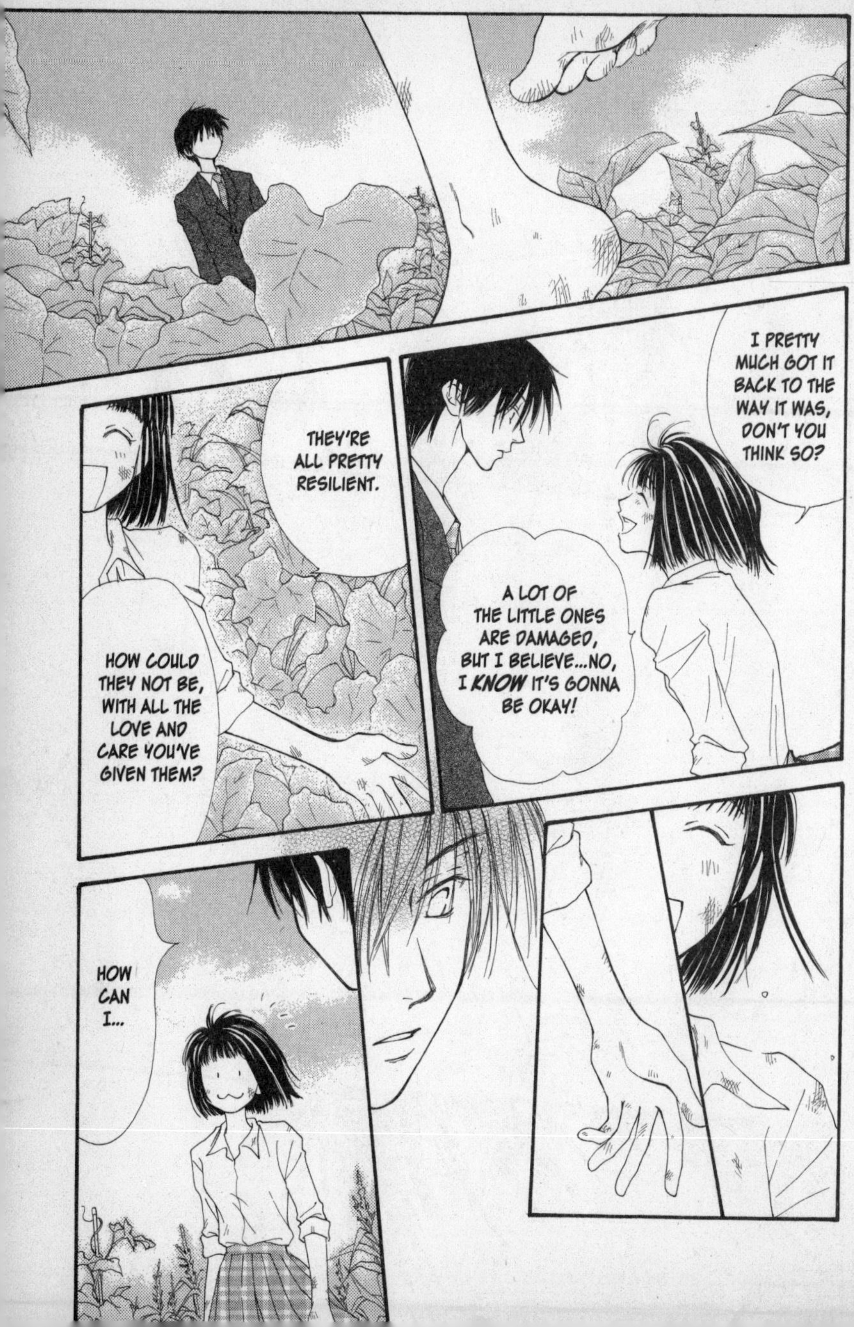
I PRETTY MUCH GOT IT BACK TO THE WAY IT WAS, DON'T YOU THINK SO?
A LOT OF THE LITTLE ONES ARE DAMAGED, BUT I BELIEVE...NO, I *KNOW* IT'S GONNA BE OKAY!
THEY'RE ALL PRETTY RESILIENT.
HOW COULD THEY NOT BE, WITH ALL THE LOVE AND CARE YOU'VE GIVEN THEM?
HOW CAN I...

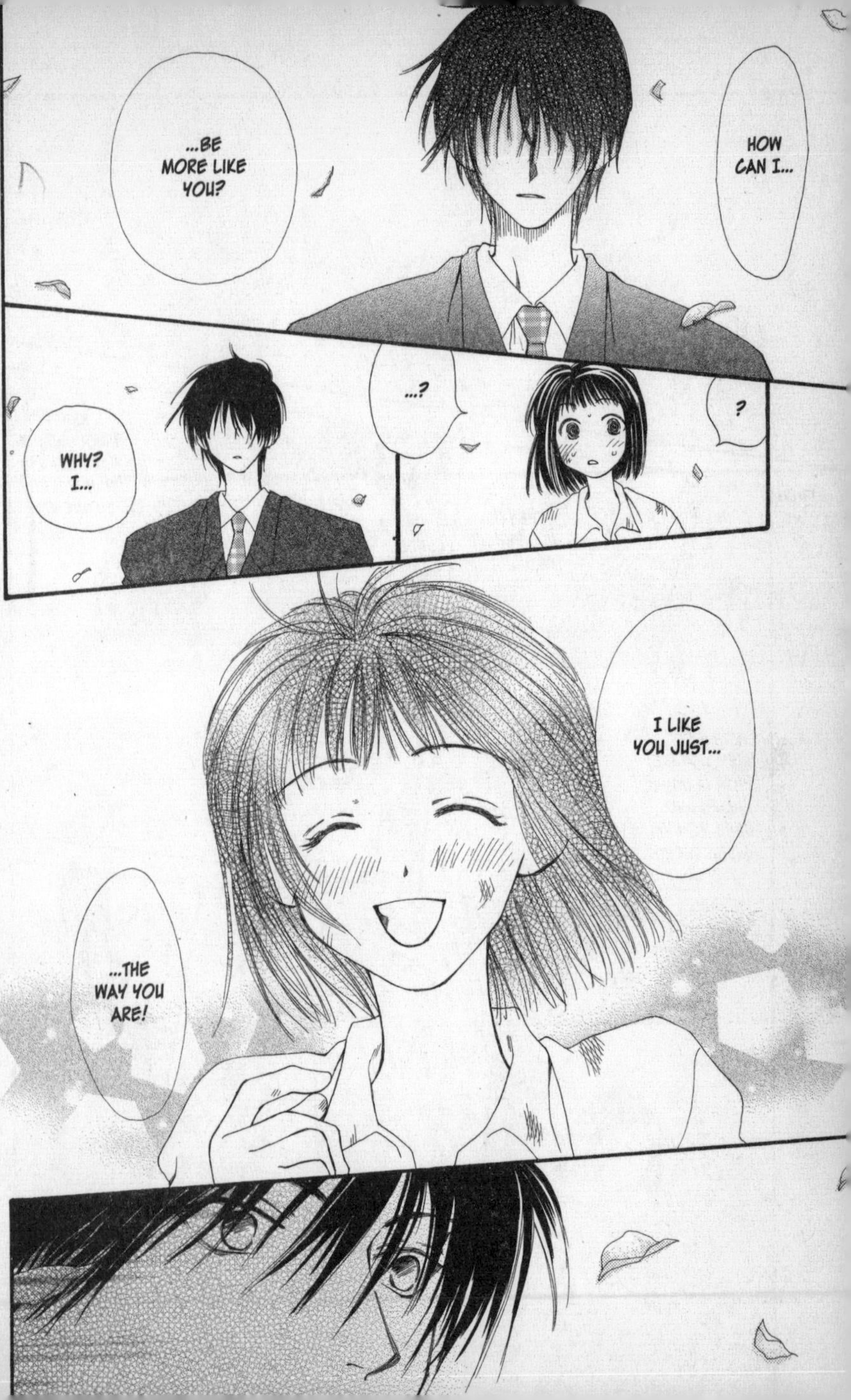
HOW CAN I...
...BE MORE LIKE YOU?
?
...?
WHY? I...
I LIKE YOU JUST...
...THE WAY YOU ARE!

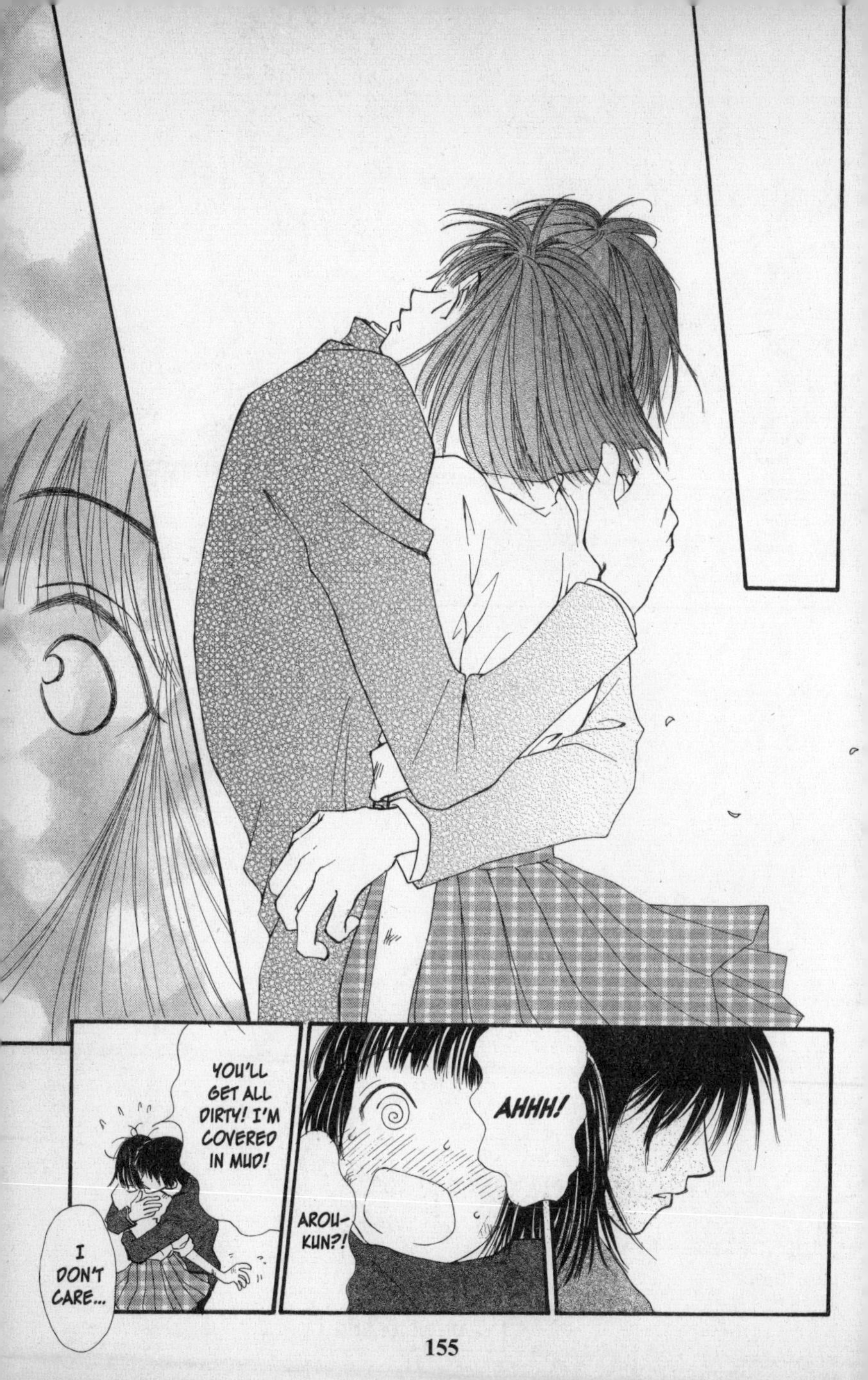
AHHH!
AROU-KUN?!
YOU'LL GET ALL DIRTY! I'M COVERED IN MUD!
I DON'T CARE...

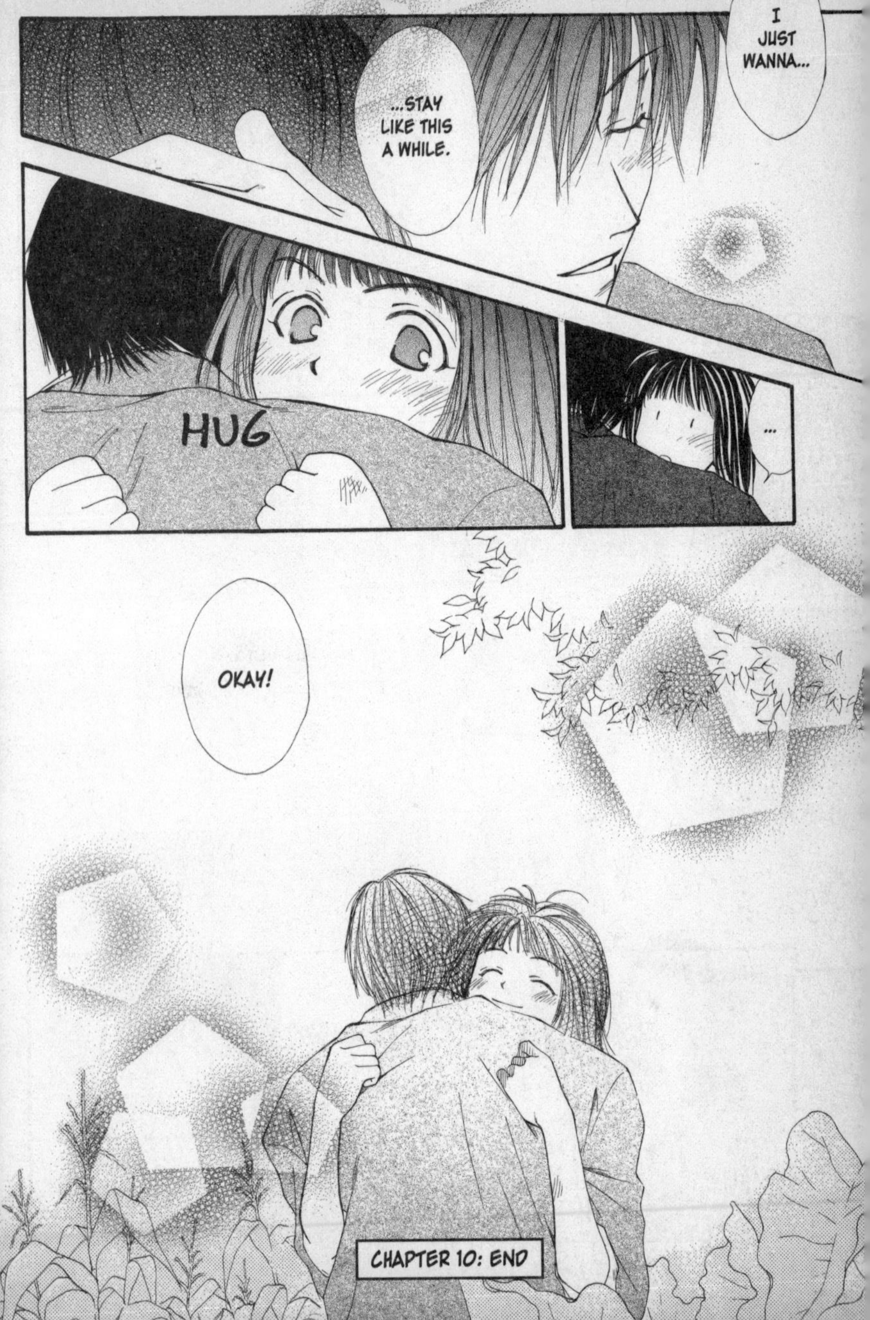
I JUST WANNA...
...STAY LIKE THIS A WHILE.
HUG
...
OKAY!
CHAPTER 10: END

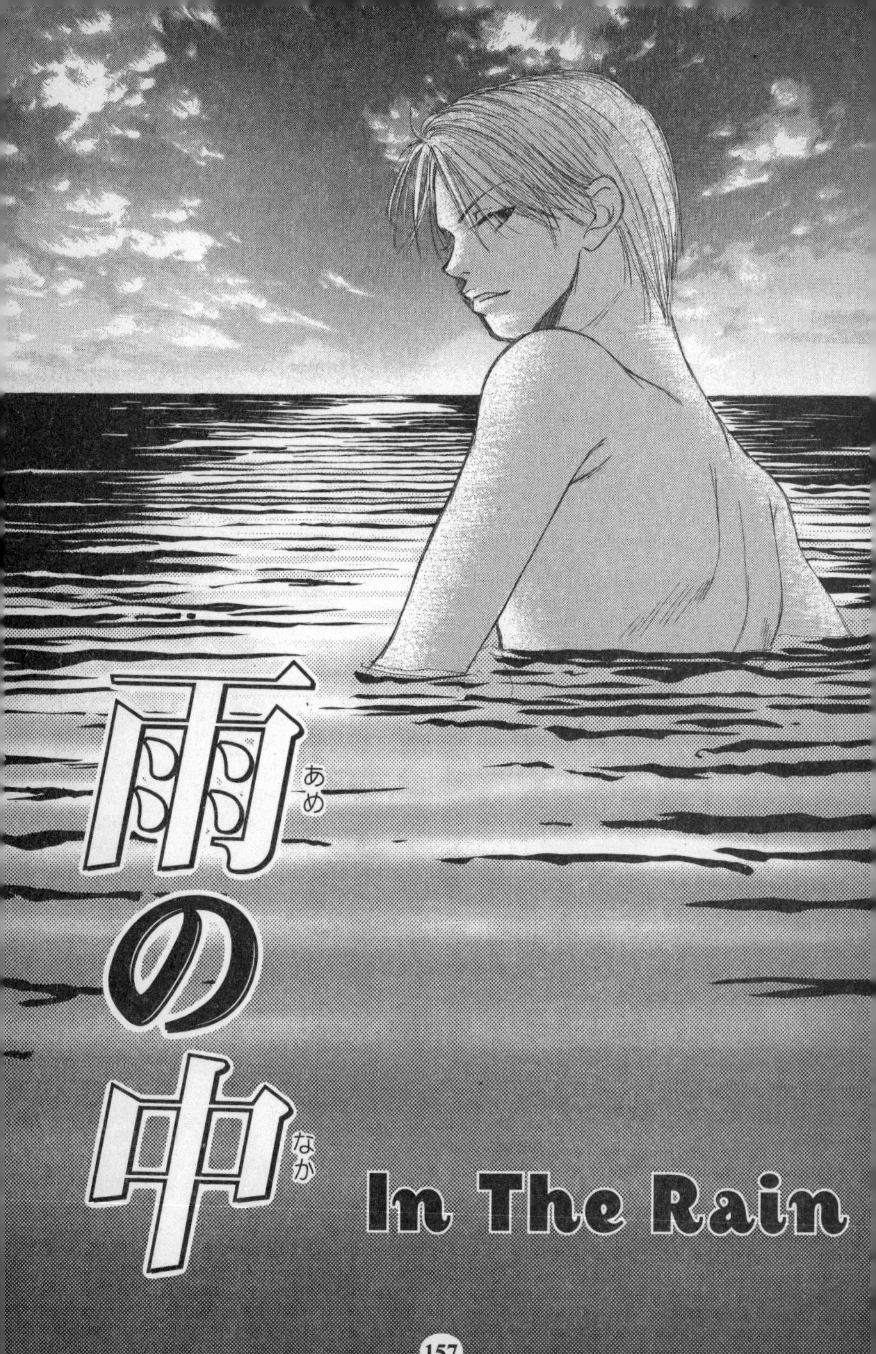
雨の中
あめ なか
In The Rain

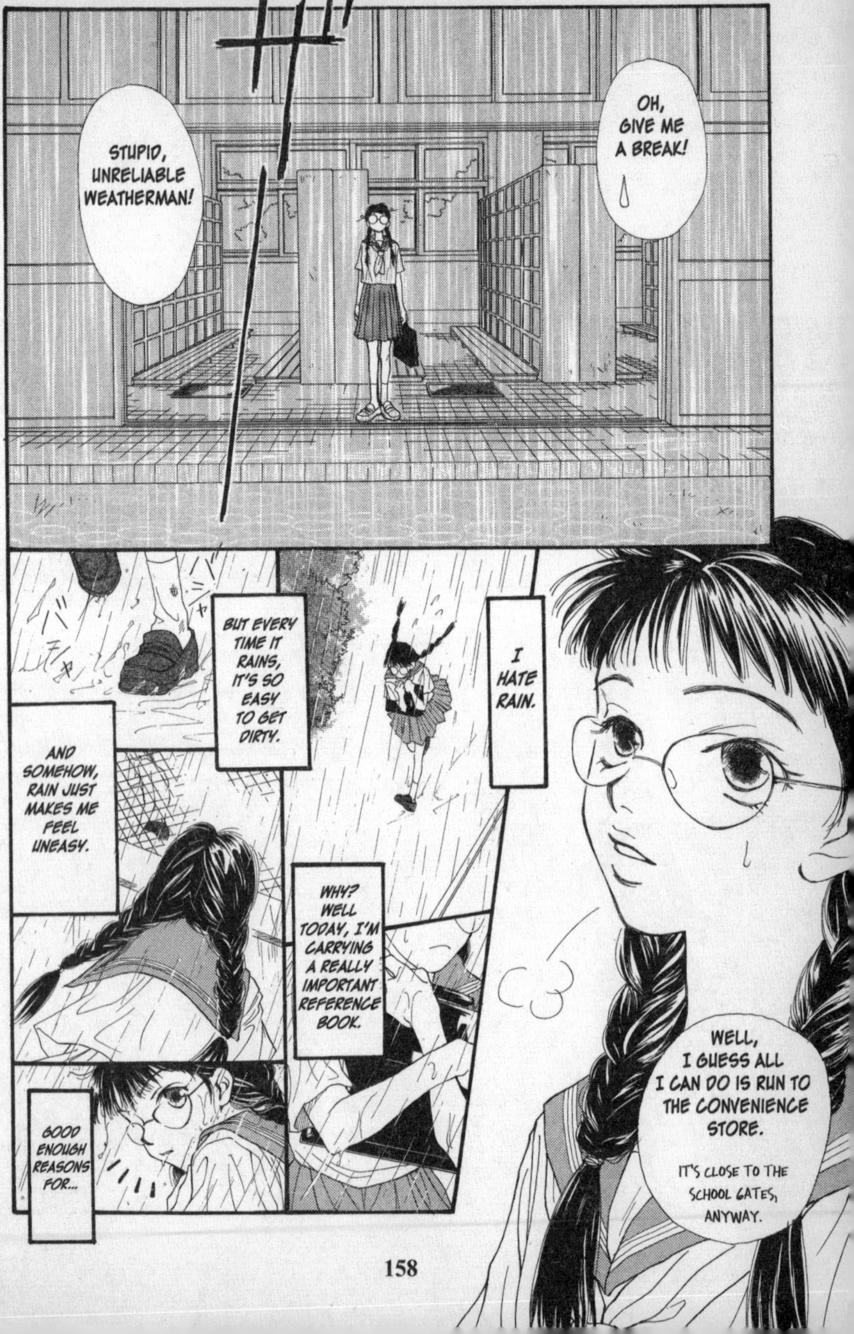
OH, GIVE ME A BREAK!
STUPID, UNRELIABLE WEATHERMAN!
I HATE RAIN.
BUT EVERY TIME IT RAINS, IT'S SO EASY TO GET DIRTY.
AND SOMEHOW, RAIN JUST MAKES ME FEEL UNEASY.
WHY? WELL TODAY, I'M CARRYING A REALLY IMPORTANT REFERENCE BOOK.
GOOD ENOUGH REASONS FOR...
WELL, I GUESS ALL I CAN DO IS RUN TO THE CONVENIENCE STORE.
IT'S CLOSE TO THE SCHOOL GATES, ANYWAY.

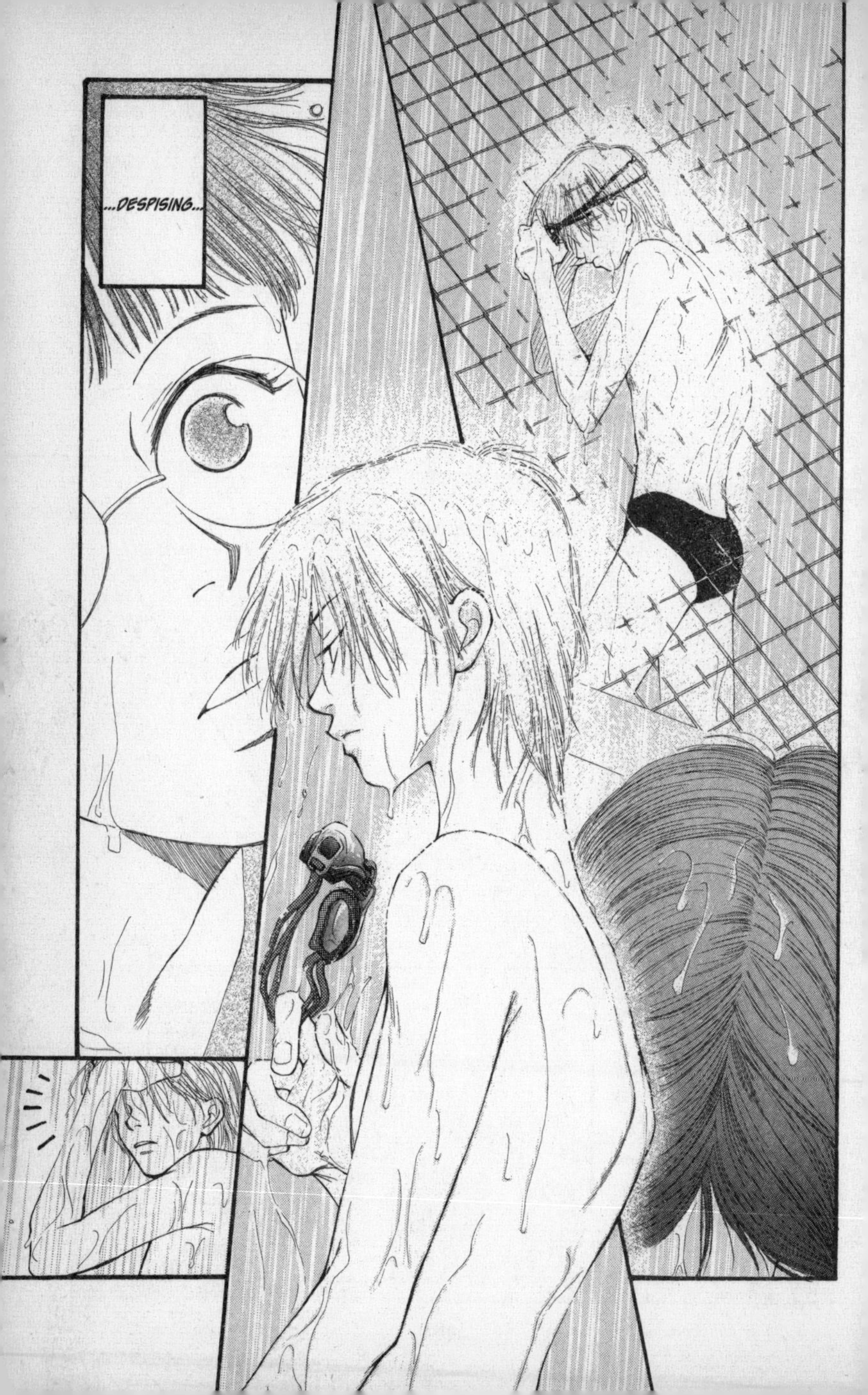
...DESPISING...

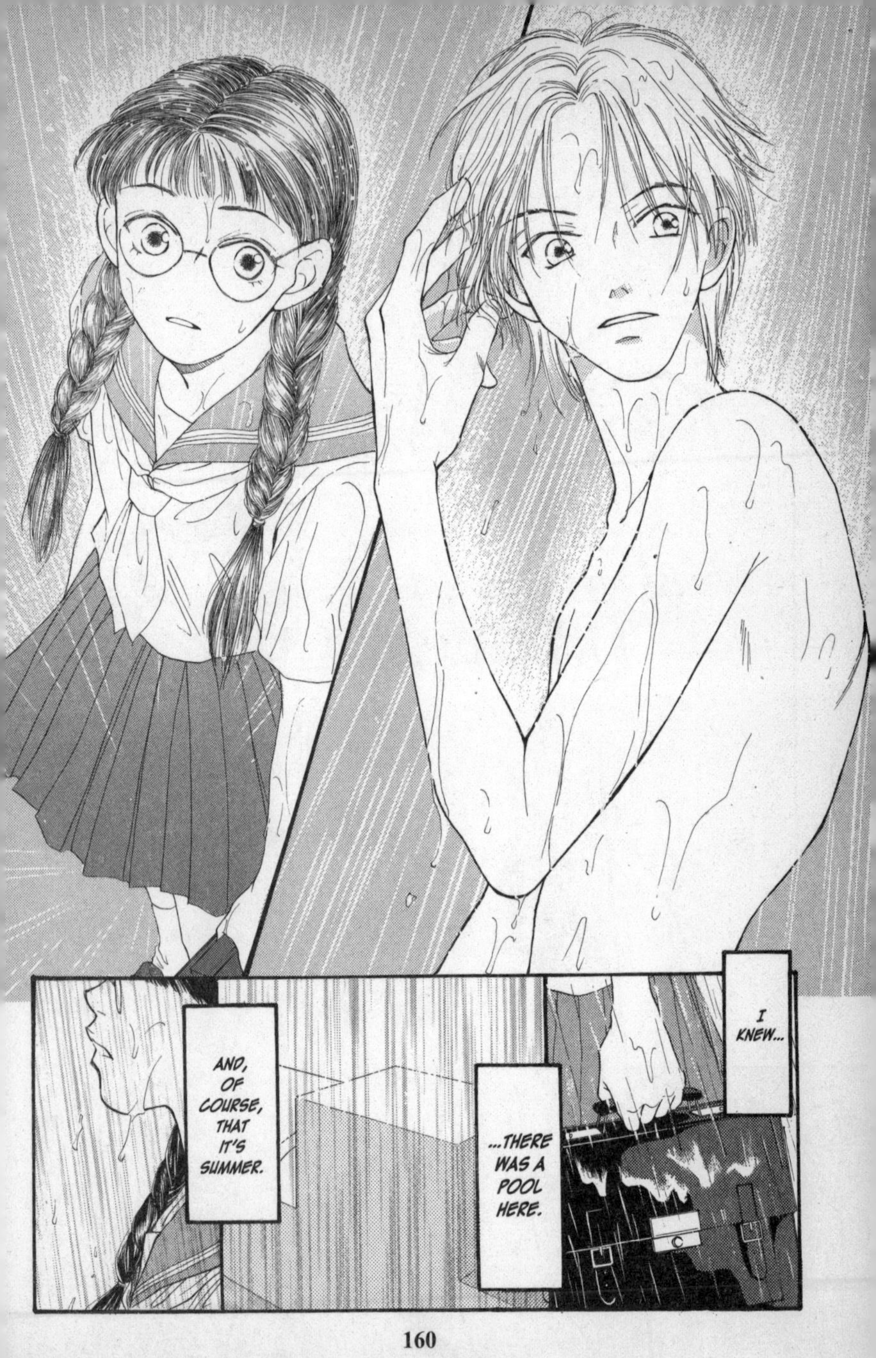
I KNEW...
...THERE WAS A POOL HERE.
AND, OF COURSE, THAT IT'S SUMMER.

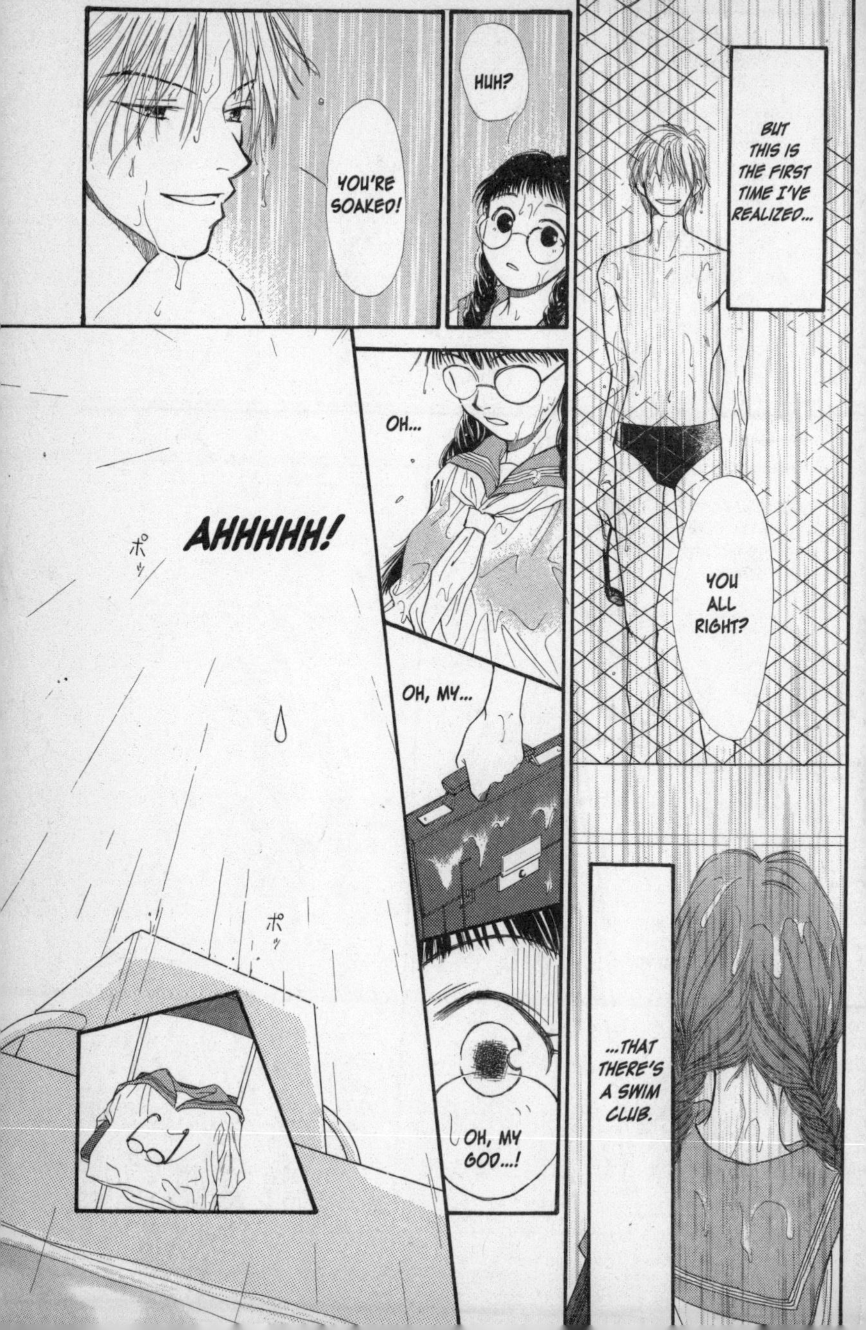
BUT THIS IS THE FIRST TIME I'VE REALIZED...
YOU ALL RIGHT?
...THAT THERE'S A SWIM CLUB.
HUH?
YOU'RE SOAKED!
OH...
OH, MY...
OH, MY GOD...!
AHHHHH!
ポッ
ポッ

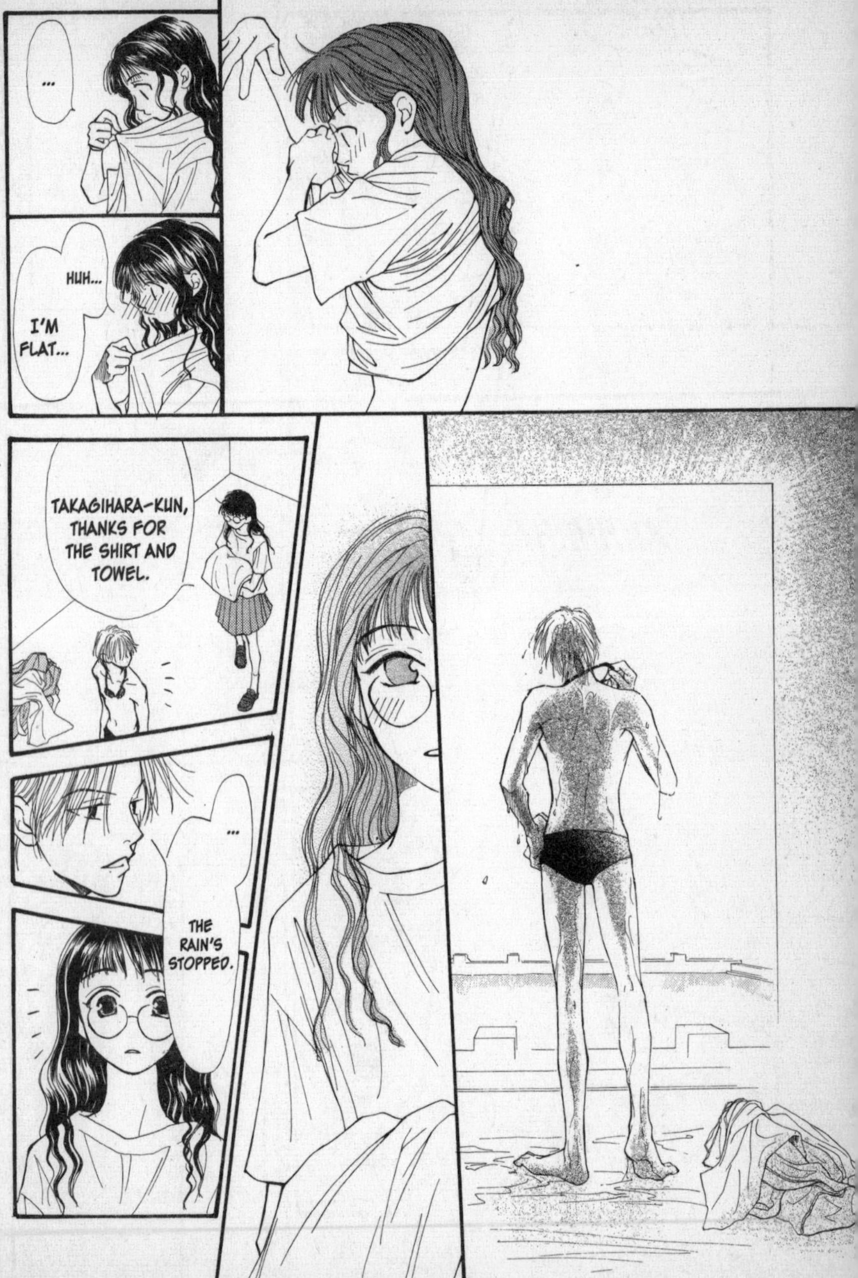
...
HUH... I'M FLAT...
TAKAGIHARA-KUN, THANKS FOR THE SHIRT AND TOWEL.
...
THE RAIN'S STOPPED.

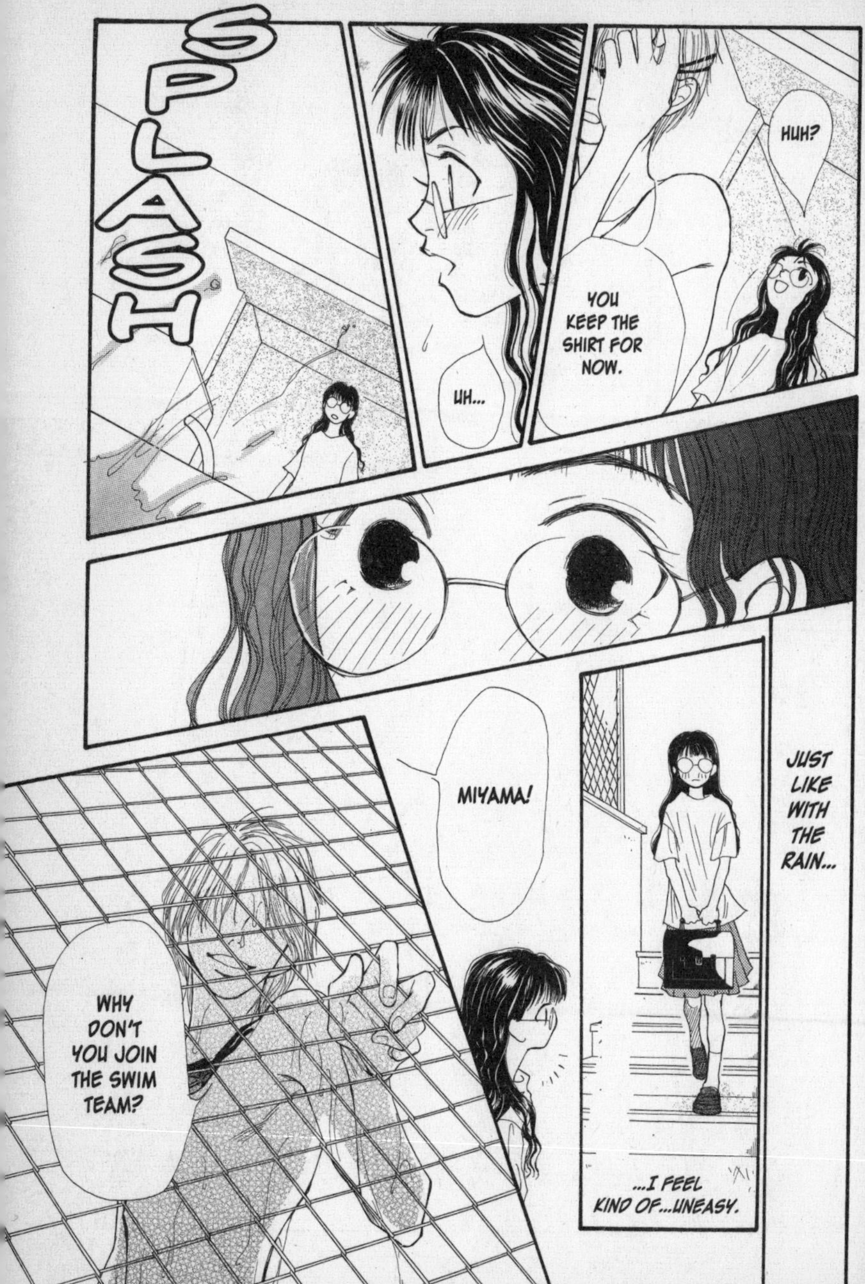
HUH?
YOU KEEP THE SHIRT FOR NOW.
UH...
SPLASH
JUST LIKE WITH THE RAIN...
...I FEEL KIND OF...UNEASY.
MIYAMA!
WHY DON'T YOU JOIN THE SWIM TEAM?

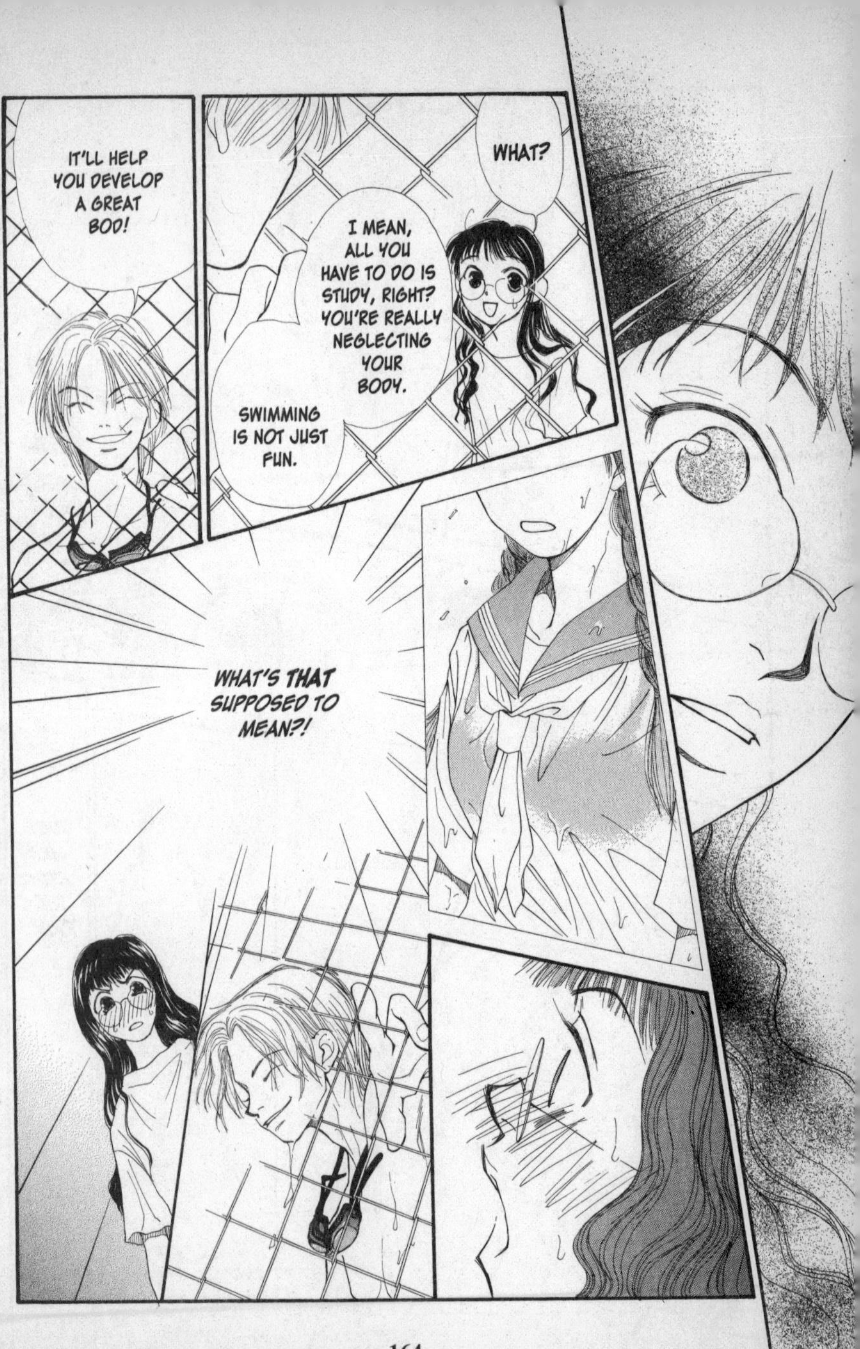
WHAT?
I MEAN, ALL YOU HAVE TO DO IS STUDY, RIGHT? YOU'RE REALLY NEGLECTING YOUR BODY.
SWIMMING IS NOT JUST FUN.
IT'LL HELP YOU DEVELOP A GREAT BOD!
WHAT'S THAT SUPPOSED TO MEAN?!

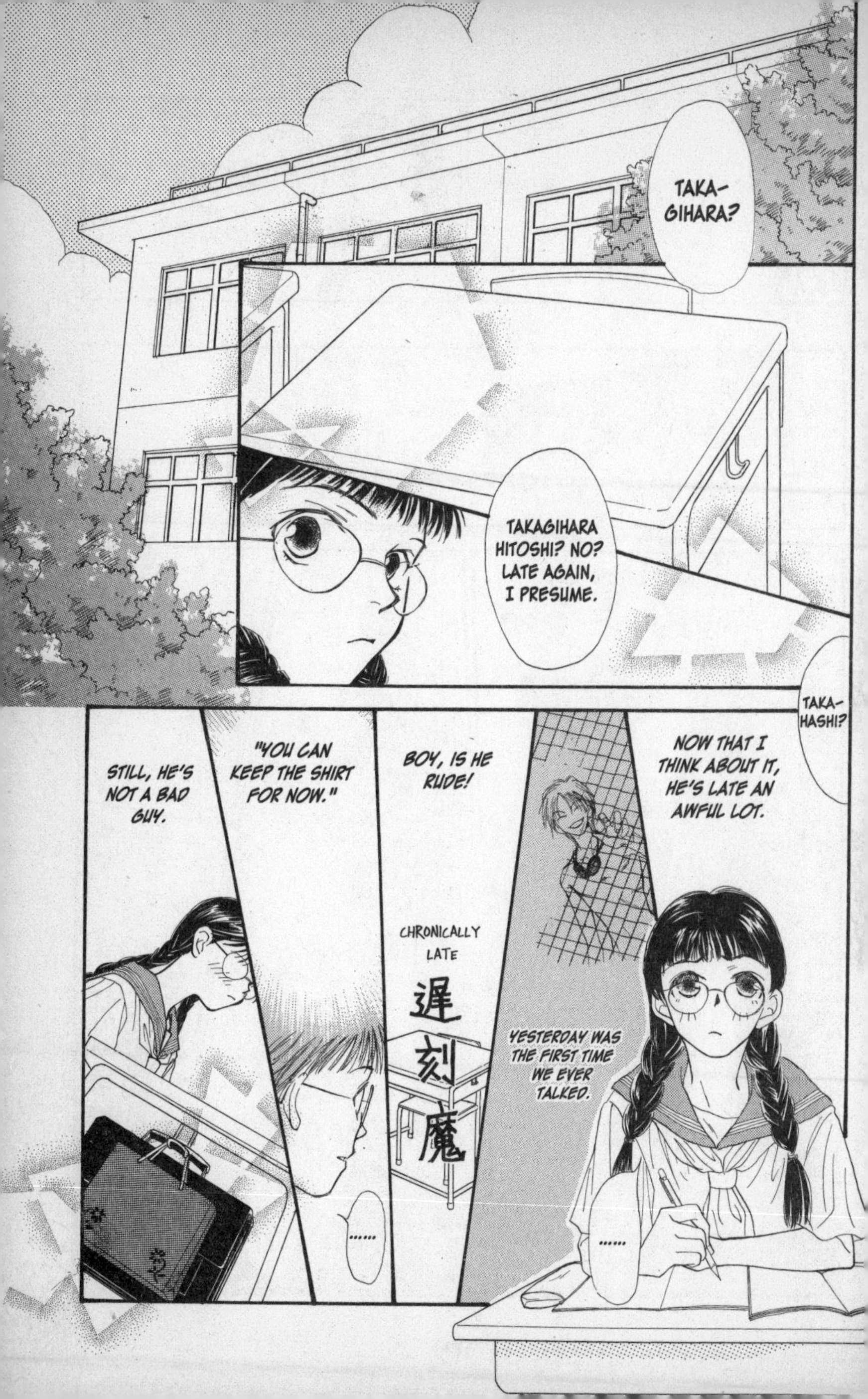
TAKA-GIHARA?
TAKAGIHARA HITOSHI? NO? LATE AGAIN, I PRESUME.
TAKA-HASHI?
NOW THAT I THINK ABOUT IT, HE'S LATE AN AWFUL LOT.
YESTERDAY WAS THE FIRST TIME WE EVER TALKED.
......
BOY, IS HE RUDE!
CHRONICALLY LATE
遅刻魔
"YOU CAN KEEP THE SHIRT FOR NOW."
......
STILL, HE'S NOT A BAD GUY.

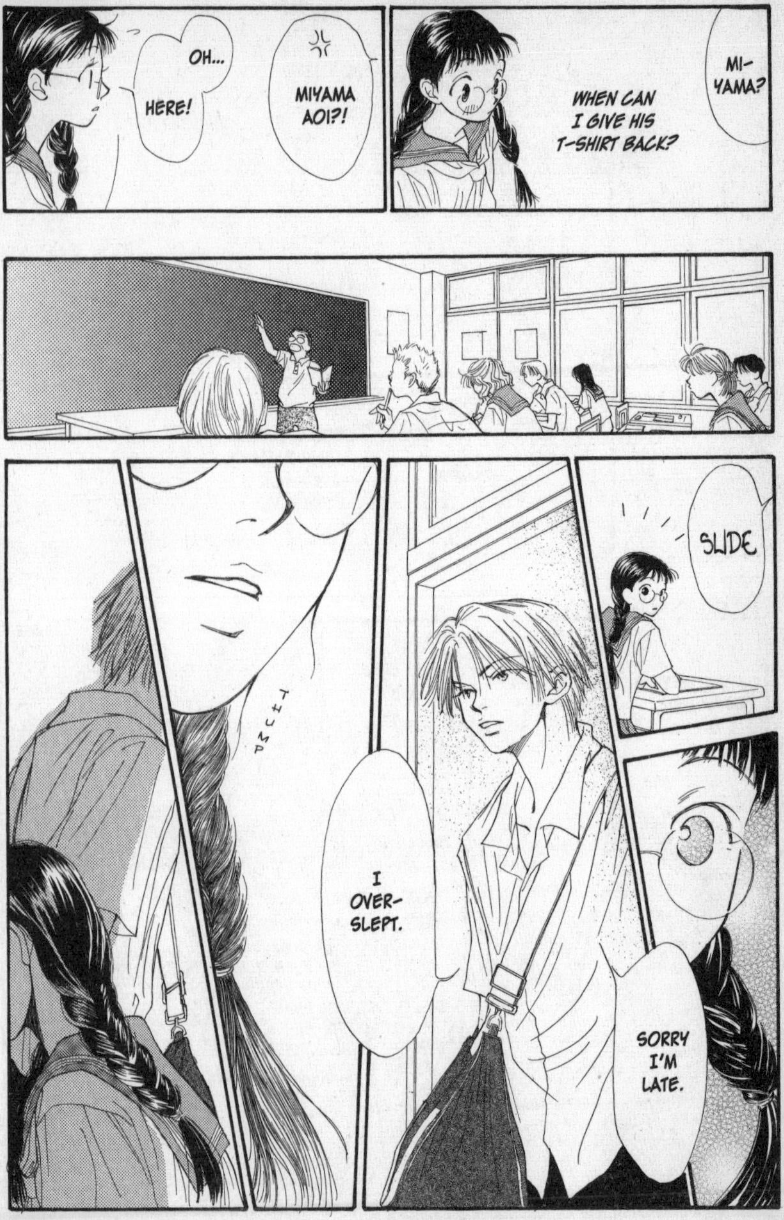
MI-YAMA?
WHEN CAN I GIVE HIS T-SHIRT BACK?
MIYAMA AOI?!
OH...
HERE!
SLIDE
SORRY I'M LATE.
I OVER-SLEPT.
THUMP

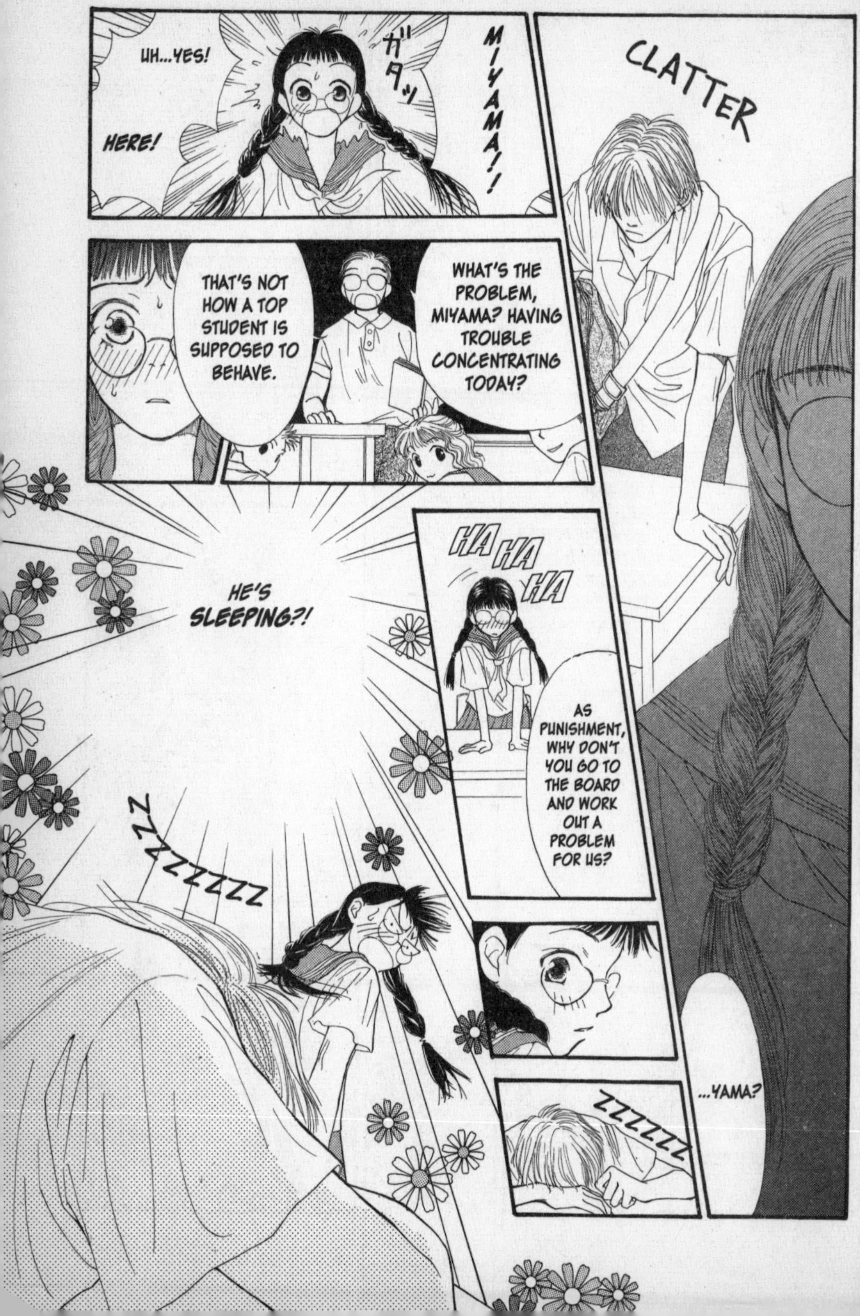
CLATTER
MIYAMA!!
ガタッ
UH...YES!
HERE!
WHAT'S THE PROBLEM, MIYAMA? HAVING TROUBLE CONCENTRATING TODAY?
THAT'S NOT HOW A TOP STUDENT IS SUPPOSED TO BEHAVE.
HA HA HA
AS PUNISHMENT, WHY DON'T YOU GO TO THE BOARD AND WORK OUT A PROBLEM FOR US?
...YAMA?
ZZZZZZ
HE'S SLEEPING?!
ZZZZZZZZ

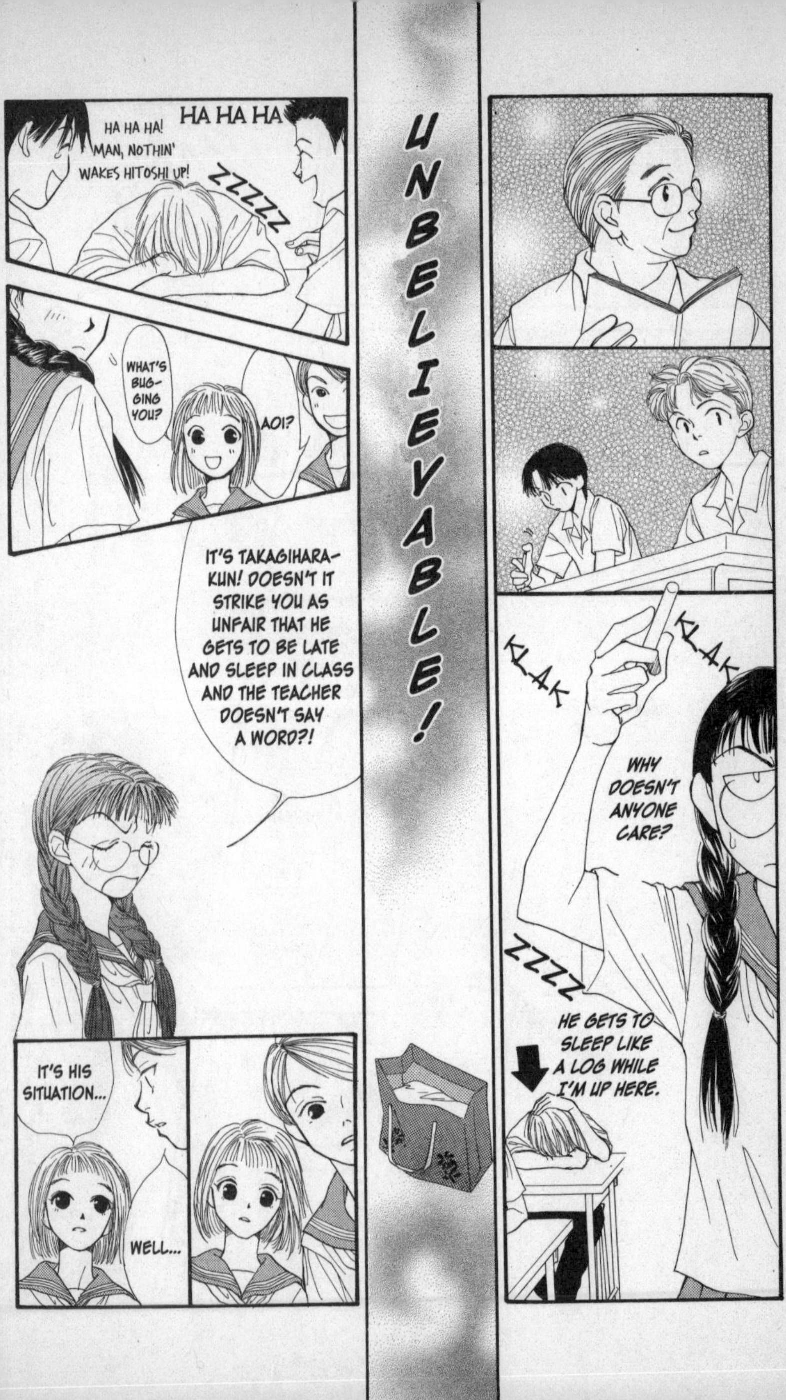
KLAK
KLAK
WHY DOESN'T ANYONE CARE?
ZZZZ
HE GETS TO SLEEP LIKE A LOG WHILE I'M UP HERE.
UNBELIEVABLE!
HA HA HA
HA HA HA! MAN, NOTHIN' WAKES HITOSHI UP!
ZZZZZ
AOI?
WHAT'S BUG-GING YOU?
IT'S TAKAGIHARA-KUN! DOESN'T IT STRIKE YOU AS UNFAIR THAT HE GETS TO BE LATE AND SLEEP IN CLASS AND THE TEACHER DOESN'T SAY A WORD?!
IT'S HIS SITUATION...
WELL...

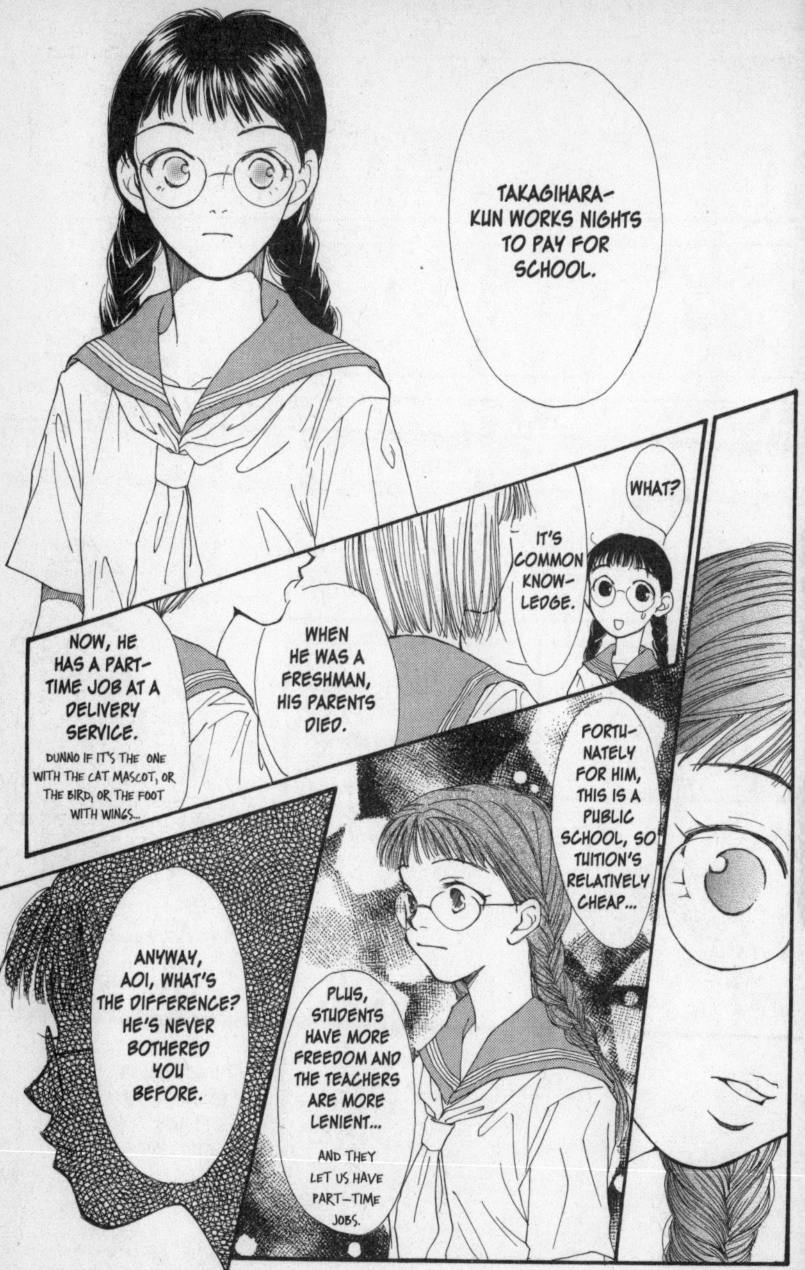
TAKAGIHARA-KUN WORKS NIGHTS TO PAY FOR SCHOOL.
WHAT?
IT'S COMMON KNOWLEDGE.
WHEN HE WAS A FRESHMAN, HIS PARENTS DIED.
NOW, HE HAS A PART-TIME JOB AT A DELIVERY SERVICE.
DUNNO IF IT'S THE ONE WITH THE CAT MASCOT, OR THE BIRD, OR THE FOOT WITH WINGS...
FORTUNATELY FOR HIM, THIS IS A PUBLIC SCHOOL, SO TUITION'S RELATIVELY CHEAP...
PLUS, STUDENTS HAVE MORE FREEDOM AND THE TEACHERS ARE MORE LENIENT...
AND THEY LET US HAVE PART-TIME JOBS.
ANYWAY, AOI, WHAT'S THE DIFFERENCE? HE'S NEVER BOTHERED YOU BEFORE.

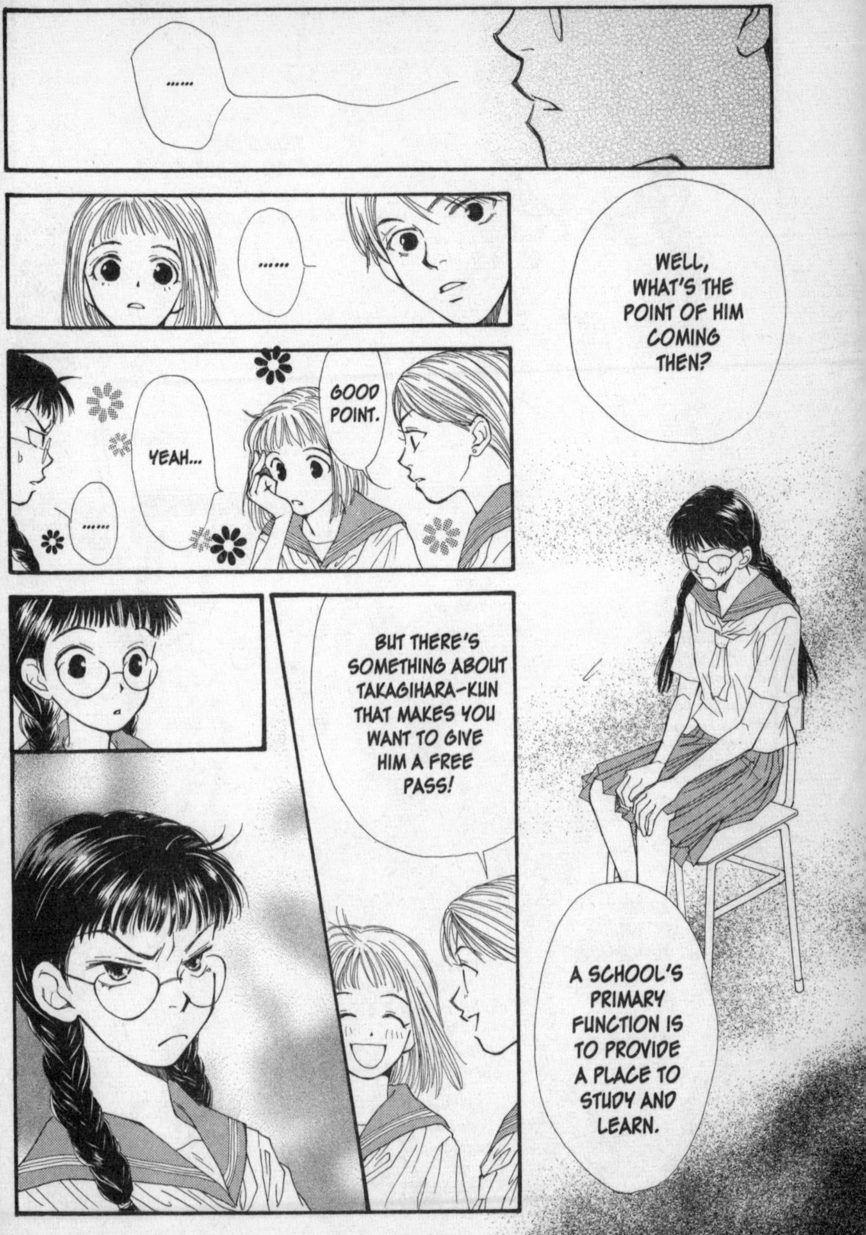
......
WELL, WHAT'S THE POINT OF HIM COMING THEN?
A SCHOOL'S PRIMARY FUNCTION IS TO PROVIDE A PLACE TO STUDY AND LEARN.
......
GOOD POINT.
YEAH...
......
BUT THERE'S SOMETHING ABOUT TAKAGIHARA-KUN THAT MAKES YOU WANT TO GIVE HIM A FREE PASS!

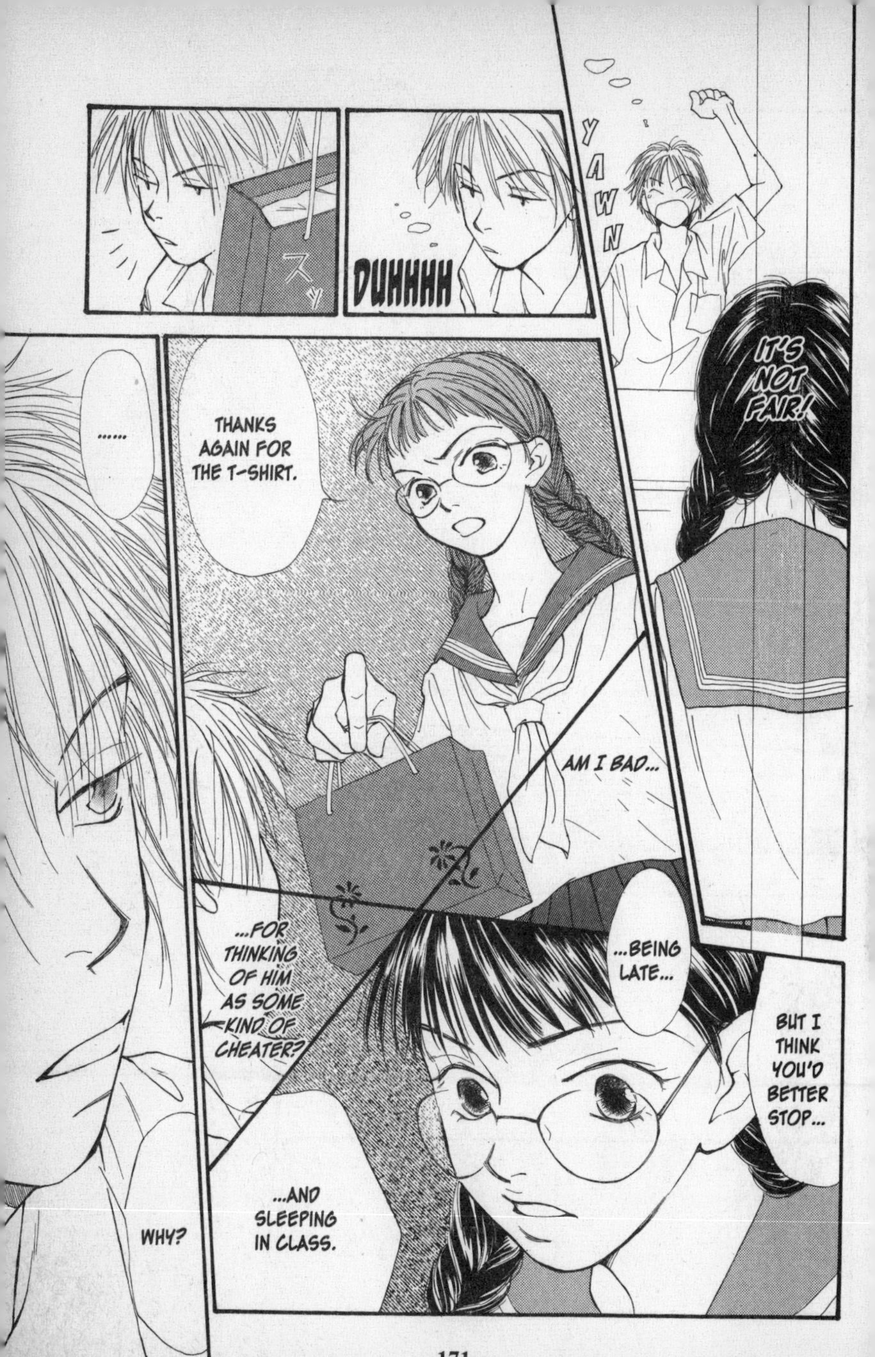
YAWN
IT'S NOT FAIR!
DUHHHH
スッ
THANKS AGAIN FOR THE T-SHIRT.
AM I BAD...
...FOR THINKING OF HIM AS SOME KIND OF CHEATER?
...BEING LATE...
BUT I THINK YOU'D BETTER STOP...
...AND SLEEPING IN CLASS.
......
WHY?

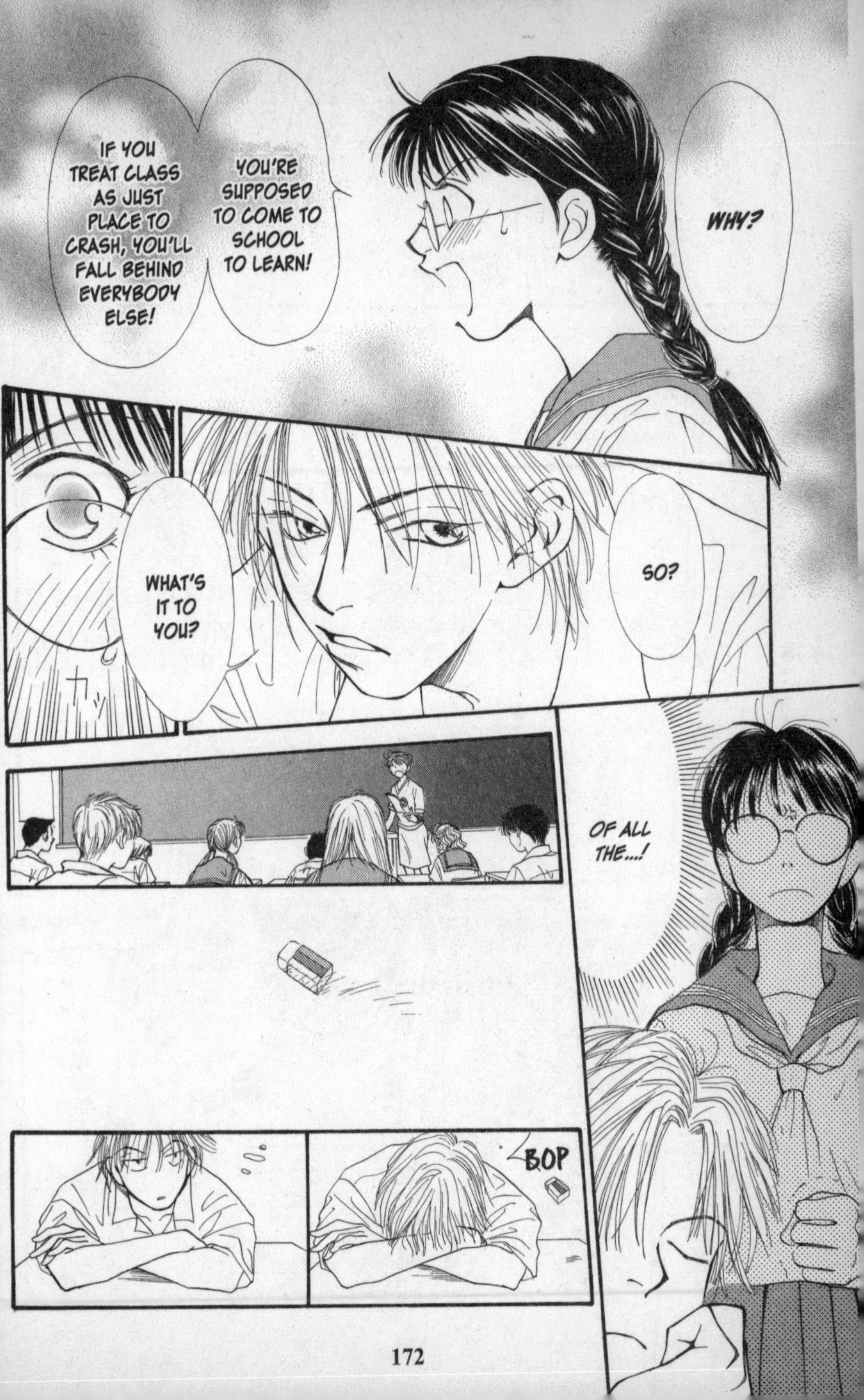
WHY?
YOU'RE SUPPOSED TO COME TO SCHOOL TO LEARN!
IF YOU TREAT CLASS AS JUST PLACE TO CRASH, YOU'LL FALL BEHIND EVERYBODY ELSE!
SO?
WHAT'S IT TO YOU?
カッ
OF ALL THE...!
BOP

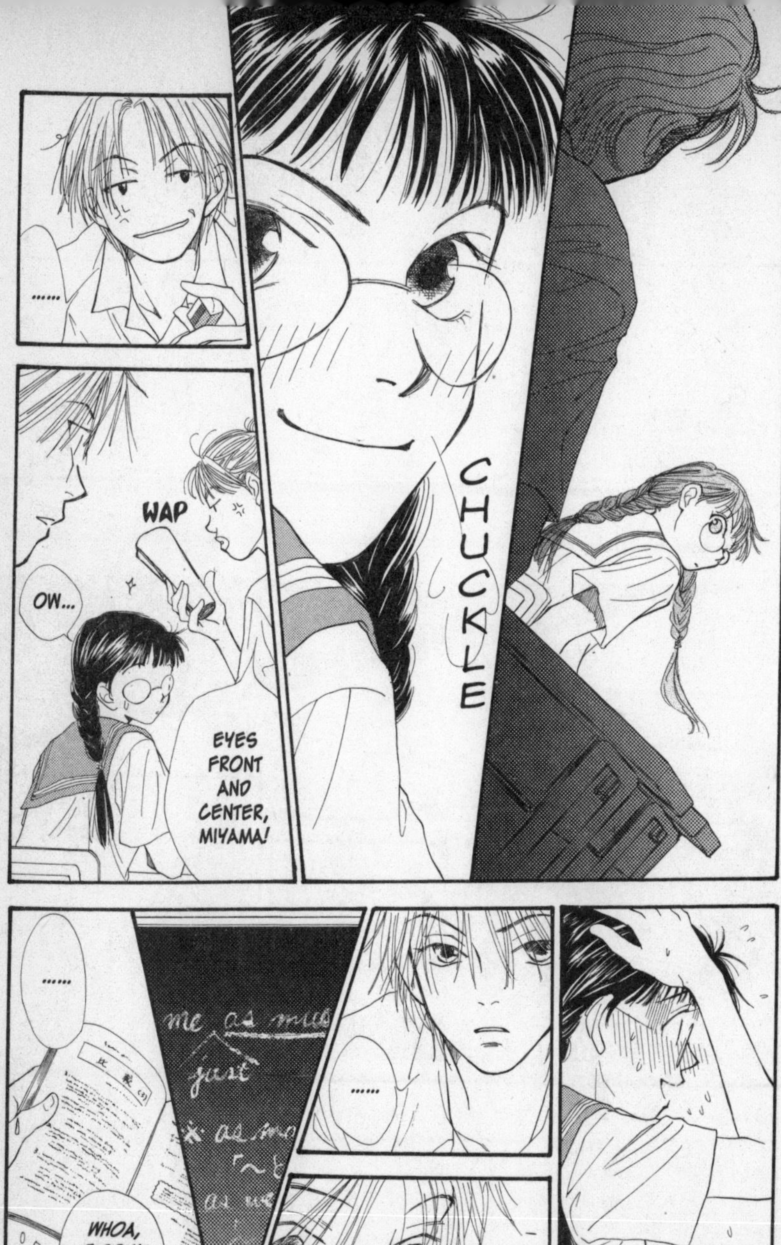
CHUCKLE
......
WAP
OW...
EYES FRONT AND CENTER, MIYAMA!
......
......
WHOA, I DON'T GET THIS AT ALL!

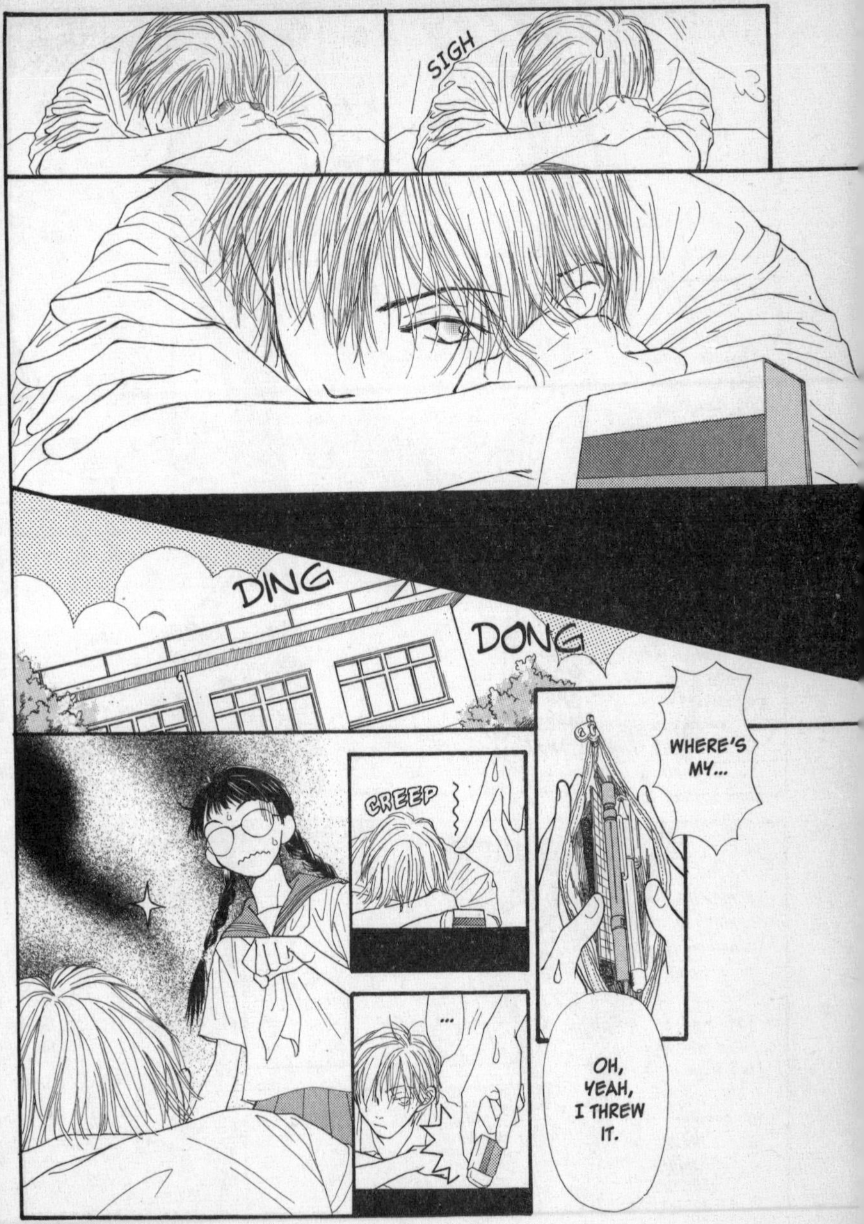
SIGH
DING
DONG
WHERE'S MY...
OH, YEAH, I THREW IT.
CREEP
...

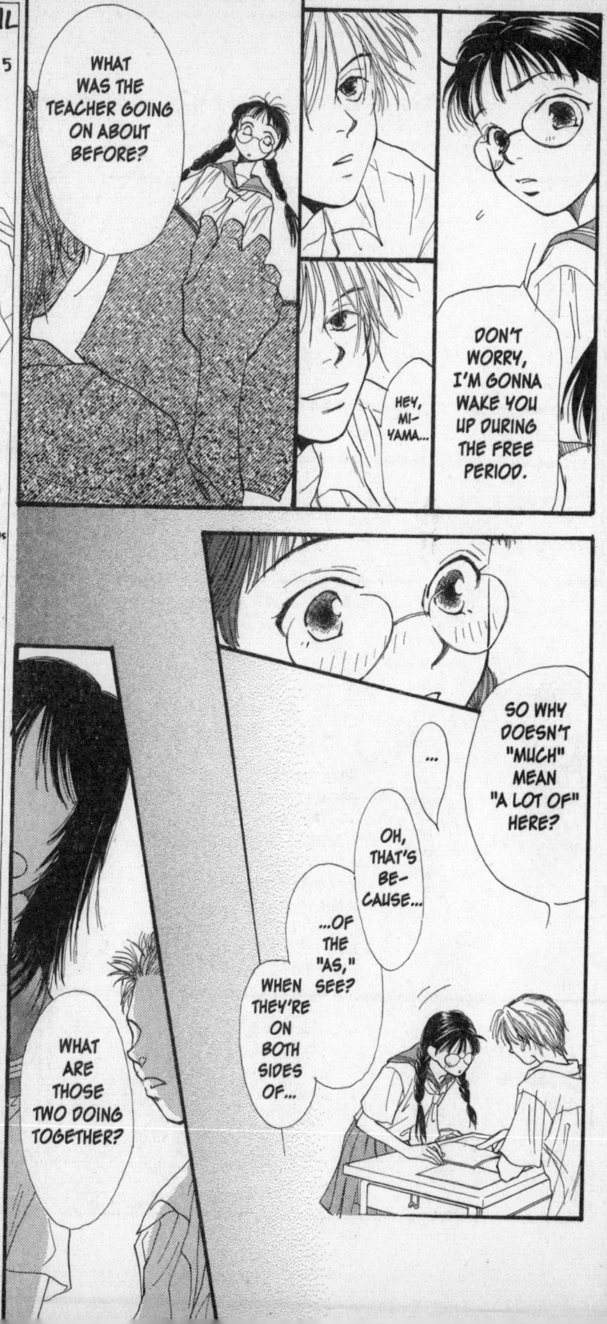
DON'T WORRY, I'M GONNA WAKE YOU UP DURING THE FREE PERIOD.
HEY, MI-YAMA...
WHAT WAS THE TEACHER GOING ON ABOUT BEFORE?
SO WHY DOESN'T "MUCH" MEAN "A LOT OF" HERE?
...
OH, THAT'S BE-CAUSE...
...OF THE "AS," SEE?
WHEN THEY'RE ON BOTH SIDES OF...
WHAT ARE THOSE TWO DOING TOGETHER?

SAKURA MAIL

NO. 5

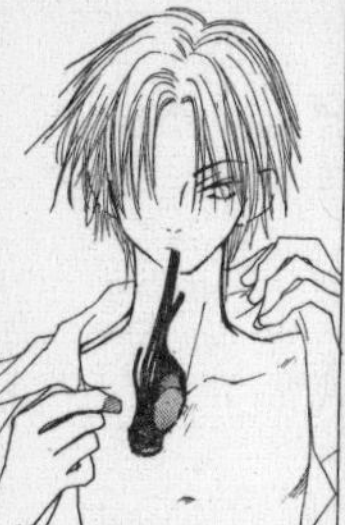

I remember having a blast creating "In the Rain," especially since I could justify drawing a half—naked guy in the story (Yeah, I've got a dirty mind. So sue me). Also, this was the first story where I put down straight into manga form what I really wanted to say. The end product, however, came out completely different and I don't think I got my message across. But when all is said and done, the story belongs to the readers, and as long as they get a kick out of it, that's enough to make me happy. When I look at the story now, I like it because I can feel the enthusiastic vibe I had while drawing it. ...Well, I'm running out of space, so I'll just sign off here. See you next time, ♡ Sakura!

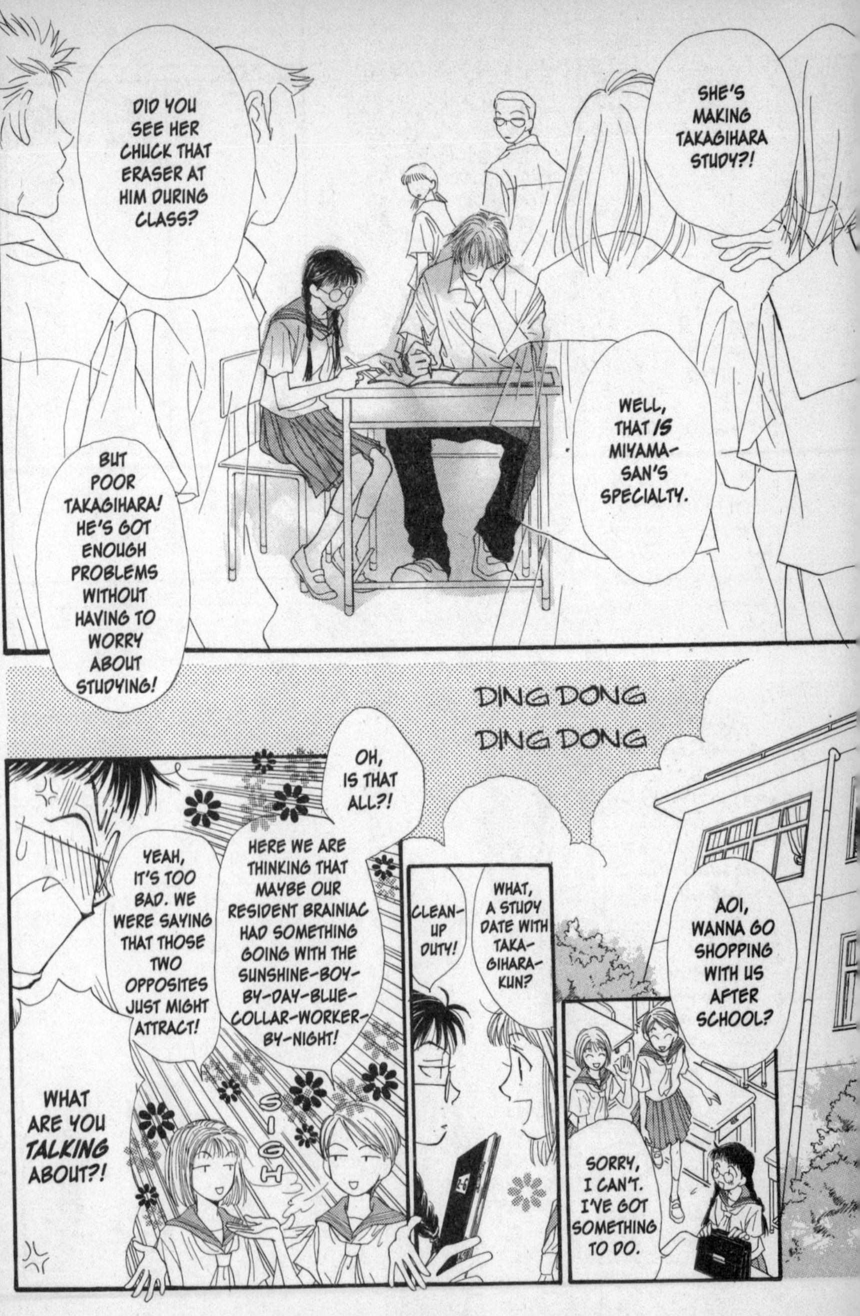
SHE'S MAKING TAKAGIHARA STUDY?!
DID YOU SEE HER CHUCK THAT ERASER AT HIM DURING CLASS?
WELL, THAT IS MIYAMA-SAN'S SPECIALTY.
BUT POOR TAKAGIHARA! HE'S GOT ENOUGH PROBLEMS WITHOUT HAVING TO WORRY ABOUT STUDYING!
DING DONG DING DONG
AOI, WANNA GO SHOPPING WITH US AFTER SCHOOL?
SORRY, I CAN'T. I'VE GOT SOMETHING TO DO.
WHAT, A STUDY DATE WITH TAKA-GIHARA-KUN?
CLEAN-UP DUTY!
OH, IS THAT ALL?!
HERE WE ARE THINKING THAT MAYBE OUR RESIDENT BRAINIAC HAD SOMETHING GOING WITH THE SUNSHINE-BOY-BY-DAY-BLUE-COLLAR-WORKER-BY-NIGHT!
YEAH, IT'S TOO BAD. WE WERE SAYING THAT THOSE TWO OPPOSITES JUST MIGHT ATTRACT!
SIGH
WHAT ARE YOU *TALKING* ABOUT?!

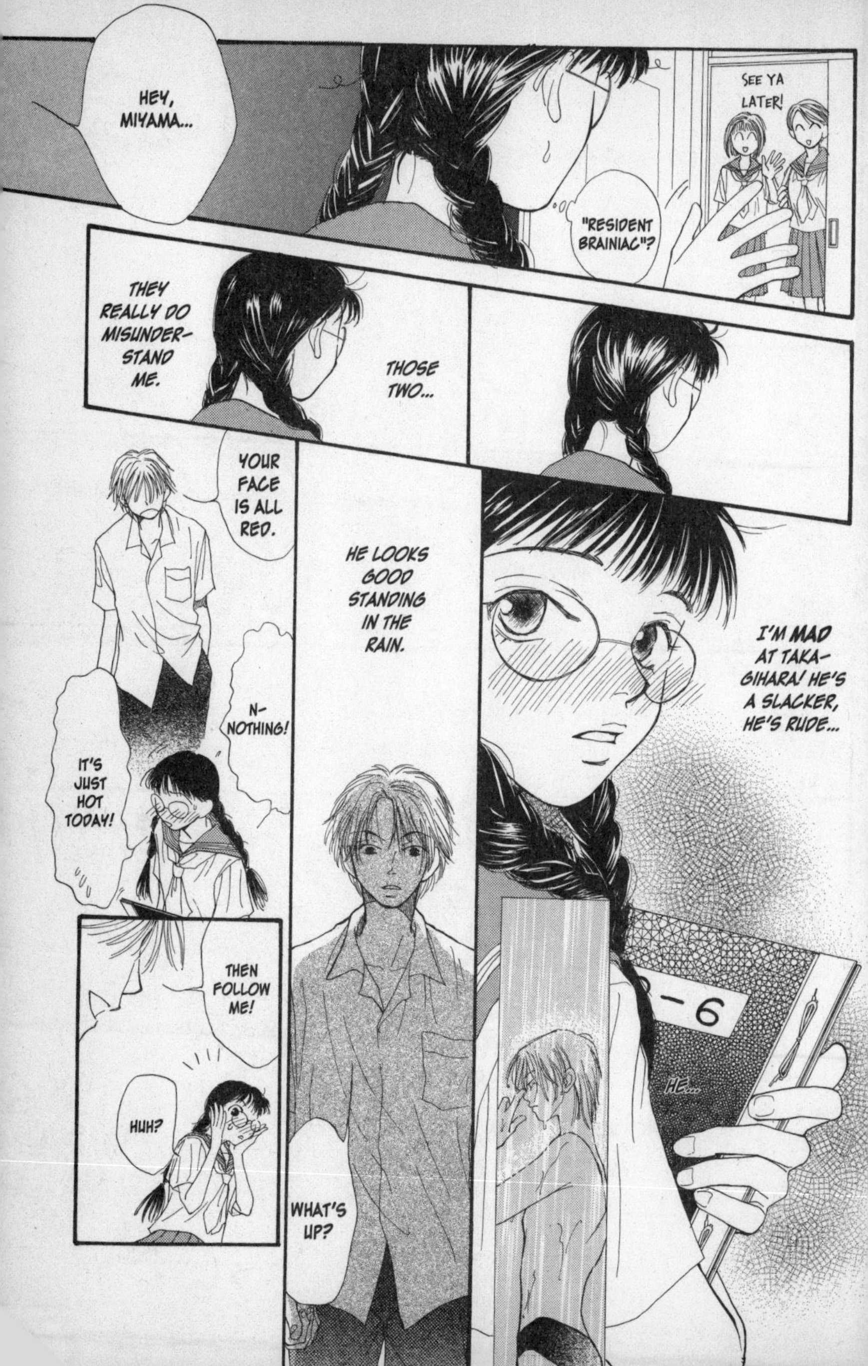
SEE YA LATER!
"RESIDENT BRAINIAC"?
HEY, MIYAMA...
THOSE TWO...
THEY REALLY DO MISUNDERSTAND ME.
I'M MAD AT TAKA-GIHARA! HE'S A SLACKER, HE'S RUDE...
HE...
HE LOOKS GOOD STANDING IN THE RAIN.
WHAT'S UP?
YOUR FACE IS ALL RED.
N-NOTHING!
IT'S JUST HOT TODAY!
THEN FOLLOW ME!
HUH?

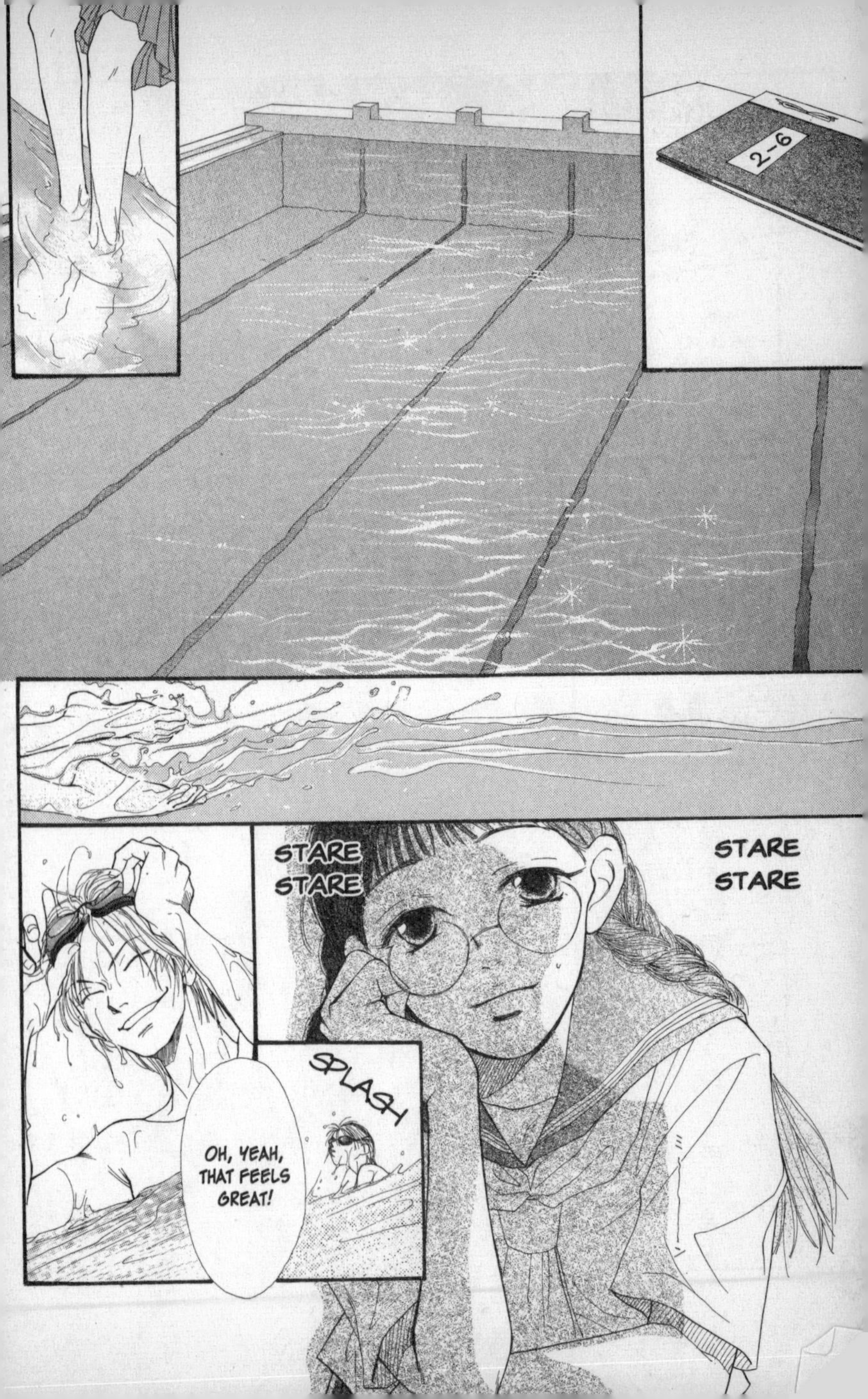
2-6
STARE
STARE
STARE
STARE
SPLASH
OH, YEAH, THAT FEELS GREAT!

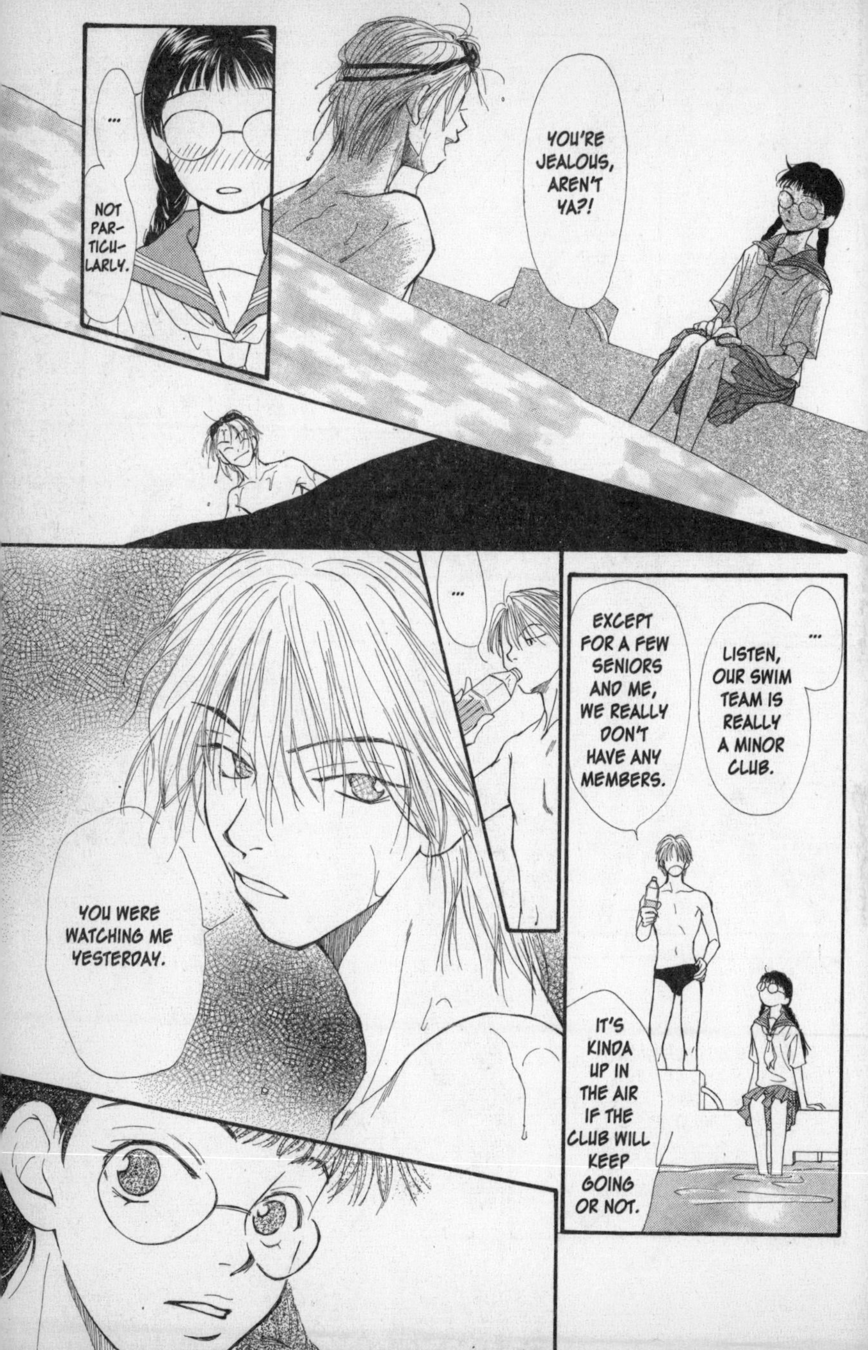
YOU'RE JEALOUS, AREN'T YA?!
...
NOT PARTICULARLY.
...
LISTEN, OUR SWIM TEAM IS REALLY A MINOR CLUB.
EXCEPT FOR A FEW SENIORS AND ME, WE REALLY DON'T HAVE ANY MEMBERS.
IT'S KINDA UP IN THE AIR IF THE CLUB WILL KEEP GOING OR NOT.
...
YOU WERE WATCHING ME YESTERDAY.

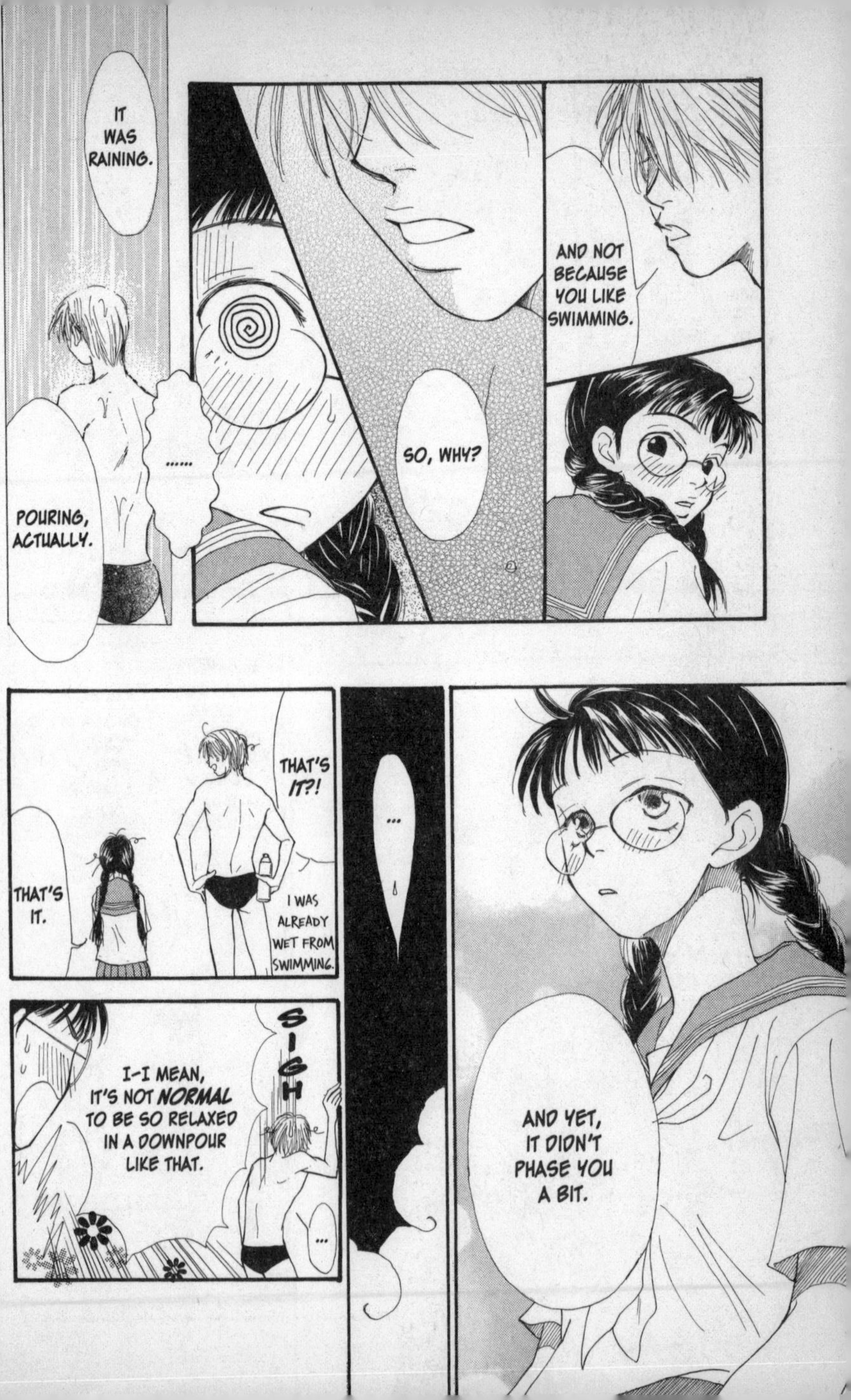
AND NOT BECAUSE YOU LIKE SWIMMING.
SO, WHY?
......
IT WAS RAINING.
POURING, ACTUALLY.
AND YET, IT DIDN'T PHASE YOU A BIT.
...
THAT'S IT?!
I WAS ALREADY WET FROM SWIMMING.
THAT'S IT.
SIGH
I-I MEAN, IT'S NOT NORMAL TO BE SO RELAXED IN A DOWNPOUR LIKE THAT.
...

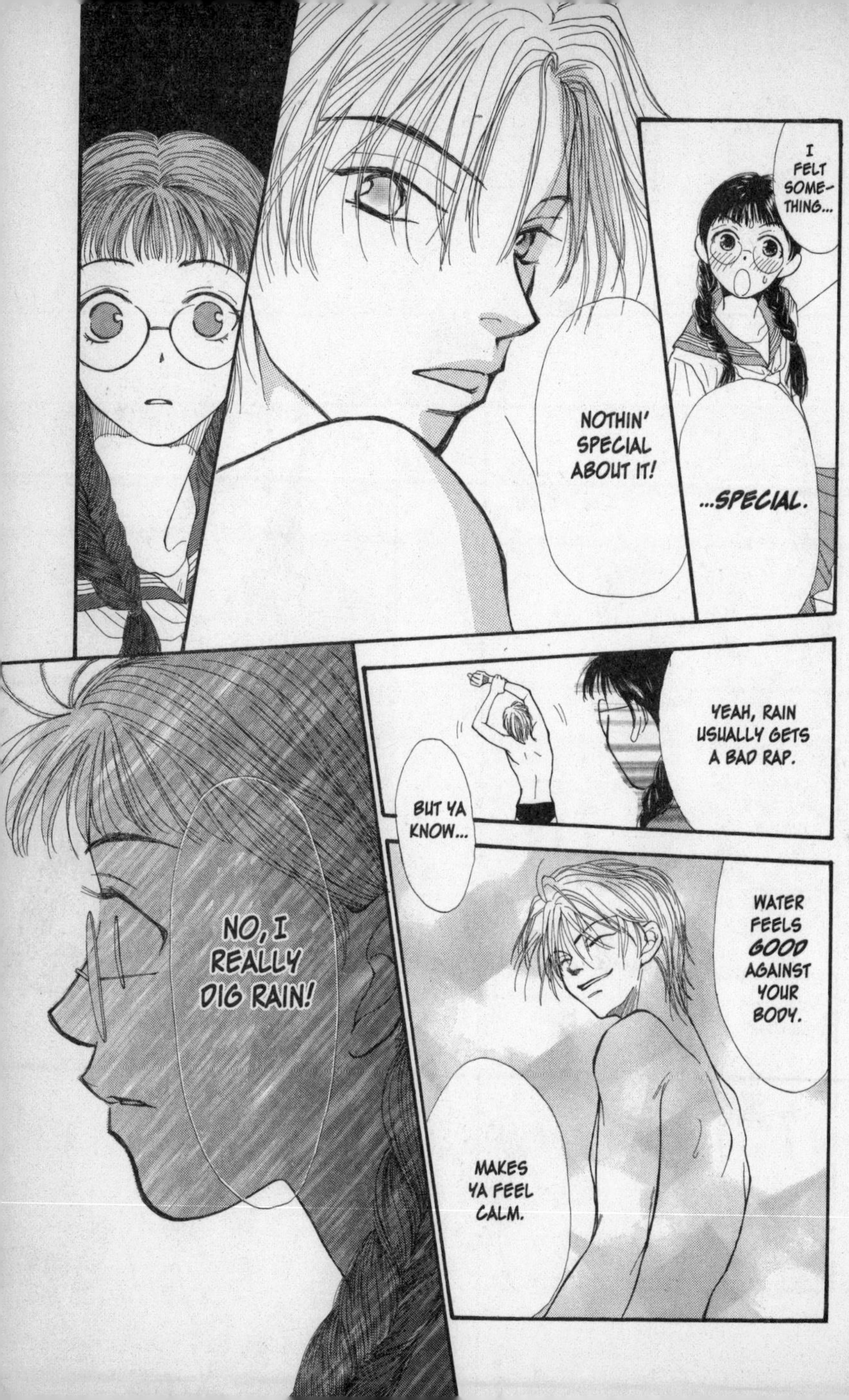
I FELT SOMETHING...
...SPECIAL.
NOTHIN' SPECIAL ABOUT IT!
YEAH, RAIN USUALLY GETS A BAD RAP.
BUT YA KNOW...
WATER FEELS GOOD AGAINST YOUR BODY.
MAKES YA FEEL CALM.
NO, I REALLY DIG RAIN!

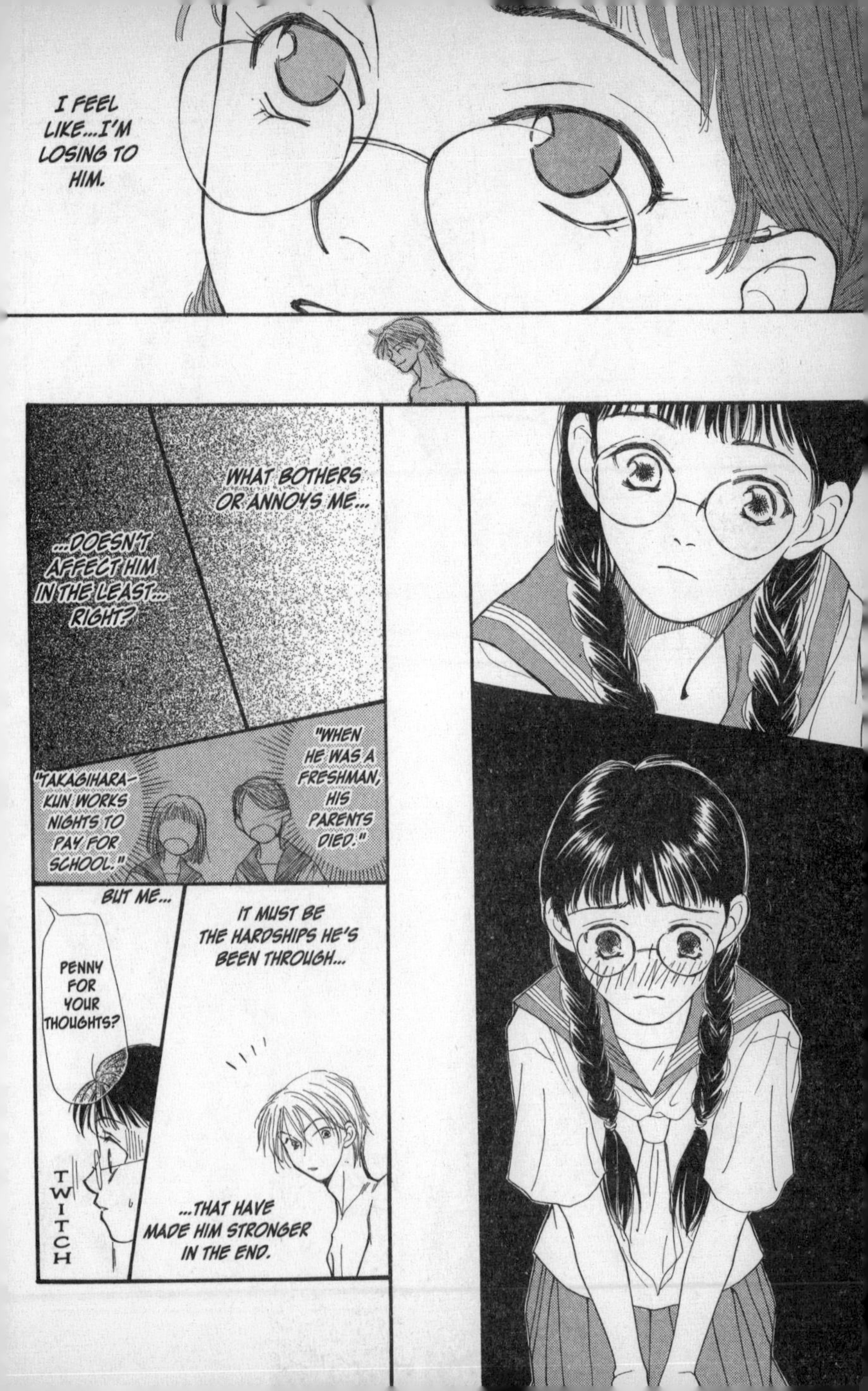
I FEEL LIKE...I'M LOSING TO HIM.
WHAT BOTHERS OR ANNOYS ME...
...DOESN'T AFFECT HIM IN THE LEAST... RIGHT?
"WHEN HE WAS A FRESHMAN, HIS PARENTS DIED."
"TAKAGIHARA-KUN WORKS NIGHTS TO PAY FOR SCHOOL."
IT MUST BE THE HARDSHIPS HE'S BEEN THROUGH...
...THAT HAVE MADE HIM STRONGER IN THE END.
BUT ME...
PENNY FOR YOUR THOUGHTS?
TWITCH

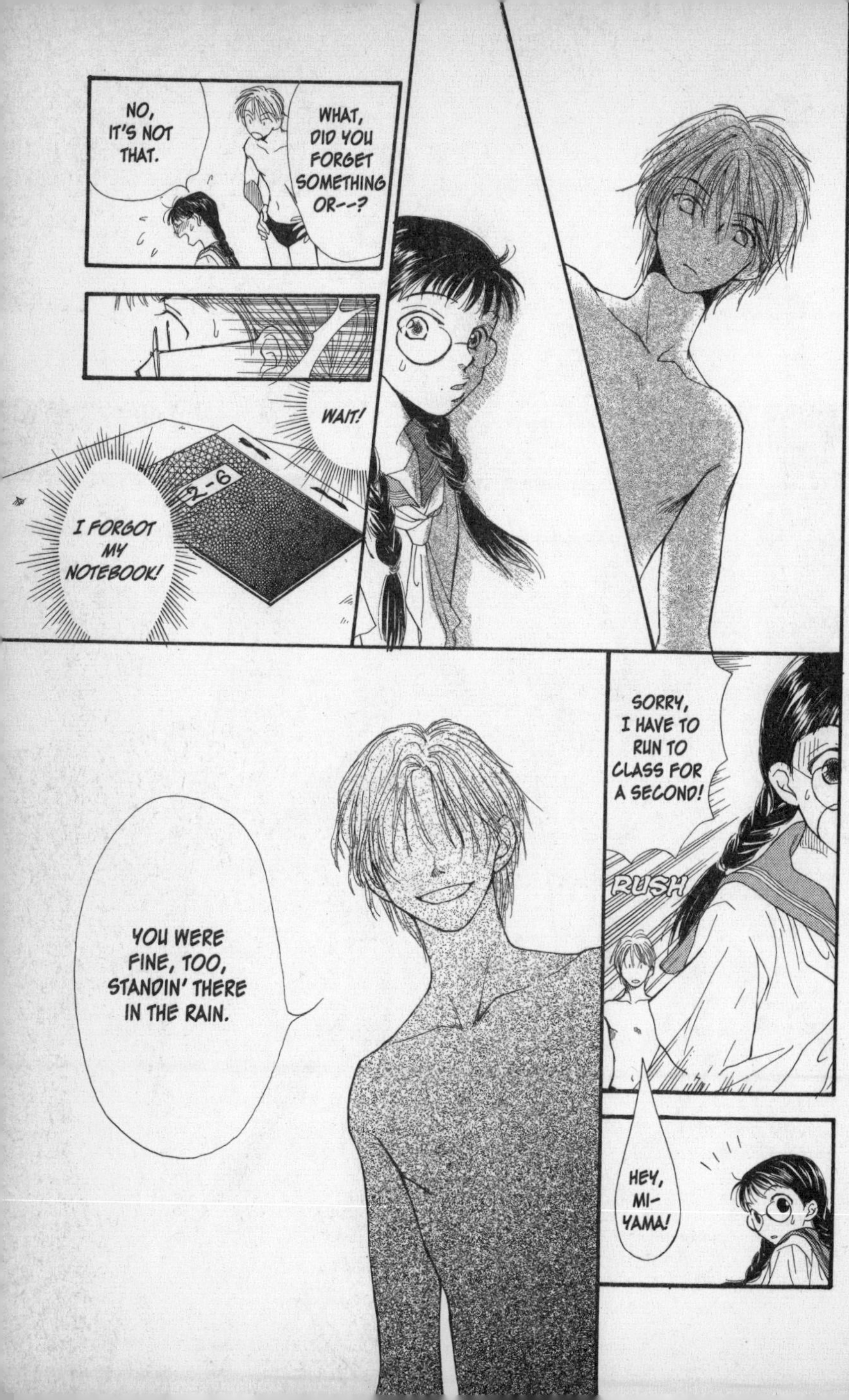
WHAT, DID YOU FORGET SOMETHING OR--?
NO, IT'S NOT THAT.
WAIT!
I FORGOT MY NOTEBOOK!
2-6
SORRY, I HAVE TO RUN TO CLASS FOR A SECOND!
RUSH
HEY, MI-YAMA!
YOU WERE FINE, TOO, STANDIN' THERE IN THE RAIN.

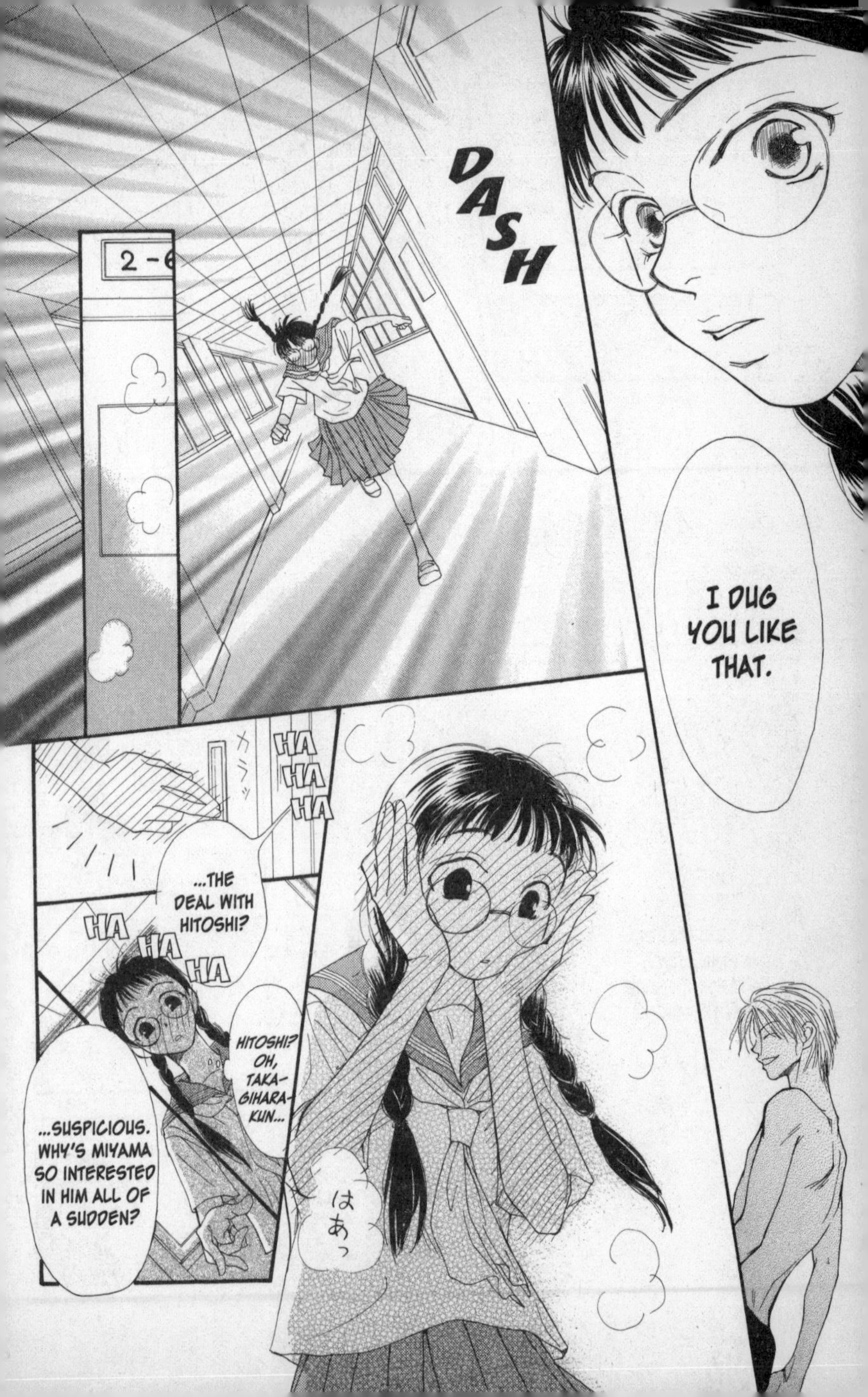
I DUG YOU LIKE THAT.
DASH
2-6
はあっ
カラッ
HA HA HA
...THE DEAL WITH HITOSHI?
HA HA HA
HITOSHI? OH, TAKAGIHARA-KUN...
...SUSPICIOUS. WHY'S MIYAMA SO INTERESTED IN HIM ALL OF A SUDDEN?

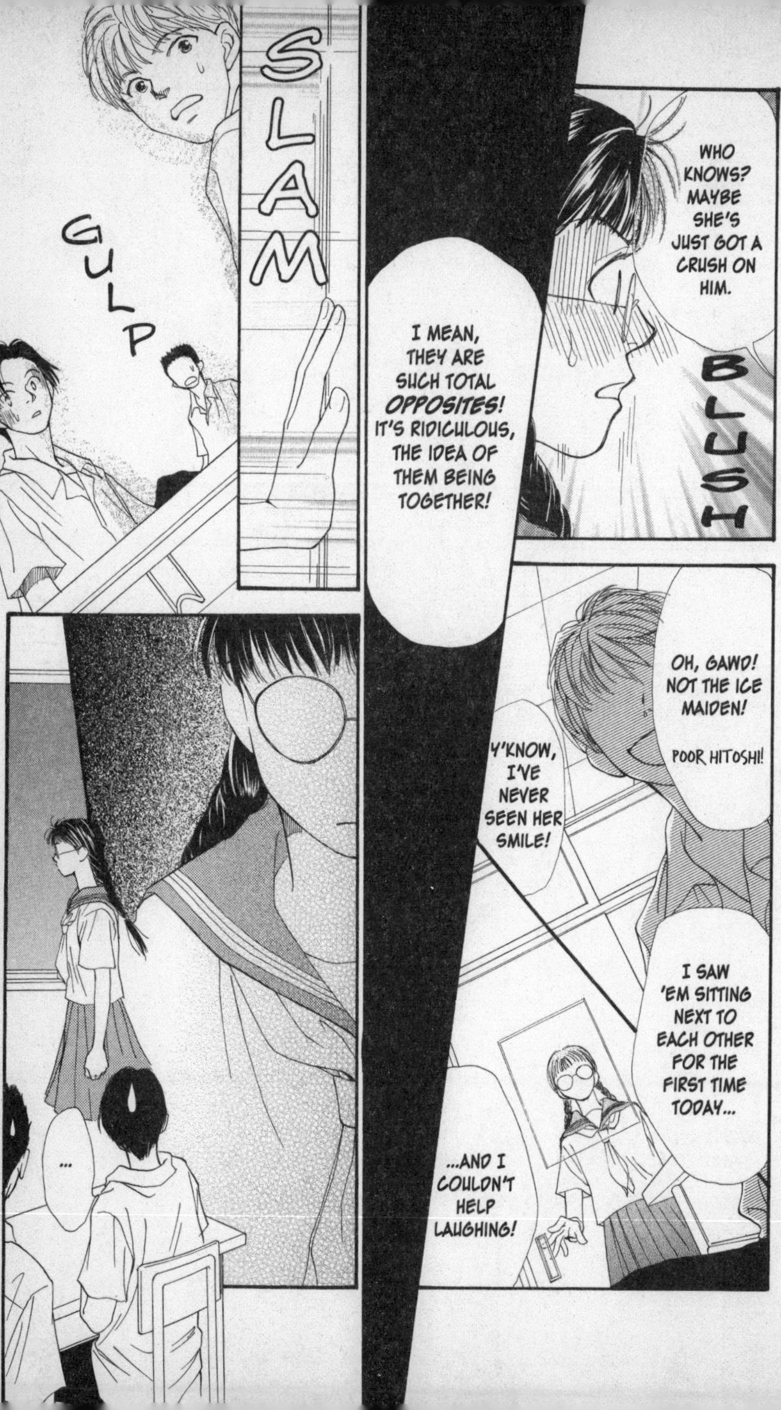
WHO KNOWS? MAYBE SHE'S JUST GOT A CRUSH ON HIM.
BLUSH
I MEAN, THEY ARE SUCH TOTAL *OPPOSITES!* IT'S RIDICULOUS, THE IDEA OF THEM BEING TOGETHER!
SLAM
GULP
OH, GAWD! NOT THE ICE MAIDEN!
POOR HITOSHI!
Y'KNOW, I'VE NEVER SEEN HER SMILE!
I SAW 'EM SITTING NEXT TO EACH OTHER FOR THE FIRST TIME TODAY...
...AND I COULDN'T HELP LAUGHING!
...

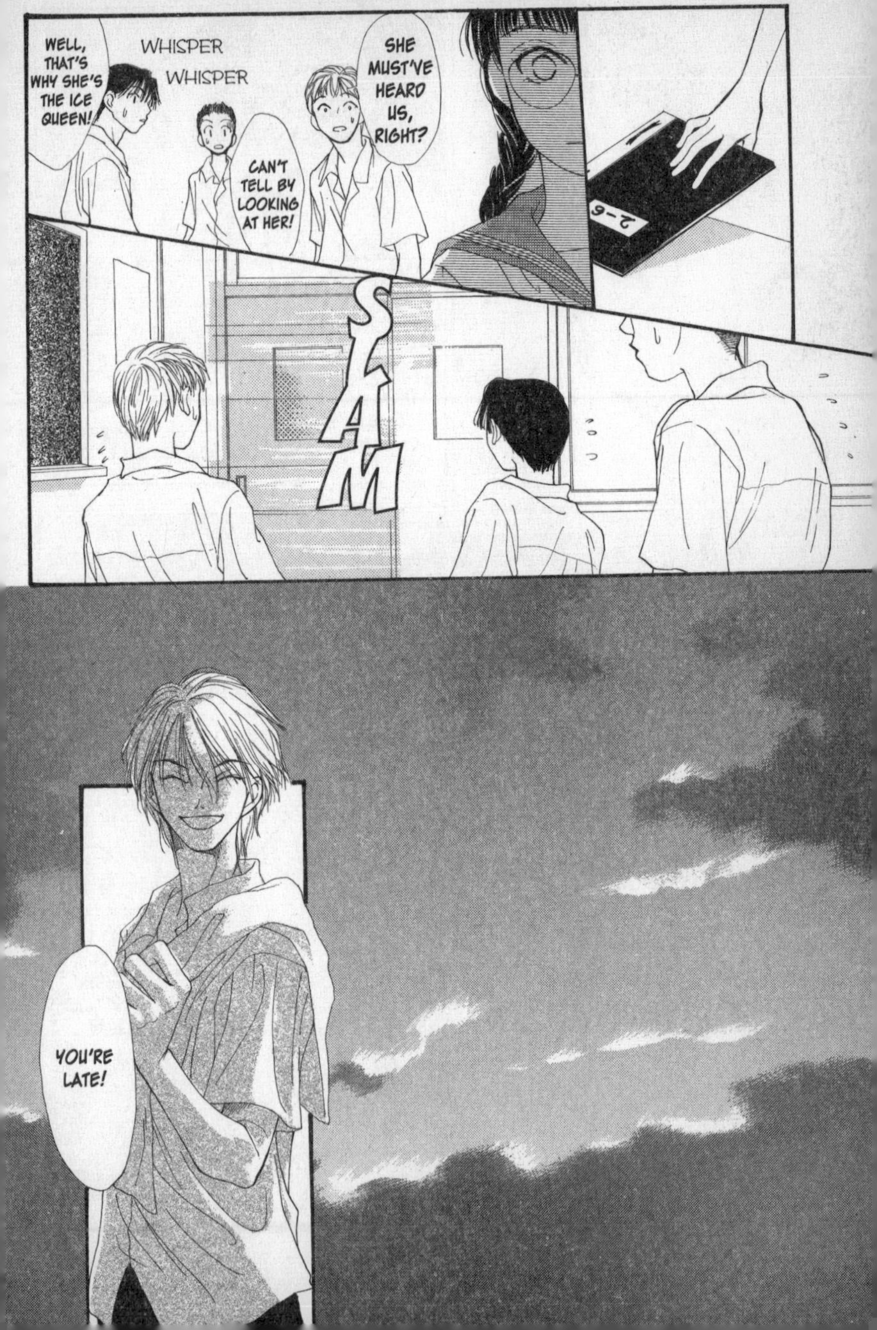
SHE MUST'VE HEARD US, RIGHT?
CAN'T TELL BY LOOKING AT HER!
WHISPER
WHISPER
WELL, THAT'S WHY SHE'S THE ICE QUEEN!
2-6
SLAM
YOU'RE LATE!

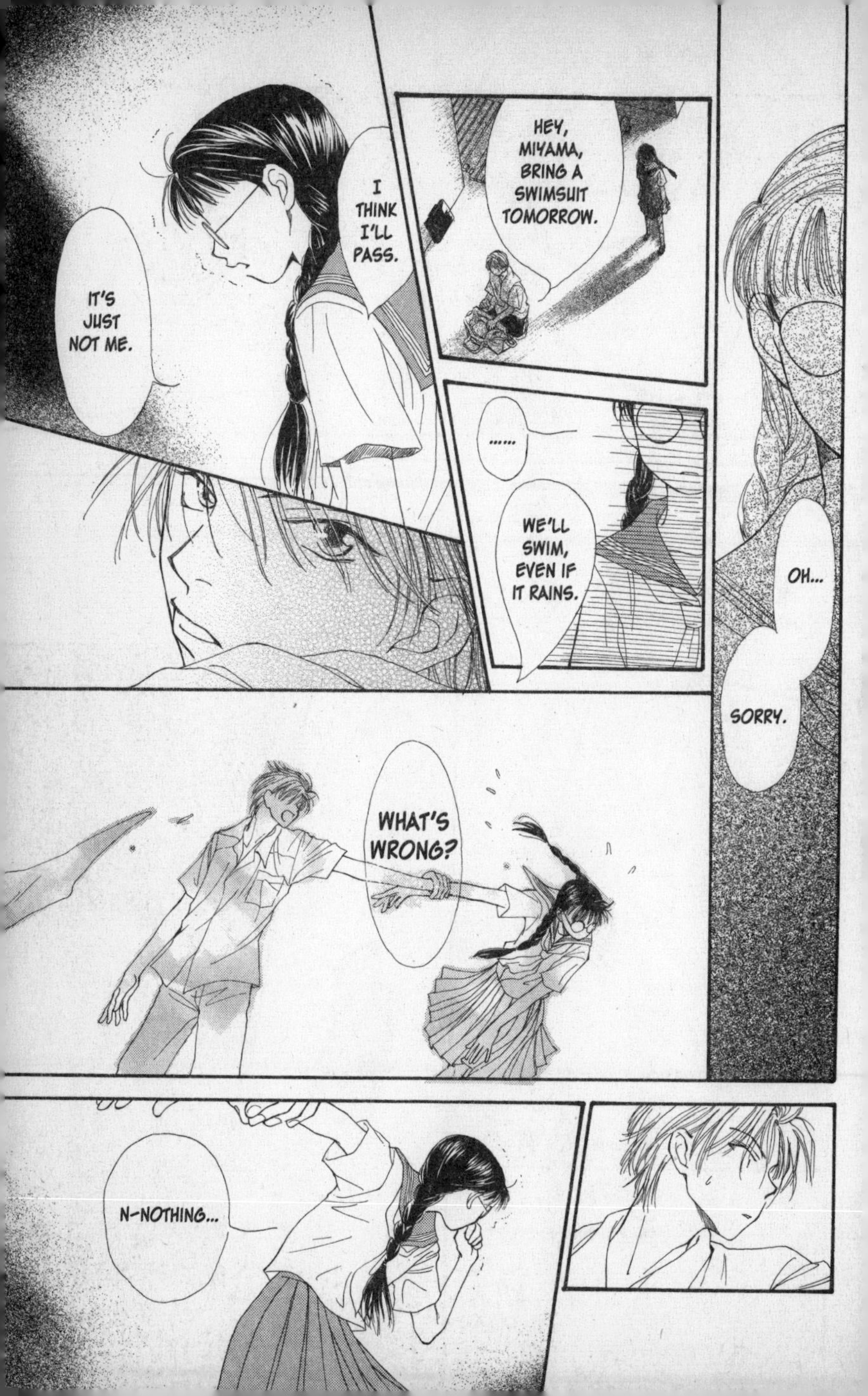

OH...
SORRY.
HEY, MIYAMA, BRING A SWIMSUIT TOMORROW.
I THINK I'LL PASS.
IT'S JUST NOT ME.
......
WE'LL SWIM, EVEN IF IT RAINS.
WHAT'S WRONG?
N-NOTHING...

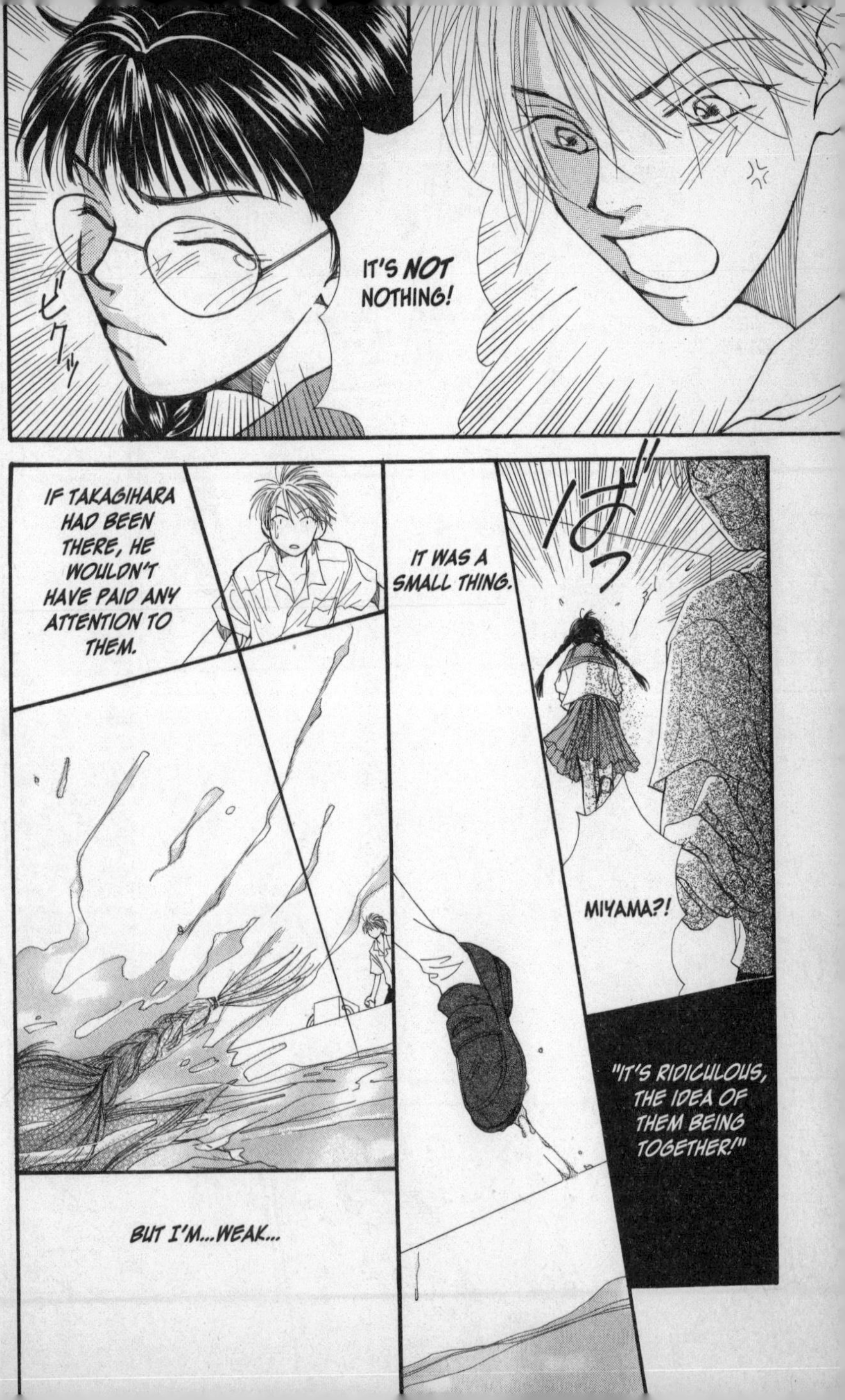
IT'S NOT NOTHING!
ビクッ
ばっ
MIYAMA?!
"IT'S RIDICULOUS, THE IDEA OF THEM BEING TOGETHER!"
IT WAS A SMALL THING.
IF TAKAGIHARA HAD BEEN THERE, HE WOULDN'T HAVE PAID ANY ATTENTION TO THEM.
BUT I'M...WEAK...

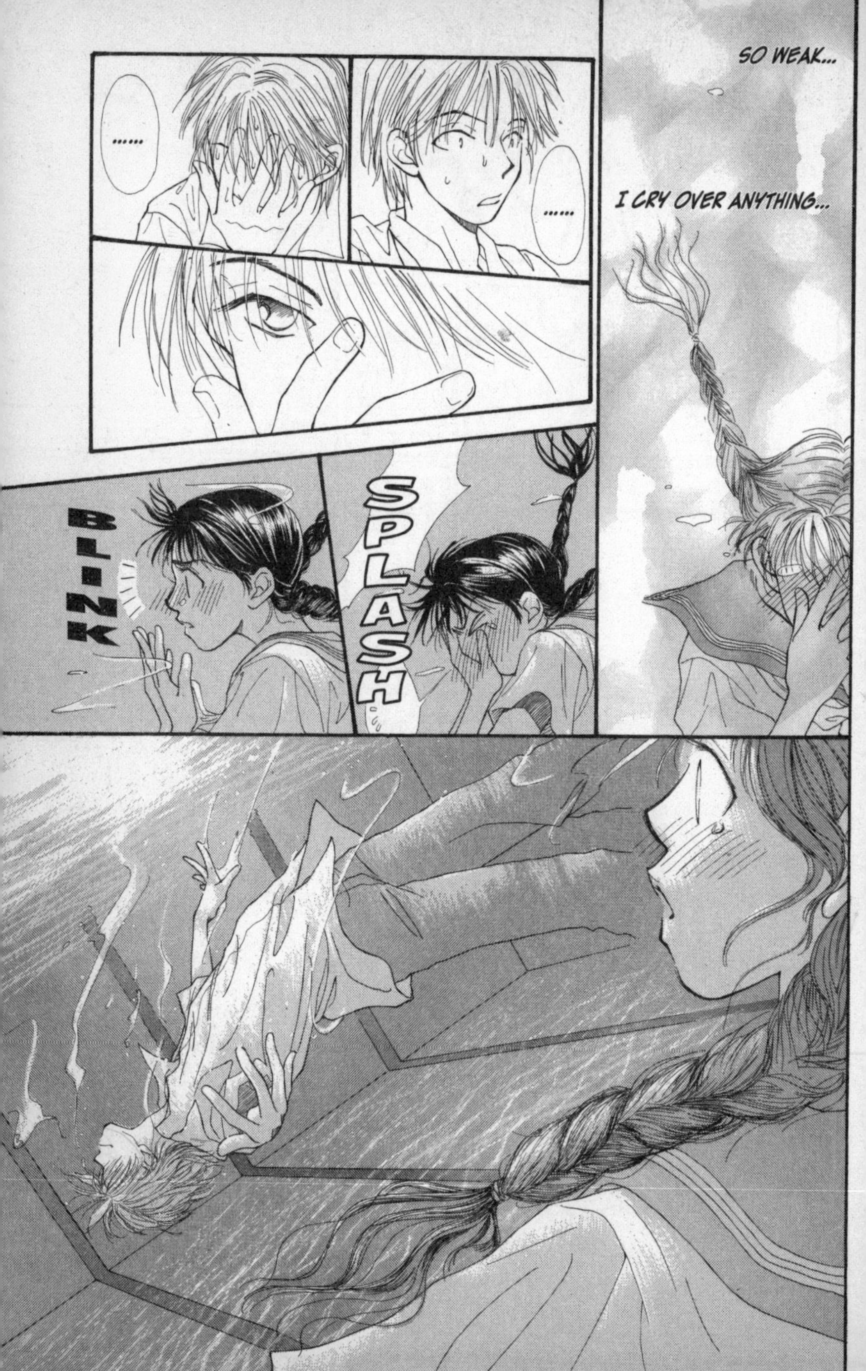
SO WEAK...
I CRY OVER ANYTHING...
......
......
SPLASH
BLINK

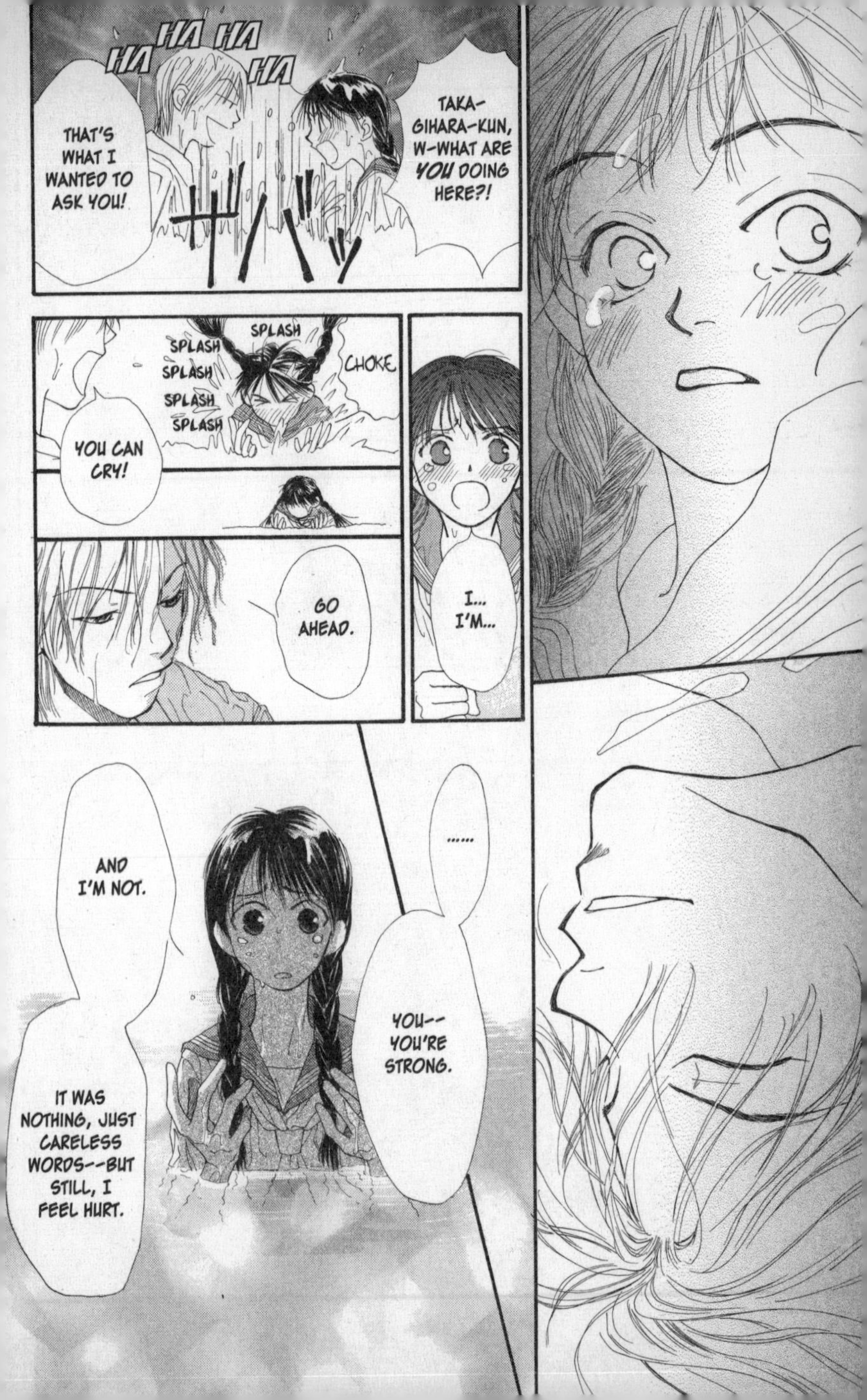
HA HA HA HA
TAKA-GIHARA-KUN, W-WHAT ARE YOU DOING HERE?!
THAT'S WHAT I WANTED TO ASK YOU!
I... I'M...
SPLASH
SPLASH
CHOKE
SPLASH
SPLASH
SPLASH
YOU CAN CRY!
GO AHEAD.
......
YOU-- YOU'RE STRONG.
AND I'M NOT.
IT WAS NOTHING, JUST CARELESS WORDS--BUT STILL, I FEEL HURT.

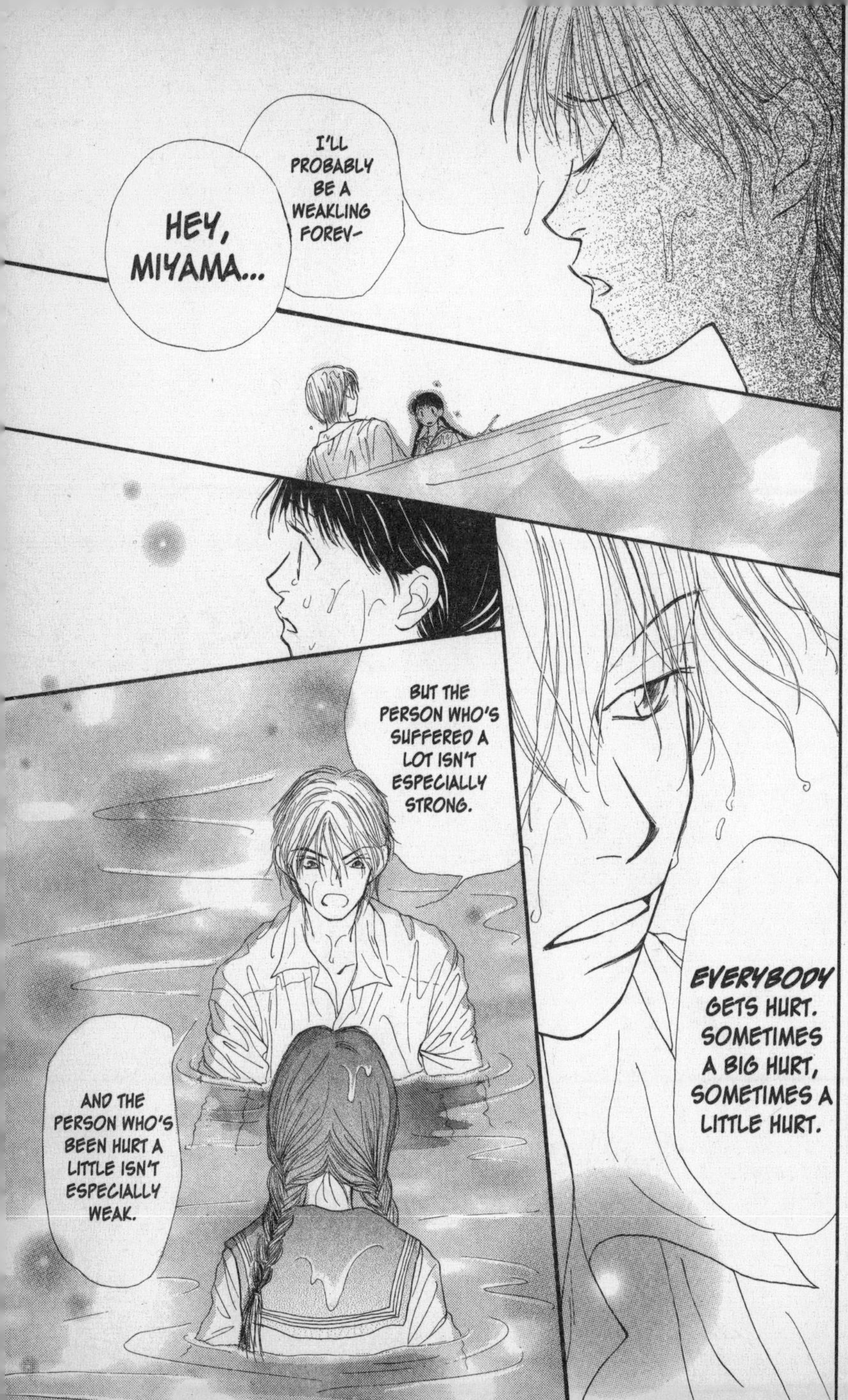
I'LL PROBABLY BE A WEAKLING FOREV-
HEY, MIYAMA...
EVERYBODY GETS HURT. SOMETIMES A BIG HURT, SOMETIMES A LITTLE HURT.
BUT THE PERSON WHO'S SUFFERED A LOT ISN'T ESPECIALLY STRONG.
AND THE PERSON WHO'S BEEN HURT A LITTLE ISN'T ESPECIALLY WEAK.

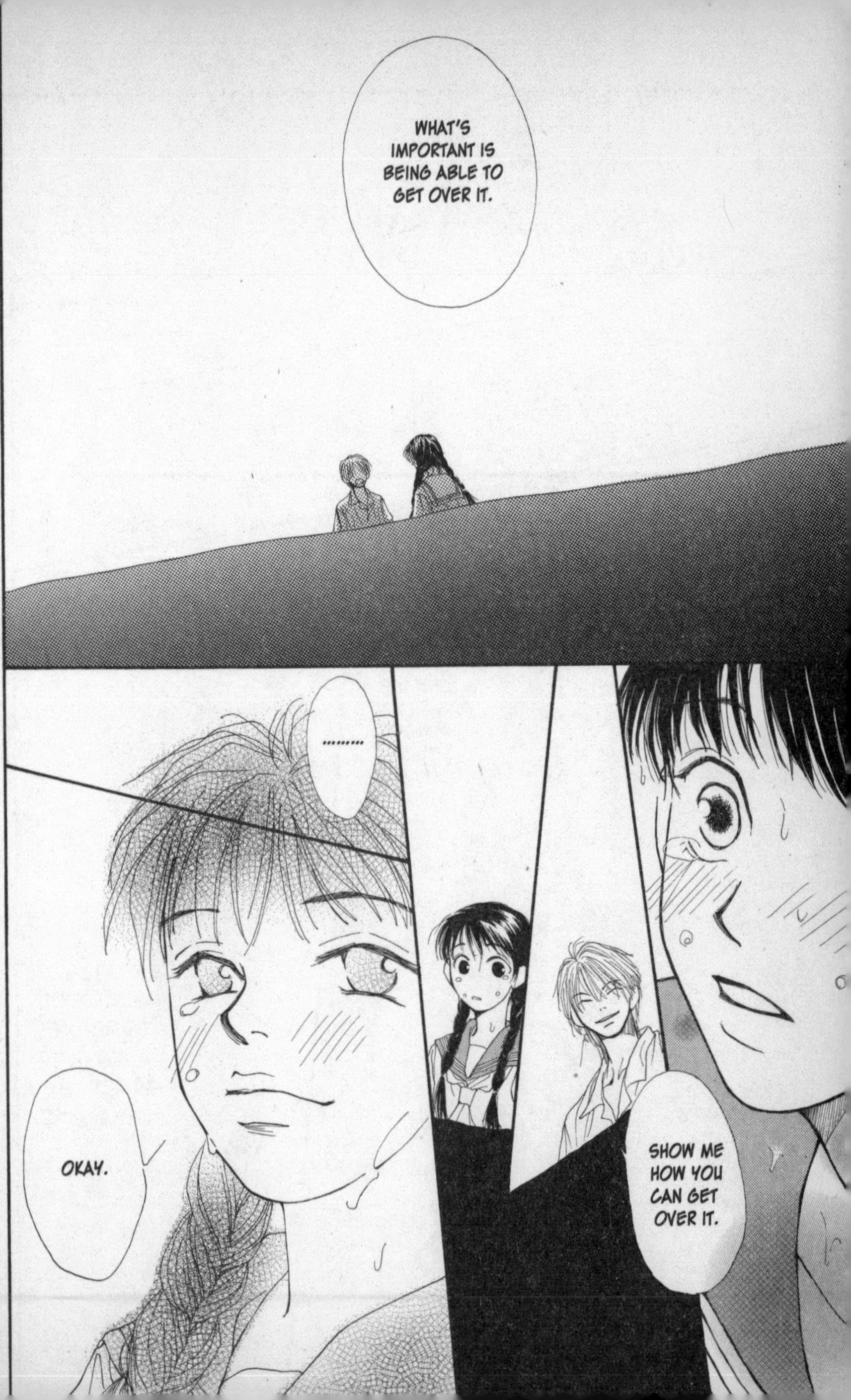
WHAT'S IMPORTANT IS BEING ABLE TO GET OVER IT.
SHOW ME HOW YOU CAN GET OVER IT.
....
OKAY.

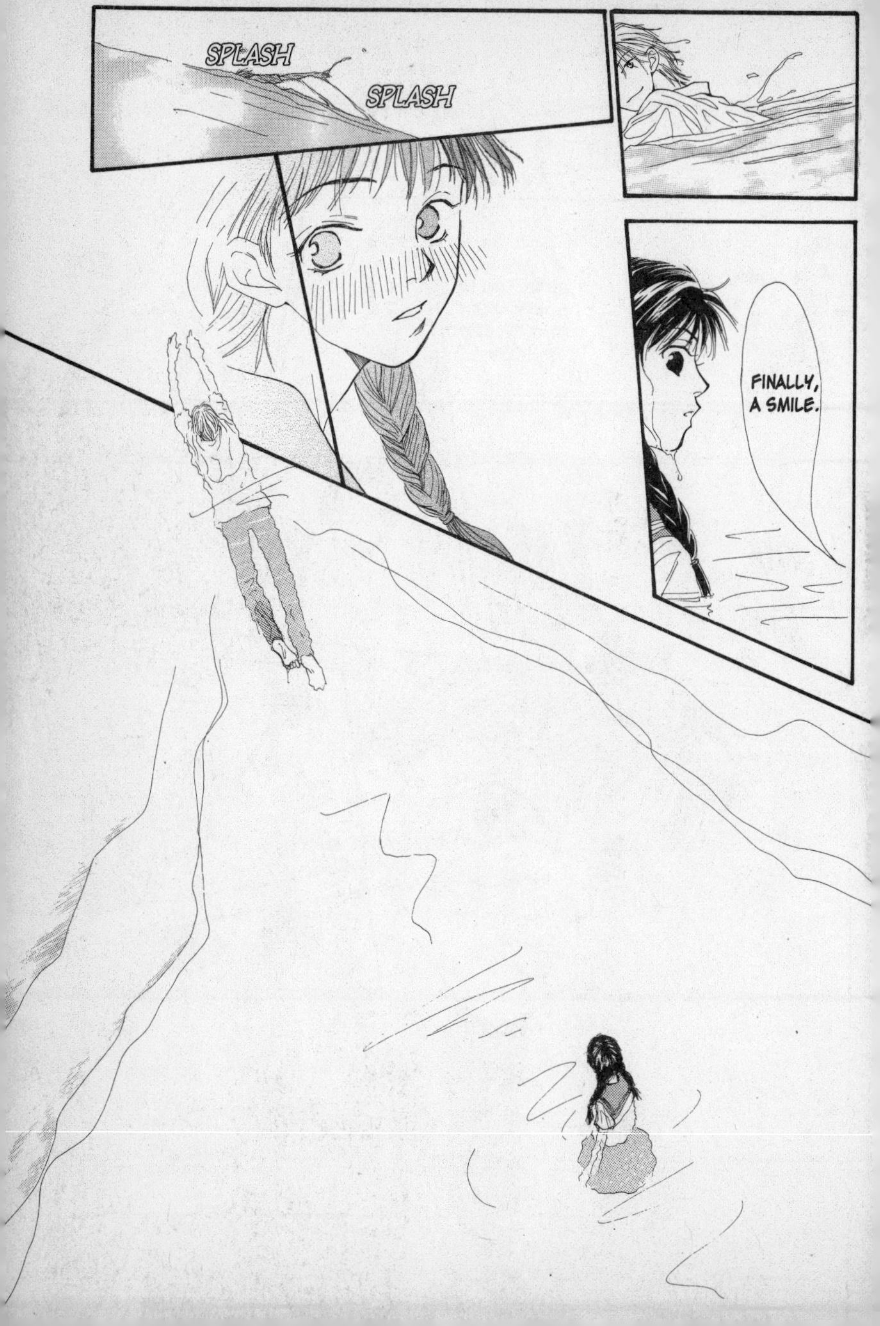
SPLASH
SPLASH
FINALLY, A SMILE.

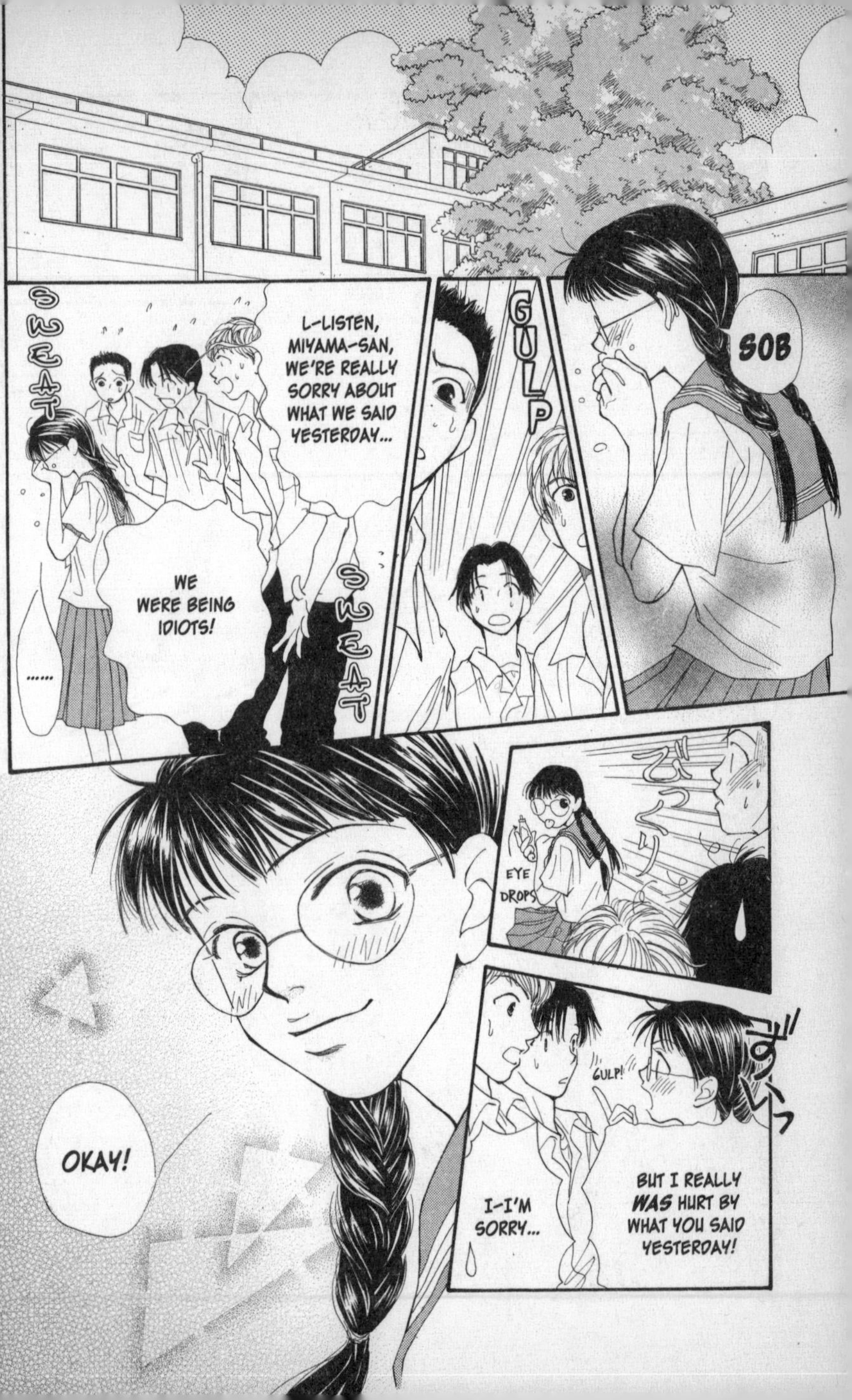

SOB
GULP
L-LISTEN, MIYAMA-SAN, WE'RE REALLY SORRY ABOUT WHAT WE SAID YESTERDAY...
SWEAT
WE WERE BEING IDIOTS!
SWEAT
......
びっくり
EYE DROPS
GULP!
BUT I REALLY *WAS* HURT BY WHAT YOU SAID YESTERDAY!
I-I'M SORRY...
OKAY!

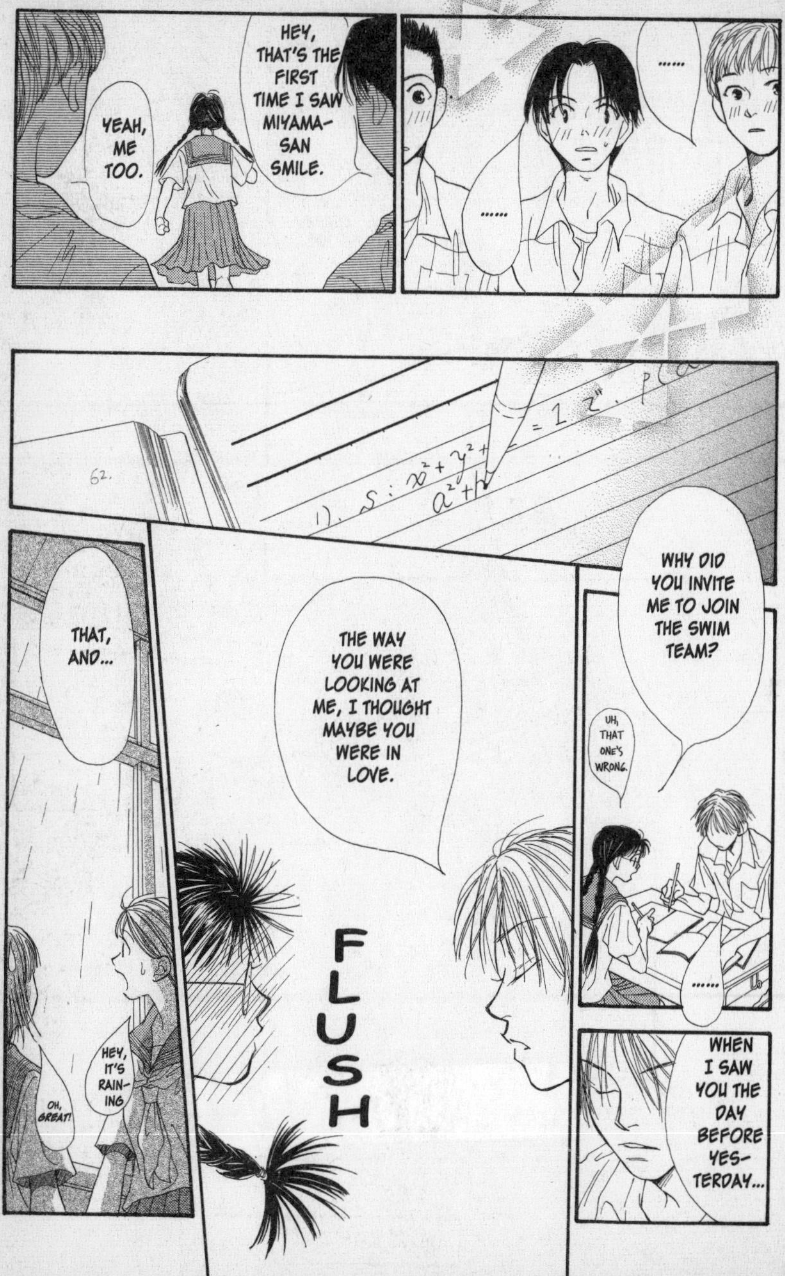
......
......
HEY, THAT'S THE FIRST TIME I SAW MIYAMA-SAN SMILE.
YEAH, ME TOO.
62.
WHY DID YOU INVITE ME TO JOIN THE SWIM TEAM?
UH, THAT ONE'S WRONG.
......
WHEN I SAW YOU THE DAY BEFORE YES-TERDAY...
THE WAY YOU WERE LOOKING AT ME, I THOUGHT MAYBE YOU WERE IN LOVE.
FLUSH
THAT, AND...
HEY, IT'S RAINING
OH, GREAT!

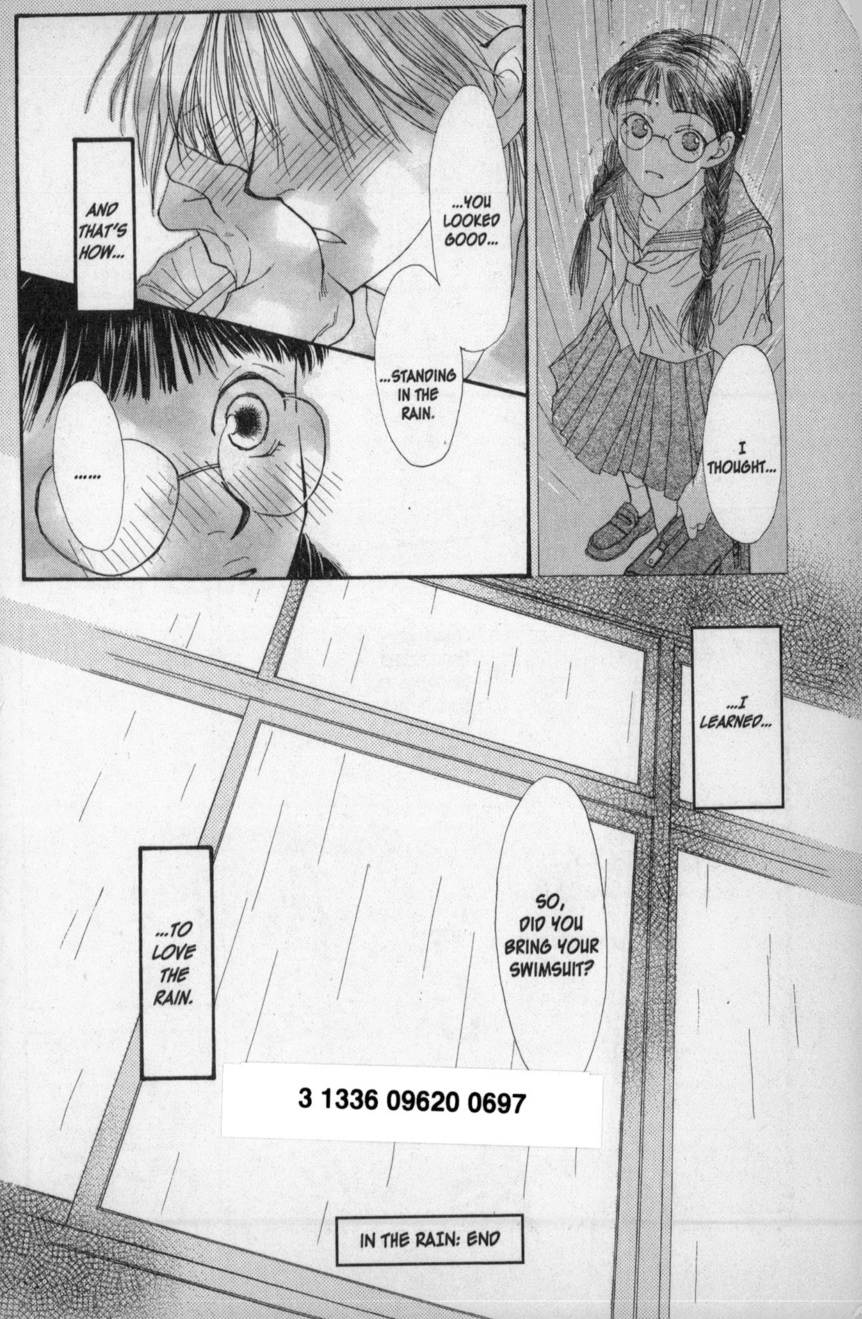
I THOUGHT...
...YOU LOOKED GOOD...
...STANDING IN THE RAIN.
AND THAT'S HOW...
......
...I LEARNED...
SO, DID YOU BRING YOUR SWIMSUIT?
...TO LOVE THE RAIN.
IN THE RAIN: END

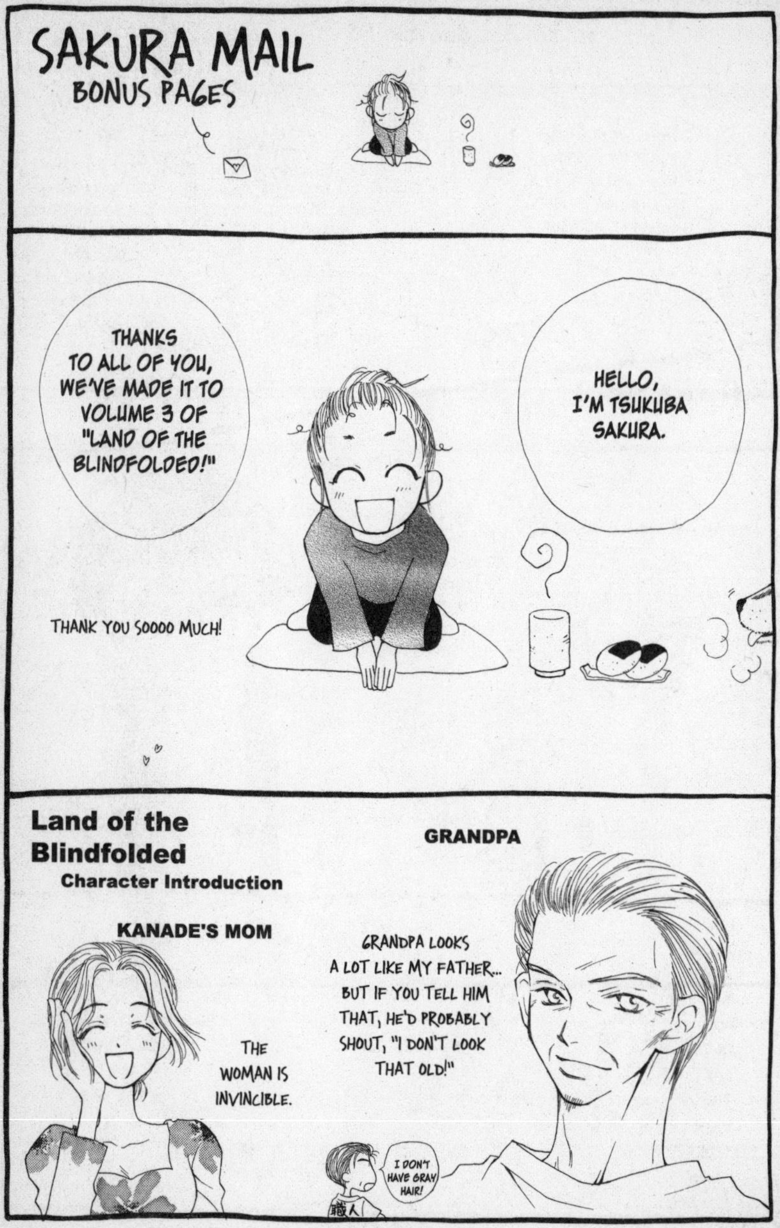
SAKURA MAIL
BONUS PAGES
HELLO, I'M TSUKUBA SAKURA.
THANKS TO ALL OF YOU, WE'VE MADE IT TO VOLUME 3 OF "LAND OF THE BLINDFOLDED!"
THANK YOU SOOOO MUCH!
Land of the Blindfolded
Character Introduction
GRANDPA
GRANDPA LOOKS A LOT LIKE MY FATHER... BUT IF YOU TELL HIM THAT, HE'D PROBABLY SHOUT, "I DON'T LOOK THAT OLD!"
I DON'T HAVE GRAY HAIR!
職人
KANADE'S MOM
THE WOMAN IS INVINCIBLE.

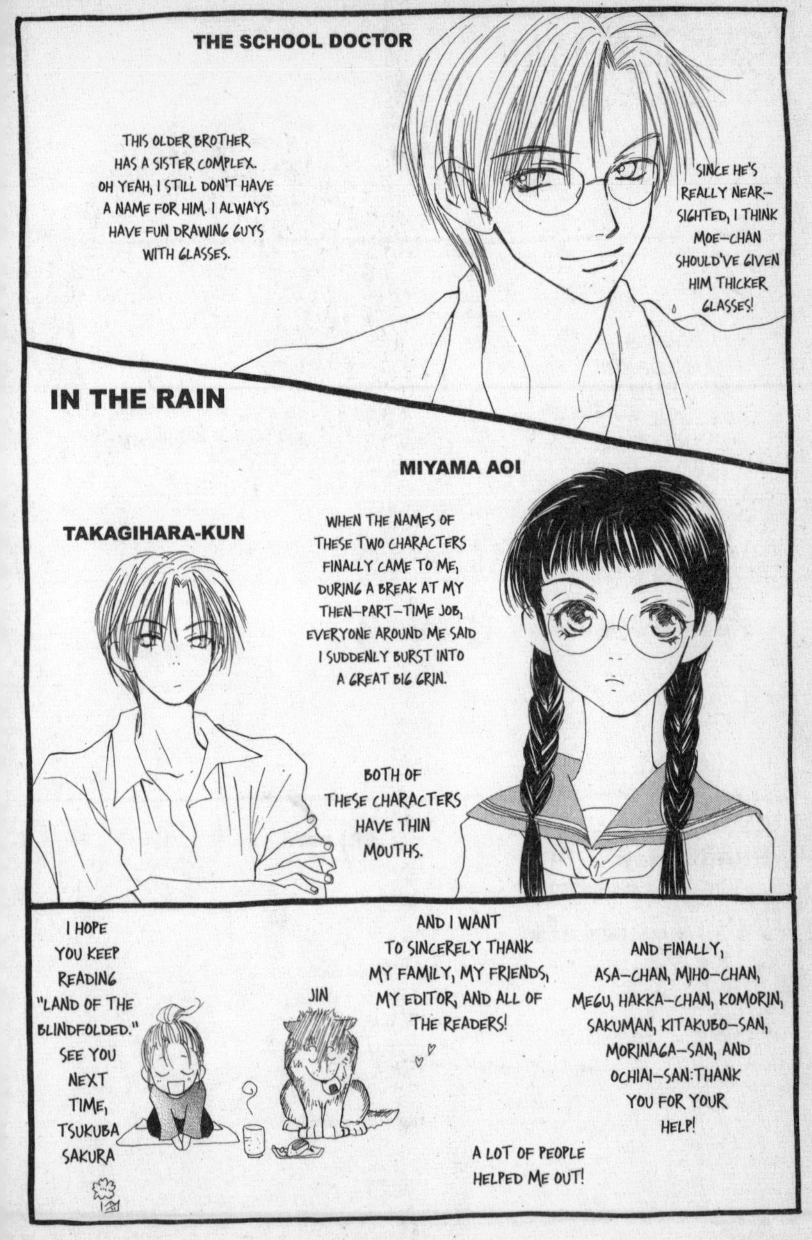
THE SCHOOL DOCTOR
SINCE HE'S REALLY NEAR-SIGHTED, I THINK MOE-CHAN SHOULD'VE GIVEN HIM THICKER GLASSES!
THIS OLDER BROTHER HAS A SISTER COMPLEX. OH YEAH, I STILL DON'T HAVE A NAME FOR HIM. I ALWAYS HAVE FUN DRAWING GUYS WITH GLASSES.
IN THE RAIN
MIYAMA AOI
WHEN THE NAMES OF THESE TWO CHARACTERS FINALLY CAME TO ME, DURING A BREAK AT MY THEN-PART-TIME JOB, EVERYONE AROUND ME SAID I SUDDENLY BURST INTO A GREAT BIG GRIN.
TAKAGIHARA-KUN
BOTH OF THESE CHARACTERS HAVE THIN MOUTHS.
AND FINALLY, ASA-CHAN, MIHO-CHAN, MEGU, HAKKA-CHAN, KOMORIN, SAKUMAN, KITAKUBO-SAN, MORINAGA-SAN, AND OCHIAI-SAN: THANK YOU FOR YOUR HELP!
A LOT OF PEOPLE HELPED ME OUT!
AND I WANT TO SINCERELY THANK MY FAMILY, MY FRIENDS, MY EDITOR, AND ALL OF THE READERS!
JIN
I HOPE YOU KEEP READING "LAND OF THE BLINDFOLDED." SEE YOU NEXT TIME, TSUKUBA SAKURA

MEKAKUSHI NO KUNI Volume 3 © 1998 Sakura Tsukuba.
All Rights Reserved. First published in Japan in 2000 by
HAKUSENSHA, INC., Tokyo.

LAND OF THE BLINDFOLDED Volume 3, published by
WildStorm Productions, an imprint of DC Comics, 888
Prospect St. #240, La Jolla, CA 92037. English Translation
© 2005. All Rights Reserved. English language translation
rights in the United States of America and Canada arranged
with HAKUSENSHA, INC., Tokyo, through Tuttle-Mori
Agency, Inc., Tokyo. The stories, characters, and incidents
mentioned in this magazine are entirely fictional. Printed on
recyclable paper. WildStorm does not read or accept unso-
licited submissions of ideas, stories or artwork. Printed in
Canada. SECOND PRINTING.

DC Comics, A Warner Bros. Entertainment Company.

Sheldon Drzka – Translation and Adaptation
Ryan Cline – Lettering
Larry Berry – Design
Jonathan Tarbox – Editor

ISBN: 1-4012-0526-7
ISBN-13: 978-1-4012-0526-3

TEEN

All the pages in this book were created—and are printed here—in Japanese RIGHT-to-LEFT format. No artwork has been reversed or altered, so you can read the stories the way the creators meant for them to be read.

FLIP IT!

RIGHT TO LEFT?!

Traditional Japanese manga starts at the upper right-hand corner, and moves right-to-left as it goes down the page. Follow this guide for an easy understanding.

For more information and sneak previews, visit cmxmanga.com. Call 1-800-COMIC BOOK for the nearest comics shop or head to your local book store.

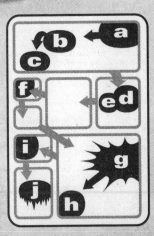